Selling the Lower East Side

Globalization and Community

Dennis R. Judd, Series Editor

Selling the Lower East Side

Culture, Real Estate, and Resistance in New York City

Christopher Mele

Globalization and Community / Volume 5
University of Minnesota Press
Minneapolis London

The companion Web site to *Selling the Lower East Side* includes photographs, text, video, and links to related sites. Visit the book's Web site at http://www.upress.umn.edu.

Published by the University of Minnesota Press
111 Third Avenue South, Suite 290, Minneapolis, MN 55401-2520
http://www.upress.umn.edu
Printed in the United States of America on acid-free paper

Library of Congress Cataloging-in-Publication Data

Mele, Christopher.
    Selling the Lower East Side : culture, real estate, and resistance in
New York City / Christopher Mele.
    p.   cm. — (Globalization and community ; v. 5)
Includes bibliographical references and index.
ISBN 0-8166-3181-6 (hc) — ISBN 0-8166-3182-4 (pbk.)
    1. Urban renewal — New York (State) — Lower East Side (New York)
2. Lower East Side (New York, N.Y.) — Social conditions.   3. Lower
East Side (New York, N.Y.) — Economic conditions.   I. Title.   II. Series.
HT177.N5 M45   2000
307.3'416'097471 — dc21   99-057397

Printed in the United States of America on acid-free paper

The University of Minnesota is an equal-opportunity educator and employer.

11 10 09 08 07 06   8 7 6 5 4 3

Contents

Preface

The origins of this book date back to the 1980s when I was living on the Lower East Side of Manhattan while attending graduate school. As a resident and a critical observer of neighborhood change, I was struck by the paradox of at least two different worlds that inhabited the identical streets and avenues around me. Over time, I lived in a half dozen apartments east of Avenue B, alongside mostly poor Puerto Rican families who had managed to maintain a tight-knit community called Loisaida (Spanglish for Lower East Side) in the wake of severe economic decline a decade earlier. Other neighbors in the same buildings were graphic designers, feature writers, and service industry workers who paid exorbitant rents for renovated apartments. To them, Avenue B and the adjacent avenues and streets were known as Alphabet City — a relatively recent invention that represented a "rejuvenation" of a landscape scarred by abandonment, arson, poverty, and a rampant illicit drug economy. The expensive apartments, restaurants, and boutiques that comprised Alphabet City stood in sharp contrast to the homeless encampments in empty lots, the ethnic groceries, and the worn tenements associated with Loisaida. A turf battle between working-class and middle-class residents and old and new uses of urban space played out before me. The area had begun to "turn around," to borrow from the terminology of the real estate industry, as the ravages of abandonment in the 1970s that left numerous buildings burned out and bricked up slowly gave way to reinvestment and middle-class development. Yet a simple gentrification narrative could not fully capture the area's transformation. While clearly catering to an upscale clientele, the aesthetic designs of new apartment buildings as well as the themes of local nightclubs and other commercial spaces seemed to gesture toward and even mimic the look and feel of the very social elements they threatened to displace.

The characterization of the Lower East Side—as unique, culturally diverse, exhilarating, and frightening—has figured predominantly in neighborhood struggles over residential change and displacement since the nineteenth century. Most recently, images, iconography, and symbols of the Lower East Side's ethnic minority communities and of neighborhood battles against upscale development were reworked as place themes to attract a particular kind of middle-class resident. Such incorporation of "difference" in the marketing of place was wholly symbolic since the new residential and consumption spaces were economically prohibitive to poor residents. As a resident, I also observed my neighbors' various organized and unorganized forms of resistance against redevelopment. These ranged from demonstrations and protests that often ended in violent confrontations with the police to less spectacular everyday presence in and control over public spaces. Municipal policies and "quality-of-life" initiatives, meanwhile, actively furthered redevelopment through surveillance and regulation of public expressions of cultural and political differences. Thus, while the police enforced mandates to eject squatters from city-owned buildings and drug dealers, prostitutes, and the homeless from sidewalks and other public spaces, private developers gestured toward these very same "social ills," providing a sanitized and commercialized sensibility of urban despair to the young, affluent middle class drawn to the neighborhood's "alternative" allure. The display of affluence depended on the existence of poverty, desire on the presence of fear, and mainstream acceptance on a corporate fantasy of marginality. In short, the contemporary redevelopment of the Lower East Side is premised on the *symbolic inclusion* of the characteristics long associated with the Lower East Side—among others, continual political activism, the working-class struggle for survival, and the presence of marginalized subcultures and the avant-garde.

Looking to the past, we see these very same characteristics take on a different kind of relevance to prior episodes of development. With few exceptions, the real estate industry and state actors defined their purposes, plans, and ambitions to transform the Lower East Side *in opposition* to prevailing representations of the neighborhood as a marginal, inferior, and threatening space. Middle-class residential upgrading required the displacement of the neighborhood's working-class residents *and* its reputation, reflecting not only the political and economic differences between social classes but cultural dissonance between them as well. As accounts of neighborhood changes in subsequent chapters of this book will show, the past negation of cultural, social, and political differences contrasts sharply with their present symbolic inclusion. Yet past and present episodes of political and economic restructuring have in common the deliberate efforts of the real estate industry, the state, and local residents to employ prevailing representations about the Lower East Side to facilitate and legitimize their actions. The motivation to speculate, invest, or disinvest, as well as the determination to target particular classes of suitable renters, is influenced by the dominant discourses about the Lower East Side as a slum, a ghetto, or an incipient artists' colony. Likewise, municipal housing policies and state development plans draw on the existing characterization of place as a pretext to justify local land-use changes and their social consequences. In ways both intentional and unintentional, the dominant representations of the Lower East Side work their way into the various resistance tactics of local organizations and residents.

This book is an examination of a century of neighborhood change on the Lower East Side. It has a dual purpose. First, a study of land-use struggles over time serves to underscore the significance of cultural representations of place to political economic processes of urban restructuring. The analysis of land-use changes draws on the critical scholarship of the new urban sociology, which emphasizes the roles of the real estate industry and the state in the production of urban space. I maintain that cultural representations and discourses about the Lower East Side are integral to the configuration of both political economic processes of spatial change and to the resistance of residents against such changes at various times in the neighborhood's history. Images, symbols, and rhetoric about the Lower East Side have considerable influence on how the real estate industry and state actors construct their plans to reinvent (or, at times, ignore) the Lower East Side and how locals develop collective and unorganized forms of resistance. By examining a century-long trajectory, I emphasize that the cultural dimension to urban political economic changes (which has received considerable attention among scholars of contemporary urban restructuring) is as important to past transformations. Second, the narrative of the struggle over the Lower East Side in the past century emphasizes the very features that make the area a fascinating place — its cultural and political histories, including the emergence of a rebellious legacy and the local influence of bohemians, beats, hippies, punks, and artists, among others, to the neighborhood's identity. These details bring to life and deepen the relevance of cultural representations and discourses about the Lower East Side to the (very) material struggle over decent and affordable housing. By extension, the inclusion of a cultural history in a study of community struggle and change addresses the important yet indeterminate role of the avant-garde and subcultures in the middle-class redevelopment of working-class neighborhoods.

Chapter 1 introduces the theoretical and conceptual framework for the examination of the struggles over space on the Lower East Side. Chapters 2 through 9 present a narrative of these struggles from the late nineteenth century to the present, examining changes in the prevailing discourses and representations that define the Lower East Side's reputation and the actions of the primary stakeholders — the real estate industry, the state, and residents. It is beyond the scope of this book to deal exhaustively with the many issues raised in the narrative, such as immigration, the development of public housing, and deindustrialization, to name a few. These processes are addressed insofar as they influence the contested struggle among local stakeholders in different times in the past century or provide the important context in which such struggles transpired. Before we turn to the story of neighborhood struggles on the Lower East Side, however, it is necessary to briefly identify the geographical boundaries and place-names of the study area.

Liquid Place: Lower East Side Geography

Perhaps most indicative of the cultural dimension of the struggle over space is the contest over the place-names of various parts of the Lower East Side. The area between Fourteenth and Houston Streets and Avenue A and the East River, for example, is referred to as part of the Lower East Side, Loisaida, Alphabet City, and part of the East Village. The contemporary use of four different place-names for the same area reflects the immediacy of past and present battles over place, not confusion. The first name, Lower East Side, referred to New York's old working-class residential and industrial area that expanded northward in the nineteenth century as a tenement district. For the city's upper classes during the Gilded Age, the Lower East Side was a feared, chaotic, and threatening space that housed the great "unwashed" foreign masses. In the midst of waves of immigration, newcomers from various Euro-

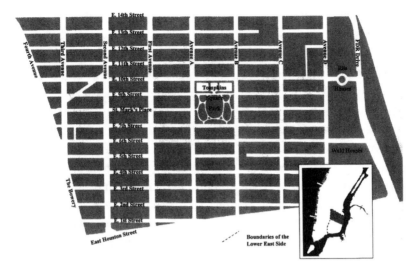

Map 1. The East Village. Map constructed by Neil Wieloch.

pean destinations carved out ethnic spaces, such as Little Italy, which later contracted and became primarily a tourist zone. For many, the contemporary use of Lower East Side to describe the area north of Houston Street emphasizes a commitment to maintaining the district as a working-class neighborhood. Loisaida also has cultural and political meanings; it refers to the Puerto Rican enclave east of Avenue A formed in the late 1950s and early 1960s. The area's present minority residents (Puerto Ricans, Dominicans, other Latinos, and Blacks) refer to their neighborhood as Loisaida, as do many housing activists and community organizers and other low- and moderate-income residents who weathered the ravages of abandonment in the 1970s and redevelopment in the 1980s. Loisaida is synonymous with community action, hope, and resistance.

As mentioned earlier, Alphabet City refers to the same area as Loisaida (Avenues A, B, C, and D) and emerged in the late 1970s and early 1980s in connection to the arts scene that soon attracted real estate investors to an abundant supply of devalued tenement buildings. The somewhat playful name Alphabet City concealed the area's rampant physical and social decline and downplayed the area's Latino identity. The name East Village, which appeared with the earlier hippie movement and signified the opposite to the stodgy, middle-class West Village, was quickly appropriated by real estate brokers and developers.

An "East Village" disassociated the identity of the area north of Houston Street from its working-class past and the less developed streets and avenues to the south. Since realtors, hippies, and other newcomers together referred to the northern part of the Lower East Side as the East Village, its use was picked up by the local, national, and international media. In the 1970s and 1980s, East Village was synonymous with downtown underground culture. For many local activists, the name retains the distinct meaning of real estate development and displacement. That all these names continue to be used is strong testimony to the importance of cultural representation to neighborhood restructuring and resistance. In the late 1990s, the symbolic boundaries of the East Village have dipped below its Houston Street border, as renovated apartments, new bars, and trendy nightclubs proliferate in the narrow streets of the old Lower East Side. In fact, those curious about the development of the East Village in the early 1980s need only visit south of Houston Street to see a similar phenomenon transpiring, as urban decay and development coexist in an awkward and uneasy form.

There are no natural borders to the neighborhood, save for the East River. There are only the invented borders, whose location and place-names signify a century of cultural, political, and social struggles over neighborhood. The geographical focus of this study is equivalent to the contemporary East Village (Houston to Fourteenth Street and Avenue D to Fourth Avenue). The decision to treat this area and not the entire Lower East Side reflects important historical changes since World War II. The political, economic, and cultural processes that produced the modern Chinatown in the southern tier are strikingly different from those that developed the East Village a short distance to the north. I use Lower East Side, however, to describe the same area when historically appropriate (pre-1960s), and I use Alphabet City and Loisaida to refer to the subcommunities within this same space.

Such fluidity of places and their defined borders within a fixed geographical space has significant implications for conducting research about the area. Quite simply, changing borders disallow a neat longitudinal study of demographic indicators tied to boundaries of census tracts, health districts, voting districts, or community boards. These and other governmental geographic inventions never reflected the borders of areas such as Loisaida, Alphabet City, or, to date, the East Village. Even a simple and parsimonious table of population changes in the entire

Lower East Side from 1900 to 2000 would overstate certain trends, such as the expansion of Chinatown in the southern tier, and disguise others, such as the severity of urban depopulation in Loisaida north of Houston Street. In reconstructing the narrative of social conflict on the Lower East Side, I have tried as best as possible to utilize primary and secondary data relevant to the area north of Houston Street and to subsections or communities within this region — the East Village, Loisaida, and Alphabet City. In the period prior to 1960 none of these subdivisions existed; thus, documents related to this era refer only to the entire Lower East Side.

While obstacles to data collection exist, I have clearly benefited from a wide range of material, including archival sources, newspapers, handbooks, government commissions proceedings, mimeographs, novels, films, Web sites, and an abundance of scholarly treatments of the neighborhood. These include the work of the Tenement House Commission (1880s–1900s); Leo Grebler's study of land utilization on the Lower East Side (1920s–40s); the historian Suzanne Wasserman's dissertation on changes during the initial decades of the twentieth century; the organization Mobilization for Youth's survey of land use and population conditions (1950s–60s); Abeles, Schwartz and Associates' "Forging a Future for the Lower East Side," prepared for the New York City Planning Commission (1960s–70s); urban geographer Neil Smith's work on tax-arrears and urban investment (1970s–80s); and Frank DeGiovanni's study of community displacement (1980s). My own analysis of real estate transactions and demographic changes covers the most recent changes (1980s–90s). In addition to primary and secondary scholarly sources, the analysis of the politics, economy, and culture of social conflict since the mid-1980s draws on my notes and experiences from interviews and fieldwork.

Acknowledgments

I owe different kinds of thanks to many individuals. My warmest and deepest thanks are reserved for Janet Abu-Lughod, to whom I am grateful for acting as mentor while I pursued my studies at the New School for Social Research and for remaining a close colleague and friend ever since. I owe a special thanks to Cindy Cooper, my graduate research assistant at the University at Buffalo, who meticulously read and provided perceptive and critical comments on the first, last, and innumerable drafts in between. Her assistance was crucial to all aspects of the production of this book.

My ideas benefited from the suggestions of the following colleagues, who read parts or the entirety of earlier versions: Sharon Zukin, Dennis Judd, Ira Katznelson, Charles Tilly, Gail Radford, Mark Gottdiener, Vera Zolberg, and John Eade. I thank them for prompting me to clarify and improve on my central arguments. I take sole responsibility for the remaining shortcomings.

Several persons were instrumental to seeing the project to fruition. Carrie Mullen, Douglas Armato, and Mary Keirstead of the University of Minnesota Press provided good-natured and expert guidance from start to finish. Daniel Webb, a graduate student at the University at Buffalo, worked long hours assembling documents, photographs, and video and writing text for the affiliated Internet Web site. I acknowledge Kurt Reymers's important part in technical assistance for the Web site. I appreciate Robert McFarland and Marlis Momber for allowing me to use their wonderful photographs, Neil Wieloch for producing the maps, and Robert Slammon for assisting in copyright permissions. I remain indebted to the librarians at the New York Public Library, the municipal archives, and my current and former universities.

Finally, I am grateful to many individuals for their continued support and friendship while I completed this project. I especially thank

Alex Aguilar, Eleanor Bader, Kelly Crean, Caroline Egan-Strang, Dorien Greshof, Monica Jardine, Val Marie Johnson, Patrick Kearns, Krystal Kelley, Donna Lee King, Laurie Lanning, Diane Levy, Jan Lin, Caroline Lord, Jonathon Lowery, Robert McFarland, Victor Mirando, Monica Murero, Tammie Robbins, and Amy Taylor.

Various funding resources allowed me the time to research and write. At the New School, a grant from Research About Lower Manhattan (REALM) supported my analysis of land use and real estate transactions as well as research in the municipal archives. Ethnographic work took place while I was a fellow at the National Development Research Institute (NDRI). Research and travel grants from the University of North Carolina at Wilmington, the University at Buffalo, and the Baldy Center for Law and Social Policy allowed necessary return trips to the field and to various libraries. The Julian Park Publication Fund at the University at Buffalo funded the costs of photographs and reproduction fees.

CHAPTER ONE

The Struggle over Space

As this book is being written, the musical *Rent* plays eight times a week to a packed Nederlander Theater in New York City's Broadway district. For a few hours, the staple Broadway patrons — white upper-middle-class residents of the tonier suburbs of Long Island and Westchester County — follow the lyrical narrative of urban struggles with AIDS, heroin addiction, homelessness, squatting, forced evictions, real estate gouging, and the dilemma of "making art" or "selling out." The cast represents a particular cross section of young urban dwellers: an aspiring filmmaker, a rock musician, a drag-queen dancer, a landlord villain, and, among others, the homeless. This updated version of Puccini's *La Bohème* is set not in Paris but in the East Village, thirty blocks south of the theater and considerably farther from the experiences of many of those in attendance. The success of the musical has prompted the opening of a "Rent" clothing boutique at Bloomingdale's, the upscale department store on the Upper East Side. There customers may familiarize themselves with an "East Village look" and an accompanying attitude by consuming high-priced sartorial reproductions of secondhand clothing. MTV, the music television network, offered a one-year lease of an East Village apartment as part of a promotion for a film about a white male tenement dweller's love/hate relationship with his cockroach-infested walk-up. In the mid-1990s, another cable network, Comedy Central, televised its "alternative" and caviling stand-up series from Tompkins Square Park, the site of earlier unrest over neighborhood renewal between locals and police. On the Internet, curiosity in the East Village has prompted the appearance of a cyber soap opera that bears the neighborhood's name. In this virtual East Village, Web browsers interact with plot lines of the fictionally disenfranchised, the struggling artist, and the strung-out drug addict. Several travel-related Web sites survey the neighborhood's nightspots and after-hours clubs, including Web pages in Japanese, German, and Dutch. All of these representations — the theatrical, the commodified, and the virtual — are played out at Life Cafe, an actual restaurant in the East Village featured both in the Broadway show and the cyber soap, where patrons with laptops may browse the Web and virtually experience the place where they are eating their lunch.

The representations of the East Village spun by *Rent* and its boutique, formed through the daily exploits in cyberspace and on television and chronicled in trend-setting magazines, yield a specific rendition of the neighborhood and the everyday experiences of its residents. Primarily through media exposure, middle-class visitors encounter, become familiar with, and appreciate an illusion of the East Village lifted from bits and pieces of an otherwise complex interplay of ethnic, racial, class, political, and sexual social relations. Symbols, images, and rhetoric typify local social life as "peculiar" or "offbeat" but always aesthetically pleasing and penetrable to the inquisitive (and acquisitive) middle and upper classes. The latest symbolic representations that ennoble the community's cultural differences mark a dramatic shift from those of the past. Beginning in the nineteenth century, popular notions had fixed on the area's entrenched poverty, ethnic plurality, political activism, and "low" culture in ways that elicited feelings of revulsion and fear among the city's elite and middle classes. The contemporary symbolic transgression of traditional cultural boundaries of poverty and plenty signifies the erosion of cultural distinctions between social classes — the consumption of discrete categories of commodities, including commercial and residential spaces, can no longer be identified with any one class in particular. This form of transgression is symptomatic of long-term changes in middle-class consumption patterns,[1] the increasing sophistication of advertisers and other "cultural intermediaries,"[2] the economic importance of the production of cultural objects or goods,[3] and the consumption of subcultural forms as a basis of social identity.[4] Advertising, promotion, and the niche marketing of "difference" have transformed once threatening and scorned subcultural aesthetics, such as rap, hip-hop, drag, and queer, into more or less readily available, consumable lifestyles.

Representations that imaginatively venerate the ethnic, racial, sexual, and cultural diversity of place but intentionally understate the material dimensions of structural inequality have become increasingly prominent in forms of urban development in New York and similar Western cities. In the East Village, real estate developers have translated the symbolic value of cultural difference into economic value, attracting middle-class renters, diners, and shoppers who find allure in this edgier version of "bohemian mix,"[5] flush with modern living spaces and other amenities. Developers of spaces labeled "slum" or "ghetto" are no longer required to produce or market images of place that, in effect, compete with the suburban ideal. Instead the real estate sector has produced housing that aesthetically targets various middle-class lifestyles. Past and present struggles over poor living conditions mounted by diverse religious, ethnic, racial, sexual, radical political, and environmental groups are not excluded or disavowed in such representations but are included *symbolically* under the rubric of marketable "difference."

The architectural features and interior designs of the East Village's new, high-end commercial and residential spaces produce a contrived sense of urban grittiness and feel of "downtown" without the risks and inconveniences of poverty. The effects are a symbolic gesture toward (but ultimately a rejection of) the surrounding landscape of tenement apartments occupied by poor and low-income families and individuals. The aesthetic intent of these new spaces is to suggest the disappearance of the boundary between the neighborhood's exterior/public (dark, dangerous, ethnic, uncontrolled) landscape and interior/private (exclusive, expensive, white, safe) places. An engraving in the frontispiece of a newly constructed apartment building on East Sixth Street memorializes the site's diverse and sometimes cheeky past. It reads, "Dedicated in celebration of all those who came to watch, rock and dance," commemorating previous uses as a turn-of-the-century immigrant theater, the Fillmore East rock club in the hippie 1960s, and the Saint, an oversized gay dance club popular in the early 1980s. The building's developers sought not to reproduce the bizarre and the spectacular but rather to briefly reference them as a source of fascination and allure. On East Houston Street, Soviet-era Moscow and Lower East Side political radicalism of the early 1900s inspired the facade of the multistory Red Square apartments. An installation of automobile parts, steel machinery, and scrap metal atop the adjacent high-end retail complex mimics the look of the formerly squatted Rivington Street sculpture garden that once stood nearby. Real estate marketing announcements, tourist brochures, and neighborhood shopping guides refer to cross-dressing festivals, past incidences of riot and social conflict, and a long history of ethnic diversity as adding to the neighborhood's unique appeal.

The symbolic middle-class embrace of the cultural practices of the categorical "Other" through consumption has not improved the precarious housing situations many local residents face. Representations of the East Village circulated and consumed by the inhabitants of suburban Westchester, the browsers of cyberspace, some new residents, and curious tourists are simultaneously derived from and superimposed on the social and cultural lives of residents who include, among others, immigrants, Latinos, the poor, squatters, and the homeless. In this embrace of difference, local cultural practices and social interactions provide the symbolic matériel for the representation of the neighborhood as attractive and alluring. In recently opened restaurants, boutiques, and apartment houses, gestures toward inclusion of "local color" are purely token as these spaces (and their intended patrons) remain detached from the impoverished social and economic conditions that continue to plague many area residents. The effect of this latest form of urban development is the gated community without the gate — the symbolic inclusion of difference coexists with its material exclusion. Thus, the basic components of inner-city urban development — political economic processes that threaten to displace poor and working-class residents — remain but are justified or glossed over by powerful representations of local cultural diversity.

The contemporary redevelopment of this traditionally working-class neighborhood is premised on powerful actors' wholly symbolic inclusion of its once marginal identity and reputation as culturally deviant and politically defiant. This seemingly ironic condition serves as a point of departure for a historical analysis of the relationship between cultural representations of the inner city and urban restructuring. In a historically impoverished area like the Lower East Side, efforts at urban development certainly are not new. In the past century, the real estate industry and government actors have periodically tried to restructure the neighborhood, displacing its working-class and minority populations and character and replacing them with middle-class ones. And while the symbolic inclusion of local cultural differences to sell real estate is novel, representations of place have always been relevant to the production and transformation of urban space. Representations of place — historically particular sets of images, rhetoric, and symbols that circulate and signify a particular neighborhood identity — are not simply cultural expressions that sit atop or reflect political economic processes of urban change. Instead, as I argue in this book, they are intrinsic to the entire process of restructuring, including producing built environments, attracting new kinds of consumption, and mounting and countering local resistance to such changes. A central theme is that stories, reports, rumors, and reputations that comprise popular discourse and representations about the working-class, minority inner city have had demonstrable influences on the contours of struggles over neighborhood restructuring among stakeholders.

Representations serve as critical sources of legitimacy for investment decisions and urban development policies that bring about a community's renewal or abandonment. Through the deployment of certain place representations and not others, real estate investment actions and state development policies are presented as compulsory, the subsequent social costs are exculpated, and residents' resistance and counterclaims to neighborhood changes or neglect are disregarded. Likewise, a central feature of resident resistance against development involves the rejection or affirmation of the prevailing sets of images and symbols of the neighborhood, its people, and their lifestyles.

Following this introductory chapter, I present a historical narrative of struggles over space on the Lower East Side since 1870, focusing on episodes of conflict that pitted the interests of urban accumulation and, often, political regulation against working-class residents' demands for affordable and decent housing. An analysis of this contentious history suggests how we might more successfully read and interpret the diverse ways in which the symbolic realm of reputations and characterizations of place are implicated in the material production and consumption of urban space. In tracing these struggles and their varied outcomes over time, I demonstrate the ways that dominant images, language, and other cultural signs that "stood for" the neighborhood framed the political and economic strategies and tactics of three groups of stakeholders: the real estate sector, state actors, and residents. In chapters 2 through 6, I reveal the ways symbolic representations of the ghetto and the slum as different and inferior facilitated certain exploitative real estate investment actions and governmental urban development policies from the 1870s to the 1970s. The real estate sector banked on dominant and negative cultural representations to portray both urban investment and disinvestment practices as natural, rational, and logical (if, at times, beneficial, desirable, or unfortunate). In the material realm, such actions produced land-use changes that uniformly displaced the poor and ethnic and racial minorities. These representations of the ghetto also sustained a legacy of radical political and cultural activism that was not only frequently successful against development efforts but became a central characteristic of the neighborhood's identity. Community residents often mounted organized resistance to threatened changes and unmasked the discourse of development to reveal the social costs to working-class and minority residents. Conversely, some residents, including various avant-garde or subcultural groups who lived in the neighborhood, indulged dominant representations of Lower East Siders as different and/or inferior, thus sabotaging and subverting the images and rhetoric of a "new and improved" middle-class neighborhood concocted by developers and the state. In chapters 7 through 9, I recount the shift in representations of subcultural differences from the maligned margins to the middle-class mainstream and, consequently, the shift in the characterization of the Lower East Side from the deteriorated ghetto to the desirable urban niche. This turn in representational style, rooted deeply in the neighborhood's history but fully manifested only since the late 1970s, has influenced the present conditions of struggle on the Lower East Side, creating opportunities for the real estate sector and challenges for local resistance to development.

In the following sections of this introductory chapter, I introduce and develop an approach that considers place representations as instrumental to the political economy of urban restructuring. Drawing on the theoretical advances of contemporary urban sociology, I first introduce the political economic interests and motivations of the real estate industry, the state, and working-class and ethnic and racial minority residents. Next I briefly examine representations of urban places and how they are manipulated, deployed, and contested by these groups of stakeholders to promote their different agendas.

The Struggle over Space: Lower East Side Style

The past century has been marked by turf battles on the Lower East Side, with real estate capitalists and state actors largely interested in "improving the use" of the prized real estate sandwiched between lower Manhattan/Wall Street and Midtown, and working-class and minority residents concerned with bettering their housing and their community. Before I posit the ways symbolic and cultural representations of place influence how these struggles have transpired, I must first introduce some general characteristics of the struggle itself and identify categories of its central actors. The subject matter of this book is a particular dimension of urbanization — the restructuring of the inner city, in which political economic actions alter the built environment and transform the class, as well as ethnic, racial, and cultural, composition of neighborhoods. Over the past century, powerful social forces operating at the global, national, and regional levels and ranging from industrialization to the dominance of the service sector in the urban economy periodically have driven efforts to transform the use of space in inner-city neighborhoods. Episodes of urban restructuring involve three key stakeholders — the real estate sector, the state, and residents — whose interests and actions guide the historical narrative of social change on the Lower East Side.

The real estate sector comprises a major stakeholder in that its varying and sometimes contradictory economic interests and actions *initiate* processes that seek to alter the neighborhood's built environment and its class and cultural identities.[6] The real estate sector includes thousands of independent landlords, speculators, developers, brokers, and management companies as well as construction firms, banks, savings and loans, and other lending institutions. Their activities, namely capital investment and disinvestment in neighborhood property and efforts to promote new, profitable forms of consumption, have remained the primary catalysts of social conflict and change on the Lower East Side for two reasons. First, the dominant form of ownership of the area's commercial and residential spaces has been and remains the absentee landlord who treats tenements, commercial buildings, and lots as income-generating properties rather than as primary residences. Absentee ownership increases the propensity of conflict with tenants since landowners' investment decisions are solely profit driven and reflect no attachment or commitment to home, block, or neighborhood typically associated with owner-occupiers.

The geography of the built environment has also influenced the kinds of real estate actors who operated on the Lower East Side and the range of actions in which they engaged. Most Lower East Side property consists of small parcels typically 25 feet wide by 100 feet deep. Historically, the small lot size has limited the scope of profits from real estate transactions and development. This, in turn, has repelled certain kinds of real estate actors and attracted others. The city's largest real estate companies and the recent international property investment and management companies have rarely shown interest in the local land market because of the limited profitability of smaller parcels and, as outlined in the following chapters, the difficulty of assembling individual lots for large development projects. The actions of large developers in other areas of Manhattan have nonetheless had tangible effects on the value of centrally located Lower East Side property. Most apparently, their investments in adjacent districts have typically generated interest in the neighborhood's middle-class development. The middle range of the real estate sector, including brokers, holding companies, and development firms, have entered and exited the local land market as such expectations have periodically risen and fallen. In periods of renewal, individual maverick speculators have been the initial players, buying undervalued parcels and selling them within months at increased prices. Small to middle-sized firms of private landlords, developers, and real estate and holding companies have typically followed on the heels of speculators. In periods of limited or stagnant real estate activity, Lower East Side landlords have tended to be individual petty capitalists who anticipated handsome returns for relatively modest investments. Combined, landlord absenteeism and the relatively modest investment in, and limited return from, small property created a fluid real estate environment in which cycles of investment and disinvestment were both rapid and frequent. Historically, this volatility in local real estate activities has increased the potential for land-use struggles to erupt as property owners sought to make good on their investments in ways that typically threatened the housing circumstances of working-class and minority renters.

Like the real estate sector, the federal, state, and local governments played determinative roles in the restructuring of the Lower East Side and were directly implicated in the periodic conflicts over changes in the built environment. Over the course of a century, the state's institutional mechanisms varied as diverse agencies, planning authorities, and commissions formed and disbanded, leaving imprints on the neighborhood landscape. Frequently, control over the regulatory resources of the state was a source of struggle itself. Both the real estate sector and organized residents' movements attempted to "capture the state" through political struggle and curry favor for their opposing standpoints. Given higher levels of political organization and greater economic resources at their disposal, property owners typically held more leverage than tenants over the shape of urban policies, incentives, regulations, and laws. Residents and community activists nonetheless consistently mobilized to demand that the state use its regulatory capacity to improve neighborhood conditions or to curb the discretionary power of property owners over tenants. Urban development policies, however, were not consistently or uniformly synchronous with the interests of either real estate capitalists or residents. Instead, state autonomy in urban development affairs surfaced often throughout the past century. New York development politics have ranged from aggressive promotion of private urban development to progressive or lukewarm reformist sanctions of community-based resident initiatives.[7] The longevity of political machines, especially the Tammany Democrats, was testimony to the influence of electoral politics on development decisions for neighborhoods like the Lower East Side. At the end of the nineteenth century, progressive and reformist forces at the state and local level implemented laws and created public administrative agencies to regulate working-class housing. Zoning, land-use planning, building codes, and other institutional and regulatory instruments soon followed to check real estate practices (although their selective application and enforcement would always remain governed by *political* considerations). State and federal intervention in urban development during the 1930s did not eliminate local machines but forced them to adapt to increasingly institutionalized and bureaucratized state structures.[8] The machine form continued to influence the ways in which various institutions and agencies distributed urban development and housing programs and expenditures.[9]

In the immediate postwar era, the capacity of the Lower East Side to exert political influence over development issues waned, largely due to changes in its demographic (and therefore electoral) base. The area's newest migrants, Puerto Ricans, possessed little political capital in a local system traditionally dominated by European immigrants or their offspring.[10] In the grassroots political backlash against costly and oppressive development of the late 1950s and 1960s, urban social movements on the Lower East Side and elsewhere flourished, demanding, among other things, affordable decent housing and winning some institutional legitimacy as agents of neighborhood change. In the 1970s, the politics of fiscal austerity and neoconservative retrenchment replaced the "redistributive liberalism" of the 1960s.[11] By the close of this urban fiscal crisis, the pendulum of institutional politics had swung away from community-based development and citizen reform coalitions and fully toward incentives for private commercial and residential development. It has remained there since.

Of late, the city administration has employed non-development-oriented agencies — the parks and police departments among others — to enforce "quality of life" measures that facilitate middle-class renewal of poorer neighborhoods. During the Giuliani administration in the 1990s, pro-growth politics have been combined with the ardent zeal of public officials (especially the mayor) to put to use new or existing (but relatively inexpensive) policies to "improve" the city's image and, consequently, middle- and upper-class property values. This brief overview of urban development politics suggest two things: that state actions fostered the interests of other stakeholders at different times and that state actions were often dictated by autonomous electoral and institutional interests. With these points in mind, the state, in its infinite complexity over the past century, clearly has existed as a stakeholder in its own right in the struggle over space and not simply as a passive tool for other actors.

The investment actions of the real estate sector and many of the state's development policies set off protracted struggles with residents, namely working-class and ethnic and racial minority renters. Efforts to produce new uses for existing residential and commercial spaces invariably threatened to displace East Siders from their homes. The success of middle-class redevelopment plans hinged on widespread displacement of existing poor residents.[12] Likewise during periods of urban decline, real estate disinvestment and inadequate urban policies brought about dramatic decreases in neighborhood population and housing abandonment. Faced with the threat of displacement incumbent to urban restructuring, working-class and minority residents had an interest in the maintenance and improvement of their neighborhood. As the following chapters show, however, the political disposition of residents cannot be imputed from their class, ethnic, and racial positions. Although opposition to neighborhood changes often developed within class, ethnic, and racial boundaries, certain issues fractured solidarities within groups and created alliances between them. The relationship between white ethnic and Latino residents in the 1950s, for example, was antagonistic, despite roughly similar class statuses and mutual interests against urban displacement. In the 1980s, Latino housing activists and organizations ignored their overlapping political interests with young white squatters, whom they regarded as outsiders or troublemakers rather than allies. During the same period, many older ethnic residents aligned themselves with middle-class newcomers over quality-of-life issues, despite displacement pressures on the former group. Such social divisions frequently were bridged, however, and Lower East Side residents organized against actions and policies that, left unchecked, forebode a loss of community. Developers, landlords, and local government agencies typically found themselves battling working-class resistance sustained by an ongoing legacy of defiance that began to define a core feature of the neighborhood's identity. An admixture of politics and culture, Lower East Side resistance often stalled proposed land-use changes and regularly confounded the halcyon images of a revitalized, middle-class community proposed by investors and zealous city officials.

Thus far we have considered the important political economic interests and motivations of the three stakeholders in the struggle over space with brief mention of the cultural tactics employed by residents engaged in resistance to land-use changes. This book focuses on the process of urban struggle and, in particular, the cultural frameworks that shape the strategies, tactics, and more spontaneous actions of each of the key neighborhood stakeholders. As the narrative will reveal, turf battles on the Lower East Side were embedded within historically specific cultural discourses about the inner city that, in turn, fundamentally shaped the configuration and outcomes of local struggles. In the following pages, I first define representations as historical articulations of social power that shape public awareness of cities and neighborhoods. Representations of the inner city steer public commentary about neighborhoods, their residents, and the events and activities that take place there. Next I develop an approach that explores how these cultural symbols, images, and rhetoric are employed in struggles over space. My intention is not to reconstruct cultural notions about the Lower East Side per se or to portray them as simple expressions of political economic conflicts. Instead, I intend to show how real estate capitalists, state actors, and residents engage representations of place to legitimate and facilitate their actions in transforming or defending the neighborhood.

Representations of the Inner City and the Struggle over Space

In the following chapters, I demonstrate the complex relationships between prevailing discourses, images, rhetoric, and symbols that, together, shape representations about the Lower East Side and the political and economic processes of restructuring that form the basis of neighborhood struggles since the late nineteenth century. Before doing so, it is important first to distinguish place identities from representations and to show how the latter develop and change over time and correlate to social and political processes well beyond the scope of the neighborhood. Finally, I spell out the ways representations are employed by the different community stakeholders engaged in the struggle over space.

The connection between place-related cultural images and symbols and economic processes of urban land use and changes was referred to in the first human ecology writings of the Chicago School of urban sociology in the early 1920s. Sentiments, affective meanings, and attachments to place as well as sustained social interaction and activities within a territory over time comprised a cultural dimension or sense of place that, like economic competition, influenced urban spatial processes.[13] The sense of place, or place identity, is formed from "people's subjective perceptions of their environments and their more or less conscious feelings about those environments."[14] Within a short while, however, human ecology emphasized exclusively the centrality of economic competition in its approach to the study of the city; place identity and other cultural variables were relegated to the category "nonrational factors." Since Chicago's heyday, sociologists, largely working within the human ecology framework, have periodically reasserted the importance of cultural factors in spatial change.[15] Yet the relationship between sentiments, place identities, and shared attachments and so-called rational factors that drive land-use change remains awkward largely because the human ecology framework ontologically separates cultural forms from economic processes that determine land rents, housing demand, and property values.

An entirely different framework for understanding the connections between cultural images, symbols, and rhetoric and political economic restructuring has developed from the influences of new urban sociology and poststructuralist theories.[16] A distinction is made between place identities and representations of place and how the latter are formed and circulated. As the early ecologists noted, place identities are constructed from sentiments, attachments, and patterns of social interactions among residents and other users over time. Through patterns of social interactions, streets, sidewalks, parks, and buildings that comprise a neighborhood's built environment are encoded in localized and historically specific systems of sociospatial semiotics. Social groups that share class, ethnic, religious, or cultural backgrounds engage in patterned interactions that tether cultural significations to particular features of the built environment. Repeated social interactions in buildings, streets, and entire neighborhoods produce territorial meanings (e.g., "community"[17]) and a sense of privilege and ownership of place. The formation of place-names, such as Loisaida or Jewish Broadway, reflects this process. Because dozens of social groups typically use identical urban spaces for similar and different purposes and imbue them with innumerable meanings, place identities may quietly overlap or radically conflict. Various social groups construct their own territories with known borders within public spaces; elderly residents, for example, carve out safe sections of parks to create their own recreational enclaves, and members of a party circuit share a geography of worthwhile clubs, bars, and restaurants that do business in the early morning hours. Neighborhoods have identities—that is, they are vested with meaning—through patterns of social interaction and attachments among their frequent users, most notably residents. We will return to the discussion of place attachments later in this chapter in the section on community resistance to urban restructuring.

While both share sets of images, symbols, and language, representations of place form in a manner radically different from identities of place. Representations "stand for" place and offer an alternative to immediacy and experience as a means to know about a neighborhood and its residents. The range of particular images, symbols, and rhetoric that visitors, observers, and outsiders use to refer to or describe a neighborhood as pleasant or dangerous are constructed neither necessarily by the gazers themselves nor by those with firsthand knowledge through use of such spaces. Instead, people come to know of and about places through the circulation of predominant representations and popular notions. Anselm Strauss noted this in his 1961 publication *Images of the American City*. Select symbols, according to Strauss, act as simplified shorthand that most people recognize and associate with otherwise infinitely complex spaces. Representing place is an exercise in making sense out of chaos and providing a consensual understanding that facilitates "organized and relatively routinized" social interaction in the city.[18] "The city, as a whole, is inaccessible to the imagination," he wrote, "unless it can be reduced and simplified."[19] The significance of Strauss's work is his focus on the characterization of place as defined by public consensus formed around particular symbols, rhetoric, and images rather than from direct exposure or experience. The inclusion and exclusion of particular symbols to represent a place, the kinds of interpretations they intend to elicit, and the means by which they are circulated are not problematized, however. For Strauss, the dominant symbols that come to represent place identity emerge almost spontaneously from the place itself, typically from the outstanding features of its landscape, such as landmark buildings or bridges, or from defining historical moments. Striking differences between the kinds of interpretations of place prompted by representational symbols and images and those spurred by actual experience seem inevitable to Strauss. Such disjunctures are an unfortunate but benign consequence of representations that try to integrate complex realities into a few intelligible symbols. The disparity between the representation and reality of place — oversimplification or exaggeration — is bound to occur.

A preferable approach is to view the construction of representations, the means by which they are circulated, and the often glaring discrepancies between simplification or exaggeration and the complexity of place as expressions of social power and contestation rather than as ad hoc by-products of consensual place image making.[20] Symbolic representations of place that characterize local cultures as different and marginal *cannot be divorced* from the class, ethnic, and racial expressions of social power at any given time. Outstanding themes in place representations in any given historical period are reflective of wider political and social currents. These guideposts make sense of "different" places, people, and social interactions in ways that cannot be considered neutral but rather are bound to political, economic, and cultural dimensions of inequality. They guide popular interpretations in ways that are often but not invariably conducive to the interests of "ruling groups [who] attempt to fashion the whole of society according to their own world view, values system, sensibility and ideology."[21] Representations collapse multiplicity and diversity into simplified sets of assumptions that tend to reinforce, rather than contradict, prevailing ideologies that explain away social inequalities and legitimate the political and economic processes that create them. On the Lower East Side, the descriptors "slum," "ghetto," "urban renewal zone," "downtown," and "arts district," among others, were more than faulty or inadequate labels to identify a place at a specific time — they masked both social and cultural diversity and political and economic conditions, such as the exodus of capital, that fostered inequality. The French urban sociologist Henri Lefebvre considered symbolic representations in relation to hegemony — as a means to explain urban resistance as exceptional rather than commonplace:

> The silence of the "users" of space. Why do they allow themselves to be manipulated in ways so damaging to their spaces and their daily life without embarking on massive revolts? . . . It is difficult to see how so odd an indifference could be maintained without diverting the attention and interest of the "users" elsewhere, without throwing sops to them in response to their demands and proposals, or without supplying replacement fulfilments for their (albeit vital) objectives. Perhaps it would be true to say that the place of social space as a whole has been usurped by a part of that space endowed with an illusory special status — namely, that part which is concerned with writing and imagery, underpinned by the written text (journalism and literature), and broadcast by the media; a part, in short, that amounts to abstraction wielding awesome reductionist force vis-à-vis "lived" experience.[22]

Unlike the fixed grip over society implied by domination, representations are hegemonic processes that tend to pervade the everyday consciousness of non-residents and residents alike. As the narrative of urban struggle that follows this chapter shows, representations are likely to be contested, shifted, or reformed as well as reproduced.

Multiple images, symbols, and discourses "familiarize" individuals with neighborhoods and contribute to the emergence of place reputa-

tions. As such, representations of places do not consist of a singular collection of symbols emanating from or authored by one source or circulated through one particular medium. Rather, representations exist *only*
through their expression and circulation in society, appearing in a variety of forms and flowing from a number of social institutions.[23] Symbols, images, and rhetoric circulated in films, novels, serials, television
news broadcasts, newspapers, magazines, crime reports, sensational jour-
nalism, photographic exhibitions, advertising, music, visual arts, Internet Web sites, and other entertainment forms create, affirm, and change
public perceptions and impressions of place. Government institutions
produce plans, reports, and evaluations that present factual data that
typically validate one form of discourse about a region, its dominant
and minority groups, and interpretation of their behavior over others.
Less authoritative sources cite these governmental reports as a basis to
speak on behalf of a neighborhood, its people, and their lifestyles. Representations that concoct a sense of place in vivid detail are especially
powerful. With each new advance in technology and the ever broaden-
ing scope of media circulation, representations evolve from crude sub-
stitution to what appear as "authentic" simulations of "real" neighborhood experiences.

   Increasing technological sophistication elevates multimedia as a credible means for the curious, the visitors, and other "outsiders" to make
sense of different peoples and places. Despite the various sources from
which place representations emanate, however, they do not float disconnected or remain meaningfully distinct and separate from each other.
Instead, dominant themes emerge from the repetitive circulation of
images and symbols and from mutual references and citations across
sources. Bits and pieces of images, symbols, and rhetoric tied to a particular place begin to exist as sets or "regimes of representations," as
Stuart Hall, taking the lead from Michel Foucault, has labeled them.[24]
These sets of interpretive cues together form reputations, parables, and
legends that impart a range of interpretations of place. Representations,
then, classify and essentialize place, presenting it in symbolic shorthand
to the visitor, the potential resident, the curious voyeur, or, in short, the
interested public. Across history, representations of the city's wealthier
districts and the Lower East Side have appeared as mutually reinforcing binaries. Paired opposites account for differences not only in social
geography (uptown and downtown) but in political economy (rich and

poor), social groups (Self and Other, each coded in the prevailing ethnic and racial terminology of the historical period), and social behavior (moral, normal and evil, deviant). These distortions stereotype and
fix the otherwise complex and vastly changing social realities of the urban environment. Typification reifies and objectifies people, places, and
social interactions: locals are not invisible but rather appear as a cast of
characters who inhabit roles in scripted performances not of their making. Places, people, and activities are marked and assigned as "safe," "dangerous," or "up and coming," while social interactions that form local
identities are often "drowned out," twisted, or distorted in the realm of
mediated discourse.

The recurrent circulation of particular images, symbols, and rhetor-
ical forms sets broad parameters for the public's awareness and understanding of place. Representations exist not simply as description but
also as ready explanations of the social, economic, and political features of a given place. As images, symbols, and rhetoric circulate, fictive
accounts merge with "factual" ones, creating place narratives that broadly
spell out the characteristics of the individuals who live there, the sets of
factors that have caused certain conditions, and the likelihood of the
neighborhood's improvement or distress. The language and intonation
associated with such classifications (e.g., cultural difference as hope-
lessly deviant or evil) impart a wide range of corresponding emotive
responses (e.g., fear, pity, revulsion, or forbidden desire) to the consumers of such representations. These responses are powerful insofar
as they influence public disposition toward prescriptive and proscriptive
actions and policies that seek to remedy, improve, or neglect a neighborhood's existing social, economic, and political conditions.

Employing Symbolic Representations in the Struggle over Space

Various reputations and popular cultural notions about inner-city life
do not exist simply as inadequate impressions with insubstantial consequences for urban change. The significance of cultural representations
lies in the ways they are employed by stakeholders in the struggle over
neighborhood restructuring. A constructed popular knowledge of place
influences critical aspects of social actions that are taken to change place,
including investment, disinvestment, development policies, and community resistance. In any given historical period, dominant cultural
representations of the Lower East Side have shaped the contours of

struggle over urban restructuring, influencing the ways changes in land use have been proposed, rationalized, legitimized, and contested. Popular place images, rhetoric, and symbols have been employed to frame proposed land-use changes as desirable, inevitable, logical, or, conversely, imperfect and unjust. In this section, I provide a brief overview of the ways representations were engaged in the neighborhood struggles detailed in the narrative that follows this chapter.

For the real estate sector and state actors, the necessity and desirability of urban change are conveyed primarily in two ways. First, popular notions of the inner city are drawn on to define the neighborhood's status quo condition as unacceptable and plans for urban restructuring as beneficial. Thus, representations that emphasize the Lower East Side as different and inferior factor into these stakeholders' legitimacy claims for (dis)investment and the presence or absence of development policies. In addition, constructing the status quo as intolerable and restructuring as logical (and even natural) often neutralizes residents' public protest of the social costs of changes to their community. Second, symbolic representations of place are employed to target redevelopment toward a preferred market of consumers. Real estate capitalists typically employ cultural symbols and signs to attract upscale consumers to newly constructed or renovated commercial and residential spaces. Place-marketing or more historic forms of civic boosterism demonstrate how myths, legends, or other desirable notions are concocted to communicate and build support for plans to renovate, rebuild, tear down, or modernize a neighborhood's built environment.[25]

Drawing from larger representations of the inner city, the real estate sector and state actors concoct narratives of neighborhood change in which their desired political economic action appears as the best and most credible conclusion. An intrinsic component of the political economy of neighborhood change is the definition and presentation of the neighborhood's existing status as *problematic* and urban restructuring as *ideal or necessary*. Representations of the inner city as a site of social disorganization serve to normalize and facilitate the political and economic practices of both urban investment or disinvestment and municipal development incentives or negligence. During periods of urban investment, development is presented as the elixir for a set of defined urban social problems. As chambers of commerce, mayors' offices, and real estate firms have pronounced throughout the history of the modern city, private urban development offers what the public perceives as "run down" neighborhoods, immigrant warrens, and "dilapidated" ghettos the best chance at progress and improvement. Conversely, during periods of urban decline, disinvestment and the curtailment of policies are rationalized by the existence of often the very same social problems (now represented as overwhelming and incurable). The frequency of local crime or rampant drug sales or use defines neighborhood character or reputation at certain times and not others, independent of actual rates of increase or decrease. Hence, the measurable scale of social problems—the occurrence of various crimes, the number of abandoned housing units, and so on—is not by itself a sufficient condition for understanding why certain community concerns are addressed during periods of restructuring and others are not. As the following chapters show, what constitutes the characterizations of the inner city as slum or ghetto rarely matches empirical observations of demographic, social, and economic conditions. Rather, the characterization of neighborhood in such discourse is largely dependent on the land-use interests of real estate developers and the state and their assessment of challenges to such plans from existing residents. Within a discourse of restructuring the presentation of community issues and social problems is, therefore, subordinate to the need to rationalize and legitimize political economic development interests and to neutralize potential resistance.

Particular neighborhood *social* problems, including drug dealing, crime, and juvenile delinquency, are hence conceptualized as *spatial* problems that either can be cured through private redevelopment or appear to necessitate private disinvestment. Real estate capitalists become enshrined as the agents best suited to correct the social problems of the ghetto or the slum (or, during periods of decline, they represent themselves as guileless victims of such ills). Private urban development is presented as a more desirable and "practical" solution to urban social ills than government policies, such as low-income housing subsidies or welfare programs. Such proclamations appear more attractive when situated within a broader discourse that purports the limited capacity of government to intervene in social justice issues such as decent and affordable housing. Subsidies for private development, in the forms of tax incentives, abatements, and the provision of urban infrastructure, such as highways and parking lots, are discounted. Proclamations of social problems that come from institutional sources, such as planning agencies or civic leaders, also tend to validate and legitimize the frequently coercive practices that accompany restructuring. Representations are employed to legitimize residential displacement ("bulldozing," evictions, resident relocations) and serve to exculpate the many social costs of restructuring. Residential displacement is conceptualized — indeed, naturalized — as an "unfortunate but necessary" consequence of progressive change. Thus, in the symbolic realm, urban investment or disinvestment practices appear as natural and logical. In the material realm, such actions produce land-use changes that uniformly displace the poor and ethnic and racial minorities. The engagement with prevailing representations also helps build consensus around transformation among capitalists,[26] state actors, some residents, and broader publics.

Referring and often contributing to prevailing notions and reputations, developers and state actors have historically portrayed the status quo on the Lower East Side in ways that favor their political economic interests. In addition, they have presented development not only as a solution to the status quo but in terms that would attract prospective middle- or upper-class residents. The attraction of new consumers is dictated not only by the physical renovation of living spaces but the invented symbolic characterization of place as desirable. That is, pouring considerable amounts of real estate capital into a working-class minority neighborhood alone will not change long-standing perceptions of fear or danger that exist within public discourse about "the ghetto." In episodes of renewal, the reinvention of place as alluring becomes essential to attract higher forms of consumption and, therefore, to valorize property. Existing reputations and characterizations of "different" places have to be replaced or reworked with more suitable images to attract middle-class consumption. Preferred place representations often derive images from an ennobled past or selectively appropriate symbols from the present to market place. Images and symbols of the ideal neighborhood introduce and inculcate the real possibility of "neighborhood comeback" or "renaissance" to targeted consumers. The middle classes appear in such propositions mostly as a *constructed category* — the coveted but elusive ideal outcome of urban restructuring perpetrated by developers and city agencies. To attract newcomers, developers refer to certain middle-class aesthetic attributes and consumption patterns in the representations of an ideal, renewed Lower East Side. They attempt to spatialize these fictive assumptions about the middle class — that is, through investment and use of state policies, they try to reconfigure the landscape materially and symbolically to match the supposed consumption desires of preferred consumers. Quite expectedly, the characteristics of the middle classes, their residential preferences, and the neighborhood preferences assumed and produced by developers and the state shifted over the century, as did the real estate sector's strategies to allure upscale consumers. Across time there was stability in that the social and cultural characteristics of the targeted middle class were typically defined as contrary to those of existing residents. For most of the neighborhood's history, the symbolic representation of the preferred middle-class consumer was not stipulated in economic terms but rather in idealized notions of cultural aesthetics defined *in negation* to those of existing residents. In addition to being *not* poor, the desired new tenants were *not* working-class, *not* ethnic, *not* deviant, or *not* minority depending on prevailing discourses of difference in any given historical moment.

The sector of society that "fit" the constructed categories and assumed aesthetic sensibilities of the desired middle class ranged from white-collar Wall Street workers in the 1920s, white families drawn to the new and highly subsidized suburbs in the 1950s, suburban youth who seemed to offer the real estate sector the prospect of a much larger middle-class revival of the inner city in the 1960s, Wall Street workers once again in the 1980s, and, later, the growing market among the young, middle-class media- and arts-based workforce. Thus, the elements of a new place identity and the types of new consumers featured in redevelopment plans are not arbitrarily defined but are derivative of prevailing societal notions of middle-class aesthetics and desirability. Conjuring images of radically improved quality of life or substituting a new place-name (East Village, Alphabet City) for an existing one (Loisaida or Lower East Side) connected fantasy and desirability to the transformation of space. Positive and hopeful futurist representations that circulate in the media also shift attention away from the coercive means of restructuring (community disruption, displacement, and loss) to its desired outcome (modern, clean, better urban neighborhoods).

Within such discourses of a neighborhood's renaissance or rejuvenation, the political economic interests that drive land-use changes appear sublimated to a more noble abstraction of community betterment. The expected outcome of investment and development is coded in signs and rhetoric of an improved "quality of life" for *all* without specifying the intended class, race, or ethnicity of desired residents. Urban development is made more persuasive and acceptable when promises of local improvements such as enhanced neighborhood appearance and increased public safety are universalistic and appeal across social boundaries. Thus, the human costs of development — the displacement of working-class and minority residents — are not addressed in such discourses but are further disguised by claims of collective community betterment. Depending on the believability of such claims, they may divert residents from collective action and deflate otherwise potent forms of local resistance. Development is represented symbolically as beneficial to all residents. Yet, the intended land-use changes and the development of the built environment aim for the middle- and upper-class residents who can afford them. Real estate and state actors gain further legitimacy for urban restructuring through the invention of a neighborhood vision that correlates to their pragmatic intentions to restructure space. By controlling the discourse of neighborhood vision through access to the media and through public decrees and proclamations, they limit or simply exclude the possibility or feasibility of other options for neighborhood improvement, such as those put forth by residents.

In the narrative of urban restructuring concocted by the real estate sector and state actors, notions of a neighborhood's *existing* conditions, its *future* potential, and the desired class of residents who *should* live there typically impugn current land uses and place identities as formed by residents and other users. But representations of locality also play a central role in the production and reproduction of frequently effective cultural and political resistance, from riots and rent strikes to graffiti and squatting. Neighborhood reinvestment and disinvestment entail both physical displacement of residents and a symbolic dislocation of "home" and "community." Residents often mobilize and act collectively to resist threatened changes to their neighborhood, street, and individual apartment buildings.[27] Historically, residents borrowed many of the tactics of organized resistance from struggles in the workplace (e.g., the rent strike). Solidarities, nonetheless, were formed around interests specifically related to community.[28] The most visible tactics, such as rent strikes, tenant demonstrations, and building takeovers, threatened to curtail development ambitions or, at minimum, to force developers and state actors to acknowledge and address displacement and the consequences of urban restructuring. Political economic repression *and* cultural marginalization repeatedly inspired a local insurgent social solidarity. When faced with very tangible threats of displacement, locals have invented repertoires of resistance that either reject or put to use the various representations that have portrayed the Lower East Side as a different, rebellious, and exotic place.

Faced with threats of residential displacement, community-based organizations, resident councils, and other organized resistance groups bring to bear their own representations of community to counteract and delegitimize threatened changes. Organized forms of local resistance typically employ recognizable community symbols and images to legitimize their right to control the uses of space and to prevent community displacement. Existing cultural practices and dense social networks are often refitted to accommodate resistance. Social networks organized for religious, ethnic, and artistic exchanges, for example, often double as political action networks, combining cultural and political strategies. During episodes of urban restructuring, residents typically engage in a highly visible and vocal public defining of place. Grassroots agencies collapse and define local interests into global notions of "community," "home," or "low-income neighborhood." Tenant-based organizations, for example, define their agenda in the struggle over space (e.g., the popular Lower East Side refrain, "This land is *our* land") to encompass widely diverse communities whose interests they claim to represent. Such resistance discourses rarely represent a united neighborhood front against threats of social and spatial change. Rather, grassroots organizations' definitions of community are competitive and reflect the often fractious relationships among different groups of residents. At various times, then, in the neighborhood's history, ethnicity, religion, race, age, length of residential tenure, or political persuasion has provided the basis for some to speak on behalf of all or to silence others. Infighting and the lack of consensus among disparate groups have the recurrent effect of diluting the potency of resistance against the real estate sector or state actors. Predominant representations and ethnic and racial stereotypes of the homeless, the poor, and others may be reproduced locally in the competition for control over turf.

Alongside highly focused forms of resistance (rent strikes, riots, etc.), locals also engage in a range of symbolic or cultural resistance forms that may thwart the restructuring plans of the real estate sector and the state. By viewing conflict over space in its symbolic as well as material dimensions, the realm of social resistance is broadened to include actions and experiences that do not address directly or are not defined explicitly in opposition to forms of political economic domination.[29] In many instances, the symbols, images, and rhetoric of the everyday lived experience of marginalized social groups confounded the intentions of real estate capitalists or state actors to invent and package the Lower East Side as a desirable middle-class neighborhood. Restructuring, inclusive of the cultural strategies of stakeholders described earlier, encoded working-class and minority *neighborhood presence* with political meaning.[30] Working-class and minority presence served as an effective deterrent to sociospatial embourgeoisment of the Lower East Side. The practices and ordinary activities of working-class and minority residents often countered the preferred middle-class image of neighborhood concocted by developers and state actors. The commonplace activities of the much maligned "Other" — the immigrant, the working-class ethnic, the racial or ethnic minority, the drug addict, the criminal, and the sexual deviant — existed as subversive acts but *only* in the context of intensive efforts to represent and invent the Lower East Side as a mainstream, middle-class district. The most routine expressive behaviors, such as walking to work and playing in a park, formed *countervailing* images to the middle-class representations imposed by developers and the state. The commerce of pushcart vendors who crowded the streets of the Lower East Side in the 1920s, for example, was characterized as an obstacle to middle-class redevelopment. Young Latinos hanging out in a park changed from ordinary to threatening only when developers expressed interest in rehabilitating the low-income neighborhood in the 1980s. Our analysis of social resistance during periods of restructuring, then, must include the everyday actions of residents — control and use of streetscapes, parks, foyers in buildings, as well as cultural and artistic endeavors such as parades, feast days, and murals that *do not correspond* to the desired place images synthesized by developers and the state. In the face of residential displacement, everyday actions did not happen as intentional forms of resistance, but they were often effective against the development plans of state actors and real estate capitalists. In short, when powerful actors attempt to reinvent place and, thereby, threaten its existing meanings and interpretations, the lived experiences of residents who maintain such local cultural attachments to place become *potentially* subversive.

Insiders or Outsiders? Cultural Changes and the Avant-Garde in the Struggle over Space

Prevailing representations of class, ethnic, and racial differences were drawn into the political and economic efforts to transform the Lower East Side. The real estate sector and state actors presented their development agendas in opposition to dominant representations and posed alternative images and symbols tied to "higher and better uses" for the neighborhood. Organized resident groups protested the many stereotypes about the Lower East Side that circulated through the media and popular culture. Often unwittingly, the everyday practices of working-class and ethnic and racial minorities also challenged or short-circuited the plans of developers to portray a glossy, middle-class East Side to potential residents. Clearly, political economic struggles over space were cultural ones as well, and the continuity of such battles contributed to the area's reputation as a space of inventive political resistance and creative expression against powerful forces of urban change.

For most of its history, representations that characterized the Lower East Side as marginal, threatening, dangerous, or abnormal, as stipulated earlier, were influential to the unfolding of local struggle. Although middle- and upper-class outsiders held considerable disdain for social and cultural conditions on the Lower East Side, there was a consistent fascination or obsession among the elite and middle classes with the unpolished or obscene qualities of the "Other." In representations of cultural differences, locals loomed as unique objects of scorn and derision. But these same representations fueled the public's obsessive curiosity with the everyday lives of Lower East Siders. Images and rhetoric that portrayed parks, streets, tenements, bars, and nightclubs as nefarious and forbidden appeared consistently throughout the area's history. As later chapters recount, the middle-class intrigue with the East Side was satiated through sensationalist reports and novels and secretive outings, or "slumming." As early as the 1920s and into the current day, tourists in search of the unusual and bizarre trekked south of Fourteenth Street to briefly consume the spectacle of the slum, the ghetto, the art colony, or downtown and decide for themselves if the area lived up to the image presented in the media.

Also drawn to the cultural contest were middle-class subcultural groups who ideologically embraced the subversive elements of existing discourses about the Lower East Side and its "typical" residents as different or unusual. Subcultures, whose identity, social practices, and rituals intentionally embraced and espoused cultural difference, ranging from the bohemians in the 1920s, the beats in the 1950s, the punks in the 1970s, to the queer subculture in the 1980s, found the East Village reputation propitious to the expression of alternative lifestyles. These groups expressed their opposition to bourgeois society by rejecting familiar and comfortable surroundings and taking up residence among the "undesirables" in the urban "abyss." Rather than treat their presence in the neighborhood as incidental (i.e., simply drawn there by cheap rents) or sociologically irrelevant,[31] I examine each of these avant-garde movements and subcultures in its relation to conflict over restructuring the Lower East Side.

The Lower East Side emerged as a preferred *site* for subcultures and avant-garde movements in New York City primarily because the struggles between insiders (ethnic and racial working class) and outsiders (white, middle and upper classes) became a *source* of inspiration and expression of a critique of capitalist culture and, in particular, of a bourgeois lifestyle.[32] Put bluntly, the drama of the disenfranchised struggling to make do and to counter economic and political exploitation enticed avant-garde movements and subcultures to settle on the Lower East Side. "The intellectual history of the vanguard movements is the history of their degrees of hostility to middle-class society, a hostility that extends from outright assault to self-exile," wrote the critic Harold Rosenberg. "An avant-gardist who ignores conventional opinion wishes it known that he ignores it; his indifference to middle-class values is a maneuver in a war of nerves."[33] The representation of the Lower East Side as marginal, exotic, and different suited the image and the identity of romantic artists as "frontier scouts" of culture, moving ahead of their contemporaries into uncharted territories where they would undergo privation and sacrifices.[34] The consistent middle- and upper-class cultural and political marginalization of the Lower East Side added to its attraction as a space of authentic resistance to the numbing sameness of bourgeois society. Adherents to the different artistic subcultures viewed the lifestyles of the marginalized urban poor, prostitutes, drug addicts, and others as *the* authentic critique of bourgeois society. Local practices and styles were selectively emulated as the blending together of "class signifiers was central to the formation of the avant garde sensibility."[35]

The following chapters explore whether insurgent art, literature, music, and style associated with avant-garde or subcultural movements can be recast as more focused forms of resistance against neighborhood restructuring and its correlate, residential displacement. The narrative of a century of changes on the Lower East Side elicits a contradictory verdict. The cultural subversion of avant-gardism contributed to the East Side's identity and reputation as different, marginal, and persistently anti-bourgeois. Subcultural movements consciously aligned themselves with working-class and minority residents in the struggle against profit-driven realtors, developers, and a recurrently unsympathetic and unresponsive local government. Since subcultures were *located* on the Lower East Side and *interacted* in varying degrees with neighborhood residents, their practices, rituals, symbols, and rhetoric were often shaped and transformed by the active medium of place. The presence of subcultures affected local processes of struggle among capitalists, the state, and working-class residents as well. Conversely, the avant-garde critique of bourgeois culture through symbolic (and temporary) attachment to disenfranchised cultures and lifestyles was, of course, limited and itself thoroughly bourgeois.[36] By idealizing (and idolizing) the "indigenous" and the "authentic," the subcultures partly reproduced cultural stereotypes of working-class people and places. Few among the poor and the marginalized adhered to notions of their economic and political exploitation and oppression as a lived critique of middle-class society. The avant-garde movements often self-identified culturally with locals, but unlike most residents, their composition was predominantly middle-class white youth. Support among the various subcultures for local political causes faced mixed reactions from working-class residents (especially those belonging to organized resistance groups), who often dubiously regarded the lasting intentions of middle-class "outsiders." Despite proud sentiments and attachment to their neighborhood, many of the poorest Lower East Siders equated social mobility with departure from the tenements. The notion of middle-class youth choosing to live in destitution and privation was unsettling and, often, insulting to their struggle to "move out and move up."

Given the diversity among subcultures, it is not propitious to characterize an unchanging relationship between the avant-garde and the process of struggle over space on the Lower East Side. Rather, adequate explanations depend on identifying the social organization of the individual subcultures, their predilections to interact with locals, the form of their cultural critique, and their relationships to mass society and institutions such as the media. The bohemians of the 1920s and 1930s and the beatniks of the 1950s were drawn to the East Side to immerse themselves in a local life whose meaning they (rather than the locals) had constructed as anti-bourgeois. Both groups remained voyeuristic, operating largely as place spectators who moved relatively unnoticeably in the interstices of the Lower East Side's different social worlds. In short, they fabricated self-serving place identities from the everyday struggles of the working class, but their presence on the Lower East Side had little immediate effect on its social and physical landscape or the efforts of outsiders to change it. In their cultural and (somewhat) political rejection of mostly suburban, middle-class lifestyles and expectations, hippies converged on the Lower East Side and, in doing so, constructed an East Village as their own countercultural space. Like the bohemians and beatniks, the hippies were drawn to the East Side's traditions of pluralism and resistance. But unlike their predecessors, the hippie movement purposefully engaged communities on the East Side and sought to transform them. They also ushered in a new era in which subcultural groups sought to colonize the East Village to simultaneously consume and contribute to constructed fictions of anti-bourgeois reality. Painters, musicians, poets, writers, and other artists whose identities (and work) existed outside the mainstream joined the ranks of demonstrators and local activists. Yet the very presence of these *middle-class* cultural dissidents provided a glimmer of hope to desperate landowners who sought to develop a new identity for the Lower East Side that was decidedly neither working-class nor ethnic.

Cultural shifts that emerged in the decades following World War II would have significant consequences for the impact of post-1970s subcultures on urban restructuring on the Lower East Side. Complex changes in mass media, especially advertising, and the eventual redefinition of the distinction between high and low cultures transformed the critical stance of avant-garde movements vis-à-vis mainstream society. Product marketing and advertising became pronounced in the overheated postwar consumer society as television and other new means of communication promoted the manipulation of images in the selling of goods.

Capitalists found in subcultures innovations that they themselves could not produce. Despite its functionalist undertone, Thomas Crow's summary of the postwar relations between capital and subculture is quite helpful:

> In our image-saturated present, the culture industry has demonstrated the ability to package and sell nearly every variety of desire imaginable, but because its ultimate logic is the strictly rational and utilitarian one of profit maximization, it is not able to invent the desires and sensibilities it exploits.... This difficulty is solved by the very defensive and resistant subcultures which come into being as negotiated breathing space on the margins of controlled social life. These are the groups most committed to leisure, its pioneers, who for that reason come up with the richest, most surprising, inventive and effective ways of using it.[37]

Corporate and the subcultural realms grew increasingly intertwined. Art forms developed initially from critically avant-garde movements in the late 1950s and early 1960s seeped into advertisements and product packaging and vice versa, as best exemplified in the pop art of Andy Warhol. Changes in the art world, especially the ascendancy of New York as a cultural capital, provided space both literally and figuratively for more experimental (i.e., "low") artistic styles including pop, minimalism, photorealism, and neo-Expressionism.[38] With the progressive rise of consumer culture, the "average" middle class has become increasingly engulfed in "cultures of difference," as commodities associated with particular subcultures have been consumed worldwide, and tourism has allowed visitors to participate in the spectacle of different places. Circulation of "difference" in mass media as well as postwar governmental and corporate subsidies to artists provided new opportunities for the avant-garde to present "hidden" or "subversive" cultural forms and to gain public recognition. The increased exposure and subsequent middle-class acceptance of subcultural forms jeopardized the subversive foundation of avant-gardism. The avant-garde functioned less as a vanguard and increasingly as the broker between subcultural forms and practices and an expansive culture industry.[39] Assimilating the symbols, images and rhetoric of subcultures into a more expansive bourgeois aesthetic "denuded the American avant garde of cultural concerns and reduced the movement to celebrity, lifestyle, status and fashion."[40]

The formation of subcultural enclaves on the East Side in the 1970s and 1980s reflected these cultural changes as painters, musicians, and other artists unwittingly or intentionally contributed to the neighbor-hood's growing appeal among elements of the middle class. An "arts district" that gained the attention of the middle classes challenged ex-isting adverse representations of the East Side and translated them into possibilities for upscale redevelopment (that ultimately displaced the artists themselves). Despite the continued subjective desires among members of subcultures to take up the causes of their poorest neighbors, the appropriation of cultural differences as commodities has threat-ened the historical alliances of the avant-garde with working-class resi-dents. The final chapter addresses this phenomenon and its implica-tions for community restructuring and resistance.

Given the framework just outlined, it is now possible for us to analyze the ways representations, which define the broad parameters of per-ceptions of the inner city, are directly implicated in the political econ-omy of urban restructuring. By viewing the histories of spatial con-flicts as cultural as well as political and economic, we can visualize the powerful ways actors represent and utilize images of place to further the production and consumption of the inner city as a middle-class space. A focus on the cultural dimensions also compels a definition of types of local resistance to include the manifold experiences, rituals, and practices of subordinate groups in everyday life. Such a focus does not serve to diminish the significance of political economic processes in restructuring. Rather, it deepens our understanding of the ways op-posing stakeholders utilize cultural forms to advance their respective interests, actions, and policies over time. The framework also allows us a means to address the dilemma first posed in the opening pages of this chapter — how is it that cultural differences emerged as symbolically central, rather than marginal, to middle-class urban development in the East Village? Each of the following chapters maps the importance of cultural symbols, images, and rhetoric in both the workings and out-comes of neighborhood conflicts among stakeholders. Particular atten-tion is paid to the ways in which local stakeholders manipulate images of class, ethnic, racial, and sexual differences over time to facilitate neigh-borhood change or to prevent it.

CHAPTER TWO

Different and Inferior:
The Ghetto at the Turn of the Century

New York has consistently been described as two cities, one rich, the other poor; the citadel and the working-class ghetto. In the closing decades of the nineteenth century, the segregated city was of grave concern to the middle and upper classes, who economically benefited from the teeming masses "downtown" but simultaneously feared and despised them. Writings from the period between 1870 and 1925 refer to such concerns in vivid detail. In a passage from his novel *Manhattan Transfer,* John Dos Passos describes an episode in which a respectable young woman leaves her pampered and secluded lifestyle of uptown New York to embark on charitable work deep in the densely crowded streets of the Lower East Side.[1] Clearly overwhelmed, she collapses in disgust at the sight and smell of a group of street urchins she encounters in Tompkins Square Park. T. S. Arthur's *Cast Adrift* tells the gruesome tale of Flora Bond, a young woman new to the city and inexperienced in its ways, who upon entry into the ghetto, immediately falls in with the wrong crowd and eventually dies as a consequence of her depraved ghetto lifestyle.[2] The protagonist in David Graham Phillips's *Susan Lenox: Her Fall and Rise* is redeemed from a sinful and debased condition and, therefore, certain death only after she escapes the impurity that was rampant downtown.[3] In these and other novels and in journalistic accounts and government reports, New Yorkers learned the moral geography of their city in which differences between uptown and downtown were acute. Whereas uptown contained the elite shopping and residential districts, downtown consisted of overcrowded blocks of cheaply constructed tenements with densities of over 250,000 persons per square mile.[4] As the center of New York immigrant and working-class society, the Lower East Side loomed as a dreadful netherworld, a place to be feared and reviled, inhabited by peculiar, if not dangerous, "Others" whose immoral behavior needed to be controlled or, at best, reformed. Representations of the unwashed masses and the spaces they inhabited were the antithesis of the social world that the urban bourgeoisie had constructed and were determined to defend.

Bourgeois representations of working-class immigrants and the spaces they inhabited were both a reaction to the growing economic and cultural divisions between social classes and a means to legitimize political and economic processes that fueled the exploitative conditions within the Lower East Side ghetto. With the expansion of industry and population through foreign migration in the second half of the nineteenth century, differences between New York City's social classes grew sharper and more defined spatially as well as socioeconomically. The rise of an industrial class-structured society generated a specific urban form — the ghetto — in which working classes were geographically segregated from other classes, and their residences were increasingly separated from their workplaces.[5] Within the framework of spatial segregation, the Lower East Side developed its own distinctively working-class housing economy, patterns of community building, and repertoires of social resistance. The contours of these local economic, social, and political processes, as this chapter shows, were culturally defined and influenced by a discourse of the exotic and the unequivocally inferior in need of salvation, isolation, or reform. Bourgeois representations, it is argued, collapsed the complex cultural realities of the immigrant ghetto into categories and stereotypes of the dysfunctional and untamed. Such views of immigrants and their spaces, as circulated in authoritative circles and popular culture, favored the reproduction of housing exploitation, legitimized the long absence of progressive regulations, and shifted the explanation and blame for the social problems of misery, overcrowding, and disease on to the least powerful, the immigrant tenants themselves.

Cultural Representations and the Objectified Ghetto

The stark socioeconomic inequalities between the residents of the "uptown" and "downtown" worlds were matched in degree by representations of vastly different cultural landscapes that were invented by and circulated among upper- and middle-class institutions, social reformers, and politicians, and to a very small extent, Lower East Siders themselves. Those who inhabited upscale homes in the finer neighborhoods of Manhattan rarely ventured onto the Lower East Side or came into personal contact with residents but nonetheless remained (mis)informed of the political, ethnic, and cultural goings-on within the nearby canyons of poorly built tenements south of Fourteenth Street:

> A localization of class life in this period tended to lock the wealthy, wage earners and the impoverished into distinct areas of the city. By the 1890s, each had acquired a name and a recognizable mythos, much as the Bowery, whose reputation lingered on, had done in the antebellum period. New neighborhoods, characterized by distinctive types of housing such as the apartment house and purpose-built tenement, made their appearance during these years, and tended to set off the style of working-class life from that of the middle and upper classes.[6]

Save for the experiences of those who actually ventured onto the Lower East Side, most New Yorkers' contact with the neighborhood came from an abundance of symbols, images, and rhetoric produced by the city's diverse publishing industry, which flourished in the decades following the Civil War.[7] Upper-class New Yorkers contrasted their own familiar world with the strange world of others in comics, guidebooks, newspaper columns and exposés, magazines, and popular fiction. Dailies, such as the *New York Journal* and the *New York World,* and magazines, such as *Harper's,* regularly featured stories about the metropolis's "dark side." Early-nineteenth-century guidebooks tellingly ignored those zones where behaviors considered impertinent to the middle and upper classes transpired. In oversized descriptions of the city, such as *The Secrets of the Great City,* first published in 1868, readers were presented with both the virtues and vices of the city. As a rule, the tone of these treatments of vices constituted a mix of the reproachful with the sensational. This is clearly the case in *Darkness and Daylight, or Lights and Shadows of New York Life.* Its publication was a milestone in the genre of sensationalist representations that mapped the city's moral geography and detailed the lives of thieves, prostitutes, tramps, tenement dwellers, and others deemed "less fortunate." The book's 251 illustrations were drawn from photographs rather than from sketches made hastily at the scene or by artists' recall. This innovation, which promised a more intensive (i.e., "realistic") experience for the reader, was extolled in the publisher's preface:

> The dark side of life is presented without any attempt to tone it down, and foul places are shown just as they exist. . . . In looking on these pages the reader is brought face to face with real life as it is in New York; *not* AS IT WAS, but AS IT IS TO-DAY. Exactly as the reader sees these pictures, just so were the scenes presented to the camera's merciless and unfailing eye at the moment when the action depicted took place. Nothing is lacking but the actual *movement* of the persons represented.[8]

Sensationalist accounts uniformly characterized downtown life as different and odd, and they often sounded the alarm against a recusant and morally bankrupt populace. In the fictional, the imaginary, and the sensational, the immigrant working classes were not composed of agents complete with work and home lives that were richly complex and diverse but were merely one–dimensional objects formed from the forces of moral decay, rampant industrialization, and social disorganization. Second-Wave immigrants, who made up the bulk of the Lower East Side population by 1910, were portrayed as racially "darker," socially inferior, queer in appearance and customs, and ultimately unassimilable. Descriptions of the dress, ceremonies, and social customs among Jews, for instance, were used to incite malevolence against a "barbaric eastern invasion" that threatened Christianity along with Western values and culture. Journalistic depictions, some mundane, others sensational, recounted the chaos of the streets where numerous bizarre activities unfolded daily in cheaply built cheek-by-jowl tenements. Hucksters peddled their wares in an endless din of shouts, husbands and wives aired marital grievances, often violently, children played and teenagers loitered without supervision, prostitutes solicited customers, and gamblers, drug addicts, and alcoholics engaged in their respective habits in full view.

The discursive marginalization of class, race, and ethnic differences was instrumental to the articulation of bourgeois identity. One's middle-class status and prestige were measured not only by degree of economic success but by political, social, and cultural superiority over the working masses. Representations of the "Other" or the marginal depicted terrifying outcomes of life outside bourgeois society. That these moral tales were spatialized made them all the more "real." Middle-class read-

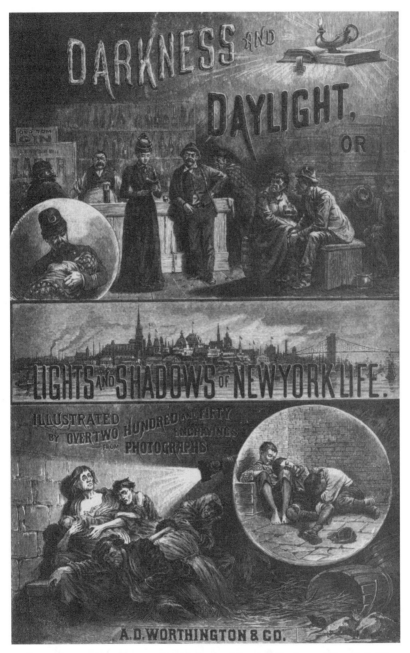

Figure 1. Cover of *Darkness and Daylight, or Lights and Shadows of New York Life*, by Helen Campbell (New York: A. D. Worthington, 1892).

Figure 2. Sketch of flophouse from photograph in *Darkness and Daylight, or Lights and Shadows of New York Life,* by Helen Campbell (New York: A. D. Worthington, 1892).

ers could locate the netherworld on a map, pointing to the landscape downtown as the site of deviance, immorality, and inferiority. Traversing from uptown to downtown marked a fatal crossing of cultural boundaries between good and evil. Vivid and thick descriptions of depravities of the ghetto affirmed the superiority of the middle-class urban world over that governed by violence, decadence, and poverty. Several novels of the period described the dire consequences that inevitably resulted when (mostly female) characters disavowed the structure, predictability, and security of bourgeois society for the unseemly thrills of the ghetto.[9]

The tone evoked in representations of cultural and ethnic differences ranged from revulsion to pity, fear to empathy, and disdain to sympathy. Sympathy and pity were reserved for those depicted as the deserving poor, especially children. With only vague mention made of the causes and conditions of poverty, Lower East Siders were often depicted as uncaring, mean-spirited, and exploitative individuals and, therefore, undeserving of charity or assistance from private and governmental institutions. Gamblers, pimps, and prostitutes were viewed as especially godless creatures whose criminal behavior demanded containment and social control. The small businessman was also scorned. Pushcart hucksters, whose practices of bargaining and price haggling transgressed bourgeois notions of civility and merchandising etiquette, were singled out as dishonest, vile, and lewd. The discourse of "cultural inadequacies" espoused by the middle and upper classes implicitly offered an explanation for the impoverished living conditions on the Lower East Side. The absence of economic considerations diverted explanations for poverty away from class inequalities and toward cultural differences. Thus, "real-life" exposés, as diverse as those found in the more sensationalist *McClure's* magazine or the more "objective" Committee of Fifteen's 1902 report on vice, similarly reinforced the public's overall perception of the evils of the slum and the threats its residents posed to the larger society. Unabridged "true-grit" stories of life on the Lower East Side did not challenge middle- and upper-class ideological perspectives of poverty among the "lower" classes, they reinforced them.

Representations of the Lower East Side not only framed the processes that created and maintained the immigrant ghetto from the mid-nineteenth century to 1925, they were ideological expressions of them. Individuals and institutions incorporated cultural and ideological notions of the immigrant "Other" into justifications for actions and policies (or the absence of them). Prevailing attitudes that marginalized the Lower East Side rationalized the exploitative behavior of real estate actors and the convenient silence of a disinterested government. Public notions of the inferior "Other" suffused the operation of the slum housing economy, allowing greater leeway of exploitation to those whose economic interests were tied to construction and management of working-class tenements. "Outsiders"' impressions of immigrants and their neighborhoods worked their way into ethnic community building and in the types of resistance residents mounted against repression in the workplace and, pertinent to this discussion, in the home. For most of the nineteenth-century, slum landowners successfully countered the complaints of tenants and housing reformers in part due to the prevalence of this pejorative discourse. When middle-class social reformers gained headway in their efforts to reform the slum, they either endorsed extant representations of the immigrant world or imposed their own charitable but no less inchoate characterizations. Finally, the constructed dichotomies of good/evil, superior/inferior, and uptown/downtown served as allure to the more adventurous subsections of the middle class. Each of these scenarios is discussed below.

The Production of the Downtown Abyss

Late-nineteenth-century cultural discourse expressed most vividly and conspicuously upper- and middle-class apprehension toward the immigrant working classes and the space they occupied, the Lower East Side. The origins of the district's stigmata were rooted, however, in the course of New York City's urban development in the first half of the nineteenth century. Population increases and urban congestion in lower Manhattan in the early 1800s pushed the city's locus of land development upward toward the northern wilds of the island. In 1811, a land-use plan with long-lasting consequences subdivided Manhattan (most of its area yet to be developed) into a rectilinear grid of twelve avenues running the length of the island (north-south) and dozens of narrow streets spanning its width (east-west). During a time when individual homes were the residential construction norm, property lines were drawn within these blocks to create 25-feet-wide by 100-feet-deep parcels. Alleyways, courtyards, and rear access streets (found in Philadelphia and other older cities) were not factored into the 1811 plan. As the city's economy and population continued to expand, nearly every lot on every block was enveloped by residential, commercial, or industrial development.

With the passage of decades, commerce and industry pushed northward along the streets and avenues adjacent to Broadway, where factories and garment lofts replaced stores and homes. The city's expanding labor force, fueled by increased immigration from Europe, first overwhelmed the early working-class neighborhoods found near the quays along the East River. The residential area adjacent to the notorious Five Points on the east side (near present day City Hall) then pushed northward. Motivated by their disdain and fear of the working masses, the city's wealthier residents, followed by the middle classes, fled the overcrowded and increasingly impoverished conditions downtown and built spectacular residences farther and farther uptown. "As our wharves become crowded with warehouses, and encompassed with bustle and noise," noted an 1857 commission on the expanding city, "the wealthier citizens, who peopled old 'Knickerbocker' mansions near the bay, transferred their residences beyond the din."[10] Commercial districts catering to the upper classes followed suit over the ensuing decades, pushing bour-

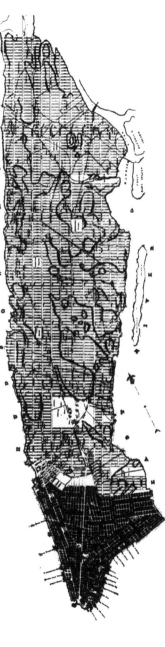

Map 2. Manhattan Plan of 1811. From Committee on the Regional Plan of New York and Its Environs, *The Building of the City* (1931), 50.

geois shopping districts from Fourteenth to Twenty-third to Thirty-fourth Streets.

As the city's elites colonized the northern stretches of Manhattan, sweeping away squatters and erecting streets, parks, businesses, and homes in their path, speculators and developers transformed their former neighborhoods into an enormous working-class manufacturing and residential district. On both the east and west sides of lower Manhattan, homes once occupied by upper- and middle-class residents were torn down to make room for factories or were quickly converted into cheap rooming houses for the working poor. On the Lower East Side, tracts of open land just below Fourteenth Street were carved up for speculative development. Tidal marshlands that formed parts of today's East Village were drained. Peter Stuyvesant's farm north of Ninth Street, the Minthornes' farm, which reached from Avenue B and Tompkins Square Park to First Avenue and Fourth Street, and the Leanderts' south of Fourth Street were all parceled into shoebox-sized, 25-by-100-foot lots as dictated by the 1811 street plan.[11]

Throughout the remaining decades of the nineteenth century, the twin forces of rapid industrialization and expanding immigration buttressed the expansion of the city's working-class housing market. Growth in lower Manhattan's light manufacturing and textile industries increased steadily in the early decades of the century but trebled following the Civil War. Between 1860 and 1880, employment in garment production more than doubled from twenty-nine thousand to over seventy thousand, and in printing and publishing the total workforce grew from seventy-five hundred in 1860 to over fifteen thousand in 1880.[12] Speculative buying and selling of working-class housing hyperinflated the land values of the 25-by-100-foot parcels in areas adjacent to industry, warranting a condition in which unbridled exploitation was a prerequisite for a profitable housing market. In his 1903 study of real estate practices in working-class neighborhoods, Lawrence Veiller concluded that "such a system [of speculative development] is detrimental to the welfare of the community, that it increases the value of property in an artificial manner, [and] that it makes it almost impossible to properly house working people of this city."[13] Given the considerable gap between high land values and the limited housing budgets of working-class residents, the degree of systematic exploitation of tenants through overcrowding and high rents determined earnings for both builders and landlords.

The interests of several different real estate actors coalesced in the development of the Lower East Side working-class slum. Occasionally, a few of the city's largest real estate players dabbled in the working-class housing market, but established, reputable firms rarely specialized in the buying and selling of "low-end" properties. "Building land operators,"[14] a single hybrid form combining the practices of speculator, construction contractor, and, often, builder, controlled most Lower East Side housing development. Operators typically purchased tracts that they either developed themselves or sold for considerably higher prices to builders or developers.[15] One such operator, Philip Braender, combined his role as speculator with his trade as mason to purchase and build on hundreds of Lower East Side lots. Contractors and structural iron, brick, and lumber supply owners also expanded into speculative working-class housing development in the latter half of the nineteenth century.[16] Building land operators frequently acted as lenders to other operators, providing financing for both the purchase of the land and construction costs. The firm Weil and Meyer bought East Side lots in the 1870s and financed purchase and construction loans to developers (in the 1880s the firm developed the lots on its own, constructing fifty new buildings a year).[17] Failed land deals and business foreclosures were not uncommon, and other organizations intervened to support the working of an overinflated market. The Material Men's Mercantile Association, for example, insured building material dealers for credit extended to possible ill-fated and unscrupulous builders.

By consolidating their control over much of the Lower East Side's speculation, building, and lending, operators maximized profits by inflating the costs of buying, building, managing, and renting working-class housing. A builder's or buyer's expenses were recouped and a handsome profit was often made at each level of operation. For builders, profits were made by erecting structures quickly and cheaply and by optimizing rental occupancy. The tenement design best utilized the 25-by-100-foot lot size for the maximum number of tenants. Although tenements emerged as a built form in New York City in the 1830s,[18] the quick pace and enormous scale of tenement construction and the subsequent high degree of absentee landlords was unique to the Lower East Side, especially north of Houston Street. In block after block, single builders simultaneously constructed rows of three to twelve tenements within six to eight months.[19] Initially unfettered by housing legislation and building codes, which were not enacted until 1867 (and not enforced until the 1890s), builders erected tenements cheaply by cutting corners in construction from start to finish and providing the barest essentials. Shoddy construction was the norm as builders typically purchased the cheapest materials and employed poorly experienced laborers, such as "lumpers" — underpaid and often unskilled bricklayers. Both design and construction of the tenements were central components of the working-class housing economy, allowing for the heaping together of dozens of men, women, and children in ill-suited and undersized quarters. Tenements, as the state tenement house commission reported in 1900, were "calculated to foster the most undesirable characteristics of these immigrant people, and to choke out to a very decided degree the good characteristics they might develop."[20] Prior to 1879, variations of front and rear, barrack-style, and railroad tenements prevailed, ranging from four to six stories high, with no access to light or air in interior rooms. Tenement plumbing proved structurally defective and incapable of handling the sanitation needs of sixteen to twenty-four families per building. "School sinks" — rows of water closets housed in rear yards — contributed to foul air, pestilence, and outbreaks of epidemics. Indoor common hall sinks and water closets appeared later but continued to present risks to public health due to tenant overcrowding.[21]

With the ultimate goal of paying off mounting debts owed to the former landowner plus making a profit by selling the tenement upon completion, builders constructed the type of tenements that would sell — those that optimized revenue generation. Once tenements were built, the pattern of exploitation continued in the rental market. Depending on levels of debt owed to builders or operators, landlords could expect a 12 to 12.5 percent gross return from rents. But the profitability of tenements was often the subject of debate. Veiller and other reformers focused on the costliness of a long-term investment. Cheaply built tenements were ill suited to withstand the high densities and frequent turnover of tenants. Repairs, evictions, and vacancies cut into the buildings' incomes.[22] Yet few tenement owners held onto their properties for long periods of time, and ownership changes were common. Continued demand from an exploding population of immigrants reinforced a perception that slum housing was good business. As Moses Rischin wrote, "the Lower East Side tenements soon came to be recognized as the most lucrative investment in the city. Nowhere else did the speculator's market in tenement properties flourish as luxuriantly as it did here."[23]

The operation of the tenement and its labyrinthine profit-extracting schemes created a parasitic hierarchy with exploitation built into several levels. Beyond the original landowner who collected debts from a tenement's builder, who, in turn, earned money from the purchasing landlord, one or two sublandlords, tenant subleasees, and borders were involved. The majority of Lower East Side landlords were absentee owners who were primarily former residents and hereditary property owners. A 1903 study found that "many if not most of the large tenement houses now going up for the accommodation of Jewish immigrants are erected by Jewish speculators, who, in many cases, themselves began life in this country in tenements. And Italian tenement house property is largely owned by Italians of a similar class."[24] Absentee landlords often subcontracted apartment leasing to subleasees (referred to by tenants as "cockroach landlords") who came into direct contact with tenants. The cockroach landlord typically paid a set price to the landlord; thus profit was made by raising rents and by overcrowding buildings. Participants of the 1908 rent strike complained of tenant bidding wars compelled by the subleasees. When an apartment became available, the sublandlord would take the highest price bid for it (typically well above the means available to a working-class family).[25] Cockroach landlords were locals no different from tenants. Citing the same 1903 study: "He and his family are often steeped as low in depravity and discomforts as any of his tenants, being above them only in the possession of money, and doubtless often beneath them in moral worth and sensibility."[26] And commenting on the levels of exploitation, the report's author wrote, "The man who has just succeeded in climbing one round of the ladder is the first to kick down, if he can, the man just below him."[27] Cognizant of high demand for housing, the attitude of the sublandlord was "take it or leave it."[28] Near the bottom of this metaphorical food chain was the tenant. Pressed by high rents, tenant families were forced to take in boarders. Tenants sublet the closets and hallways within their apartments or adjacent spaces in common hallways, beneath the stairway, in the basement, or even on the rooftop (what Henry Roth called "that silent balcony on the pinnacle of turmoil").[29] A passage in a 1905 account of Jewish life on the Lower East Side describes a family consisting of husband, wife, and six to eight children whose ages range from less than one to twenty-five years each. The parents occupy the small bedroom, together with two, three or even four of the younger children. In the kitchen, on cots and on the floor, are the older children; in the front room two or more (in rare cases as many as five) lodgers sleep on the lounge, on the floor and on cots, and in the fourth bedroom two lodgers who do not care for the price charge, but who desire to have a separate room to themselves.[30]

This system of subletting to strangers rankled the moral probity of social reformers and the upright middle and upper classes. The prevalence of multiple families in a single apartment and mixed-sex living conditions were singled out as evidence of rampant immorality, but the economic necessities that created such arrangements were usually ignored.

Landlords also capitalized on the nexus of frequent resident turnover and the continued strong demand for housing by newly arriving immigrants. Owners seldom improved the living conditions of their buildings unless required to do so by emerging housing legislation. Tenants' requests or demands for repairs went unanswered by insalubrious landlords or their local agents. "We asked to have the walls cleaned, but were told they would be painted in the spring, so we submitted."[31]

Prevailing middle- and upper-class representations of the slum and its occupants bemoaned the dismal material conditions but tolerated, if not encouraged, the continued exploitation of tenants by landlords. As social reformers and some state legislators began to pressure for housing improvements, blame was deflected from landlord practices to the reproachful morals of tenants. Accusations of immigrants spending their wages in saloons and gambling houses or on prostitution and liquor rather than rent fit squarely into dominant middle- and upper-class images of the poor and reinforced their suspicions of licentious behavior. Disdain for the immigrant communities and indifference to their exploitation translated into both limited culpability for landlord exploitation and, as we shall see, weak political resolve to legislate housing reforms.

Constructing Community in the Margins

It gave you an odd feeling to learn that many dwellers in the area below 14th Street passed their lives without ever once crossing that barrier, or seeing the wonderful metropolis that lay north of it. New

York had become a metropolis virtually invisible, if not unknown, to millions of its own residents.

Lloyd Morris, "Cosmopolis under the El"

By the final decades of the century, legions of immigrants crowded into jerry-built tenements that stretched northward to East Fourteenth Street — the border of starkly contrasting worlds of "uptown" and "downtown" and of middle-class constructions of "goodness" and "evil." Between the late 1870s and the early 1920s, wave after wave of immigrants from mostly eastern and southern Europe settled on the Lower East Side and formed homes and communities in overpriced conditions provided by landlords and paid for with meager wages. Ethnic communities emerged under the scornful gaze of the city's elites whose political and economic interests and policies reproduced the exploitative conditions for the poor. Although the Lower East Side housed the economic lifeblood of the growing city, its reputation among the middle and upper classes remained embedded in cultural expressions of ethnic inferiority and difference and the (mal)adjustment of newcomers to urban living. Despite the gross disparity in material conditions between Lower East Siders and the better-off classes, mainstream commentary on the lifestyles of the poorest immigrants dealt very little with issues of income and living costs and more with what were perceived as consequences of inadequate virtues and immoral practices of the poor.

Although "morally licentious" activities were prevalent throughout Manhattan, vice was, like most things on the Lower East Side, more concentrated and visible than in other neighborhoods. The uptown prostitute trade blended in with its respectable surroundings, and while street solicitation certainly occurred, a considerable portion of the sex trade was conducted discretely in houses run by reputable madams. Downtown prostitution was far more public and, therefore, the brunt of moral outrage by the city's upper classes and political scrutiny by a number of vice commissions. In the 1890s Second Avenue gained notoriety as "Pimp Row" for the dozens of bold working-class prostitutes who solicited passersby day and night.[32] The Bowery was, of course, the city's premier avenue of sinful transgression lined with saloons, drug dens, and flophouses frequented by sailors, criminals, thrill seekers, the hopeless, and the occasional "innocent gone wrong." Accompanying legends,

THE MOST DENSELY POPULATED SPOT IN THE WORLD — THE LOWER EAST SIDE
OF NEW YORK.

Figure 3. "The Most Densely Populated Spot in the World — The Lower East Side
of New York." Frontispiece for Robert W. DeForest and Lawrence Veiller, editors,
The Tenement House Problem (New York: MacMillan Company, 1903).

tales, and half-truths of the wayward and colorful unconventional acts
(some propagated by Lower East Siders such as saloon keepers)[33] sustained the cultural image of the netherworld that formed the basis of outsiders' impressions of Lower East Siders. Indeed, a prevalent theme in
official reports and in period novels was a place whose inhabitants operated under their own perverse rules and moral codes. In some of the

popular novels of the period, including Stephen Crane's *Maggie: A Girl of the Streets*[34] (1892) and David Graham Philips's *Susan Lenox: Her Fall and Rise* (1917), inhabitants of the ghetto first appeared as innocent victims accursed of misfortune but were soon revealed for their true nature as villains. Shop girls were cruel gossips, housewives were nasty drunks who drove away their husbands, and feeble old women used their trifling income gained from picking rags to buy not food but narcotics and liquor to satisfy their addictions. In Nathan Kusay's *The Abyss* (1916), a most heartless and abusive head of a family of beggars fooled naive contributors into believing his deformed four-year-old daughter was an exotic and talented monkey.[35] To the horror of the book's main character, her street performances entertained many and earned the family a steady revenue. As innocence was questioned and doubted, the ghetto emerged in the middle- and upper-class mind as an alien place with its own values, mores, and social rules outside the bounds of and ultimately threatening to respectable society. Its institutions were gambling and opium dens, and its cathedrals, saloons. In this "anti-community," as sensational reports contended, middle-class sentiments of charity and caring were signs of weakness. The ethos of the street—hustling, selfishness, and greed—ruled supreme. In Reginald Kaufmann's popular *House of Bondage* (1910), a lawyer, himself struggling to gain status in upper bourgeois society, evoked a social Darwinist argument to explain ghetto behavior as non-American, a product of foreign (lesser) stock.[36] And in Owen Kildare's (1905) *The Wisdom of the Simple,* the depravity and hardships of tenement living were a consequence of bad morals and the weak work ethic of lazy citizens.[37] Ghetto life on the Lower East Side was not simply a poorer version of the middle- and upper-class world but a different space altogether—a dangerous and fearful abyss.

Liberal attitudes did exist toward the immigrant neighborhood and the polyglot of ethnic cultures that would call the Lower East Side home. The most positive of upper- and middle-class representations of the Lower East Side characterized the neighborhood as a space near the threshold but without the possibility of ever becoming fully "American." Spaces like the East Side functioned as "immigrant portals" and "staging areas" where newcomers embarked on the journey toward assimilation—a sociocultural process of shedding antiquated and dangerous "Old World" customs and idiosyncrasies and mastering the enlightened and refined habits and ways of middle-class society. In this version held by many social reformers, the neighborhood's position in flux and transition, as a space existing between the old and the new, between the backward and the modern, explained the chaos and disorder exhibited in the behavior of inhabitants of the East Side. The process of assimilation played out in the tenements and streets of immigrant ghettos and climaxed only in the act of one's leaving behind such neighborhoods along with their debased cultural habits. Thus, the process of Americanization was just as much spatial as it was cultural and economic, a point noted by early urban sociologists at the University of Chicago who studied immigrant dysfunction and assimilation.[38] The assimilationist view argued that places like the Lower East Side played an intrinsic function in the socialization of new Americans. Yet there was little room for social and cultural accommodation of such places in situ and without the radical social and physical transformation that was the clarion call of the reform era.

A dominant thread that ran through these and other impressions of the immigrant ghetto was the incapacity to cede a positive role for agency and everyday control over living and lifestyle to the slum dwellers. Horrible things tended to happen to the "victims" of the ghetto, or they were "driven" into rampantly available cultures of hedonism or criminality. In the most flattering accounts, the poor survived but had few ambitions, no desires, weak support networks, and, at best, unreliable friends. Families were represented as dysfunctional, as expressions of the prevailing immorality: parents neglected or abused their children, and adolescents were only a few years shy of their inevitable criminality.[39] Prevailing discourses gave little or no mention to ethnic and religious solidarity, fraternal organizations, or self-help societies. Because they were different (dangerous, foreign, lower-class, among others in a long list of derogative descriptions), the ghetto dwellers were trapped in near-constant misery that seemed only to worsen — a condition that further elicited either scorn or pity from the upper classes. Consequently, all aspects of middle-class-defined civilization — social networks, status, peers, and moral orders — were devoid in the ghetto.

Making Community

Stereotypes and uninformed impressions of the Lower East Side influenced the everyday experience of its residents, their social and cultural practices, and the ways they made community.[40] For them, the

East Side was a world constructed from a dynamic interplay between the castigation of the outside world — the factory boss, the policeman, the moralizing settlement worker — and their own efforts to harness paltry wages and create and retain a sense of dignity about where they toiled, slept, ate, raised children, socialized, and died. In the manufacture of fictive "Lower East Sides," the rapid and profound changes in social diversity in a small area over a brief period of time were ignored or overlooked. Distinct communities based on cultural and religious diversities between and within groups of Germans, Jews, and Italians were, more often than not, collapsed into a convenient and singular category — "the dangerous classes" or "foreigners" — in contemporary discourse. Within this mind-set, all ethnic cultures shackled immigrants to "Old World" values and practices that prevented them from successful assimilation and maintained abject poverty. Representations of the Lower East Side promulgated unidimensional, cookie-cutter renditions of what was a complex, highly stratified, and rapidly changing web of microcommunities situated in a small area of lower Manhattan. Objectification of the social life of the "other space" combined ignorance with a refusal to recognize both obvious features and less pronounced nuances and the numerous social, economic, and cultural differences among legions of newcomers. Indeed, within this excluded zone, vastly different communities were constructed from dense social and cultural networks based on ethnicity and religion. The process was untidy but had long-term consequences for how Lower East Siders continued to form community and act politically.

Communities within the Lower East Side were formed in a social and physical space constantly redefined by flows of ethnic and religious groups with markedly different cultural practices. The inflow and settlement patterns of social groups inhabiting the East Side during the peak immigrant era (1880–1925) were elastic and fluid; rapid changes occurred in the length and site of settlement and the way community life was organized.[41] Each new immigrant cohort merged elements from its existing cultural and religious practices with the economic and social requisites for survival in an ambiguous environment. Ethnic and cultural successions consistently enveloped and transformed communities in the blocks north of Houston Street. The relatively small area — fourteen streets crossed by six avenues — was home to a polyglot of Irish, Germans, Austro-Hungarians, and Italians along with Russian, German and Polish Jews, and a handful of other ethnic and religious groups. Within the short span of six decades, these ethnic and religious cohorts arrived as part of larger migration "waves," first settling in the interstitial spaces of existing ethnic enclaves and eventually overwhelming and all but displacing them. Irish immigrants had first settled Manhattan's east side in the mid-nineteenth century, pushing northward as their numbers swelled and the city expanded. By the mid-1860s, the Irish had begun to colonize other parts of the city, and a wave of German immigrants settled en masse the area east of the Bowery from Houston to Twelfth Street in the 1860s, constructing the tenements and forming social and cultural foundations along St. Mark's Place, the spine of *Kleindeutsch-land* (Little Germany). With the second wave of eastern and southern European migration, Italians established an enclave in the north end of the neighborhood near Twelfth Street and First Avenue. Jews, bursting out of the overcrowded warrens of the southern Lower East Side, pushed beyond Houston Street and resettled the northern tier.

Within these ethnic enclaves further subcommunities existed, each defined by homeland region, religious preferences, and class distinctions. Encompassing entire blocks or perhaps a particular set of tenement buildings, these spaces were most significant. The cultures that dominated these microcommunities framed the everyday experiences of most Lower East Siders. The immediate spaces of tenement buildings and streetscape were sites of community identity formation—where a familiar dialect was spoken, favorite foods were prepared, and parenting styles and notions of social propriety and impropriety were shared. A mere block away typically represented a totally foreign world devoid of familiar signs and references. An overview of the German, Italian, and Jewish enclaves provides a glimpse of the varied social and cultural practices that contributed to the remarkable vitality of the Lower East Side. These vast changes in social and cultural formations inscribed a cosmopolitan legacy of diversity within the Lower East Side.

In the 1860s, groups of German immigrants first established footholds in the eastern half of the northern tier of the Lower East Side, in the streets intersecting Avenues A, B, and C. Once the dominant ethnic cohort, the Catholic Irish presence eventually was confined to a small remnant lower-class community along Thirteenth and Fourteenth Streets east of Avenue A. Although their population numbers dwindled, the Irish remained influential in the social and political life of the Lower

East Side, acting as policemen, Tammany officials, and saloon keepers.[42] As levels of immigration increased, *Kleindeutschland* expanded west beyond Second Avenue, which came to be known as the Great German Thoroughfare, with its German butcher shops, beer halls, and theaters. Rather than a homogeneous single entity, *Kleindeutschland* was a patchwork of distinct German subcommunities. Immigrants referred to themselves by their region of origin — as Bavarians, Brandenbergers, Hessians, Swabians, or Prussians. Seventy-seven microcommunities comprised of northern and Protestant Germans and southern and Catholic Germans founded their own churches, small businesses, and social organizations. In turn, German religious-based enclaves were further subdivided into social-spatial networks that reflected lower-, middle-, and upper-class affiliations.[43] Upper-class German Protestants, for example, clustered in the northwestern fringes of the Lower East Side, near Third and Fourth Avenues, while lower-middle-class German Protestants settled farther east, around St. Mark's Place and Ninth Street near Avenue B.[44] Each of these subcommunities shifted in size and location, expanding and alternately decreasing with the surrounding ebb and flow in the numbers of fellow Germans, other Germans, and, later, Italians and German and eastern European Jews. Such flux and volatility affected the ways residents and subgroups interacted with each other and how social organizations were formed and functioned. Responsible for maintaining home life and generating outside income, working-class women of similar religious and ethnic backgrounds formed networks through everyday interaction in familiar spaces: on the front steps of tenements, at the street market, in the park.[45] Commercial spaces, such as billiards parlors, penny arcades, saloons, candy stores, and other leisure spaces, functioned as ad hoc meeting places and, on occasion, formal headquarters for both short-lived and long-term social organizations and self-help societies.[46] Rather than creating spaces exclusively defined for community political and social purposes, German immigrants intertwined community business and leisure with cultural remembrances of village and home country. As patrons of social organizations relocated, so too did their organizations and meeting places. *Vereine* (community associations) provided sickness benefits and burial services and were organized around occupations and German region of origin.[47] German veterans (of the 1870–71 war) formed a social club at a casino at 12 St. Mark's Place. Other voluntary associations, such as the German Odd Fellows, met at various saloons and similar leisure spots.[48] Moralists among the middle and upper classes and less enlightened social reformers misread a good portion of the immigrants' enthusiasm for public leisure spaces (saloons were seen as especially sordid) as evidence to support views of the limited redemptive qualities of the poor. Churches, on the other hand, as fixed institutions in a highly mutable social environment, "were often sign posts of those who *once lived there,* rather than those who were still living in the neighborhood."[49] The spectacular St. Brigid's Roman Catholic Church located on Eighth Street and Avenue B ministered to resident Germans for only a short time before mostly Jewish and, decades later, Puerto Rican residents came to occupy the adjacent streets in the neighborhood.

During the 1890s, a Second Wave of European migration (from the south and the east) brought dramatic changes in the profile of ethnic enclaves on the Lower East Side and in the German settlements in the northern tier in particular. The Italian presence in the northern tier appeared in the 1890s when the mass migration from southern Italy began in earnest. The enclave, centered on Eleventh and Twelfth Streets between Avenue A and Second Avenue, was considerably smaller in size than the numerous German subcommunities; the largest and most well-known Italian enclave of Little Italy was located several blocks south and east of *Kleindeutschland.* The Italian settlers, with few exceptions, were Catholic peasants (*cafoni*) from southern Italy. Upon settlement in New York, they labored as mostly unskilled workers in low-end retail (selling fruits, candies, and flowers), the building trades, and the garment industry. Like the Germans, the Italians first settled in patterns reflecting social and cultural patterns adopted from their home country. New arrivals were directed to streets and apartment buildings according to town or province of origin.[50] Likewise, one's village or region of origin remained an important factor in cultural practices and group attachments.[51] Much of Italian group life was localized and maintained by the influences (positive and negative) of the local *padroni,* or leader. *Padrone* played multiple roles as middlemen between immigrants and key institutions and individuals in Italy and in the United States. They facilitated connections between locals and homeland, provided bank services and advanced loans to newcomers, matched immigrant laborers with employers, and shuttled New Yorkers to work sites in other cities across the northeastern and midwestern United States.[52] Italian self-help

and mutual aid societies were also active in organizing community social life—once again, taking advantage of leisure spaces, such as Fratel-
lanza Marsico Nuovo on Avenue A, as places to meet. Middle-class observers of immigrant communities assumed that ethnics produced within
their respective enclaves precise replicas of social institutions and customs from their homeland. These "Old World" practices, characterized
as regressive or backward "foreign incursions" that were inherently an-
timodern, explained the dismal condition of ethnics and why they could
not break free from reins of poverty. Indeed, immigrant groups such as
the Italians re-created in their new environment homeland institutions
such as the *societa di mutuo soccorso* (mutual aid societies), which en-
sured emergency aid, sponsored religious activities and feasts, and supported recreational activities. These institutions were far from identical
to their native forms, however, as their functions changed to reflect the
needs of a populace transformed by urban and industrial living.[53]

The largest immigrant cohort to settle in the northern tier of the Lower
East Side between 1880 and 1925 was comprised of mostly Jewish eastern Europeans. The Jewish cohort was also the most diverse in ethnicity (from Germany, Austro-Hungary, Poland, Russia, and the smaller
states in the east) and in religion (a multiplicity of Reform, Orthodox,
and secularist factions). More than two hundred thousand eastern European Jews entered the United States in the 1880s, another three hundred
thousand in the 1890s, and one and a half million between 1900 and
1918.[54] The settlement stronghold of this burgeoning complex of communities was the congested southern tier of the neighborhood, along
the corridors of East Broadway and Grand and Delancey Streets. By the
mid-1890s, scores of new arrivals encroached on the turf of the German Christian enclaves, pushing north beyond Houston Street along
Avenues B and C to Seventh Street. By decade's end, Jewish residential
communities were settled throughout the northern tier. Poorer eastern
Europeans (predominantly Hungarians) settled along Avenues B and C
as far north as Tenth Street, while more affluent German Jews colonized
the blocks intersecting Second and Third Avenues.[55] By 1910 the Lower
East Side was packed with more than a half million persons[56]—of whom
a significant number were the Second Wave migrants from the east.
The newcomers from eastern Europe dramatically reshaped the already
diverse social and cultural landscape of the Lower East Side. The variety of subcommunities defined by affiliations between religious prac-

tices, ethnic backgrounds, and class positions trebled, leaving the Lower East Side remarkably cosmopolitan. Newly arrived German Orthodox Jews and Reform Jews carved out independent social and physical spaces between a mix of established German Catholic, Protestant, and secularist communities. Religious differences kept the German communities apart, but ethnic antagonism toward the encroaching eastern Europeans — described as "wild Asiatics"[57] — often formed a bond between them.[58] Within a decade, the older German communities succumbed to demographic and cultural changes and abandoned the Lower East Side for upper Manhattan (Yorkville) and Brooklyn.[59] Formed from unique historic circumstances within their home countries, Jewish immigrants' efforts at community building were more intensive than those exhibited by the older ethnic groups. Eastern European Jews sought to reproduce a semblance of the densely networked *shtetl,* or small village, life permanently left behind.[60] The Lower East Side in the first decades of the twentieth century teemed with Jewish *lansmanshafts* (self-help organizations) and larger charitable and philanthropic societies that underwrote the founding of numerous synagogues, loan societies, Hebrew schools and other educational centers, hospitals, and cultural centers. Jewish women founded ladies' auxiliaries to the male-dominated fraternal organizations.[61] Unlike the Italian immigrants, Jewish immigrant labor arrived in the United States largely skilled. Significant numbers took skilled positions in the garment trades, jewelry and watchmaking, the print industries and leather works, and as shopkeepers and merchants.[62] Many others were employed in less than desirable jobs available in garment factories and home work.

As the Jewish presence increased, the cultural landscape of the Lower East Side was once again reinvented. Unlike members of previous immigrant cohorts, the Jewish newcomers toiled to create a lasting community structure that *expressly* integrated social life with the advance of education, politics, and culture. Saloons and dance halls, once popular among older ethnics, were replaced with delicatessens, coffeehouses, political and educational halls, libraries, small printing houses, and theaters. Moses Rischin claimed no less than 250 coffeehouses existed on the Lower East Side in 1905, providing space for political debate, friendly discussion, and respite from the dark cramped interiors of the tenements.[63] Jewish intellectuals, who emerged to address social and economic injustices at the workplace and at home, contributed to a surfeit

Figure 4. "East Side Street Professions: Hardware Department." Samuel Zagat, *Jewish Daily Forward*, 1920.

of socialist and anarchist organizations with headquarters or branches across the Lower East Side. The headquarters for the Industrial Workers of the World was located on East Fourth Street, and a growing anarchist movement held its meetings on East Sixth Street. Emma Goldman and Abraham Cahan gave speeches at the Ferrer Center and School on St. Mark's Place.[64] Numerous Yiddish presses served a multitude of political, religious, and cultural subcommunities on the Lower East Side and spawned a literary tradition that countered the images of despair and social chaos that appeared in bourgeois novels about immigrants. In addition to conveying information to the Lower East Side's large Jewish community, writers and editors for the *Jewish Daily Forward* presented partly romantic and partly realistic accounts of the immigrant experience to outsiders. Abraham Cahan's *Yekl: A Tale of New York* and *The Rise of David Levinsky* emerged as popular stories of ethnics coming to terms with the loss of Old World culture, the harsh trials of Lower East Side living, and the romantic promise of assimilation.

Along with the appearance of numerous coffee shops, synagogues, and libraries, popular Yiddish theater transformed the neighborhood's cultural landscape. Founded in Romania in 1876 and banned in Czarist Russia in 1884, Yiddish theater's core was the Lower East Side from 1885 through the 1920s. German theaters that lined the Bowery, beginning with the Old Bowery Garden in 1885, were reopened as Jewish theaters, transforming the street into the "Yiddish Rialto."[65] For outsiders (save for the bohemians), Yiddish theater, with its common-man themes and boisterous audiences, appeared unrefined and vulgar. Within the Jewish communities, it served several social and political purposes. "Greenhorn" theater featured comical stories of the tribulations of new arrivals' adjustment to New York. The ubiquitous tenement stoops, rooftops, and fire escapes were re-created as sets in plays that explored in a more serious fashion the alienation of the bittersweet transition from Old World to New.[66] For the mass of Jewish immigrants, the theater briefly swept away "the loneliness outside [and] schooled folk in the rough surfaces of city living and knowingly familiarized them with the tenement wilderness."[67] Beginning in 1912, the heart of Yiddish theater moved farther north to Second Avenue—the "other Broadway"[68]—adjacent to Jewish restaurants, coffeehouses, and delicatessens. Eventually, Yiddish and other ethnic theaters centered on the Lower East Side migrated beyond the boundary of Fourteenth Street, affecting the cultural life of mainstream America.

An Emerging Culture of Collective Action and Insurgency

Immigrant groups carved out their own vibrant communities in the midst of the harsh realities of poverty, overcrowding, and the cultural disdain of the middle and upper classes. The experience of community building within such constraints politically radicalized the everyday experiences of Lower East Siders. Far from being the stereotypical passive victims or selfish profiteers of immense social changes and adjustments to urban life, residents engaged in near-continuous mobilization and resistance to dismal living conditions and threats of further exploitation. The strength of Lower East Side communities was often manifested in the ability of disparate religious and ethnic groups to put aside differences in united resolve against forms of class injustice.

Given the social and economic characteristics of its population, the Lower East Side figured predominantly in the nineteenth- and early-twentieth-century history of the U.S. labor and trade unionization movements. Home to thousands of needleworkers, dyers, printers, and workers in numerous light manufacturing industries, the neighborhood was headquarters for trade unions and workers' organizations and the site of labor mobilization and strife. Whereas the bulk of Irish immigrants were tied to the conservative Tammany regime, post-1880 Italians and Russian-born Jews on the Lower East Side were active in socialist politics. Jewish garment workers, for example, comprised one-fourth the membership of New York's Socialist Party.[69] The nascent radicalism of the labor movement was not confined to the workplace but spilled over into the spaces of home and community life. Union Square, along the northern border of the neighborhood, hosted dozens of rallies in support of workers' rights and against exploitation and ravages caused by periodic economic recessions. The Tompkins Square "riot" of January 13, 1874, is the most glaring incident that formed the foundation of lasting political activism and neighborhood mobilization.

Spurred by the particularly harsh economic consequences of the 1873 depression for local workers and their families, several thousand laborers formed the Committee of Safety to pressure an otherwise unresponsive city government to provide employment in public works projects. Workers organized a rally in Tompkins Square Park and a march to city hall to voice their protest. Unemployed workers and local labor organizations had often used the centrally located ten-acre park for rallies and speeches with minor intrusion from authorities. Concerned about increasing labor radicalism and overexaggerated reports of possible socialist and anarchist "uprisings," however, the city ordered its police force to disband the proposed gathering and prevent demonstrators from marching. On the day of the march, between four thousand and six thousand men, women, and children filled the park and surrounding streets, including twelve hundred members of the German Tenth Ward Workingmen's Association. The police response was swift and brutal. In a melee that would eerily be repeated over a century later, bands of policemen swung clubs at groups of demonstrators and bystanders in and around the park. Labor leader Samuel Gompers, present at the rally and the police attack, described the action as "an orgy of brutality."[70] In the weeks that followed, the police, city officials, and the major press maintained that the assemblage at Tompkins Square was orchestrated by "dangerous foreign agitators" who had planned "acts of outrage and violence."[71] For residents who knew otherwise, the police attack galvanized their resolve, if only briefly. A series of meetings organized by mostly German residents at the Cooper Institute (Union) conveyed the community's outrage toward police brutality. The riot and the outsiders' unsympathetic reaction reinforced the social and economic isolation of the Lower East Side and fostered the sentiment that despite their differences, residents shared common grievances and a need for action. Sentiments toward solidarity reappeared periodically, such as the case of overwhelming public turnout for protest marches following the deaths of 146 women factory workers in the Triangle Shirtwaist Fire of 1911.

Although labor issues dominated the radical political themes of the late nineteenth and early twentieth century, mobilization and resistance around residential issues were clearly present. Ethnic and religious community organizations often came to the assistance of striking workers. Local restaurants distributed free meal tickets to strikers, and Jewish congregations offered five-cent dinners to union cardholders.[72] May Day celebrations were typically festive and well-attended events on the Lower East Side. As Charles Leinenweber notes, "the Socialist movement drew strength not only from the shops, but from the rich and vibrant working class culture that flourished in the neighborhoods: in the streets, tenements, cafes, taverns, dance halls, theaters, barber shops, church basements, settlement houses and unions halls."[73] Local political action was frequently a mix of workplace politics and community organization. The language of contention around neighborhood concerns was adopted from the labor movement: rent strikes, strikers, scabs, and tenant unions.[74] Interestingly, detractors such as politicians and the mainstream press used the same language to disparage efforts (e.g., tenant uprisings).

Workplace issues often overlapped or were tied to community and quality of life themes. Alongside the calls for better wages and working conditions, Lower East Siders demanded cheaper and safer housing and lower food prices.[75] Issues of central concern to the diverse residential groups often prompted the rise of movements that took actions in the forms of rent strikes, food boycotts, and riots. These mobilizations were different from labor organizing efforts and were rooted expressly in the dense social networks that thrived in overcrowded neighborhood spaces. As we have seen, from an outsider's view, the Lower East Side at the turn of the century with its hordes of impoverished residents and over-crowded streets was a wildly chaotic place, full of noise and disorder. Cramped tenements insured that public space was often the arena for private conduct, such as the rearing of children, fights between spouses, and moments of intimacy. Within such pandemonium, however, a sense of order prevailed. The ethnic and religious groups that coexisted on the Lower East Side maintained dense social networks that were located in distinct spaces: the home, the workplace, the market, and leisure spots. There was strong probability, for example, that a Jewish family living in a particular tenement emigrated from the same village as its neighbors, practiced a similar form of Judaism, attended the same synagogue, shopped the same stores along Avenue C, Orchard Street, and East Broadway, and visited familiar coffee shops, candy stores, and theaters. Italians, Germans, and other immigrant cohorts carved out their so-ciospatial communities in a similar fashion. In short, Lower East Siders made order out of the chaotic social world around them by patterning their (exclusive) social networks through a maze of familiar residential, commercial, and religious locations. These same ethnic and religious networks that linked Lower East Side tenement apartments to street markets, shops, social and religious clubs, and workplaces proved highly useful as well to collective action and rebellion. During numerous epi-sodes of spontaneous and organized resident rebellion, networks acted as an expansive web of associations that communicated information and mobilized hundreds and sometimes thousands of residents for demon-strations, strike actions, riots, and boycotts. The spaces connected to these networks, too, were instrumental as apartments, stores, work-places, and streets became sites for organization and/or contention. When kosher butcher shops raised prices and housewives began a boycott in 1902, word of the boycott and a call for mobilization spread through factories and tenements, synagogues, and social clubs. And as the boycott spread, the heads of the highly organized *lansmanshaften* became its leaders. Likewise, eight decades later, a handful of apartment buildings, squatted tenements and, of course, Tompkins Square Park became "landmarked" as familiar sites for demonstrations, speeches, and calls for action by protesters of redevelopment and displacement. From the past to the present, popular rebellion on the Lower East Side was initiated often spontaneously but rarely willy-nilly; it was highly structured socially and spatially.

In most cases, local women maintained the networks and in times of crisis refitted them for collective action. The multiple social roles of immigrant women — as social club members, shoppers, and workers inside and outside the home — placed them in central positions of resistance. Women had key access to information and control of its dissemination throughout the neighborhood. In the 1902 kosher butcher boycott, the reaction of neighborhood women was spontaneous and intense. After butchers' efforts to pressure wholesalers to reduce prices failed, women responded by implementing and popularizing a three-week boycott of kosher meat shops.[76] Pickets were set up, and women policed the shopping of their neighbors, making violations of the boycott rare. Once the core leaders of the Jewish women boycotters formed an organization, the Ladies' Anti-Beef Trust Association, appeals were made to non-Jewish women to participate in the cause against rising food costs, and the boycott eventually spread to other parts of the city. The strength of the association was weakened eventually by the efforts of religious and secular male-dominated organizations to control and co-opt it. Nonetheless, the boycott was a success and prices were reduced, and the tactics employed by women in the 1902 boycott proved lasting.[77] The strategy of adapting sociospatial religious and cultural networks of affiliation within and between ethnic groups became a model of collective action on the Lower East Side that was repeated in subsequent food boycotts in 1917 and in citywide tenant actions immediately following World War I.[78] The use of solidarity networks that were reinforced by social isolation and cultural marginalization has since proven to be a well-suited strategy for Lower East Side protestors. Squatter protests in the 1980s and 1990s utilized similar social networks as conduits for relaying information about building takeovers and defensive actions against evictions (see chapter 8).

By far, the neighborhood issue that mobilized Lower East Siders most frequently was rent increases imposed by landlords, who loomed as villain or "czar" in the collective mind.[79] Tenement dwellers lived without leases or rent-level protections and were subjected to burdensome and arbitrary increases in rent whenever immigration levels rose and the supply of available housing was limited. Such was the case in an escalation of rents in 1904.[80] Eastern and southern European migration had pushed the population density of the Lower East Side to new extremes.

Figure 5. "She's moved from the top floor to ground floor front. She's been evicted." Samuel Zagat, *Jewish Daily Forward*, 1920.

At the same time, the housing stock declined due to massive public service projects such as the construction of the entryway to the Williamsburg Bridge that eliminated housing for seven thousand residents in 1900.[81] Subleasees of tenement landlords took advantage of this situation and gouged rents, threatening existing tenants with exorbitant increases. In response, resident members of the United Hebrew Trades, Workmen's Circle, and various locals formed the New York Rent Protective Association.[82] The strike called for by the association was successful: no tenants were evicted, and rent rolls were either reduced or maintained. A second episode of rent strikes occurred in January 1908. Rents in even the oldest of tenements had increased by a full quarter between 1902 and 1908, but no structural improvements had been made.[83] But larger issues were at hand. Organized by the Tenant's Union and the Anti-High Rent League, the strike was called in protest of the rent-farming lessee system that rewarded sublandlords for overcrowding their buildings. In comparison to the earlier strike, the 1908 action was more militant but, ultimately, less successful. The Eighth Assembly District Branch of the Socialist Party organized a strike in which tenants employed the symbolism of red flags (actually dyed petticoats) mounted from fire escapes and rooftops, and hung landlords in effigy to rouse solidarity among Lower East Siders.[84] On Sunday, January 5, 1908, landlords and police staged an effort to remove the red flags but were met with heated resistance from tenant strikers. The number of tenants participating in the strike grew beyond the expectations of organizers, and sympathy strikes were mounted by tenants on Manhattan's Upper East Side and Upper West Side and in Williamsburg, Brooklyn.[85] Political elites and the mainstream press, however, were highly unsympathetic toward the strikers and lambasted their use of socialist rhetoric.

Resembling the communities that formed them, the organizations that emerged during periods of collective activity were volatile. None of these mobilizations left an intact structure for future grassroots organization and mobilization. Rent strike and boycott committees disbanded quickly due to a transient membership and the shifting terrain of local politics. In the case of rent strikes, organizations broke up over differences in goals and strategies between socialists and non-socialists. As Jenna Weissman Joselit's study of early-twentieth-century rent strike activity points out, tenant mobilization and organization "was ad hoc and temporary; once tenants secured what they regarded as gains or were simply unable to proceed any further with their protests, the 'rental agitation' subsided."[86] Food boycotts that were initiated by women but formally organized by male members of religious institutions dissolved due to religious factionalism. As residents moved out of the neighborhood, they took with them organizations and repertoires of resistance. Russian Jews who once lived on the Lower East Side reappeared in 1917 as leaders of a rent strike in Crotona Park in the Bronx.[87]

Evidence of lasting organizations and structures may be absent; nonetheless a strong culture of resistance — spontaneous, full-throated, intensive but short-lived — had its roots in this period of wide-scale social change. Successive waves of immigrants — each unique in religious and ethnic background but sharing broad working-class membership — participated in struggles played out in the same locality over several decades. Resistance movements emerged out of existing sociospatial networks, an example of what James Scott referred to as "manipulating a realm of ordinary activity that was open to them and coding it with political meaning."[88] Thus, Lower East Side social and spatial networks that were consistently marginalized politically and culturally by mainstream society were inherently apropos for subversive mobilization and action, making the existence of an organizational apparatus superfluous. This legacy of collective action has been retained throughout the Lower East Side's history, as later chapters address.

The Culture and Politics of Immigrants, Housing, and Social Reform

Bourgeois perceptions of dangers and threats associated with the Lower East Side also reflected a sociocultural framework through which political actions and policies with regard to immigration and immigrant spaces were legitimized. The anti-immigrant ideology pervasive at the turn of the century was rooted in a host of political and economic processes, including industrialization and changes in labor force composition, the rise of trade unionism and urban radicalism, and national economic fluctuations. Rising sentiments against foreigners found their most popular expression in an aggressive nationalism that trumpeted social, cultural, and biological distinctions between "old stock," "native-born" Americans and foreigners.[89] Second-Wave immigrants, especially eastern European Jews, were the targets of a variety of anti-immigrant and antisocialist vitriol. Newspaper editorials exhorted socialist tenden-

cies and antidemocratic leanings as "innate in the Russian Jew."[90] Similar rhetoric and references to characterizations of immigrants' difference and inferiority suffused official legislation proposed in the 1890s
and again in the 1920s. Legislation proposed in 1896–97 imposed a literacy
requirement that targeted poor peasants from southern Italy and eastern
Europe.[91] The Federal Bureau of Information was formed in 1907 to coax
new immigrant arrivals to settle in cities other than New York in part
to curb the social problems within ghettos like the Lower East Side and
to discourage the population growth in existing enclaves.[92] In its recommendations and findings, the United States Immigration Commission
of 1907–11 emphasized the social, cultural, and economic differences between First-Wave (northwestern Europe) and Second-Wave immigrants.
The commission generally favored the "inborn characteristics" of First-
Wave immigrants but disregarded the different urban political and
economic conditions for each wave. The Immigration and Nationality
Act of 1924 claimed not to discriminate but to maintain a racial status
quo, but calculations of the maximum numbers of possible newcomers
from each foreign country were derived from the 1890 census, thus pre-
dating the massive influx of southern and eastern Europeans. The act
was a legislative "closing of the door" to the flow of eastern and southern European immigrants settling on the Lower East Side.

The organization of local politics, too, reflected both material conditions and the prevailing symbolic representations that described and
explained them in a routinely negative manner. Rampant patronage and
linkages among citywide political associations, local districts, and the
municipal government maintained indecent activities on the Lower East
Side and in similar immigrant neighborhoods. Although their political
actions and power were hardly grassroots or inclusive, local political
machines were structured at the street level, bringing district captains
and lieutenants (foot soldiers) in direct contact with voters for favors
and ballots. For most of the nineteenth century, municipal governments
were noticeably remiss in the provision of services aimed at improving
ghetto conditions. With the municipal government largely absent, ward
politics and the machine "boss" flourished on the Lower East Side. Following the 1821 revision to the New York State Constitution, which
abolished virtually all property qualifications for voter eligibility, male
immigrants were quickly naturalized and voted in large numbers, fa-
voring the machine politics organized around the infamous Tammany

Hall.[93] The threat of immigrant "mob democracy" alarmed the upper classes. Much to their chagrin, the most popular politicians were those who pandered to the impatient and "unruly" masses. Thus, "'militant,' 'hard-fisted,' and tough, the [political] boss's style reflected the culture of the working classes."[94] The longevity of Tammany's success among immigrants rested on a mix of social welfare provisions (which the municipality neglected) and corruption. In return for votes, machines dispensed rudimentary or emergency social services, city contracts, and lucrative jobs in unseemly businesses. Local politics were also shaped occasionally by strong reform tendencies that clearly reflected the moral outrage of the city's middle- and upper-class citizens. Widespread media coverage of the Boss Tweed Ring scandals of the early 1870s[95] further galvanized the middle- and upper-class sense of immigrant politics as corrupt and undisciplined. Although Tweed was brought down by scandals, machine politics continued with the "Honest" John Kelly regime and nine ensuing Tammany "bosses." Theodore Roosevelt Jr. was appointed Police Commissioner in a highly visible effort to end machine-based corruption in the police department, which permitted gambling and prostitution to thrive in neighborhoods throughout the city. The city's elites and middle classes were enthralled by stories of police activities in gambling and prostitution, many of which were meticulously documented in well-publicized hearings convened by a state legislative committee in 1894. In the twentieth century, the media diverted the public's attention to the link between the threat of socialism and excessive immigration. In 1919, the Joint Legislative Committee to Investigate Seditious Activities (the Lusk Committee) was formed to thoroughly investigate the extent of socialist activities among the working classes in New York and other cities, such as Buffalo. In the committee proceedings investigators frequently referenced Lower East Side locations (schools, meeting halls, etc.) and activities (rent strikes, demonstrations, etc.) as contributing to the impending "socialist threat."[96]

Characterizations of local politics as corrupt in turn furthered existing notions of the Lower East Side as different, undeserving, and threatening and legitimized the absence of a concentrated municipal or state effort at social welfare and reform. As conditions within the immigrant ghetto worsened, a generation of middle-class social reformers mounted evidence against this prevailing ideology and lobbied for public intervention in the affairs of the poor. Reformers bemoaned graft and corrupt political administration, the exploitation of women and children in the labor market, and the dearth of social programs and housing policies.[97] Yet social reform was steeped in contradictions. Most reformers who lived among the working-class immigrants were middle-class women. Their attitudes and actions straddled conflicting positions of neighborhood insider and outsider. While reformers generally understood the social evils of the slum as a product of modern industrial society, their attitudes, nonetheless, ranged from outright rejection to lukewarm acceptance of the representation of the Lower East Side as a threatening, vulgar, and chaotic space. Social reformers, such as Lillian Wald, sought to assimilate "inferior" immigrant cultures but also celebrated aspects of them. Reformers showed respect for the autonomy of immigrant cultures but at the same time called for their eventual dissolution.[98] Reformist solutions to the immigrant slums often prescribed the development of middle-class social institutions under the guise of community betterment. Housing reformers were critical of the real estate industry, but they rarely contested the logic or the "right" of real estate entrepreneurs to profit in the housing market and chose instead moral and hygienic grounds to justify government intervention. Likewise local immigrant practices were often (mis)read as unsatisfactory or deviant alternatives to bourgeois strictures. Candy stores, which stood on nearly every Lower East Side corner, were a central meeting space for social clubs and for children to congregate outside the densely packed tenements. Many reformers held the (erroneous) view that loitering in such spaces inevitably led to visits to the poolroom and, ultimately, the unruly behavior and vices associated with the saloon or bar.[99]

Social settlements offered residents much needed services and programs as well as more structured spaces of acculturation. South of Houston Street the University Settlement was founded in 1886 as the first settlement house in the United States. Influenced by London's Toynbee Hall, its founder, Stanton Coit, designed social programs that both addressed the pressing needs of the area's immigrant population and aided in much needed "cultural assimilation." The work of the University Settlement was influential in social and housing reforms, such as kindergartens and public baths, which were eventually adopted by the municipal government. Several other settlements opened before the close of the century. Lillian Wald founded the Henry Street Settlement in 1893. Grand Street, the Educational Alliance, and the Christodora House were all central institutions in both local and national reform circles. In 1897 philanthropists Sara Libby Carson and Christina McColl founded the Christodora House. The settlement provided food, shelter, and instruction each week to nearly five thousand mostly Russian, Polish, and Ukrainian immigrants. In 1928 the Christodora settlement moved from 1637 Avenue B to a new seventeen-story building at the corner of Ninth Street and Avenue B donated by Arthur Curtis James, a railroad tycoon. The "sky-scraper settlement" housed, among other facilities, a music school, a poet's guild, a dining hall, and a playhouse.[100]

Although the inadequate moral sentiments of the ghetto population were of concern, social reformers viewed them as a manifestation of larger socioeconomic problems that came to bear in the slum. Housing reformers took the lead in pressuring government intervention in alleviating ghetto problems. But the reformers' plans promulgated in the last decades of the nineteenth century received tepid interest from politicians and government bureaucrats. Reform strategies centered around campaigns for restrictive housing legislation, but such campaigns were not noticeably effective before 1901. The first state-appointed legislative commission dealing with tenements was convened in 1856. In the report, commission members devoted considerable text to discussions of the moral and hygienic consequences of overcrowding in slums. The prevalence of such problems, it was argued, constituted the social and moral basis for new legislation, although the report did mention the "rapacity of the landlord... unrestrained by conscience, and wholly unchecked by legislation."[101] Despite the imputation, the commission did not recommend any measures that would inhibit the profitability of speculators, builders, or landowners. Instead, the call for improvements in building design was stipulated in terms of health and morality: ventilation would advance hygiene, increases in the numbers of rooms would prevent prostitution and incest, and an upgrading of cleanliness and comfort would deter drunkenness.[102]

After the 1856 commission, reformers continued to rally for building codes, inspections, and enforcement, which proved most elusive to legislation and, later, enforcement. In 1867, the first tenement law was enacted. The law took the important step of defining the tenement as a built form that could be subjected to specific codes and regulations.[103] The provisions within the law were complex and exact: fire escapes, room dimensions, specifications of building materials, and standards of cleanliness were outlined and to be regulated by the city's Board of Health. Since the law did not provide for an increase in the number of health inspectors, its provisions were largely unenforced. Builders took advantage of weak inspection, and the construction of poorly built tenements continued in spite of the law. The legislation also did not challenge the existing dimensions of tenement coverage of 25-by-100-foot lots—which at the time covered approximately 90 percent of the lot.[104] It was not until the Tenement House Act of 1879 that the exploitive practices of builders and landlords were addressed in legislation. In that act, rear lot structures—unhealthy and decrepit backyard wooden "shacks"—were prohibited by the codification of specific dimensions for clear space behind tenements. The 1879 law funded the hiring of thirty additional sanitation inspectors. On the issue of density, the act limited building coverage to no more than 65 percent of a lot, but at the insistence of the real estate lobby, builders were allowed to petition for special permission to overbuild. That clause effectively nullified any real effects on controlling building size and lot coverage.

At the same time the 1879 law was sponsored and enacted, the housing construction industry adopted a new and "improved" building design—the double-decker dumbbell tenement. Given the extent of discussion about the tenement problem among reformers, ministers, and some governmental officials, it appears oddly ironic that the dumbbell design emerged from an architectural contest sponsored by a builder's periodical, *Plumbing and Sanitary Engineer*. The dumbbell was touted as a model tenement that best satisfied two requirements of the contest: to upgrade sanitation and hygiene conditions while respecting builders' demands for inexpensive construction and the maximum coverage of the 25-by-100-foot lot (the dumbbell came in at 80 percent). Builders quickly adopted the new design and its "improvements," and the dumbbell became the dominant form constructed between 1879 and 1901. In the midst of southern and eastern European migration, hundreds were constructed and immediately overcrowded.

Immediately condemned by critics as an inadequate design adjustment rather than an innovative improvement, the central feature of the dumbbell was a narrow airshaft situated between buildings to provide light and ventilation for interior rooms. The feature soon became known as "the evil of the air shaft"[105] as it compounded the spread of

Figure 6. "A Whole Block of Dumb-bell Tenement Houses Built under the Laws in Force in 1900." From Robert W. DeForest and Lawrence Veiller, editors, *The Tenement House Problem* (New York: MacMillan Company, 1903), 11.

filth and disease and trapped foul and stale air; light could not reach the lower levels of the airshaft and garbage accumulated at ground level:

> Though the house was new, the odors soon became insufferable, and the air from the shaft ... became so foul that we could not sleep in the rooms opening on it without feeling that we were taking a great risk. The stairs were usually so dirty that it was unpleasant to use them, and clothes were constantly being soiled with the contact. But how could this be helped? There was the traffic of twenty-two families, where the children had to run most of the errands, and they, of course, spilled things on their various journeys. And how could we hope to live quietly with the noise from these twenty-two families, with children running overhead and through the halls and crying, with furniture being moved over bare floors, with the housekeeper scolding careless tenants, and so on?[106]

For critics, the dumbbell was evidence that an unregulated, "free market" of tenement construction and rentals was incompatible with real improvements in density, sanitation, and hygiene. Following the imposition of this new form, reformist attitudes shifted squarely toward legislation that restricted the practices of the housing industry. Little mention was made of morals and social values of tenants in the report of a second legislative commission appointed in 1884. The report prescribed extensive redesign of tenements to address flaws cited in earlier reports (light, ventilation, plumbing, etc.). It also called for a permanent Tenement House Commission and demanded the names and addresses of tenement owners to be filed in the Department of Health.[107] All of these concerns passed in legislation as the Tenement House Law of 1887.

If reformers were to successfully convince politicians to enact *and* enforce legislative reforms, the public's conceptions about the causes of the tenement problem needed substantial revision. The reformist exposé proved to be a powerful tool that shifted the blame for ghetto conditions from residents to builders and landlords and, consequently, prompted a shift in middle-class notions of the immigrant poor. Middle-class reformist circles first vilified the landlords:

> A belief that landlords were greedy villains was a necessity for the housing reformers. Since reform laws imposed costs on landlords without reimbursing them in any way, and since no one expected or wanted rents to rise, it was morally necessary to believe that rents were exorbitant and that costs could be absorbed without giving up a fair return. It was convenient, therefore, to assume that landlords were a class of evil men, overcharging ignorant tenants and callous to the point of criminality. The fact that tenement house owners were not respectable old-American businessmen, by and large, made it easier to adhere to this notion.[108]

Sympathetic accounts in newspapers and magazines exposed the joyless lives of newly arrived immigrants consumed by the monotony of hard labor in the sweatshops and fetid accommodations of their tenement apartments. In his aptly titled *How the Other Half Lives* (1890) Jacob Riis portrayed the funereal world of the Lower East Siders. Through images and text, the meager provisions and horrid conditions of tenement interiors were meticulously detailed, including the exact measurements of tiny living spaces, the age and sex of apartment dwellers, types of furnishings, and the sanitary conditions of kitchens, bathrooms, and bedrooms. Riis's photographs documented misery in a compassionate, rather than sensationalist, way, showing, for example, residents overworked or overcrowded in windowless and airless rooms.

The popularity of Riis's series of exposés on slum conditions and the tenement house exhibition shown at 404 Fifth Avenue in February 1900 further jostled the public's support for solutions to the decades-old "tenement problem."[109] In 1901, the state legislature passed measures that radically altered the built form and challenged the prevailing method of capital accumulation through the speculation, development, and operation of tenements. The Tenement House Act of 1901 ushered in New Law tenements — air shafts became courtyards, rear yards were enlarged. Exterior windows, fire escape access, running water, and a toilet were required for each apartment, and building sizes were extended to cover several lots.[110] The response from land speculators, builders, banks and loan companies, suppliers of building materials, and landlords was swift: thirty-one bills intended to water down code inspection were introduced in the state legislature, but all failed.[111] Despite protests from the real estate sector, Lower East Side building continued through 1910. Between July 1902 and 1903, 43 percent of the city's New Law tenements were constructed on the Lower East Side;[112] the heaviest concentration occurred in the area east of Avenue B between Houston and Ninth Streets.[113] Due to increases in building lot size and costs of construction, realty partnerships rather than the traditional single owner developed New Law tenements.[114] Despite the structural improvements of the New Law tenements, living conditions remained miserable as overcrowding persisted (in part due to a housing shortage caused by slum clearance for the entry way to a newly constructed Williamsburg Bridge), and landlords compensated for costs by increasing rents (see discussion of rent strikes earlier). Although provisions of the 1901 law were originally well enforced, the mayoral election of Tammany candidate George McClellan in 1904 brought weak enforcement of building codes and maintenance inspections.[115]

Tenement regulations and, importantly, their enforcement were strengthened by new support for such measures from the city's middle and upper classes. Progressive reformers were largely successful in challenging prevailing discourses about the slum and redirecting the public's focus, at least temporarily, away from tenants to those who profited from the slum.

The Allure of the Margins

The upper- and middle-class construction of the Lower East Side as a place of exaggerated excesses, we have seen, served a number of ideological purposes reflective of class-based fears associated with rapid social change. Symbolic representations of the immigrant reaffirmed the dominant position of bourgeois class and status in late-nineteenth and early-twentieth-century New York. Life as it was depicted in the downtown netherworld contrasted sharply with the regimented and regulated existence of the Victorian and Gilded Age New York bourgeoisie. Bourgeois dictates rewarded a scripted and highly routinized lifestyle that emphasized the maintenance of social status, respectability, and adherence to public morality (although adherence was hardly uniform). Bourgeois values and morals maintained strict distinctions between public and private spaces and the appropriate activities that were to occur within each, especially with regard to gender roles.[116] The apparent attributes of the ghetto (unbridled chaos, unstructured spaces, and a blurring of private and public space) and of its residents (ill-mannered women, shiftless men, and grotesque children all engaged in vile combinations of greed, lust, laziness, and hedonism) presented an anathema to the bourgeois lifestyle. For the bourgeoisie, the proximity of the Lower East Side as a site of moral decay with debased social customs and other threats attested to the ideological and political need to secure its privileged social position. In addition, the consequences of the non-bourgeois life — rampant diseases of many sorts, unrelenting poverty, and death as portrayed in numerous novels and sensational accounts — were an important morality tale for the late Victorians.

Surely, fear of the "Other" fueled bourgeois imagination and curiosity about the Lower East Side. On the other side of middle-class fears reigned a fetishistic desire to consume or, more rarely, to mimic such base differences. Popular consumption of sensationalist novels and journalistic accounts evinced a form of bourgeois voyeurism — a temporary, if passive, retreat from an otherwise scrutinized, byzantine, and strait-laced world. Along with the predictable moralizing of the evils associated with ghetto behaviors, both fictional and "factual" accounts produced suggestive and detailed glimpses of a chaotic free-for-all of wanton women, excessive gambling, and an uncontrollable appetite for liquor and drugs. The familiar literary theme of the reluctant young woman's descent into the urban underworld, for example, provided a striking opportunity for graphic descriptions of excesses of all sorts. In *House of Bondage,* the innocent Mary is transformed into the streetwise Violet, who encounters painted "girls of the streets," "dancing girls," and other "bad girls" who loiter in cheap, smoked-filled music halls and saloons and succumb to any number of temptations.[117] Private fascination with scandalous acts may have mitigated an otherwise restless and colorless bourgeois existence. Of course, absent the moral tales, such accounts of mayhem constituted, in the eyes of the righteous middle-class, blatant pornography. Thus, accounts of fulfilled temptations and unrepressed desires were universally situated within graphic descriptions of a vile place of starvation, mounting debts, and physical and psychological abuse that reinforced bourgeois superiority and social distance above the netherworld.

Some members of the bourgeoisie, titillated by the exotica and danger to be found on the other side of rigid social, cultural, and physical boundaries, were not contented with consumption of secondhand accounts of the ghetto. Young, middle-class, well-educated men conducted individual and anonymous late-night forays downtown to engage in debauched activities of drinking, gambling, drugs, and promiscuous sex. For middle-class dandies drawn to mystery and the thrill that accompanied risk to reputation, the Lower East Side was a source of curious attraction, then amazement, and finally amusement, and a means to escape momentarily the social rigidity of bourgeois life. Warnings in guidebooks such as *Appleton's* doubled as challenging invitations to the daring. Concert halls on the Bowery, for example, offered

> a class of resorts such as respectable persons do not visit. . . . a lavish display of gas-jets and paint and tinsel outside serves to give passers-by an impression of splendor within which the reality by no means warrants. The women are seldom good-looking, vulgar as a rule, and ignorant always. The music is furnished from a badly thumped piano, the liquors served are vile, and the women insist on being treated constantly to a concoction which they dignify with the name of brandy, and for which they charge accordingly. The frequenters of these places are chiefly foolish young clerks and mechanics, who labor under the delusion that this is "seeing life." Strangers should be very careful about going into them, for the police make spasmodic and irregular raids on them under the law relating to disorderly houses; and on occasions every person found in the place is arrested, locked in a cell all night, and arraigned before a magistrate in the morning.[118]

"Slumming" allowed one to visit and consume difference, in its class, ethnic, racial, sexual, and criminal manifestations. Once satiated, the wayfarer retreated back to the familiar and well-ordered world uptown.[119] This notion of the Lower East Side as youthful playground presented another layer of objectification in which the space existed as both marginal and (perversely) alluring—a phenomenon that, as discussed in later chapters, resurfaces in the 1960s and 1980s.

Another challenge of sorts to bourgeois lifestyle culminated in the vibrant and diversely radical art, music, theater, literary, and political community of Greenwich Village, just west of the Lower East Side and, as we shall see, very influential to it. Here Emma Goldman, Max Eastman, Upton Sinclair, Harry Kemp, and a long list of other writers, artists, and political activists produced an American bohemia. Short-lived and by no means harmonious, the common thread within this subculture was a deep disillusionment and contempt for the established social, political, and cultural order on which the middle class had prided itself. As several commentators have remarked, the architects of this bohemia engaged in a voluntary, self-conscious lived experience of their critique; a premium was placed on the authenticity of the antibourgeois existence.[120]

The bohemian ideology centered on a critique of the apparent hypocrisy of the bourgeois lifestyle. In the midst of a vastly changing city ruled by an ethos of cutthroat industrial capitalism in which its role was instrumental, the bourgeoisie sought to isolate itself by constructing (and consuming) a bogus sense of grandeur, propriety, and ennobled decency. The apparent contradiction meant that bourgeois life was inauthentic and, ultimately, bound for dissatisfaction. The bohemian alternative exalted authenticity and a constant search for novel experiences that would "lift" its more enlightened followers out of the sameness of everyday bourgeois existence.[121] Thus, much of what the bourgeoisie considered vulgar, distasteful, and outright immoral formed bohemian ideals and, simultaneously, its lived critique of the middle-class lifestyle. Within this framework, it is not surprising to find the Lower East Side held a special place in the bohemian outlook: a romanticized view of the Lower East Side as different and unconventional fortified the bohemian ideology. The alleged social disorganization and deprivation that offended respectable society was recast as a source of spontaneity, passion, and creativity. Within the bohemian frame of reference, the lived experiences of gamblers, pimps, prostitutes, rag pickers, pushcart peddlers, and street gangs were neither deceitful nor obsequious. Few bohemians admired the material conditions of Lower East Side poverty, but many aspired toward a romanticized authenticity of experiences seemingly untouched by bourgeois conventions. Hutchins Hapgood was the most vociferous of the romanticizers. Author of *The Spirit of the Ghetto* (1902) and *Types from City Streets* (1910), Hapgood marveled at those few and unique spaces unfettered by the drive to secure a living and characterized by an atmosphere both easygoing and halcyon. New York City of the early twentieth century, caught up in a whirlwind of dramatic social and economic transformations, had disallowed such unhampered spaces.[122] The closest approximation was the living quarters of the newly arrived immigrants yet to be assimilated into the mainstream order reviled by Hapgood and his contemporaries. Although critical of the conditions of abject poverty within the ghetto (for which the middle classes were held responsible), Hapgood was fascinated with the everyday culture of immigrants. Unlike the bourgeois dandies' episodes of slumming, the bohemians sought to identify with and often mimic the "spirit of the ghetto." As participants rather than spectators, bohemians found in the Lower East Side a place for authentic expression of antibourgeois values. Bohemian support for ghetto culture, such as Jewish Yiddish theater, was an effort to transcend the barriers between the more middle-class Greenwich Villagers and the working-class Lower East Siders. Likewise, the bohemians' embrace of "low culture" reinforced a much desired social and cultural distance between themselves and the middle classes.

In comparison with mainstream bourgeois notions of immigrant communities, the bohemian interpretation of ghetto life was progressive and, within the framework of prevailing ideologies and attitudes toward the poor, often radical. Yet bohemian fascination with the ghetto must be considered another example of the objectification of immigrant life and community that suited the ideological and cultural goals and purposes of those living outside the Lower East Side. Meanings of liberation, adventure, nobility, and validity of the antibourgeois existence were imputed to the lifestyles of Lower East Siders. Agency was largely absent. Subjective hopes, desires, and everyday successes and shortcomings of immigrants were collapsed and stereotyped within a bohemian framework of counter-bourgeois authenticity and lived expression. Hapgood and others were apparently fascinated with the more colorful experiences of Lower East Side characters rather than with the ordinary experiences of most residents. Leslie Fishbein noted, for example, that instead of a "radical appreciation of the older, unassimilated Jewish women with a tradition of independence and strength . . . whose resourcefulness contrasted strikingly with the plaintive weakness of the Victorian ideal of the lady, radicals tended to dismiss them as quaint oddities, corsetless and periwigged."[123] Bohemian attachment to this heroic fictional Lower East Side heightened during the 1920s when mainstream disillusionment with and eventual liberalization of Victorian moral and ethical codes took place. The middle-class cultural establishment grew enchanted with all things bohemian, including poetry, music, and art. Reports of glamorous lifestyles of Greenwich Village artists and writers—existential brooding and a fondness for alcohol, sex, and all-night parties—piqued the curiosity of outsiders.[124] The popularity of once obscure local cafés and bars was soon followed by the incursion of tourists from uptown. For many Villagers, to whom such acceptance signaled the death knell of bohemia, the Lower East Side was a suitable place for exile. The economic boom of the first half of the 1920s brought upscale development and higher rents to Greenwich Village, pushing Village locals farther east.[125] The Lower East Side's cultural diversity and inexpensive rents attracted a community of artists, poets, and writers but never in the size and scale of the former Greenwich bohemia. With the onset of the Great Depression and, later, urban renewal, the bohemian presence on the Lower East Side subsided. The reputation of the Lower East Side as a refuge in its own right for countercultures would develop only in later decades.

In the decades bracketing the turn of the century, the immigrant slum on the Lower East Side appeared lasting and unchangeable. Over six decades, a rapid and steady turnover of diverse social groups used and reused the harsh landscape of overcrowded streets and tenements. By 1900, middle- and upper-class notions of this chaotic and hectic ghetto had improved only slightly; immigrants were less reviled and were shown sympathy and pity. Changes in public opinion were due largely to the efforts of reformers like Jacob Riis who "corrected" representations that had become powerful ideological forms with grave political and economic consequences. State intervention in the ghetto housing market registered modest progress in the quest to improve living conditions and, more importantly, set the groundwork for a much larger governmental role in the new century. Despite cultural and political changes, the exploitative housing economy of the slum functioned profitably, providing minimal shelter to wave after wave of impoverished newcomers and making changes in the type of provisions only when forced to do so either by the state or the collective action of residents. Within this great flux of migration, ethnic subcommunities were formed and transformed. Although immigrants formed strong and vibrant communities on the Lower East Side, the constant aspiration of the majority was to leave the terrible environment and settle elsewhere in the city or beyond. Most eventually did only to be replaced by yet another cohort of newcomers who broadly continued the pattern. The politics, culture, and economy of the Lower East Side were clearly associated with the immigrant (re)settlement pattern. The district's social and demographic flux, ironically, proved to be quite stable in a period of rapid urbanization and social change.

The nineteenth- and early-twentieth-century ideology that equated economic and social success and assimilation with departure from the ghetto was partly reproduced by the immigrants themselves, who, for obvious reasons, were anxious to leave a place like the Lower East Side. Yet the representational linkages of economic and moral failure with the space of the Lower East Side and success with departure from it had significant immediate and long-term effects. First, such representations ignored the exploitation that caused miserable conditions within the neighborhood, thus allowing them to continue for years with impunity. Second, the discourses of "remaining on the Lower East Side as failure" and "departing from the Lower East Side as success" became emblazoned in the public's connection with the area and its function. The symbolic association of social inferiority with the geography of the Lower East Side would last for decades. For as the spatial economy of the Lower East Side continued to welcome and exploit generation after generation of working-class arrivals, the rest of Manhattan was maturing into the "capital of capitalism."[126] The gradual shift to an economy less dependent on manufacturing than corporate management and administration would prove a formidable challenge to transforming the built environment and the identity of the Lower East Side.

CHAPTER THREE

Utopian Metropolis versus the Legacy of the Slum

Late-nineteenth and early-twentieth-century representations and discourses of class, ethnic, and spatial differences between the morally superior "uptown" and the opprobrious "downtown" served as ideological filters through which hegemony and exploitation in the workplace and the neighborhood were rationalized and legitimized. Characterizations of difference as marginal in countless reports from governmental commissions, novels, journalistic accounts, and urban myths and tales undergirded both the hesitancy of municipal intervention in the plight of those housed on the Lower East Side and facilitated the continued exploitative practices of the slum tenement builders, owners, and sublandlords. Likewise, the ways in which local collective action and everyday resistance against exploitation were framed, perceived, and dealt with were influenced by pervasive political and cultural representations of immigrants as inferior and dangerous. Housing and social reformers, in turn, reproduced many of these same images of baseness as a means to demonstrate an urgent need for rehabilitation of the Lower East Side's moral and physical landscape. In short, the nineteenth-century construction of the Lower East Side's identity as marginal and flawed both reflected and furthered the practices that produced and reproduced the ghetto.

In the 1920s and 1930s, significant changes in political economy swept over the New York region, bringing into question the sustainability of the working-class ghetto, highlighting its worst elements, and, in effect, demanding a resolution to the conspicuous differences between the Lower

East Side and the rest of Manhattan below Ninety-sixth Street. In the first two decades of the new century, the Lower East Side continued to operate as a way station for newcomers and a somewhat profitable, if unreliable, venture for speculators and landlords. Thousands of immigrants continued to supersede those fleeing tenement life and formed new ethnic and religious communities yet again, reproducing with few variations the hectic world of ghetto living and the rancorous connections between landlords and tenants. But as the Lower East Side reached its peak in resident population and accompanying misery (around 1910), fissures in the political economy of the slum were well in place. The many new office skyscrapers and apartment towers that surrounded the Lower East Side belied a shift in the New York economy in which the city would emerge as the world's premier center of corporate business, finance, and banking.[1] With each year came steel bridges, parkways, and public transportation projects that opened new territories and transformed old ones for a variety of business and residential uses. Although the Lower East Side remained a working-class dormitory, Manhattan's predominant form of employment slowly shifted from manufacturing to white-

Figure 7. Aerial view of the Lower East Side, 1931. From Committee on the Regional Plan of New York and Its Environs, *The Building of the City* (1931), 405.

collar office work, and the outer boroughs gained manufacturing and industrial firms.[2] The growth of the modern metropolis chiseled away at the facade of the seemingly durable edifice of the Lower East Side working-class ghetto. Following the passage of the Immigration Act of 1924, the facade crumbled as the single source of demand for tenement housing — new immigrants — was curtailed. When the flood of immigrants slowed to a hardly noticeable trickle and the routine influx of new residents was halted, the most glaring elements of the ghetto — the rapid rise and fall of teeming ethnic and religious enclaves and the tenement system — were laid bare.

This chapter recounts in two parts the tumultuous decades following the demise of the immigrant ghetto. Part one covers the years 1925 through the mid-1930s. It presents the various solutions put forth to rescue the Lower East Side from its increasing obsolescence and to rehabilitate representations of the marginal ghetto that outlasted the various exploitative purposes and practices they had fostered. The solutions to the ghetto, interestingly, would not come from housing reformers who long crusaded for changes but from the real estate sector who waged a campaign of utopian renewal to undo decades of material and symbolic marginalization. The efforts toward middle-class renewal were frustrated by economic misfortune, resistance from remaining residents, and representations that continued to signify cultural differences and inferiority long after many of the area's reputedly ignoble inhabitants had moved away. The second part of this chapter traces the significance of state intervention in urban development during the New Deal era. The local consequences of federal, state, and local government housing policies, it is argued, reinforced the neighborhood's working-class identity that, in turn, squelched the plans for middle-class renewal.

Rising Metropolis, Declining Immigration: The End of the Working-Class Ghetto?

In the early 1900s, soaring numbers of immigrants continued to fill the already dense warrens on the Lower East Side. At the same time, new working-class and lower-middle-class neighborhoods in upper Manhattan and the outer boroughs accommodated residents fleeing the Lower East Side and immigrant newcomers as well. Metropolitanization, marked by the formation of new residential communities,[3] coexisted with a vibrant, ever growing downtown residential, industrial, and commercial core. In fact, the Lower East Side's pattern of rapid succession and turnover of residential communities was partly dependent on the continued expansion and urban development of the New York City region. The Irish Lower East Siders of the 1830s to 1850s founded new enclaves on Manhattan's west side in the 1860s. Streams of Germans, who settled on the east side in the 1850s and 1860s, moved north to the Upper East Side and established Yorkville in the 1870s. For decades, each exiting group made room for "a seemingly unlimited flow of immigrants from abroad"[4] to establish new enclaves. Thus, the durability of the slum housing economy rested on a symbiotic relationship between steady or increasing population influx through immigration and the continued residential growth in upper Manhattan, Brooklyn, Queens, and the Bronx.

Such compatibility was fractured after 1910 when metropolitan expansion accelerated and the Lower East Side housing market began to lose existing residents faster than it could absorb new ones. Like earlier generations of immigrants who exited the neighborhood, residents belonging to southern and eastern European ethnic and religious communities began to drift into newer neighborhoods in northern Manhattan and the Bronx, as well as in Brooklyn and Queens. The extensive development of a regional transportation infrastructure expedited the pace of residential outmigration. By 1909, the Brooklyn, Manhattan, and Williamsburg Bridges connected the Lower East Side to Brooklyn, and within a few short years thousands of Lower East Siders were drawn to comparatively better housing opportunities across the East River. Older, smaller Jewish communities in the Brownsville and Williamsburg districts of Brooklyn witnessed tremendous growth. The city's subway lines connected new neighborhoods deep in the outer boroughs to the Manhattan core allowing for quick and inexpensive commuting. Par for the course, plans for subway expansion set off speculative construction across the boroughs, increasing the supply of new housing. As mass transportation opened new residential options for the majority of the city's working class, the Lower East Side's historic advantage of "walk-to-work" held less sway for existing residents and, for the first time, newcomers. The effect on the area's demography was felt as early as 1910. The number of immigrants arriving in New York City peaked at just over 767,000 between 1905 and 1910 — a record high. For the same five-year period, the gain of new residents in all of New York City reached a historic high of 18 percent, but the Lower East Side's increase was only 4 percent (a record low).[5] For social reformers and concerned lawmakers, any opportunity to reduce population density and its associated miseries in the ghetto was viewed as progress. Reformers heralded the exodus of Lower East Siders to modern up-to-code housing in the outer boroughs. New working-class housing was a triumph over the tenement form and was held up as an example of what could be built on the Lower East Side.

Despite the increasing competition from new working-class and lower-middle-class housing in Brooklyn, the Bronx, and Queens, Lower East Side landlords were still able to profit from tenements as long as immigration levels remained at significant levels. Once the numbers of new arrivals dropped significantly after 1924, the historic and unique arrangement of cultural, economic, and social patterns that comprised the ghetto collapsed. A series of congressional laws that culminated in the Immigration Act of 1924 produced far-reaching changes in the ethnic composition of migration flows into the United States and, subsequently, in the social composition of the Lower East Side. A literacy requirement and a series of other restrictive policies imposed between 1917 and 1924 were directed against the latest wave of immigrants from the lesser-developed southern and eastern European countries. The 1924 legislation controlled the amount of immigrants entering the United States by setting quotas differently for each country. Annual quotas on new arrivals were calculated on the basis of the national origins (ethnic composition) of the U.S. population according to the 1890 census. Such quotas favored established First-Wave immigrant groups (from western and northern Europe), whose numbers had been steadily declining since 1880. An expression of anti-immigrant hysteria, the law was premised on the idea that certain nations showed greater affinity to "American" culture and the experience of democracy than others. Its intent was to curb eastern and southern migration, which, as referenced in chapter 2, was constructed as a menacing threat to American values.

The legislation effectively cut off the massive population flows into the United States, thus sealing the fate of the Lower East Side slum. The local effect of the immigration laws was swift and remarkable. Density levels on the Lower East Side declined from 867 persons per acre in 1910 to 536 in 1925.[6] In 1928, the vacancy rate for Lower East Side tenements was estimated at 14 percent, and by 1930, it had increased to 20 percent.[7] Between 1910 and 1940, the area experienced an incredible 60-percent decline in population. For the remaining residents, the drop in demand for tenement housing loosened the economic vise grip of the landlords and increased housing options within the Lower East Side. Tenants vacated the worst units in Old Law apartments to rent increasingly available units in better buildings. Speculators, developers, and builders, astute to the emerging opportunities in residential development in other areas of the city, had already withdrawn from the Lower East Side housing market prior to the effect of declining immigration and decentralization. In the midst of a regional building boom that lasted from 1920 to 1929, only 783 new buildings were constructed on the Lower East Side. That figure represented only 1 percent of all new construction in Manhattan during this period. For landlords, the decline in demand for tenements reduced their fixed assets to costly liabilities. In the late 1920s, the average annual net return for tenement apartments fell precipitously.[8] Owners of the previously overvalued Old Law buildings were also affected by new changes in housing legislation. The adverse effect of a declining tenant base was compounded by the passage of the 1929 Multiple Dwellings Law. The provisions of the law, which included building codes for use of interior rooms, up-to-date fire safety, and a private toilet in each apartment, were grandfathered to include Old Law dwellings. Landlords were compelled by law to make extensive and expensive rehabilitation of dilapidated units spent from years of constant use and little or no maintenance. The housing policy of the LaGuardia administration included rigid enforcement of compliance with the law. By the close of the 1930s, 80 percent of the Old Law tenements owned by private individuals or financial institutions that continued to operate (were not demolished or boarded up) were in compliance with the fire codes enacted in the 1929 law. Nonetheless because they were sorely lacking in plumbing and heating, Lower East Side tenements remained housing of the last resort.[9] The law's enforcement provoked many owners of partially occupied buildings to board up or demolish dozens of Lower East Side tenements rather than be held criminally negligent or be forced to make expensive changes. Rehabilitation of surplus Old Law tenements during the onset of the depression was unthinkable. As a result, bank foreclosures increased substantially.[10] Owners of New Law tenements and buildings erected after 1900 fared little better. Shrinking demand for Lower East Side housing and the post-1929 economic hardships meant landlords found it difficult to sell off holdings.[11]

With its slum housing market frustrated by metropolitan growth in the fringe and severely curtailed immigration, the Lower East Side in the late 1920s, in comparison to most neighborhoods in New York, looked woefully shabby and obsolete. Its aged and cheaply constructed cold-water flats were ill suited to compete for tenants other than the most desperate. Discrepancies in living conditions between the neighborhood and the rest of Manhattan south of Ninety-sixth Street were far more glaring. As modern and more commodious garden apartments appeared in pristine neighborhoods in the outer boroughs, the featureless tenements and still boisterous and chaotic streetscape of the Lower East Side were glaring liabilities. Given the magnitude of the tenement problem — a significant number of Old Law tenements remained standing in the late 1920s — no new land use superseding that of the immigrant ghetto was readily apparent. In addition, the Lower East Side's reputation among middle- and upper-class New Yorkers remained fixed on nineteenth-century images of the ghetto, only slightly modified to reflect recent changes. If the Lower East Side was viewed as less frightening, its defining characteristics were, nonetheless, still ethnic and working-class. Save for the bohemians and, as we shall see, certain ethnic groups, individuals and families rarely chose to live on the Lower East Side. That stigma would work against large-scale, spectacular plans for middle- and upper-class redevelopment.

With the Lower East Side's reputation intact and demand for its walk-up tenements diminished, landlords were faced with a handful of limited options: operate tenements for low-income residents at a loss (save for brief periods of demand brought about by short-term housing shortages), abandon structures permanently (leading to foreclosure and possibly demolition) or temporarily (e.g., board them up), or modernize or construct new buildings in hope of attracting a higher socioeconomic stratum of tenants. Independent landlords played all three options in the 1920s and 1930s. For the most influential real estate actors and associated institutions, the option to rebuild the Lower East Side was most appealing.

Reinventing the Lower East Side

In the wake of diminishing demand for what was arguably the least desirable rental housing in the New York region, thousands of Lower East Side landlords were thrust into making individual decisions about the disposition of their tenement properties. The immediate probability of improved uses for existing buildings appeared dim. A lack of willing buyers of outmoded tenements added to the already existing problem of weakened demand for local housing. By the mid-1930s, as the range of different landlord decisions was realized, the effect on the Lower East Side landscape was manifest. The once uniform district marked by unvarying row after row of overcrowded tenements resembled a patchwork quilt of land uses, in which the infrequent new building was surrounded by an abundance of vacant lots, half-empty New and Old Law tenements, and boarded-up buildings. With further decline apparent, the real estate sector was faced for the first time with the cumbersome task of inventing new and profitable uses from what had become a wholly economically obsolete space. By the late 1920s the call for change was one of inventing a middle-class Lower East Side. Factions of local real estate interests as well as outside developers, planning groups, and quasi-public agencies embarked on an agenda to displace existing notions of the working-class ghetto and actively invent place images and symbols to suit more profitable uses for Lower East Side land. Their representations envisioned a modern residential district devoid of its decrepit built environment and, ultimately, its ethnically "different" and working-class residents.

Despite a dramatic drop in population density and an overall decline in immigration, the Lower East Side remained the most culturally and ethnically diverse area in New York through the Second World War.[12] The social worlds that collectively defined the ghetto had changed considerably from the immigrant heyday. Since better housing alternatives in other neighborhoods were usually available to Lower East Side tenants, the reasons for their continued residence on the Lower East Side varied considerably. The class statuses of subcommunities ranged from the very poor and destitute to the working poor, the working class, and the lower-middle class.[13] Various Second-Wave ethnic groups — primarily eastern Europeans — dominated the local cultural landscape. In addition to the ethnics, Greenwich Village bohemians displaced by rising rents on the west side continued to resettle on the Lower East Side. In 1931, for example, an optimistic observer of Lower East Side development commented on the presence of "the newly arrived musicians, writers, painters and sculptors . . . who [may] help in the revival of the East Side by starting a procession toward it."[14] For others who did have the means to leave but chose to remain, the central reasons given were cultural, religious, or attachments to the neighborhood.[15] Following the curtailment of immigration, more secular Jews left the neighborhood than did Orthodox. For Orthodox and other devoutly religious Jews, the Lower East Side offered religious, educational, and cultural institutions that would have been difficult to establish or replace elsewhere. The concentration of Orthodox schools and academies, synagogues, kosher restaurants, and cafés and proximity to Beth Israel hospital could not easily be left behind. Leo Grebler, who extensively researched land-use changes on the Lower East Side between the 1920s and 1950, noted that a large number of individuals and families who chose to remain as residents were "the people necessary to run the synagogues, the yeshivas, the Talmud Torahs, the all-day parochial schools, the stores selling religious articles and books, the homes for the aged and the sages, the ritual baths, and the whole gamut of institutions that forms such an important part of the Lower East Side landscape."[16]

Although demographic changes after 1925 made the Lower East Side less a place for newly arrived immigrants, it nonetheless retained its popular reputation as an "Old World" neighborhood. This reputation was sustained by hordes of ex-residents, visitors, and tourists who frequented the district to observe religious practices, to engage in rituals of remembrance, to buy ethnic goods and commodities, or to immerse themselves in a diverse cultural environment.[17] The Lower East Side remained *the* cultural urban center for numerous ethnic and religious cohorts whose members no longer resided there. On weekends especially, entire families returned to the Lower East Side to observe religious customs or to indulge in nostalgia for days gone by. For both religious and secular Jews who had departed, locations across the Lower East Side retained their central cultural and/or religious significance well into the 1950s. Institutions such as the Educational Alliance continued to operate and

serve both local Jews and those who had exited the neighborhood. Although their readership was geographically dispersed, both Yiddish
dailies maintained their offices along East Broadway. Throngs of shoppers still crowded the clothing stores along the narrow Orchard Street
and the produce markets of Essex Street. Crowds packed the Yiddish
theaters and delicatessens on Second Avenue. Many families still purchased furniture from warehouse-sized stores on First Avenue and Avenue A. In short, hundreds of ethnic restaurants, cafés, theaters, and
religious and cultural institutions continued to thrive largely by catering to a clientele of former Lower East Siders.

A trip to the old neighborhood for former Lower East Siders was especially meaningful. For those who had enjoyed a degree of social and
economic mobility ("to move up is to move out"), return visits rekindled
good and bad memories of life in the ghetto and the collective struggle
of "doing without." Elders pointed out their former tenements (perhaps
still inhabited or boarded up) to their grandchildren, recounting past
horrors and amusements and experiencing a sense of personal and,
perhaps, bittersweet accomplishment. After a tour that inevitably included shopping and eating, the dilapidated tenements, cluttered streets,
and impoverished residents were left behind as the "spectators" returned
to the relative comfort of their homes uptown, or in Brooklyn or the
Bronx. Ritualized pilgrimages to the Lower East Side and the attachments
to memories of place elevated the neighborhood's *symbolic* significance
and reinforced both its ethnic, "Old World" character and reputation.
Although population continued to decline, the weekend onslaught of
nostalgia seekers and religious worshipers gave the feel of a vibrant
neighborhood and disguised the anemic residential housing market.

The romanticized spectacle of a nostalgic ethnic Lower East Side that
emerged in the late 1920s did little to profit the owners of emptied tenements. Old World nostalgia was, for the real estate sector, misplaced
(and dangerously unprofitable) sympathy for a bygone era. An identity
based on immigrant working-class culture was one frozen in time and
was increasingly unsubstantiated by social and economic realities of a
changing Manhattan where new immigrant settlements were virtually
nonexistent and employment patterns had shifted away from manufacturing and toward white-collar services. Indeed, the version of a Lower
East Side that embellished and celebrated ethnic cultures, rituals, and
identities (namely eastern European and Jewish) made the prospect of

attracting a significant cohort of new and different tenants—either poor or middle-class—more difficult. In his overview of the Lower East Side housing market, Grebler posed the question of why, in spite of numerous vacancies and low rents, the Lower East Side did not attract an appreciable number of Blacks, who were migrating to New York in great numbers in the 1920s and 1930s.[18] In his response, Grebler argued that the ethnic and cultural features of the Lower East Side were so entrenched as to discourage black settlements.[19] Real estate capitalists and planning agencies focused on the negative effects of ethnic nostalgia in efforts to capture an upscale housing consumer market that would revalorize an obsolete Lower East Side. In a 1932 publication, the Lower East Side Planning Association listed the "reputation of the district created by former overcrowding and practices of exploitation" as a principal cause of the area's continued blight.[20] Local business elites decried the ways of the poor ethnic as a greater obstacle to reinventing identity than the district's abundance of decrepit housing—rehabilitating housing units, it would seem, was a much easier task than changing the behavior of immigrants and their impression on the city's middle classes.

To revitalize an otherwise stagnant housing market, the real estate sector sought to reinvent the Lower East Side's reputation. In a marked departure from the immigrant era, the social and cultural attributes of Lower East Siders were scrutinized by those individuals with an economic stake in the local land market. Self-serving representations of the Lower East Side put forth by real estate organizations, slum committees, chambers of commerce, and business elites began to invent sharp distinctions between the past (the immigrant quarter) and present (the deviant ghetto). Within this discursive narrative, the once "savage" immigrants with their base and uncivil ways were rehabilitated and ennobled only by virtue of their exodus from the Lower East Side. Echoing the dictum "to move up is to move out," the departure of older immigrant groups provided irrefutable evidence of their social mobility and success. Consequently, the vibrant and sizable ethnic communities that continued to call the Lower East Side home were cast as failures of assimilation. In the aftermath of the heroic exodus from the ghetto, those left behind were the "marooned,"[21] "the queer, the unadjusted, the radical, the bohemian, and the criminal"—"the slum is the neighborhood of lost souls."[22] In such constructions, remaining tenants who clung to arcane immigrant lifestyles formed a static "fermenting vat"[23] that encumbered the progressive rehabilitation of the slum:

> Like a migrating flock of blackbirds resting and feeding temporarily, so groups of immigrants as well as individual families and isolated individuals stop in this transitional area on their way up or down the social scale. Each of these waves leaves a residue of poverty-stricken, socially unadjusted, maladjusted defectives and delinquents which gradually accumulate into a slum population.[24]

A sociocultural discourse that drew distinctions between a mythical dignified ghetto of the past and the ignoble and dispensable slum of the present was conveniently welded to contemporary rational planning arguments to do away with centrally located working-class housing. In planning documents in the late 1920s and early 1930s, carefully detailed recommendations for new land uses were coupled with diatribes of the slum (almost always the Lower East Side) as "a breeder of crime" and a magnet for "human derelicts who foundered in more respectable sections [of the city]."[25] Slum committees (whose boards were drawn more from the banking and real estate industries than social reform organizations) constructed the need for renewal both as practical redevelopment of an obsolete district and as social responsibility to the entire city. To do so, committees and real estate associations appropriated the language, symbols, and imagery used by social reformers in their decades-old campaigns against the tenement and its social consequences. The elimination of slums was thus codified as a "public purpose"[26] for the betterment of all city residents, not just Lower East Siders and certainly not real estate capitalists exclusively. The social costs of redevelopment, such as residential displacement from the bulldozing of large tracts of tenements, were trivialized. Forced evictions or any other possible sacrifices were outweighed by the larger benefits of abstract notions of civic good and decency. As one study noted, "We are confident that a large portion of the group displaced by slum clearance will be able to find suitable accommodations *elsewhere.*"[27]

Incorporating the Former Ghetto into the Modern Metropolis

> For Le Corbusier, on his first visit to New York in 1935, the skyscrapers were too small to match the image in his mind.
> Ada Louise Huxtable, "Stumbling toward Tomorrow"

Given the social reformers' lengthy and vitriolic battle against slum conditions (as outlined in chapter 2), it seems remarkably ironic that the real estate industry co-opted and utilized nearly identical reform rhetoric to legitimize their drive to displace the working class. In doing so, real estate organizations and quasi-public planning groups came to dominate the public discourse of getting rid of the slum, posing the problem in moral and economic terms and the solutions in rational ways that profited landowners. "Official" problem-solving committees and panels were formed with representation of banking executives, captains of industry, and often social reformers who showed little concern for potential social costs of private solutions. All that was "morally reprehensible and undesirable" (decrepit housing, sanitation) was double-coded as unprofitable and improvident given the emerging economic opportunities within the city and region. The shift away from manufacturing and the rising preeminence of the corporate sector in Manhattan's economy were posed as "new realities" that demanded a solution to an economic, not simply social, problem. "Sentimentality," wrote Lower East Side social reformer Loula Lasker, "must give way to sound economic policy."[28] Thus, the decades-old reformist agenda of curing the social ills of community residents was made subordinate to the economic challenge of making the best use of underutilized and costly urban land. Tenements, it was argued, were no longer overflowing in capacity; thus, they should be pulled down and replaced with structures more suitable for "higher and better uses." Anticipated demand stemming from changes in Manhattan's residential class structure from working class to middle class determined new, profitable uses. Consequently, the remedy that emerged was not to improve the ghetto but to eliminate it entirely under the guise of "modernization" and "community betterment." Private capitalists, not social reformers, were best positioned to make such "improvements," and the appropriate role for the state was to provide expertise, legislative assistance, and subsidies for private redevelopment of housing aimed at white-collar workers.

"Fixing the ghetto" was subjected to the newly developed discipline of rational, "scientific" planning that viewed neighborhoods less as communities and more as components to be integrated into a larger spatial system, the New York region. One of the most vocal proponents for coordinated planning and the revival of the Lower East Side was the Regional Plan Association (RPA). In the first decades of the twentieth century, quasi-public organizations such as the New York City Improvement Plan (1907) and the Committee on the City Plan (1914) brought together local banking and industry leaders and political officials to fabricate a land-use agenda that would benefit particular businesses and industries. The Committee on the City Plan, for example, successfully zoned out garment shops adjacent to Fifth Avenue in favor of promoting the area's reputation for luxury shopping. (Evidently, shabby and unkempt garment workers took lunch breaks in full view of upscale shoppers.) In 1922 the Russell Sage Foundation formed the Committee on the Plan of New York and Its Environs. Over the ensuing decade numerous studies on land use, transportation, parks, and housing in the thirty-one-county New York region were commissioned and published together as a regional master plan. In 1929 the RPA was incorporated and charged with developing ways to implement the master plan.[29] The RPA, originally comprised of twelve banking and business elites, held significant influence among the area's governors, mayors, and developers, and the 1929 plan served as a broad guideline for regional development for nearly forty years. As far as the hyperrational plan was concerned, the redevelopment of the Lower East Side fit into a larger regional jigsaw puzzle, as part of the geography of Manhattan, then New York City, and, finally, the metropolitan region. Thus, local planning was subjected to the RPA's larger mandate to facilitate pro-business regional land use. The Lower East Side's condition as an increasingly obsolete, but nonetheless vibrantly chaotic, ghetto meant little, and, consequently, the desires of remaining communities mattered even less. "To the planner," wrote the president of the RPA in 1931, "there can be no beauty without order."[30]

Manhattan's land use in the RPA's blueprint was delimited as commercial and residential space dedicated to New York's corporate business economy.[31] Much of the data on the obsolescence of the tenement district were gathered by the New York Slum Clearance Committee, composed of settlement workers, architects, a bank president, realtors, and a real estate lobbying organization. The committee recommended that tenements be replaced with modern housing at rents out of range for most Lower East Siders.[32] The best land use for the Lower East Side, by virtue of its location adjacent to Wall Street, was middle-class, "white collar" residential.[33] In the late 1920s, the original target for new tenants was the former Lower East Siders who had entered the ranks of the middle classes. Planners and real estate developers soon broadened the scope of potential renters of upscale Lower East Side housing to include all white-collar workers employed in lower Manhattan. As traditional Lower East Side employers — tobacco plants, fur showrooms, men's and women's garments, and printing plants — vacated lower Manhattan for midtown west and the outer boroughs, the financial district galvanized its hold over the city south of Fulton Street.[34] Banks, the stock exchanges, insurance firms, accounting agencies, and law firms conglomerated in the Wall Street area employing a large white-collar workforce. "Are not these the logical future residents of the East Side — these thousands of middle-class folk who daily take a journey of ten to twenty-five miles in crowded subways?"[35] The Regional Plan addressed the issue of the Wall Street firms' migrating north to the newer office district of Forty-second Street:

> It is true that for persons living to the north and northeast, it may be at present more convenient to stop at 42nd Street than to travel farther south to Wall Street.... But the approaches to the Wall Street section can be greatly improved.... Consider, also, how the development of a very high-class residential district somewhere between Wall Street and 42nd Street would affect the situation.[36]

An RPA-sponsored survey of the local housing market concluded that the district's convenience to lower Manhattan would sustain a shift from a low-income market to a moderate- and high-income one.[37]

Between 1927 and the mid-1930s the more organized elements of the real estate sector expressed interest in government incentives and financial subsidies that were increasingly viewed as necessary if large-scale improvements were to occur. According to boosters, private redevelopment hinged on municipal provision of public parks, waterfront access, and, most importantly, transportation.[38] To attract investors, public works projects were planned to modernize the transportation infrastructure and allow greater access into and out of the district. The RPA called for the construction of a major north-south traffic artery to run along the east side of Manhattan. The Second Avenue "speedway" would consist of a below-ground automobile highway from Houston Street to the Harlem River. South of Houston Street to Canal Street, the speedway would convert to a parkway along the cleared Chrystie-Forsyth site.[39] Using the parkway-speedway, motorists could travel from the Lower East Side to the Upper East Side in minutes. The RPA's recommendations also included the widening of Avenue C to improve the district's

Figure 8. Proposed development of Second Avenue. From Committee on the Regional Plan of New York and Its Environs, *The Building of the City* (1931), 395.

access.[40] Neither plan was realized. In the early 1930s, planners viewed road widening and new construction as a key way to coax skeptical developers and builders to invest in luxury housing development on the Lower East Side. Another project — the proposed East River Drive — would run the length of the Lower East Side along the riverfront, connecting the relatively inaccessible eastern streets and avenues to Wall Street and midtown Manhattan. Planners found the existing disposition of riverfront property most suitable for clearance and construction of the artery. By 1929, most of the factories, piers, and lumber and coal yards found on the strip of land hugging the East River lay abandoned and contributed to the adjacent blight.[41] Unlike most areas within the Lower East Side, parcels of properties there were large, less expensive, and owned by a small number of individuals; only five owners controlled the riverfront from Fourth to Thirteenth Streets.[42] The 1929 Regional Plan also called for amenities to attract the desired well-heeled residents.[43] Corlears Hook Park was to be enlarged, and an additional park would run adjacent to the drive. Yacht basins were to anchor each end of Corlears Hook Park, at the foot of East Third Street and of Montgomery Street.[44]

In the architectural vision of a reinvented Lower East Side, the clean lines and sharp angles of the modernist skyscraper would replace the misshapen, chaotic slum dwellings. A massive project, proposed in 1931 but never built, envisioned a community of wealthy and moderate-income city dwellers who would shuttle via automobile to and from their modern high-rise apartments surrounded by vast, open green spaces. The project, named Rutgerstown, was proposed as a limited-dividend project for moderate-income housing to be constructed on a cluster of tenement-ridden blocks south of Corlears Hook. The ambitious plan called for a total reconfiguration of the landscape, including ridding the area of all of its walk-up tenements and its gridiron street pattern. Several multistory towers that would house seventy-five hundred apartments were to rise from large, empty green expanses.[45] The proposed scheme for a massive self-contained community is comparable to Bat-

Figure 9. Frank Lloyd Wright's drawing of proposed St. Mark's Place tower for *Architectural Record*, 1930. Frank Lloyd Wright drawings are copyright 1999 The Frank Lloyd Wright Foundation, Scottsdale, Arizona.

tery Park City, which was built near Wall Street in lower Manhattan in the 1980s. These mega-complex prototypes were not to be limited to the Lower East Side's waterfront. A futurist architectural exhibition at the Museum of Modern Art called for modern high-rise apartments to be erected along a widened Chrystie Street in the heart of the Lower East Side.[46] Such grandiose plans soon gave way to the harsh realities of the depression, however. The Public Works Authority eventually built a significantly scaled-down version of the highway and East River Park along the river in 1935. The adjacent luxury high-rises never materialized.

While the RPA, other organizations, and planners investigated the feasibility of the futurist automotive-based community design for the Lower East Side,[47] others were readapting the neighborhood's past walk-to-work appeal for the modern era. Two midscale high-rises, Ageloff Towers on Avenue A and Third Street and Stuyvesant Apartments on Second Avenue and Tenth Street, were constructed in the late 1920s prior to the onset of the depression. While neither project was on the scale of what ardent supporters of neighborhood modernization had in mind, both were situated on multiple lots and incorporated up-to-date apartment layouts. Rent levels for Ageloff and Stuyvesant apartments were higher than those for surrounding cold-water flats. In contrast to the surrounding tenements, clerks, professionals, and other white-collar workers filled the buildings. Ageloff and Stuyvesant, both privately developed, were but two examples of what planners and developers had envisioned as an upscale walk-to-work residential neighborhood for office workers employed in the new skyscrapers of the Wall Street area, just south of the district.

The local real estate industry, especially its organized voice, the East Side Chamber of Commerce, embraced such plans as illustrative of the virtues of civic improvement and progress. The chamber, whose members included a faction of local landlords, outside developers, and area merchants, as well as influential planners and businesspeople from across the city, ardently supported plans for upgraded land uses. The Lower East Side Planning Association, whose board consisted of numerous bank executives but no residents or settlement workers, was founded in 1931.[48] Representing an organized component of the real estate sector and pro-development government agencies, these stakeholders positioned themselves as providers of a place substantially redesigned for new middle- and upper-middle-class residents. Plans drawn up by

Figure 10. The proposed Christie-Forsyth Parkway, 1931. From Committee on the Regional Plan of New York and Its Environs, *The Building of the City* (1931), 399.

organizations such as the City Club, the East Side Chamber of Commerce, and the Lower East Side Planning Association proposed slum clearance, followed by the construction of massive middle-class apartment communities.[49] Large-scale developers and builders, in particular, saw potential profit in massive housing complexes burgeoning out of ten-city-block tenement areas razed by government-sponsored and -financed slum removal programs.[50] Real estate developers expressed initial attraction to an upscale walk-to-work development plan for the Lower East Side. The project's sponsor Fred F. French, who had successfully employed the walk-to-work residential concept in the development of the massive Tudor City complex in the East Forty-second Street office district, proposed a similar venture for the Lower East Side. Between 1928 and 1931 French used four dummy corporations to purchase nearly three hundred individual lots between the Manhattan and Brooklyn Bridges. Approximately 14.5 acres of property were amassed to erect a proposed $150-million Knickerbocker Village to house thirty thousand middle-class tenants.[51] Depression-era economics forced French to make concessions in the plan. First, French failed to secure private financing for the massive and expensive project. He appealed to New York State for financial assistance, and in 1933 the state was brought on board in a direct capacity to finance the redevelopment project. The Reconstruction Finance Corporation (RFC) provided mortgage funds for Knickerbocker Village, but French was required to operate the development as a limited-dividend corporation (profits were set at 6 to 7 percent). The RFC was federally financed but operated under the provisions of the State Housing Law of 1926, which provided tax abatements and exemptions for limited-dividend companies to develop new middle-income housing projects. French was also forced to scale back the size of the complex considerably: only two towers of a much larger plan were completed.[52] Although downsized, Knickerbocker Village was built, and it attracted lower-middle and middle-class white-collar workers from across the New York region as residents.

Knickerbocker's significance had less to do with its success as a middle-class project than its inclusion of the state as a player in a development project. The "rescue" of Knickerbocker Village elevated the state as a major stakeholder in the redevelopment of the Lower East Side. The state's terms of intervention, while initially fully in favor of middle-class development, were not dictated solely by the real estate sector. Stipula-

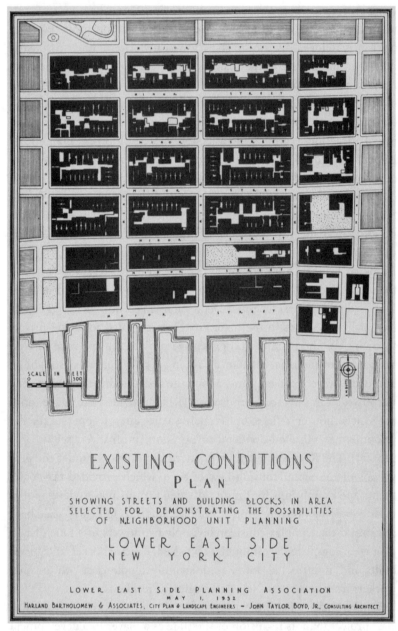

Figure 11. The limitations of the 25-by-100-foot parcel. From Lower East Side Planning Association, *Plans for Major Traffic Thoroughfares and Transit, Lower East Side, New York City* (1932), 100.

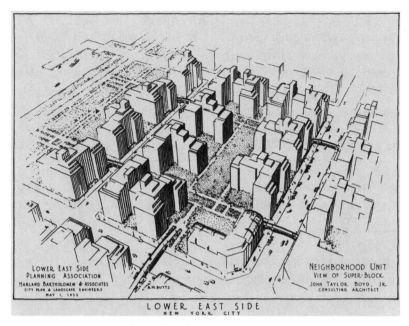

Figure 12. The proposed "Superblock" improvement. From Lower East Side Planning Association, *Plans for Major Traffic Thoroughfares and Transit, Lower East Side, New York City* (1932), 104.

tions of the State Housing Law of 1926 clearly endorsed the vision of a post-slum urban landscape sprinkled with towering middle-class apartment complexes. The law's provisions stipulated, however, that only new, large, block-level residential developments were eligible for subsidies; rehabilitations and new construction on single lots were ineligible. Again, the fragmented nature of absentee ownership of small parcels on the Lower East Side came into play as few new eligible projects were constructed. The Amalgamated Clothing Workers Union had successfully utilized the law's allowances to build a complex for three hundred former Lower East Side families in the Bronx. In 1930, new construction for a similar limited-dividend project was begun at the site of a demolished factory on Grand Street on the Lower East Side. The Grand Street project was intended for working-class residents from the Lower East Side and other areas within the city. The complex was built as a cooperative in which units were to be sold to "low-wage earning" workers at $500 per room ($150 down payment and monthly installments of the balance over ten years).[53] Such costs were well beyond the means of the typical Lower East Sider, and the complex instead drew middle-class tenants from other parts of the New York region.[54] Over half the tenants were independent businessmen, a third were professionals or government employees, and the rest were skilled laborers and salesmen.[55] Amalgamated Houses, with its modern high-rise design and units rich with amenities, stood out amidst the seemingly unending landscape of run-down nineteenth-century tenements. Upon completion in 1931, this middle-class structure surrounded by poverty and decline symbolized a future Lower East Side free of tenements — and their tenants. In later years of further urban decline, however, that symbolism was reversed: Amalgamated Houses represented the last "fortress" against what appeared to be the area's inevitable downward spiral toward despair in the 1970s.

In addition to proposing middle- and upper-class replacement housing, developers, planners, and local businessmen attempted to influence the state's relatively new powers of land-use zoning as a tool to rid the Lower East Side of its working-class and ethnic vestiges. The Lower East Side Planning Association worked for several years to have the district zoned for residential use as a means of eliminating the area's cheap, "honky-tonk" image. Although the famous open-air pushcarts were fewer in number, several streets retained a bazaar atmosphere where shoppers (including many former residents) and shopkeepers haggled over prices. Delancey, East Broadway, and Second Avenue remained congested working-class shopping and entertainment thoroughfares frequented by former Lower East Siders, current residents, and visitors from across the region.[56] The extensive commerce and bustle of these thoroughfares were hardly compatible with the upscale image planners and developers had in mind.

In the midst of the propounding of both modest and imposing redevelopment schemes, the Lower East Side remained entrenched as a materially and symbolically obsolete district. Housing stock and housing market conditions continued to falter, appearing even more outmoded in comparison to other residential communities in and around the city. The lure of early suburban-style developments pushed the effort to rebuild (rather than renovate) the older warrens of the inner city; open spaces, wider streets and avenues, bigger parks, docks, and other amenities were deemed essential to compete with new communities in the outer boroughs and "first-ring" suburbs. The sweeping aside of the old built environment and remaining residents (characterized as failures of assimilation) would, it was hoped, erase the neighborhood's outstanding symbolic association with poverty and ethnicity.

A 1931 RPA bulletin predicted that without action the Lower East Side would continue to be "a sore spot on the City's social economy and a wasted area in its assessment map."[57] Despite considerable consensus for development among key stakeholders in the real estate sector and the first signs of supportive intervention from the state, neither the "slum" nor its residents disappeared. The onset of the Great Depression not only placed nearly all urban development plans on hold but also ushered in a period of intensive and often contradictory state intervention in which the state emerged as the central stakeholder in the struggle over land use on the Lower East Side. In addition, the opposing interests of landlords, developers, and residents along with their representations and counter-representations of the Lower East Side shaped the kinds of housing programs and policies that came to redefine both local landscape and identity.

The Failure of Middle-Class Reinvention and the Rise of the Subsidized Ghetto

The strategy to reinvent the Lower East Side was a clear example of an effort, as Jon Teaford has put it, "to beat suburbia at its own game."[58] Implicit in the emerging ideology of city development was the belief that by eradicating the glaring physical differences between city and suburb, the rapidly emerging social distinctions in class, income, race, occupation, and educational levels between them could be erased as well. Given better housing opportunities elsewhere, many white ethnics (both second-generation immigrants and those foreign-born) who experienced social and economic mobility moved out of their old apartments, leaving their former neighborhood a concentrated enclave of poverty. Without capital renovations, these neighborhoods were ill prepared to reverse that trend.

Ultimately, the strategy for reinvention of the Lower East Side failed. Throughout the economically grim years of the depression, planners, developers, and local business elites managed to keep their vision of a renewed, upscale Lower East Side in the forefront of potential futures for the neighborhood. In his 1938 study on housing conditions on the Lower East Side, land economist Homer Hoyt wrote, "Most of the area . . .

has become a liability to the owners and the city. Tax delinquencies have greatly increased and many of the residents are on public relief."[59] Despite worsening conditions nearly a decade after the regional plan first appeared, Hoyt's prescription reiterated what was by then a familiar refrain: massive government intervention to create new housing for Wall Street workers.

But financial woes alone were not responsible for subsequent land-use changes that effectively axed real estate capitalists' aspirations for a middle-class, "white-collar" neighborhood. As it emerged in the 1920s and 1930s, the collective agenda to reshape the district was fraught with local political difficulties and national changes in the state's role in urban restructuring. Reinvention required a massive undertaking that demanded conformity (be it consensual or forced) in interest and action among residents, property owners, and the state. Such compliance was not forthcoming as middle-class renewal met staunch opposition from residents. In addition, the interests and class backgrounds among thousands of independent landlords owning a nearly equivalent number of small properties rarely converged with those of business elites and new developers with grand schemes of residential and commercial modernization. Finally, in its new role as an interventionist, the state experimented with policies that vacillated between subsidizing middle-class and lower-class housing projects. Each of these points is taken in turn.

In the 1930s, the Lower East Side was a polyglot of ethnicities, age cohorts, income categories, newcomers, old-timers, those who chose to live there, and those whose economic circumstances prevented them from living elsewhere. As we have seen, plans for the creation of a homogeneous middle-class residential district stood in stark contrast to this demographic reality and the dominant symbolic representations of the Lower East Side. For several subgroups existing within the neighborhood, discussion of middle-class renewal plans was interpreted as a threat of community displacement. Many of the residents who chose to remain in the neighborhood resented the cultural attack developers, planners, and, partly, social reformers launched on the retention of "Old World lifestyles." Propaganda circulated by a variety of media represented renewal as a public benefit for the Lower East Side, but there was an increasing sense among residents that they were excluded from such a future. A 1930 *New York Times* article on new housing plans in the area reported that old-time Lower East Siders were too set in their ways and exhibited signs that they would be unable to adapt culturally to the modern lifestyle such changes would bring.[60] The few new development projects that were completed did little to palliate the displacement fears of working-class ethnics. While the Amalgamated Houses and the scaled-down Knickerbocker Village were touted as successful prototypes for redevelopment, very few locals lived there. Of the 386 low-income families displaced by the Knickerbocker development, for example, only 3 resettled in the newly constructed complex.[61]

Those who remained in the tenements continued to demand decent housing conditions and to combat efforts that would further stigmatize and eventually displace the working-class community. Rent strikes, by now an honored tradition on the Lower East Side, remained frequent.[62] In the early 1930s, as the depression took hold on the city's economy, rent strikes were prevalent not only on the Lower East Side but across the city. In January 1933, landlords and police evicted a writers' and artists' colony known as Paradise Alley, on Avenue A and Eleventh Street, for withholding rent. A brief melee ensued as nearly five hundred unemployed workers came to the assistance of the colony's residents.[63] In 1934, a consortium of mothers' clubs, settlement houses, and religious organizations formed the Lower East Side Public Housing Conference to canvass support for housing reform during the height of building foreclosures and subsequent tenant evictions.[64]

Residents also mobilized against community planning initiatives that excluded their input. Given the local history of struggle for better housing conditions, long-term residents took offense at the notion of their community being reinvented for outsiders or "uptowners."[65] A significant number of residents and affiliated organizations turned out for a public hearing on the proposal to zone a large portion of the Lower East Side in March 1938. The East Side Tenant's Union, local settlement houses, the Lower East Side Public Housing Conference, and the American Labor Party rallied for the inclusion of the land uses that were glaringly missing from the new zoning proposal. No mention was made explicitly of retaining or constructing new low-income housing.[66] Locals saw the zoning issue as a ruse for the larger plan to displace them and reconstruct the Lower East Side for middle- and upper-class tenants. The zoning proposal was passed, but the effort to extend the ordinance to the entire Lower East Side was defeated.

THE RENASCENCE OF RUGGED INDIVIDUALISM

The Tenant of Knickerbocker Village Who Reverted to Neighborhood Practice

Figure 13. "The Renascence of Rugged Individualism," *The New Yorker* (1936).
Copyright The New Yorker Collection, 1936, Carl Rose; from cartoonbank.com
of The New Yorker Magazine. All rights reserved.

The most significant obstacle to reinvention proved to be an unintentional but nonetheless powerful and effective form of resistance: working-class ethnic presence and attachment to place. Locals blocked the endeavor to reinvent the Lower East Side by remaining as residents and by actively participating in the various forms of community life deemed contradictory to middle-class sentiments. Residents had formed extremely deep cultural attachments to the Lower East Side, and given the efforts to displace both residents and community identity, they showed fierce and sustained commitment to remain. Tenement families from diverse backgrounds, for example, formed strong ties of solidarity that went beyond ethnic differences or class similarities. When Old Law tenements were pulled down to make way for Knickerbocker Village, the very same families who were evicted resettled together in another building. Despite opportunities for housing elsewhere in the city, nearly 83 percent of those tenants displaced by the Knickerbocker project relocated to similar Old Law tenements within the neighborhood.[67]

Lower East Siders' commitment to place was further evidenced by their reaction to social reform policies during this era. Social reformers had embraced the reinvention and modernization agenda somewhat naively as the best chance for the reviled old neighborhood to be integrated within the mainstream cultural fabric of the city.[68] Many reformers interpreted much of the community life of the Lower East Side — the seemingly disordered street life, marketplace, and amusements — as evidence of a persistently delinquent lifestyle.[69] Given the opportunity to rid such a lifestyle, many settlement workers, for example, pondered why locals chose to cling to arcane cultural practices. Interestingly, the persistence of Lower East Siders' attachment to place solidified the prevalent theory among reformers that slum behavior was inextricably linked to dilapidated physical conditions and reinforced the prescription that slums be eliminated at any cost. A case in point was the paternalistic attitude of social reformers and the openly hostile and rebellious nature of their "clients" in the 113-unit Lavanburg model tenement built on the Lower East Side in 1930. The managerial style at Lavanburg was harsh and disciplinary; lengthy personal interviews and frequent visits to tenants' homes were conducted to monitor the "moral progress" of former slum dwellers and to weed out the undeserving.[70] During the height of the depression, residents of Lavanburg rebelled against the regulations forbidding homework and took in garment piecework to earn additional income. Lavanburg's founder, Abraham Goldfeld, bemoaned the residents' "reversion to traditional means of self-help."[71] Although many Lower East Siders took advantage of social reform and settlement house programs, they resisted the anti–working class and proselytizing attitudes of the middle-class reformers in a range of ways both material and symbolic. Local resistance and residents' strong cultural attachments to place frustrated the claims that middle-class development would put to rest the evils of the slum.

A second problem besetting reinvention was the conflicting real estate actions of self-interested tenement owners. Advisers for the RPA had singled out individual landlords, family trusts, estates, and other forms of fragmented property ownership as the chief obstacles for any comprehensive redevelopment plan. Such owners were "notoriously unenterprising" and "given to holding on and doing nothing in the hope that some happy combination of circumstances may one day bring them a boom market."[72] Such frustrations were experienced by planners and large developers throughout a decade of reinvention efforts. When landlords acted in what they concluded was their own, individual best interests in the 1920s and 1930s, the consequences were amazingly diverse. Some landlords maintained their properties and fully supported the modernization vision, but only a small number reaped the benefits of large-scale development. Newspaper articles and editorials in favor of modernization and the grand utopian designs of planners captured the public's attention but also diverted it away from the fact that numerous landlords had abandoned their buildings while others had begun to renovate them.[73] In the spring of 1936, the city's newly created Vacancy Bureau found that Lower East Siders were being squeezed out of the district because of upgrading renovations *and* evictions due to code violations.[74] The destruction of some tenements and renovations of others had the unintended consequence of causing a shortage of low-rent housing on the Lower East Side in the late 1930s. Ironically, Old Law tenements shut down or foreclosed on due to code enforcement were put back on the market and remodeled during a later postwar shortage in 1946. (Two real estate firms had specialized in the acquisition, rehabilitation, and management of such tenements.[75]) As landlords aged and eventually died, the ownership of properties was assumed by offspring as evidenced in the increase in the listings of "estates" in ownership profiles.[76] Although ownership profiles changed, the holding of one or two individual lots predominated. Two major exceptions were the lots stockpiled by developer Fred French in the late 1920s and early 1930s and those held in foreclosure by financial institutions.[77] By the early 1940s, these latter properties had been sold off individually to single buyers.

Private developers were also dismayed by the kinds of development programs offered by the state. The limited-dividend clause in existing programs circumscribed the level of profits from large complexes (e.g., the State Housing Law of 1929 and RFC funds for financing Amalgamated Houses and Knickerbocker Village). Property-owning members of the East Side Chamber of Commerce, hoping to raise the appeal of state programs, proposed an "equity trust" to spread the entire amount of start-up capital to build such projects among participating developers. With a small amount of investment from each property owner, a 6 to 7 percent profit return, it was argued, was more attractive.[78] The most active proponent of the equity trusts was Arthur C. Holden, a former worker at the Christodora House settlement, an architect of futuristic designs for a revitalized Lower East Side and technical adviser for the East Side Chamber of Commerce. Holden held meetings with property holders and tried to persuade them to pool their holdings as an equity trust and apply for government-subsidized mortgages for development. The motion found few takers.[79] Again, the fragmented nature of Lower East Side land ownership (the absence of a unified landlord or developer class) worked against a comprehensive and sustainable strategy for redevelopment with or without state intervention. Despite the promise of reinvention, the legacy (or for large developers, the tyranny) of the 25-by-100-foot lot was nonetheless retained. Striking variations in the disposition of buildings within single blocks and a matching fragmentation of property ownership meant that assembling the requisite number of parcels for large-scale middle-class redevelopment projects was very difficult to orchestrate.

Both resistance from working-class Lower East Siders and the divided interests and actions of property owners placed much of the burden of reinvention of the Lower East Side on state intervention. Indeed, the middle-class redevelopment efforts identified in earlier sections were not totally private but partly state subsidized. As chapter 2 detailed, the crusade for state action, however, had originated much earlier, during the Progressive Era, when municipal reformers and settlement workers petitioned for the rehabilitation of the slum. It was only with the bottoming out of the ghetto housing market that state support became urgent in the minds of real estate capitalists. In the 1930s, property owners, developers, and some reformers were *partially* successful in influencing state urban policy to subsidize middle-income, rather than low-income, development. In its infancy, public housing was briefly defined to include middle-income housing, but by 1934 the city and state governments had also embarked on building housing explicitly for the working poor.[80] Thus, early state urban development policy was unclear in its mandate and contradictory in its results in reshaping the city's landscape. The contradiction was largely resolved after a decade of the New Deal and subsequent wrangling between city, state, and federal governments and real estate capitalists over the government's role in housing provisions and subsidies.[81] In effect, two federal housing policies emerged by the close of the 1930s. Programs directed by the Federal Housing Administration (FHA) focused on the financing of new housing, providing a wide range of direct and indirect subsidies for builders and real estate developers and mortgage underwriting for homeowners. FHA programs channeled new middle-class housing development away from cities to the suburbs. The second program, public housing and, later, urban renewal, would come to apply almost exclusively to the landscape of the older, inner cities. The evolution of the latter programs during the 1930s had considerable ramifications for both middle-class aspirations of Lower East Side landlords and the development plans of the city's real estate sector.

Competing and Conflicting Demands on State Housing Policy

The year 1940 marked the symbolic closure of incongruous government policies that vacillated between low-income and middle-income housing subsidies for the Lower East Side. The New York City Housing Authority bought the land slated for a middle-income development and erected a massive low-income public housing venture, the Vladeck Houses. Aspirations for a middle-class renewal of the Lower East Side were effectively quashed. By 1950 the Lower East Side contained the largest concentration of government-sponsored low-income housing south of Ninety-sixth Street. Over 3,750 units were constructed on a thin strip of land between Houston and Fourteenth Street alone, and an even greater number of units were built farther south. Given that this area was considered an implausible location for large public housing developments in the late 1930s, how did such a significant reversal in site location occur? As the following section shows, the housing policy turnabout reveals the intensity and the uncertainty of urban capitalists and an interventionist state in their attempt to reframe the use and character of formerly overpopulated ghettos in the specter of urban deconcentration of industry and working-class residency.[82]

Despite intense and relatively concerted civic boosterism on the part of planners, architects, social reformers, and developers for a modern white-collar Lower East Side, state incentives for private development were limited. The earliest subsidies for middle-class housing were largely counterbalanced in effect by competing policies that expanded or improved the area's low-income housing. With the exception of the State Housing Law of 1929 and the Reconstruction Finance Corporation, in retrospect most forms of governmental intervention in the local housing market appeared to work against the plan to create a middle-class Lower East Side. At the local level, Mayor Fiorello LaGuardia continued a policy of strict enforcement of the Multiple Dwelling Law of 1929 and slum clearance throughout the 1930s. Faced with compliance or demolition, more landlords abandoned their holdings, others foreclosed, and some upgraded and raised rents. Other groups of organized landowners welcomed large-scale slum clearance to make large parcels available for subsidized housing developments.[83] Between 1934 and 1936, the square footage of vacant lots on the Lower East Side increased from 200,000 to 650,000.[84] These lots were not contiguous, however, but interspersed between occupied and unoccupied tenements, contributing to the neighborhood's tattered look. Rather than subsidize the city's residential development, most federal government development programs in the early 1930s funded the construction of bridges, tunnels, and parkways that would link the suburban hinterlands to the central core of Manhattan. Government programs such as federal road construction, in conjunction with a variety of mortgage subsidies that clearly favored suburban housing, provided the momentum for the massive wave of postwar suburbanization. Master builder Robert Moses' priorities were to extend the metropolitanization of the New York area deep into what were then the wilds of Long Island and the marshlands of New Jersey.[85]

While the state government showed lukewarm interest in the plight of the inner city, the municipal government experimented in providing housing to low-income workers, much to the chagrin of the real estate industry. Given its reputation as the most notorious slum district in the country coupled with a long legacy of housing reform, the Lower East Side towered above other sites as the most deserving of new government programs to build low-income housing. In 1935, the newly created New York City Housing Authority transformed twenty-four tenements on Avenue A and Third Streets into First Houses, the first housing in the United States built entirely by the government. By tearing down some of the existing tenements and reconstructing others, the completed First Houses consisted of 122 units in eight buildings with courtyards and shared recreation space.[86] The design of the complex differed little from the surrounding landscape of tenements: the buildings were low-rise brick with front-to-back positions perpendicular to the street.[87] Beginning with a pool of nearly fifteen thousand applicants, the Housing Authority accepted those who were deemed "in good standing" after a stringent review and inspections of their current residences.[88] Housing reformers immediately hailed First Houses in support of further government provision of low-income housing.

The experience of building First Houses was never repeated, but it shaped subsequent deliberations about the scale and design of low-income public housing locally and nationally. The extensive rehabilitation of tenements was expensive and impractical given their age and condition and the availability of cheaper technologies for more durable new construction. The low-density design severely limited the number of replacement units constructed: the list of applicants far outstripped the supply of new apartments. The arrangement of First Houses, the equivalent of today's vest-pocket or in-fill housing, regarded the severe building limitations posed by the 25-by-100-foot lots. Most importantly, resolution of the legal difficulties in assembling the parcels proved invaluable to the future of public housing in the United States. In response to the one private tenement owner's intransigence to sell, the authority condemned the properties, and a municipal court determined the price paid for the land.[89] The landlord's appeal to a state court failed, and the ruling, which set a precedent for eminent domain as a public good, stated that the "public is seeking to take the defendant's property and to administer it as part of a project conceived and to be carried out in its own interest and for its own protection."[90]

Once armed with the court-upheld power of eminent domain, local housing agencies could assemble parcels for public housing sites with

greater ease but would remain confined by the fiscal outlays to landowners for fair-market value of targeted sites. As such, the Lower East Side
appeared highly unattractive as a site for large-scale projects. Local property prices remained prohibitively expensive in part because landlords
continued to harbor expectations for more profitable, higher uses of their
obsolete holdings.[91] The position against large-scale low-income projects on the Lower East Side was shared by the city government. Public
housing projects were noticeably absent south of Ninety-sixth Street in
plans drawn in 1935 by a LaGuardia-appointed committee formed to
recommend ways to spend anticipated federal New Deal money.[92] The
committee's recommendation against such projects echoed the RPA's
contention that Manhattan's residential districts be reserved for middle-income development. The subsequent spate of new public housing
construction in the late 1930s occurred not on the Lower East Side but in
the outer boroughs and in northern Manhattan — Williamsburg Houses
(1935), Harlem River Houses (1937), and Red Hook Houses (1940). With
an increasing portfolio of completed or planned projects, site selection
and design standards grew routinized. Sites incorporated multiple and
contiguous blocks, which provided economies of scale.

The decision to build large projects in thinly developed sites appealed
to socially conscious architects, critics, and planners[93] but was hotly contested by the real estate industry, first locally then nationally. Political lobbying by the real estate and construction industries emphasized concerns that public housing would be constructed in the new middle-class
neighborhoods, such as those in Brooklyn, Queens, and the Bronx. The
New York City Real Estate Board pressured the state legislature to place
site limitations on government funds allocated for low-income housing. Funds were to be allotted to purchase and abolish slums to construct public housing but were not to be used to purchase land in the
thinly developed areas of outlying regions.[94] The dispute over site selection was largely resolved at the federal level with the passage of the
1937 United States Housing Act.[95] The act explicitly tied slum clearance
to low-income housing construction. Public housing would replace low-
income housing and not compete with it. This one-for-one proviso had
the effect of limiting new construction to areas of existing poor and dilapidated housing. It also placated slum landlords and the housing industry by eliminating their concerns about government competition
and oversupply in the low-rent housing market.[96] Politics also played

against First Houses as a model and assured what became the institutional, featureless high-rise design of most public housing buildings. On the national front, lobbyists for the real estate and construction industries appealed to the fiscal conservatism of legislators on issues of costs of building public housing. The pared-down design specifications that emerged, supposedly dictated by the high costs of slum acquisition, clearly differentiated public housing from the surrounding units, which was appealing to private landlords.[97] For years to come, large sites with multiple public high-rises would provide a visible and stark physical contrast to private housing.

As new public housing construction became tethered to the clearance of old tenements due to political lobbying, the Lower East Side once again emerged as a tenable site. Federal dollars became available for those municipalities that would meet the site and design stipulations. Drawn to such subsidies, the local government of New York embraced the offer wholeheartedly. In 1939, the city planning commission under the LaGuardia administration prescribed slum clearance and the construction of new low-rent housing for virtually all of the Lower East Side.[98] That action, in effect, zoned the area low-income residential and positioned the city's urban planning apparatus squarely in favor of public housing and against middle-class development for the future of the Lower East Side. The area became *the* favored site for new public housing construction in Manhattan south of Ninety-sixth Street. Consequently, land values, hyperinflated by aspirations of renewal, were lowered, thus making site acquisition (and, therefore, public housing construction) easier. Once targeted for subsidized housing, virtually all new housing built on the Lower East Side in the 1940s would be public low-income.

When the New York City Housing Authority bought the land that had long been scheduled for the middle-class Rutgerstown project and erected Vladeck Houses, it signaled the closure of an era of utopian planning for an upgraded Lower East Side. In 1949, the Lillian Wald and Jacob Riis Houses were constructed along Avenue D from East Twelfth Street to East Houston Street. The sites consisted of several uniform buildings, ten to twelve stories high, set in open green spaces, known as "tower in the park" style.[99] The phalanx of tall, red brick towers formed a seemingly impregnable wall between the neighborhood and the East River. Several low-income projects were built in the region of the Lower East Side south of Houston Street: Smith (1953), LaGuardia (1957), Baruch (1959), Gompers (1964), and Rutgers (1965).[100]

With such construction, aspirations for a middle-class renewal of the Lower East Side were effectively squelched. The state had accomplished what private real estate could not do: overcome the barriers for development set in place by the fragmented disposition and ownership of individual lots. But the area had embarked on an alternate course that essentially negated any remaining plans for an upscale Lower East Side. The most powerful and organized elements of Lower East Side real estate had failed to capture significant government subsidies for middle-class development that would directly benefit their interests. Public housing provided new opportunities for subsidy but not necessarily for the same group of real estate actors. The provisions within federal, state, and local subsidies for public housing provided funds for authorities to purchase lots from landowners. By linking new construction to slum clearance, housing policy had insured that some tenements would be purchased by the state for demolition. In addition, the ruling of one-for-one replacement insured that the state's supply would not compete with tenement owners, should low-income housing demand increase.

"Social Engineering" and Neighborhood Change

State intervention and low-income housing policy had multiple and substantial consequences for the built environment and the place identity of the Lower East Side. The favored application of a low-income residential policy over any other kind of urban development policy renewed and firmly secured the area's reputation as a low-income housing district. Outside of public housing construction, no other significant public works were initiated on the Lower East Side after 1940. The East River Drive — renamed the Franklin Delano Roosevelt (FDR) Drive — became a limited access freeway, and the East River Park was rendered inaccessible, for the most part, by the freeway and the adjacent long continuous row of Riis and Wald Houses. No state-sponsored incentives were offered for the development of industry or commerce despite an anticipated increase in low-income tenants to populate the new housing.[101] The continued regulation of the city's housing market (rent control and, later, rent stabilization) helped maintain the area's working-class character. Each of these consequences is examined below.

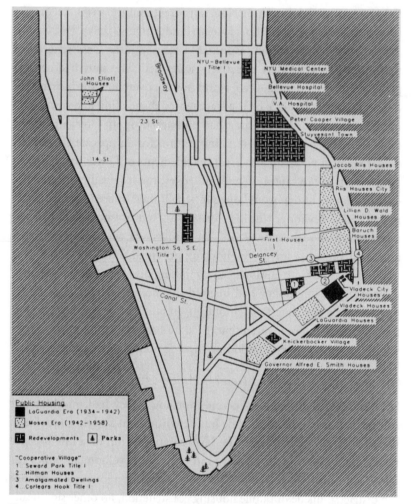

Figure 14. Redevelopment of the Lower East Side under LaGuardia and Moses. From Joel Schwartz, *The New York Approach: Robert Moses, Urban Liberals, and Redevelopment of the Inner City* (Columbus: Ohio State University Press, 1993); copyright Ohio State University Press. Used by permission.

In addition to building new housing, the state enacted tenant selection policies and rental regulations that affected the demographic composition within the area and, consequently, the place identity of the Lower East Side. The housing authority's renter eligibility rules and guidelines determined the composition of public housing resident enclaves. Selection policies established parameters for the economic and social makeup of the tenant population. The 1937 Housing Act mandate defined public housing as a temporary shelter—a subsidized boost for the deserving poor. Its purpose was stipulated as short-term assistance for the "submerged middle class."[102] In the immediate postwar years, veterans and those displaced by Moses's many redevelopment projects (e.g., those families who relocated to the Wald and Riis Houses due to the construction of Stuyvesant Town) were given preference. Racial steering in tenant placement was common into the late 1950s. In the authority's early years, black applicants were interviewed and processed in the Harlem district office of the New York Housing Authority, presumably near where most would be placed. The Fourteenth Street office processed white applicants and placed them in projects across the Lower East Side. In the 1950s, the prime criterion for selection, ceilings on family income, both calmed the real estate lobby's fears of competition with private housing and insured the creation of homogeneous low-income enclaves.[103]

The construction of enormous housing projects across the Lower East Side brought twenty thousand new residents drawn from all over the city. Compared with those residing in the surrounding private apartments, the makeup of the earliest public housing tenants showed greater ethnic and racial diversity. In 1950, over 10 percent of the occupants of Riis Houses and 16 percent of Wald Houses were nonwhite. Both projects had high rates of native-born residents as well (89 percent and 83 percent, respectively). In addition to demographic differences, public housing residents' class backgrounds contrasted with those of most Lower East Siders. The average social and economic standing of these early tenants was superior to that of residents in adjacent private housing. The median income of residents not living in public housing was from one-half to two-thirds that of the median for all of Manhattan in 1949. But the median incomes of the Riis and Wald tenants were much higher than the rest of the Lower East Side and even slightly higher than that of Manhattan. The occupational makeup of the public housing labor force resembled that of average Manhattan residents rather than the typical Lower East Sider. Census data from 1950 show male labor participation rates for public housing residents higher than for their private housing counterparts. By 1950, the largest shares of employment categories for Manhattan were in white-collar occupations. Those workers who resided in public housing also tended to hold higher-skilled white-collar jobs than their neighbors. Not surprisingly, the Lower East Side remained somewhat insulated from increases in white-collar em-

ployment save for those residing in the few middle-income housing developments, such as Knickerbocker Village or new public housing. For
the most part in 1950, the Lower East Side labor force worked at unskilled
and semiskilled jobs in the south of Houston Street manufacturing or
midtown garment districts. In the heart of the northern area of the
Lower East Side just west of Tompkins Square Park (census tracts 38
and 40), for example, between 40 to 60 percent of women in the labor
force were listed as operatives, well above the Manhattan average of
22.9 percent. Many of the first generation of public housing tenants were
war veterans whose housing options were limited by a citywide rental
shortage. The experience of one of the first tenants of the Lillian Wald
Houses, Albert Shamey and his family, was representative of those of
most new tenants. Shamey was a veteran returning from a tour of duty
with the army and was employed as a cost clerk at the United Fruit Company. Unable to afford their own apartment in the midst of the postwar
housing shortage, the couple applied for subsidized housing and was
selected to live in the Wald Houses in 1949.[104]

Given the profile of the earliest tenants, little indicated that the large-
scale introduction of public housing during the 1940s would portend
further declines in the socioeconomic composition of the Lower East
Side. Such favorable characteristics in income levels and occupational
categories for public housing tenants were short-lived, however. It is
important to note that the 1950 data construct a fleeting snapshot of
the characteristics of public housing residents as somewhat better-off
than the rest of Lower East Siders. Tenant turnover was high, especially
for veterans and their families who were eligible for any one of a number of federal housing subsidies that offered city apartment dwellers the
opportunity to become suburban homeowners. As the postwar housing shortage began to ease, the residential composition of public housing
was radically changed. More importantly, the city's social and economic
opportunities for working people in general and minority working people in particular were considerably altered (as outlined in the next chapter). During the 1950s, the authority's guidelines for choosing tenants
were also modified to reflect the changes in the population in need of
subsidized housing — an increasing number of minority newcomers who
faced new forms of structural poverty related to significant shifts in the
urban economy. As racial and ethnic changes in public housing occupancy grew more pronounced, minority segregation within the city in-

creased since most housing sites were clustered in poorer areas throughout the city. An influx of minority residents into public housing on the Lower East Side reintroduced racial/ethnic segregation to a long-standing condition of socioeconomic marginality. For residents both old and new, the Lower East Side community was further marginalized both materially and symbolically when racial discrimination joined forces with limited economic opportunities.

While the construction of thousands of public housing units fabricated new kinds of communities, rent regulation policies helped to maintain the area's prevailing social composition by according existing renters some degree of tenure rights. In New York City, rent control was effectively put into law in 1943 as an interim device to regulate rents during an acute shortage of vacant apartments. It continued in the first few years following the war to prevent landlords from raising rents in response to intense housing demand generated by returning troops and their new families. On the Lower East Side, the tenement apartment market was quickly rejuvenated but soon returned to its anemic condition as the housing crisis eased. In 1947, Congress enacted the Federal Housing and Rent Act to encourage new construction of rental housing in cities. That act exempted apartments in buildings with six or more units built after 1947 from rent control, thus allowing open-market rents for new construction. The act's provisions echoed already polarized sociospatial distinctions in New York City because the abundance of pre-1947 apartments existed in poorer areas like the Lower East Side and developers were inclined toward new construction in the city's better-off neighborhoods.[105] It was not until 1969, when rent regulations were modified significantly by New York City, that the distinction between pre- and post-1947 constructed buildings was addressed.[106] Apartments in buildings constructed after 1947 and formerly decontrolled units in buildings with six or more apartments were subject to a new form of municipal oversight—rent stabilization—that provided protective measures for tenants.[107] As stated in the beginning of this chapter, little new private market housing was constructed on the Lower East Side, and the abundance of tenements were built prior to 1920. Thus, the majority of occupied apartments on the Lower East Side were rent controlled. This rent ceiling protected tenants on fixed incomes from arbitrary rent increases, which were customary during episodes of housing shortages.

The impact of public housing policy on the social and cultural land-scape of the Lower East Side was pronounced. As the area's tenements, shops, and clubs, and the resident's cultural attachments to them were demolished and new "island communities" were imposed by governmental decisions, the traditional immigrant/ethnic character of the Lower East Side faded. This threat to community did not go unnoticed by Lower East Siders. In 1949, tenants picketed against the Housing Authority's mass evictions, which destroyed the fabric of the neighborhood.[108] Women residents protested the authority's lack of guarantees for the rebuilding of communities. They were skeptical of the promise of new housing and questioned (to no avail) the policy of demolition before funding for replacement housing was approved.[109] Clearance for the construction of the Baruch and LaGuardia Houses involved the dis-placement of 1,650 persons in 1953–54. But LaGuardia Houses was not completed until 1957, and phase two of Baruch not until 1959. Entire blocks were cleared and remained unoccupied for years. Businesses, so-cial organizations, churches, and other community institutions on ad-jacent blocks were forced to close as people were displaced or simply left. Thus, slum clearance eliminated not only homes and businesses but community attachments to such places.[110] Microcommunities were swept away as a result of state intervention in local housing disposition; some were reconstituted in other regions of the Lower East Side or other parts of the city, and others were simply eliminated forever. As a conse-quence of slum clearance and public housing construction, place-based self-help and community organizations that had traditionally operated along the Lower East Side were weakened.

What emerged from the debris of former tenements and shops were not subcommunities formed by residents with shared ethnic back-grounds or cultural interests (the classic immigrant enclaves) but col-onies of low-income families constituted by the housing authority's res-ident eligibility requirements and, often, the positioning of applicants on apartment waiting lists. Thus, within a short period of time, new and more-fragmented communities emerged on the Lower East Side as thousands of residents who shared little more than similar socioeco-nomic statuses were placed together in towering public housing com-plexes. The prosaic and uninspiring layout of public housing projects was "designed to prevent spontaneity and variety; they [planners, de-signers and the city housing authority] succeed[ed] altogether in blocking the community feeling and the liveliness that was the one redeeming feature at least of some slums."[111] These constructed low-income communities did give rise to public housing tenant associations and movements, but the scope of their goals and claims never rivaled in breadth and popularity those of the earlier enclaves. Public housing tenant movements typically were formed out of grievances with the overbearing management style of the housing authority. In an attempt to inculcate middle-class values and behavior, authority managers regulated tenants' private living spaces, setting rules for the number of guests and the length of visits, prohibiting air conditioners, and determining when the volume of a radio or television was inappropriate. Tenant associations, founded primarily by white ethnics, specifically formed in reaction to such institutionalized paternalism and sought ways to wrest some control over the daily lives of residents away from the housing authority managers.[112] The old Lower East Side, once threatened by real estate aspirations to create a middle-class district, remained situated as a poor, working-class district through changes in the built environment and cultural landscapes brought on by government housing policies. The newly constructed neighborhood was ill prepared for a host of new social forces that coalesced in the 1950s — the loss of middle-class residents to the growing suburbs, deindustrialization, new migration streams, and the destruction of long-standing communities due in part to urban renewal efforts.

CHAPTER FOUR

Reengineering the Ghetto: Ethnicity, Race, and Cultural Divisions in the 1950s

Immediately following World War II regional and national demographic and economic shifts ushered in a new era of change on the Lower East Side and in much of New York City. In tandem with growth and prosperity in the United States, New York City emerged as the undisputed economic and cultural world center of postwar capitalism. Social changes and spatial development in parts of the city between 1945 and 1960 reflected the concentration of multinational corporate administration, finance, and related services. In midtown Manhattan, newly constructed International Style glass and steel towers added millions of square feet of office space to house firms' corporate headquarters. Consequently, Manhattan's employment of white-collar professionals and office workers accelerated. The Upper East Side, once a lower-middle- and working-class district, offered new and expansive luxury housing for the city's executive class and expensive shopping boutiques along Madison Avenue. With such extravagance and wealth came a growth of cultural institutions dedicated to music and art that insured New York's leading position as cultural capital. Uptown, the traditional locus of high culture, contained a network of art museums, dealers, and galleries that featured the works of Willem de Kooning, Mark Rothko, and Franz Josef Kline, among others.[1]

During the time of the city's rising corporate-based economic stature, regional deconcentration of manufacturing and the suburbanization of the city's middle-class residents continued unabated. Bridges, tunnels, and expressways decades in the making now connected the far corners of an expanding metropolis, linking the multiple new suburban hamlets of Long Island, Connecticut, and New Jersey to the city's center. Numerous federal government programs that subsidized a mass housing market pulled city dwellers from their urban apartments to affordable single-family homes constructed on former farmlands. Many of those employed in Manhattan's expanding corporate service economy dwelled in outer-ring suburban "bedroom" communities. The exodus of the middle class unfolded in conjunction with the mass production of consumer durables, including the automobile, for newly formed households. Mobility and consumption were fused and facilitated by an expanding individualist commodity culture that trumpeted images and symbols of a desirable suburban lifestyle often at the expense of city living.[2]

Back in the city, regional demographic and national political economic trends were realized in an increasingly bifurcated social, economic, and cultural landscape. The city's middle-class housing market suffered the effects of diminished demand and the suburban lure of real estate capital investments. At the same time as white middle-class residents were drawn outside the city, minorities continued to relocate to its core from the South and Puerto Rico in flows originally prompted by recruiters of cheap labor. Mostly poor, undereducated, and unskilled migrants resettled the old working-class enclaves, forging vibrant residential communities in places largely departed by first- and second-generation European immigrants, and causing concern and consternation among the city's politicos and elites. As early as the 1950s, social and spatial changes encompassing Manhattan disturbed city officials, led by master builder Robert Moses as head of the Mayor's Committee on Slum Clearance.[3] In particular, the substantial increase in low-income housing projects and the rising population of poor minority residents, the building of luxury housing units on the Upper East Side, and the growing middle-class exodus to the suburbs together threatened to create a vastly divided city of rich and poor devoid of a middle-class.[4] Emboldened by new land-use powers, urban policymakers took on the role of social and spatial engineers in the 1950s. A decade of spatial reorganization, however, only added to class, ethnic, and racial divisions within the city.

It is within the context of this social, economic, and cultural tug-of-war between forces of corporate agglomeration and deconcentration that we situate in this chapter the sociospatial changes and escalation of racial and ethnic cleavages that occurred on the Lower East Side in the 1950s and early 1960s. The chapter first recounts the influx of Puerto Rican migrants who settled and created a vibrant cultural community on the Lower East Side over a two-decade period. Puerto Rican migration and settlement, according to representations dominant at the time, resembled the embellished "rags to riches" narrative of their former European counterparts' urban experiences. On the Lower East Side, movie houses along Grand Street, once a prime avenue for Jewish culture, now featured Spanish-language films. *Bodegas* (corner grocery stores) and *carnicerías* (butcher shops) popped up on streets and avenues around the Lower East Side, especially along Avenue C, a key commercial corridor for the emerging enclave. In the face of economic changes and postwar urban development policies, however, the often romanticized comparison of Puerto Ricans with previous immigrant groups soon soured. Deindustrialization of the city's already shrinking manufacturing base ensnared Puerto Rican and other minority blue-collar workers in conditions of long-term poverty. In tandem with the economic decline, the chapter discusses how the city's postwar urban renewal policies further concentrated Puerto Ricans in marginalized social and spatial conditions.

The chapter's second half constructs the often convoluted story of social conflict among tenants, landlords, and the city in the 1950s. With the growth of the low-income Puerto Rican community, the area's cultural and ethnic diversity rivaled that of an earlier age. Yet the distinctions among the different resident groups—namely, age, ethnicity/race, and class—were more pronounced than ever primarily due to state intervention in the production of the urban landscape. The city's housing policies had formed large poor minority zones and very few middle-class white "islands" in the midst of private apartments occupied by working-class ethnics. As a result, older ethnics, new arrivals from eastern Europe, and native-born Whites were segregated by class, but their interests often combined in antagonism toward their Puerto Rican neighbors. An enclave of artists, writers, poets, and other artistic types who flocked to the Lower East Side in the 1950s also lived within the interstices of these fragmented groups. While the artists had little *immediate* effect on the conflict among landlords, state actors, and working-class residents, their establishment of a community, as later chapters will demonstrate, reinforced the area's avant-garde identity and influenced the settlement of subsequent cultural movements. Finally, given the opportunistic exodus of real estate capital to the suburbs and the worsening central city housing market, tenement landlords represented themselves and the neighborhood within a discourse of urban decline that both mirrored and reproduced the area's poverty-stricken social and economic conditions. In reaction to this discourse of urban decline, landlord exploitation, and ethnic in-fighting, residents formed community organizations and revived the Lower East Side's legacy of collective action.

The Brief Return of the Tenement District: Post–World War II Migration from Puerto Rico to the United States

When Leo Grebler's team of researchers fanned out across the Lower East Side in 1950–51, they detected a sprinkling of Puerto Rican residents scattered between the dwindling first- and second-generation eastern European immigrant communities. While some of the newcomers were housed in tenements throughout the area, most lived in the public housing projects—the Wald and Riis Houses—along Avenue D.[5] Within a decade, however, that configuration would change, and entire Puerto Rican subcommunities composed of recent arrivals and families from across the city would form in both the northern (along Avenues C and D) and southern tiers of the Lower East Side. Changes in the region's manufacturing economy and the city's massive undertaking to redefine the racial, ethnic, and class spatial boundaries of Manhattan propelled the formation and development of the Lower East Side Puerto Rican communities in the 1950s.

The negligible presence of Puerto Rican residents that Grebler observed on the Lower East Side was anomalous for a neighborhood reputed for large ethnic enclaves formed from massive population flows. The status of Puerto Ricans as citizens (conferred in 1917 by the Second Organic Act, or the Jones Act) caused settlement patterns in New York City to differ from those of previous newcomers. Unlike the Germans, Italians, and eastern European Jews, Puerto Ricans "burned no bridges" coming to the mainland and could return without hindrance to the island for personal or economic reasons (an option chosen by a large number in the 1970s). Without the threat of curtailment, Puerto Rican migration trickled and, at times, swelled over the course of the past century.[6] New York City had become the chief port of destination for Puerto Ricans, following the building up of small enclave communities by island nationals in the last quarter of the nineteenth century. Compared to the massive European migration occurring at this time, these mini-enclaves appeared inconsequential except that they provided a locational foothold and information network for the continued movement of Puerto Ricans to the mainland.[7] The early settlers (businessmen, artists and poets, political outcasts and cigar makers) established enclaves in the interstitial spaces between the many European ethnic communities in East Harlem and Brooklyn.[8]

Several factors affected the fluctuations in migration and return-migration levels, although the severity of economic conditions in Puerto Rico and opportunities on the mainland were most determinative. The substantial increase in Puerto Rican migrants from seven thousand to sixty-one thousand that occurred between 1920 and 1940 corresponded with the dwindling flow of immigrants from abroad.[9] The war economy in the mid-1940s drove a second surge in island-to-mainland migration.[10] But in 1947, as combat troops were demobilized and returned in very large numbers to the mainland labor force, migration levels fell. Subsequent declines in the number of arrivals transpired during recessions that beset the mainland economy in 1949, 1954, and 1957. Job opportunities in lower-echelon manufacturing industries in New York and social changes related to industrial and agricultural policies in Puerto Rico accounted for periods of significant migration such as those of 1950–53 (more than a 50 percent increase over the previous half decade) and 1955–56.[11]

The demand for labor that stemmed from the cutoff in immigration in the 1920s was amplified during and immediately after World War II. Wartime labor shortages in manufacturing in the industrial Northeast and the rustbelt were largely filled by Blacks migrating from the South. In New York, the shortage of unskilled workers was also assuaged by Puerto Rican labor. When demand for cheap labor swelled, firms aggressively promoted Puerto Rican migration to the mainland. Several industries, including New York apparel firms, recruited laborers in Puerto Rico, offering them jobs and placing them in housing. Government agencies also encouraged migration. In 1948, the Migration Division of the Puerto Rican Department of Labor was formed to monitor the recruitment practices used by the numerous U.S. labor contractors operating

on the island. The division maintained branch offices in New York and
Chicago to facilitate employment placement. In New York, the Puerto
Rican Commonwealth Office and the Mayor's Commission on Puerto
Rican Affairs assisted in establishing commercial air routes to San Juan
and aided unemployed new arrivals by placing them in manufacturing
jobs.[12]

The passage from the island to the city and the adjustment to harsh
and unfamiliar social and economic conditions prompted the inevitable
comparison with the European migrations of the recent past. On the
surface, there were similarities. The neighborhoods where newcomers
resided, the poor conditions of their housing, and the low-level unskilled
and semiskilled jobs they took resembled the plight of earlier generations of arrivals. Reports commissioned by the city's welfare office emphasized the resemblance between Puerto Rican and black migrations
and prior immigration and attributed the social problems of the former to the slow process of acculturation and assimilation.[13] In a document addressing the "Puerto Rican problem," the city's Department of
Welfare commented that

> the Puerto Ricans in New York exhibit many of the characteristics of the
> older waves of strangers who came to these shores. . . . Now the Puerto
> Rican is the man behind the scenes. He changes the beds, scrubs the
> floors, washes dishes, tends table, launders clothes, harvests and cans
> vegetables and fruit, cuts and sews milady's unmentionables and
> summer dresses, makes cookies and candy, paper boxes, and a thousand
> and one other commodities. He cleans apartments and office buildings,
> and sails the seven seas in the merchant marine. In other words, he
> performs the services without which life in the metropolis would be
> much less enticing. He is, in general, on the bottom rung of the
> occupational ladder; the place at first occupied by all other waves of
> newcomers. He is "the last to be hired and the first to be fired."[14]

Such constructions, when played out, implied that given a period of time,
the latest poor masses would assimilate into the social fabric of the city
or "climb the ladder," as reputedly so many others did before them (according to revisionist representation of the immigrant era). Belief in
conformity and replication between the plight of old and new migrations
also served to legitimate initial political *in*action in the arenas of housing
and labor — despite growing evidence that social and economic problems were caused by radical changes in the city's manufacturing sector.

By the mid-1950s, however, labor market opportunities in the urban economy were so different from prewar conditions that meaningful comparisons between past groups and Puerto Rican New Yorkers were impossible to sustain. An appreciation of these structural liabilities to the low-wage economy is essential to understanding the constraints on housing choices and the building of community for Puerto Ricans on the Lower East Side.

Manufacturing Decline and the Consequences for Community

Following the war, Puerto Rican migration was viewed as crucial to salvaging small firms with slim profit margins, such as garment shops, which were dependent on a supply of low-wage labor.[15] Puerto Ricans' labor market participation rates were similar to those of the general laboring population of the city. In 1950, for example, 76 percent of Puerto Rican males fourteen years of age and older were in the labor force, as compared to 75 percent of the total male working-age population of New York City; and 40 percent of Puerto Rican women were in the labor force, as compared to 35 percent of New York's female working-age population.[16] Dominant occupational categories tended to cluster in center-city blue-collar positions left behind by the exodus of workers to new industries in the suburbs or by the occupational advancement of existing workers. The types of employment positions for new arrivals were segmented by gender. Unlike their female counterparts, male workers employed in light industries were unable to capture any sizable niche in the unskilled and semiskilled labor market. Males tended to be employed as low-skilled operatives dispersed throughout the city's light manufacturing industries, loading and unloading fabrics, operating heavy machinery, and delivering finished garments from factory floors to nearby showrooms. Males were also employed in light assembly jobs such as manufacturing toys, plastic flowers, and costume jewelry and electric plating.[17] While some jobs remained concentrated in lower Manhattan's manufacturing districts (today's SoHo and TriBeCa), many others had moved to midtown.[18] The occupational structure for Puerto Rican females was less differentiated. Garment industries were the largest employers of Puerto Rican women. Most occupied unskilled and poorly paid positions as operators and floor workers. By the mid-1950s, Puerto Ricans comprised the largest ethnic category of women employed in the least skilled and lowest paying jobs in the garment trades. Their membership in garment union locals multiplied; workers in Local 23, the skirt-makers' union, were chiefly operators, special machine operators, and floor workers — generally low-paying, female-held jobs with high turn-over rates. Membership figures from 1957, for example, reported that Latina/os (most of whom were Puerto Rican) comprised half the rank and file of Local 23. In addition to positions in light manufacturing, significant numbers of Puerto Rican men and women were employed as service workers in hotels, hospitals, theaters, and the restaurant industry.[19]

Puerto Rican migrants' quick and significant progress in entry-level manufacturing jobs was short-lived as a result of both the downgrad-ing and decline of manufacturing employment within the city.[20] Be-tween 1950 and 1960, over one hundred thousand manufacturing posi-tions were lost; the biggest drop was in the apparel industries as the production of less stylized and more uniform garments, such as under-wear, brassieres, and children's clothes, relocated offshore (ironically, of-ten to Puerto Rico).[21] In a ranking of factory wages in cities across the country, New York was fourth in 1950 and dropped to seventy-ninth in 1960.[22] At the bottom of the pay scale in 1960 were textiles, apparel, and leather — industries in which a disproportionate number of employees were minorities.

Despite the gains Puerto Ricans had made in capturing the garment labor market and despite their numerical strength in union member-ship throughout the 1950s, the garment industry failed to provide them with the path toward mobility it had earlier presented white ethnics. Historically, immigrants had entered the labor market in low-wage and unskilled positions as pressers, cleaners, ironers, and shipping clerks. Through union membership and seniority, these workers gained job security, structured wage increases, welfare benefits, and employment training. Within a few decades, Jews, Italians, and others utilized the In-ternational Ladies' Garment Workers' Union (ILGWU) and propitious labor rulings of the New Deal era to cement employment gains in the garment industry, gains that translated to increased socioeconomic mo-bility. Employment in the industry changed radically in the 1950s and 1960s. Production previously done by full-time employees in-house was farmed out to subcontractors who paid for work by the piece to be done at home. Garment employers downgraded high-wage skilled and craft positions to semiskilled positions with little chance for promotion. What were once considered entry-level jobs with potential for advancement were recast, with the consent of the ILGWU, as permanent low-wage positions. Racial and ethnic discrimination practices, combined with fears of plant and shop closures, also led to a series of deals between the ILGWU leadership and the apparel industry in the late 1950s and early 1960s. "Sweetheart" contracts traded concessions in wage increases and promotions for industry promises to remain in the city.[23] Puerto Rican women employed after 1950 in coat and suit making, an industry previously dominated by Italians and Jews, were hired as semiskilled laborers and paid wages well below their predecessors.[24] Between 1960 and 1965, the real earnings of the rank-and-file members of the ILGWU (again, most of whom were Puerto Rican and Black women) dipped below the poverty level for New York City families, even though two wage contracts between ILGWU and garment employers had been negotiated.

Many of the small manufacturing shops that remained in New York were subjected to vagaries of national and international competition, seasonality, and narrow profit margins.[25] A large proportion of Puerto Ricans were employed in exactly those industries most affected by restructuring. Assembly jobs in plastic flower making, electric plating, costume jewelry, and furniture making in nearby SoHo and TriBeCa declined appreciably beginning in the 1950s but continued to linger well into the late 1970s, before manufacturing firms there were displaced and their industrial spaces transformed for new use as upscale housing, art galleries, and retail spaces.[26] Those industries had employed Puerto Rican labor from the Lower East Side. For example, Puerto Ricans comprised 48 percent of textile and apparel workers employed in the remaining plants in SoHo in 1962.

Sectoral changes in the manufacturing economy were instrumental in transforming the working-class character of the city.[27] Many of the newly created entry-level jobs in the 1950s and 1960s were low-wage service or better-paying government positions. Prior generations of immigrants had fought and earned significant employment footholds (especially unionized ones) that allowed socioeconomic and residential mobility. Structural limitations in employment and promotion opportunities that emerged fully in the postwar era blocked historic mobility possibilities for low-wage workers. In addition, such limitations froze low-wage workers into new forms of deprivation that were more lasting — "a permanent condition of semipoverty."[28] Soon after their arrival, the "golden door"[29] of social and economic mobility that had worked for a significant portion of earlier generations slammed shut in the face of many Puerto Rican workers, further limiting, among other things, their residential choices.[30]

Urban Renewal and the Call to Eliminate the Ghetto

Thus far our survey of the formation of the Puerto Rican community has focused on the marginalization of its labor force. Structural shifts in the economy relegated a considerable number of Puerto Ricans to long-term poverty conditions and consequently limited their housing opportunities. A second precondition of the growth and expansion of the Lower East Side enclave was the city's effort at class and racial segregation through spatial reorganization policies in the 1950s. As previously mentioned, Puerto Rican newcomers did not numerically overwhelm and carve out large neighborhood enclaves similar to their European predecessors because migration streams were discontinuous. Settlement was more piecemeal: a few apartments within a building, later a few buildings on a block, and eventually a few blocks in a neighborhood.[31] Consequently, communities were geographically smaller, more numerous, and heterogeneous (diverse social composition). The primary settlement of Spanish Harlem, one of the earliest Puerto Rican enclaves, was the notable exception. In the early 1950s, Puerto Rican residents rarely constituted 50 percent of the total population of any single area outside Spanish Harlem.[32] That changed, however, when municipal policies were employed, in effect, to carve the city into ethnic, racial, and class zones.

With a dramatic increase of migrants between 1950–53 and, later, the declining economic opportunities in the manufacturing economy, political leaders in New York referred to the dire conditions as the "Puerto Rican problem."[33] The ensuing construction of Puerto Rican migration as a threat to political stability and a drain on economic resources echoed previous calls for immigration curtailment in the early 1900s. Most of the public discourse, circulated in the city's press, in special reports, and in-depth exposés, chose not to focus on the economic circumstances that contributed to poor labor conditions but on the size of the migrant flow and the decision to relocate to New York. In short, according to this discourse, the inflow of Puerto Ricans, not the excesses of the private low-income housing market or labor market instability, *caused* the reemergence and spread of the slum. Robert Moses and Philip J. Cruise, chairman of the City Housing Authority, claimed that Puerto Rican migration explained why slum conditions were worse in New York than in other cities.[34] By 1953, as Puerto Rican in-migration peaked, city officials, planners, and slum committees were pressed to deal with the growing "Puerto Rican problem." Their solutions were sorely deficient. The Robert F. Wagner mayoral administration spent considerable time and other resources trying to convince Puerto Ricans on the island to relocate to cities other than New York.[35] In 1959, criminal court judge Samuel Liebowitz claimed that Puerto Ricans were responsible for the rise in the city's juvenile delinquency rates and posited that the city should make every effort to discourage continued migration.[36]

Through their press releases, writings, and correspondence, official committees, politicians, and planners constructed the problem of slum conditions in social rather than economic terms. The overcrowding, the filth, and the decaying physical *environment*, and juvenile crime, gang rumbles, drug abuse, and other deviant *behaviors* were rarely conceptualized as the possible consequences of exploitative housing conditions or structural conditions of poverty. Instead, a wide range of social problems and deviant behaviors were uncritically coupled to the slum and the character traits (or flaws) of its residents. That is, space and social behavior were interconnected to define the *slum condition*. Slums bred crime, disease, and multiple other pathologies. Problem youngsters — labeled the "shook-up" generation — sprung from such environments.[37] Representations that conflated spatial attributes and behavior called for and validated certain kinds of solutions. Namely, the physical displacement of existing poor neighborhoods would do away with associated marginal behavior. With increasing circulation of representations of the slum condition in the city's press, slum clearance efforts appeared more palatable to the middle and upper classes.[38] Robert Moses' slash-and-burn policies of redoing the city were enacted in part due to his ability to tap into and manipulate fears that poor minority neighborhoods were expanding and threatening to overwhelm middle-class ones.

Throughout the 1950s, Moses wielded federal funds that allowed the city to engage in middle-class redevelopment of working-class districts (slums).[39] Title I provisions of the 1949 Housing Act allowed for the construction of developments geared toward *middle-class* use, such as medium-rent housing, new office buildings, parking areas, and transportation improvements. The Title I program provided an avenue for older cities to alter land use by allowing local governments to assemble large sites through condemnation and to resell the parcels to private builders.[40] While maintaining the initiative to remove slum areas, postwar housing policy had shifted its central mandate from subsidizing low-income housing to financing middle-class uses for urban space.[41] Making use of Title I, the city embarked on the development of middle-income housing with the goal of retaining or attracting residents who had been squeezed out by the extremes of luxury and low-income housing construction. Moses — "the villain of Title I"[42] — used the program to stave off the spread of deterioration in what he considered salvageable neighborhoods in Manhattan, sites such as Lincoln Square and the Coliseum on Manhattan's west side and Washington Square Village adjacent to New York University.

Moses' policy of dismembering older, working-class neighborhoods and creating new "communities" segregated by class, ethnicity, and race offered a default solution to what had been discursively constructed as the "Puerto Rican problem." If poor migrants from Puerto Rico could not be discouraged from coming to the city, the government could wield land-use policy to determine those areas where they could and could not afford to live. Once sections of older neighborhoods were slated for demolition and renewal, already poor housing conditions tended to deteriorate further and at a faster pace. Absentee landlords withheld maintenance and vital services as a method to maximize profits before condemned buildings were scheduled to be pulled down. The displacement effects of urban renewal policy were pronounced. Urban renewal projects, nicknamed "Puerto Rican Removal Plans," forcibly relocated thousands of Puerto Rican families from one poor neighborhood to another.[43] Displaced families doubled up and tripled up with friends and relatives in substandard apartments, moved into private low-income apartments in other neighborhoods, or waited for occupancy in the city's public housing units. Once renewal projects were completed in a given neighborhood, rents in new buildings were far too prohibitive for low-income families to return. Renewal, then, dispersed low-income minorities from certain areas and concentrated them in others. Increasing numbers of Puerto Rican residents encountered a tightening supply of low-income housing units confined to the poorest areas of New York, such as the satellite *barrio* on the Lower East Side.

In addition to urban renewal policies, changes in public housing legislation exacerbated class, ethnic, and racial segregation in the city. Public housing became a necessity for increasing numbers of Puerto Ricans displaced by urban renewal and trapped in a stagnant low-wage economy that limited housing options. After the passage of the 1949 Housing Act, the mandate of temporary subsidized housing for the "worthy poor" was abdicated, and public housing "became clearly defined as permanent housing for people who were more or less separated from society's mainstream."[44] While demand for low-income housing was increasing due to urban renewal displacement and overcrowding, the 1953 Congress proposed the elimination of public housing financing. The measure failed, but the ambitious plans for an increase in federal low-income housing construction in New York and other cities were scaled back. Between 1953 and 1956, the number of Puerto Ricans living in public housing projects across the city increased 150 percent.[45] On the Lower East Side, the number of Puerto Rican residents in the Wald and Riis Houses (as well as in other projects in the neighborhood's southern tier) increased rapidly.

Decline in the city's manufacturing sector and the spatial concentration of minority, unskilled, and semiskilled blue-collar workers reinforced each other, creating zones of entrenched poverty conditions. According to a 1963 federal study of the city's labor force, poor ratings in employment, income below the official poverty level, and educational attainment indices were concentrated in neighborhoods densely populated by Puerto Ricans and Blacks (the study included the Lower East Side).[46] Consequently, as limited economic means caused by structural unemployment "have taken their toll on the Puerto Rican housing situation, these housing conditions themselves have had an important reciprocal effect on the employment and class condition of Puerto Ricans."[47]

Flush with public housing units, both built and proposed, and a surfeit of old and dilapidated tenements, the Lower East Side appeared to fit squarely into the city's policy of casting off certain neighborhoods as a means of salvaging others. But by the close of the 1950s, the success of Moses' plan to carve up the city's landscape into upper- and middle-class, predominantly white zones and minority poverty zones was limited, in part because of a growing resistance at the neighborhood level and the difficulty of marshaling resources to implement his agenda. Landscapes formed from decades of community building and place attachments were not easily swept away by the not-so-invisible hand of urban policy. Nonetheless, the city's urban policy and the sectoral decline in the low-wage economy did have noticeable consequences for the demographic makeup, the built environment, and the cultural identity of the Lower East Side. By 1960, the spatial policies of the state had directly engineered the residential patterns of different ethnicities and classes on the Lower East Side. Consequently, state urban policies had a significant effect on the interactions among the different groups of residents and between locals and property owners.

"Island" Communities and the Interactions among Them

A decade of urban renewal policies and economic sectoral changes resulted in a social and physical "balkanization" of the Lower East Side. State intervention invented and reinforced the isolated residential enclaves defined by ethnicity/race and class. Segregation erased traditional bonds among Lower East Siders that historically transcended their ethnic and religious differences and formed a basis of place identity and community attachments. Thus, the late 1950s and early 1960s marked a new Lower East Side social landscape defined not only by similarities within each community *but by the differences between them.* The smallest self-contained communities were comprised of middle-class cooperative apartment dwellers. Two dominant and very different resident (sub)communities — the white ethnic working class and the Puerto Rican working class and poor — maintained mostly separate areas on the Lower East Side. The sometimes hostile relations between these latter groups partly defined the neighborhood's character and reputation. In addition, another middle-class cohort — painters, sculptors, and other artists — staked out turf in the interstices of the working-class and ethnic landscape. Although their numbers were negligible, the artists' presence, as we shall see, presaged future struggles over the neighborhood's identity.

Middle-class, mostly Jewish former tenement dwellers lived in a handful of newly built self-contained middle-income housing developments scattered about the area. Although Moses had fought to limit Title I to "salvageable" neighborhoods, one of the first middle-income projects funded under the program was built on the Lower East Side at Corlears Hook, near the Williamsburg Bridge. Erected in 1956, the ILGWU co-operatives joined the Amalgamated Houses as an anchor of an upper-working-class or middle-class Jewish presence in the midst of an increasingly poor and minority neighborhood.[48] In 1958, Seward Park Houses, another middle-class cooperative, broke ground on East Broadway. It, too, was built with Title I funds. Middle-class Jews comprised more than 75 percent of the residents of the union-sponsored middle-class housing (ILGWU and Amalgamated Houses) and a considerable percentage of the Seward Park development, thus retaining some semblance of the area's Jewish cultural past.[49] These modern middle-class "islands" and the social makeup of their residents stood in contrast to the surrounding tenements.

In addition to the few, scattered high-rises that formed middle-class enclosures, the visual landscape of the postwar Lower East Side was dominated by tenements in assorted states of disrepair, and public housing towers separated by a cordon sanitaire of expansive green spaces. The impoverished and younger Puerto Rican population formed communities in public housing projects and in adjacent, less attractive tenements. White ethnics who lived in private tenement apartments ranged from destitute to stable working class. Census data from 1960 show patterns of ethnic distribution in the local geography. If we subdivide the area north of Houston Street (today's East Village) into three north-south strata — the Wald and Riis public housing running along Avenue D to the east, the streets between Avenues B and D in the center, and the streets between Avenue B and Third Avenue to the west — ethnic groupings appear in each. In the eastern strata of public housing, 7.8 percent of the residents were foreign-born (white ethnics), and 36.2 percent were either born in Puerto Rico or were of Puerto Rican ancestry. In the center strata, we see a more even mix of 26 percent foreign-born and 30 percent Puerto Rican, as the latter established a foothold in the neighborhood adjacent to the public housing developments. Finally, in the western strata, 34.6 percent of the residents were foreign-born, and only 15.8 percent were Puerto Rican. Thus, a gradient was formed in which the percentage of minority residents declined with greater distance west of the Riis and Wald public housing. That pattern remains today, although the proportions of Whites to minorities changed dramatically between 1960 and 1990, as we shall see in subsequent chapters.

Age differences were also apparent. White ethnics in the tenements were predominantly elderly married or widowed, while Puerto Rican residents were significantly younger.

Differences in class and status, cultural practices based in ethnicity and lifestyle preferences, and needs linked to age cohorts tended to keep apart the three dominant communities. As mentioned, the sizable eastern European community of the Lower East Side was less well-off economically than the residents of ILGWU Houses or Knickerbocker Village but shared common religious and ethnic bonds. The Lower East Side remained the cultural center of eastern European Jewish and non-Jewish life, although the presence of ethnic- and religious-based theaters, restaurants, coffee shops, and social clubs declined steadily as patrons both local and from outside the neighborhood grew older, died, or lost interest. The working-class white ethnic community received a boost from Russian, Austrian, Romanian, and Ukrainian newcomers who arrived under the provisions of the Displaced Persons Act of 1948. The law allowed for the admission of over four hundred thousand refugees left homeless by World War II and the imposition of Soviet communism in eastern European countries.[50] In the 1950s and 1960s, other special bills were passed to grant admittance to political refugees from communist countries. The Ukrainian community was concentrated between Third Avenue and Avenue A and between Fourth and Eighth Streets.[51] Several Ukrainian and Polish religious and cultural institutions were housed along Second Avenue and on St. Mark's Place. With the inflow of eastern Europeans, community life was reinvigorated around St. Stanislaus Church on East Seventh Street. Several Polish butcher shops dotted the expanse of First Avenue (a few are still there). St. Mark's Place offered Ukrainian bookstores and a labor home.

Middle-class and working-class white ethnics shared a common antipathy toward the rising numbers of Puerto Rican residents. Interaction between the older middle- and working-class white ethnics and the younger, poorer Puerto Ricans was often frictional. Through nostalgic memories and everyday practices, older ethnics viewed themselves as the caretakers of the quickly vanishing old Lower East Side, to which they remained staunchly attached. But by 1960, many of the landmark Lower East Side cafés and shops celebrated by Hutchins Hapgood in his early writings on the immigrant ghetto had closed. Although several Yiddish newspapers remained in circulation, only one of the four original

Italian newspapers remained in print in 1959.[52] For old-timers, the Puerto Rican newcomers threatened to hasten the old neighborhood's disappearance and to replace it with a culture that seemed uncharacteristic and menacing. A Jewish woman resident of East Sixth Street expressed such sentiments in 1959:

> "It's not the same the neighborhood now. This block is all right, but you just walk a block over to Avenue A and you're in a different world.... in the mornings you hear them walking across from Avenue A, and then again when they come home at night you hear them, all speaking Spanish, all at once, going by right under your window. We've got to move, at least for our daughter's sake. It's got so you don't dare go out alone at night."[53]

A significant cause of the friction between old-timers and newcomers was rooted in discrepancies in age and family size rather than differences in income or class. Old Ukrainians and other eastern Europeans had weathered years of neighborhood population decline and, in the process, had laid proprietary claim to the use of parks, commercial avenues, and streets. As with previous ethnic successions, new groups engendered new uses for the built environment that conflicted with those of the prior dominant groups. Although the living conditions of Puerto Ricans resembled those of the immigrants of the turn of the century, the older white ethnics resented the encroachment on their turf.

For many Puerto Rican families, their neighbors' attitudes toward their arrival was yet another expression of the discrimination and disdain they experienced at workplaces and in public spaces throughout the city. Although contention between old-timers and newcomers was largely over lifestyle differences, the conflicts were played out and expressed in *racial and ethnic terms,* thus reflecting and reproducing larger discourses of ethnic and racial hostilities in the inner city. Both older ethnics and mainstream press accounts viewed such chafing not as consequences of age and cultural differences but as racial and ethnic antagonisms. As expressed by one middle-aged Jewish Lower East Sider, "Urination in elevators, light bulbs taken out, dirty remarks on the stairs. But let me ask you? Compared to the Puerto Ricans and Negroes, did we ever get such good places to live when we first came to New York?"[54] As resentment mixed with fear of minority youths, many older ethnics retreated from their usual engagement with community cultural and political affairs. In a social survey of elderly community concerns, researchers noted that

> several older adults . . . volunteered the information that they were afraid to leave their homes in the evening. One couple said they would not risk attending programs at a golden age center that took place after dark. One old gentleman locked himself in his room every night and refused to open his door, and an old lady reported that she dropped her membership in a local political club because she no longer felt safe participating in evening activities.[55]

Since the earliest days of the working-class Lower East Side, ethnic and (somewhat less so) racial diversity had formed a hybrid neighborhood identity always in flux and fraught with episodes of conflict and compromise. Within the political and cultural climate of the 1950s and 1960s, however, spatial segregation based on race and ethnicity translated into fractured communities where interaction was often conflictive. Spatial segregation, itself part product of city housing policy, reinforced hostility and anxiety toward those who were different culturally, ethnically, and/or racially. Such feelings, in turn, reproduced and enhanced spatial cleavages leading to turf wars both benign and violent. In the urban crime scare of the late 1950s, the Lower East Side was demarcated into various "no-man's-zones," the locations of which were spread by word of mouth among wary residents. While the elderly white ethnics tended to avoid the streets and avenues east of Avenue B, Puerto Rican shoppers, as many commentators remarked, were fond of the old Jewish shopping districts along Orchard Street and East Broadway. Numerous newspaper articles and social service agency reports from the 1960s circulated representations of a neighborhood fraught with vehement antagonisms between minority newcomers and white ethnics. English language newspapers ran sensational stories that presented readers with images of Puerto Ricans as criminals.[56] A widely publicized "racial" incident occurred in July 1964 between the owner of a tenement rented exclusively to white middle-class tenants and a group of Puerto Rican neighbors on East Third Street between Avenues B and C. All of the building's tenants fled in fear of repercussions of an earlier fight between their white landlord and their Puerto Rican neighbors. A unit within the building was set aflame after a scuffle over the prevalence of gambling and ball playing in front of the property.[57] A week later, demonstrations against charges of landlords' racial discrimination drew hundreds of protestors and spectators.[58]

Incidents of muggings, stabbings, and petty theft enacted on white ethnics, especially the elderly, by newcomers were pervasive, as were juvenile crime and gang-related violence. Turf wars were common between minority youth gangs. Seven such gangs—the Sportsmen, Forsyth Boys, Smith Boys, Centurions, Dragons, Pitt Street Dragons, and Junior Centurions—were said to operate on the Lower East Side in the late 1950s and early 1960s.[59] In the late summer and fall of 1959, the death of two teenage gang members and several rumbles between the Forsyth Boys (mostly Puerto Rican members) and the Sportsmen (Puerto Rican and black members) shook the neighborhood. Social workers familiar with the street gangs questioned the assumption that all gangs were equally violent. Nonetheless, such perceptions of violence between minority youths ran rampant. The city's overall level of gang violence reached record highs in the late 1950s, capturing the attention of mayoral and gubernatorial agencies.[60] Although the rise in delinquency between 1951 and 1960 among Lower East Side juveniles was the highest of any neighborhood in New York City,[61] by the fall of 1960 local community activists hailed the dramatic decline in gang-related incidents.[62] Still, older residents' perceptions of juvenile delinquency remained much higher than that indicated in official statistics.[63] Despite such evidence, perceptions of newcomers culled from the everyday experiences on streets, in parks, and in other public spaces and more rarely in violent episodes such as gang rumbles created a sense of unease, discomfort, and alienation for the older, working-class, white residents on the Lower East Side.

The survivor/predator image came to dominate accounts of the Lower East Side in the mainstream press, official documents, and other media influential in shaping public opinion (including that of property owners). The old and familiar Lower East Side—the remaining ethnic cafés, restaurants, shops, and theaters—increasingly appeared as a relic of some glorified past now threatened and intimidated by newcomers. Although they inhabited the identical squalid apartments, the dwindling cohort of foreign-born and first-generation eastern Europeans now moved through a more unfamiliar terrain of streets, parks, and shopping districts controlled by "others." They were the survivors who struggled to retain some semblance of their once vital ethnic communities:

they were victims of change. The flip side of this image was that of preda-
tor newcomers who encroached on the white ethnics' troubled sanctuary. Unlike past neighborhood social and cultural transformations, this
succession from one dominant culture to another was punctuated by
outright fear and distrust. Thus, one version—arguably the dominant
one—of the place identity of the late 1950s and early 1960s portrayed a
polarized community marked by anxiety, suspicion, social isolation, and
cultural retrenchment among the old-timers, and an emerging vibrant
diasporic ethnic community for Puerto Ricans. In her novel *The Golden
Spur*, Dawn Powell described a Lower East Side worn-out and weary
from change. In a visit to the old neighborhood, one of the novel's characters "walked around Tompkins Square while he waited, dropping
into the Czech bar for a beer, buying a bagel at the Polish delicatessen,
and thinking that for all its many nationalities and mixed customs it
was a mean, thin-spirited, hostile neighborhood."[64] As dusk settled and
street lamps were lit, the change in light "made madonnas out of the
fat old shrews yelling out windows for their children or dragging them
along the streets with a whack and a cuff; it made kindly peasants out
of the suspicious, foxy merchants waiting in the doors of their shops to
short-change any crippled blind man, especially if he was a brother."[65]
In Powell's Lower East Side one could live "all your life and still be a
stranger."[66]

Such characterizations of the Lower East Side based loosely on obvious and muted conflicts between segments of the population were not
shared by all Lower East Siders. Puerto Ricans, like generations of immigrants before them, sought to make the best of their new community in the face of limited economic circumstances and ethnic and racial
discrimination. The size of the Puerto Rican settlements on the Lower
East Side expanded rapidly following 1953 and record migration from
the island. The effect of urban renewal policies—a combined contraction and spatial concentration of the city's low-income housing supply—positioned the Lower East Side as a major recipient of the newly
arrived or the dislocated. Much to the advantage of local tenement
landlords, demand for unrenovated Old Law tenements, especially in
those blocks adjacent to the public housing towers, such as Avenues C
and D, increased. As Puerto Ricans established a presence on the Lower
East Side, social clubs and community action groups emerged. In the
earliest years of migration, Puerto Rican political culture was devoted

primarily to island issues (e.g., independence for Puerto Rico), reinforcing a collective sense of (or desire for) the stay in New York as a temporary experience.[67] Eventually, several organizations were formed to address local social issues. The Puerto Rican Forum and the Congress of
Home Town Clubs dealt with local educational issues. Organizations
addressing poverty issues, such as the Puerto Rican Family Institute, As-
pira, and the Puerto Rican Community Development Project, were active as well.[68] Most of these organizations emerged from neighborhoods
with the greatest Puerto Rican residential concentration, such as East
Harlem and areas within Brooklyn. More militant groups surfaced briefly
in the middle to late 1960s, raising Puerto Rican consciousness but having little success in bettering the material conditions for Puerto Ricans.[69] New York affiliates of The Young Lords, a politicized youth gang
from Chicago, were very active in social and political issues in Spanish
Harlem and on the Lower East Side.

The Avant-Garde of the 1950s

> "Art lives here cheek by jowl with all else but glamour."
>
> Ronald Sukenick, *Down and In: Life in the Underground*

While tensions among the resident groups increased in the 1950s, the
Lower East Side's long history of pluralism had, nonetheless, created an
atmosphere that indulged (rather than merely tolerated) differences in
ethnicity, race, politics, religion, and culture. By the late 1950s, it was
apparent that no singular group could brand its own version of identity on the Lower East Side in ways that immigrants had done (if only
temporarily) some fifty years earlier.[70] The core neighborhood of Puerto
Rican culture was East Harlem, not the Lower East Side, and Jewish life
(especially the intellectual community) was increasingly centered in
bookstores, coffee shops, and apartment houses on the Upper West
Side. Also missing in the 1950s was the shared experience of immigrant
adjustment found in the period from the 1870s to the 1920s, or the collective sense of struggle that had transcended the different ethnic backgrounds and religious affiliations of the former Lower East Siders. The
Lower East Side of the 1950s, then, was a patchwork of Puerto Ricans,
Jews, Ukrainians, refugees, postwar émigrés, Blacks, and Italians inhabiting strikingly different social and cultural worlds within a small phys-

1950s Beat Hangouts

a. Hudson's Army–Navy Store
b. St. Mark's Church
c. Le Metro
d. Ukrainian National Home Bar
e. The Dom
f. Stewart's
g. McSorley's Old Ale House

h. Ratner's
i. Original Five Spot
j. Rapoport's
k. Deux Megots, Paradox
l. Stanley's Bar
m. Old Stanley's
n. Engage Coffeehouse
o. Annex Bar

p. Vazac Bar
q. Old Reliable Bar
r. Slug's

— · — "Tenth Street" artist enclave
– – – Ukranian enclave
——— "White ethnic" working-class enclave
············ Puerto Rican enclave

Map 3. Avant-garde cultural sites and the landscape of the 1950s. Map constructed by Neil Wieloch. Source: Sukenick 1987.

ical space. Such ethnic and cultural diversity was a source of consternation for older, white ethnic residents and an everyday, but not necessarily pleasant, social reality for newer minority residents. For a third group—a growing population of young adults who embraced countercultural movements of the time—the Lower East Side's entangled ethnicities, classes, and cultures were a source of allure and inspiration.

Like the bohemian movement that flourished in the 1920s, the postwar New York avant-garde—the beatniks or beats[71]—was centered in Greenwich Village. As the movement matured, the Lower East Side setting emerged as an alternative or, for some, a corrective to the more popular west side beat scene. The beat movement was a collection of several diverse subcultures each centered around a cultural, and not terribly political, critique of bourgeois society. As such, the beat movement, like its 1920s counterpart, formed an idealized disengagement from the mainstream rather than an active *counter*culture to it. The beats comprised an eclectic mix of white, Latino, and black urban dwellers as well as the first generation of frustrated young, middle-class refugees from the idyllic suburbs.[72] The beat style of dress, the idiomatic expressions, the proclivity toward drugs and casual sex, and the expressive genre of literature and music were signifiers of an antibourgeois lifestyle played out in the Village's coffee shops, jazz clubs, and taprooms.

As the Greenwich Village "scene" attracted the attention of first the local then the national press, the jazz clubs and coffee shops grew more popular and expensive as tourists and curious onlookers flocked to witness the spectacle of the urban rebellious. Overexposure pushed the "postwar disaffected"[73] eastward. In addition, the antagonism of Greenwich Village ethnics (Italians, in particular) toward their unconventional neighbors estranged many beats. Several incidents of street fights, vandalism, and verbal harassment occurred in the summer of 1959 as Italian residents lashed out against the beats in general and the movement's racial and ethnic inclusiveness in particular.[74] A crackdown on narcotic use at Greenwich Village bars and clubs and in public spaces (e.g., a strict enforcement of a midnight curfew in Washington Square Park) in the late 1950s fueled an exodus to the less-surveilled Lower East Side.[75]

While changes in Greenwich Village compelled the move eastward, many beats were also attracted to the Lower East Side's cheaper rents and ethnic restaurants, and the unpretentious ways of its locals.[76] By the mid-1950s, painters, writers, musicians, and curious spectators colonized the ethnic restaurants, coffee shops, saloons, and cheap "cold-water" tenements along the streets and avenues of the Lower East Side:

> Some newer coffee shops are on the lower east side (out of the Village
> proper) and a couple of that neighborhood's restaurants have also
> become fairly beat. In part this is the result of low-income Villagers
> moving eastward in the face of rising Village rents. But these shops cater
> also to beats from various parts of the city who want to avoid Village
> tourists.[77]

With the appearance of beatniks on the Lower East Side, a few Yiddish theaters, closed down since the mid-1950s, reopened as "off-Broadway" theaters.[78] A handful of Lower East Side cafés—Hassans, Port Afrique, Les Deux Megots, among others—hosted beat poetry readings and jazz jam sessions.[79]

In addition to the beats, the Lower East Side was also home to the loosely connected art colony on East Tenth Street that formed part of the avant-gardist New York School.[80] While the first generation of expressionists, including Jackson Pollock and Mark Rothko, had departed the downtown art scene by 1951, other artists, such as Willem de Kooning and Franz Kline, showed their work in studio lofts and storefronts along East Tenth Street near Fourth Avenue[81] — thus the label, "Tenth Street Movement." A 1956 exhibition titled "Painters and Sculptors on Tenth Street" featured the works of twenty-five artists who lived on the street. At their peak a handful of cooperative galleries, such as the Tanager and the Hansa, which was founded in 1952 and later moved uptown, claimed over two hundred artist members.[82] Such movements, intentionally experimental and oppositional to mainstream art and the art market, found solace in and inspiration from the Lower East Side atmosphere of heightened diversity, social chaos, and disorder.[83] The Five Spot, a bar on Cooper Square, at the western fringe of the Lower East Side, began to attract a "subterranean" crowd in the mid-1950s. The artists de Kooning and Larry Rivers frequented the bar, as did the beat writers Jack Kerouac and Frank O'Hara and jazz bassist Charles Mingus and saxophonist Sonny Rollins.[84] Franz Kline, along with several other abstract expressionists, were habitués of the Colony, a bar on the corner of East Tenth Street and Fourth Avenue.

Although the Tenth Street artist colony had its favored cafés, bars, and lounges (some, like the Cedar Tavern on University Place, were outside the Lower East Side), its members eschewed notions of community identity, in part to prevent a "Greenwich Village effect" taking hold on the Lower East Side. "Our showing up on Cooper Square," wrote poet and playwright Amiri Baraka, "was right in tune with the whole movement of people East, away from the West Village with its high rents and older bohemians. Cooper Square was sort of the border line; when you crossed it, you were really on the Lower East Side, no shit."[85] According to an article printed in the 1954 Art News Yearbook, "The absence from Tenth Street of fixed group identities, whether of nationality, race, class, ideology, or age is one of the superiorities of this colony and its novelty.... Tenth Street is the opposite of a community." The intentional reticence of the heterogeneous "tribe"[86] of artists also reflected an aesthetic disinterest in corrupting the spectacle of public cultures on the

Lower East Side, which itself was a corrective to the numbing effects of mass culture:

> On Tenth Street the ancient relation between art and the antisocial has attained a curious evolution. Instead of hoodlums — bums. Living on the street, the working stiff is the most conspicuous human feature of the Block of Artists. This transposition of underworld substances in the environment of its creation reflects the changed social character of art in our day.[87]

The Tenth Street art colony faded by the early 1960s as most of the artists began to exhibit uptown. With the increasing mainstream prominence of Tenth Street in the late 1950s, according to Irving Sandler's history of the New York School, an abundance of mediocre exhibitions steadily dissolved its underground character such that it was no longer fashionable to exhibit there.

The everyday struggle of older white ethnics, Puerto Ricans, and other residents on the Lower East Side fascinated and perhaps stimulated the beats and those affiliated with Tenth Street. Nonetheless both were indifferent toward blatant political discourse in general and local social conflicts in particular. The prevailing ideology of 1950s subcultures was that artistic rejection of atrophied suburban bourgeois norms was itself "socially beneficial" and, therefore, political.[88] Despite their presence, neither subculture immediately affected the place identity of the Lower East Side or representations of it in ways that factored into conflict or change in the dominant uses of space. However, the presence of the beats and the Tenth Street artists did have long-term effects on the progression of avant-gardism and, later, the restructuring of the Lower East Side. Like avant-garde movements before and since, the 1950s subcultures were comprised of disaffected middle-class individuals who, in effect, mediated the cultural divide between "high" and "low" cultures. "High" culture embodied in uptown galleries and museums was connected, of course, to New York's emergence as a world-class city. The hidden and "off-beat" qualities of downtown "low" culture were buttressed by the social and spatial consequences of the deconcentration of manufacturing, people, and capital. Yet, since both beats and abstract expressionists earned great recognition outside their immediate social circles, their works *translated* parts of the downtown experience in art forms for middle- and upper-class consumption. The gradual mainstream acceptance of avant-garde work, however, cannot be said to have had an immediate effect on the marginal reputation of the Lower East Side. The influence of artistic subcultures on local political and economic development was pronounced beginning in the 1960s, as chapter 5 details.

The Discourse of Decline, 1955–65:
Neighborhood Disinvestment and Community Resistance

With the privilege of hindsight we may see how community changes in the 1950s were shaped by forces of corporate agglomeration, blue-collar decentralization, middle-class suburbanization, and urban renewal policies. At the time, however, neighborhood changes were represented in images and rhetoric of urban decline that were often coded in solely racial and ethnic terms. On the Lower East Side, the mass influx of Puerto Rican residents, the sprinkling of middle-class complexes, and the interest of beatniks and other nonconformists in the neighborhood's apartments factored heavily into the investment decisions of property owners. Their perception of the Lower East Side was that of long-term poverty, chaos, and disorder that virtually assured an unprofitable housing market. Contemporary discourse about the "death of the city," the squalor of such older neighborhoods, and the romanticized images of suburban life fostered an atmosphere ill suited for long-term investment in places like the Lower East Side. Conversely, residents resisted the fatalist construction of their community and the landlord actions that furthered urban despair.

The demographic changes that occurred on the Lower East Side throughout the 1950s factored into the interests and actions of tenement landlords. City policies had targeted certain neighborhoods for middle-class urban renewal while cordoning off others, such as the Lower East Side, for concentrations of low-income and minority residents. Large numbers of subsidized low-income housing units limited landlords' opportunities to reinvigorate an already anemic housing market. The negative consequences of the city's policy appeared mitigated, however, by a sudden and sharp demand for low-income housing. For struggling Lower East Side landlords, the flood of impoverished Puerto Rican migrants into New York was a boon. Puerto Ricans increased demand for otherwise unwanted cheap and dilapidated housing. Indeed, expectations were high enough to spark speculation in tenements on the Lower East Side and in other, similar neighborhoods in the city.[89] Seeing the housing of a growing number of displaced and newly arrived Puerto Ricans as a profitable venture, "unscrupulous real estate speculators bought heavily in the receiving areas where newcomers were most likely to relocate, such as East Harlem and the Lower East Side."[90] The story line of overcrowding, exploitation, and profits seemed to be repeating itself but proved short-lived. The settlement and migration patterns of the new migrants and, more importantly, the drastic decline in employment opportunities offered to them soon proved significant constraints to profit making for landlords who hoped for a windfall from the return of low-income housing demand. Despite landlords' attempts to profit from this new wave of poor, working-class migrants, their investments soon soured as they became proprietors of a neighborhood that housed an economically idled population. For absentee landlords, who judged the suitability of tenants solely by their existing and future capacity to pay rents, the downturn in the economic fortunes of their tenants meant declining rent revenues and more vacancies. The small influx of beatniks into the neighborhood had little appreciable effect on landlords' outlooks and strategies. In a testimonial given in a report on the local real estate market, one landlord griped about the beatniks: "They're worse than the ones who came before. You rent an apartment to a young girl and next thing you know there are 14 girls living there and they're taking marijuana."[91] Finally, the city's middle-class migration to the suburbs contributed to landlords' malaise. The phenomenon of suburbanization created a hostile investment atmosphere for the inner-city land market. The production of new housing units in the city's outer region offered safer and more lucrative opportunities for speculators and developers, as well as for banks and other lending institutions. All of these factors contributed to landlords' fatalism about the future, which was manifest in their behavior as property owners.

The Lower East Side's growing reputation for social problems, especially crime, was an additional source of concern among landlords. Petty crimes and gang violence lowered landlord confidence in the neighborhood's long-term prospects. In the late 1950s, the Lower East Side and similar low-income neighborhoods across the city experienced an escalation in robberies, muggings, petty larcenies, pickpocket crimes, the buying and selling of stolen goods, and the stealing of valuables, such as copper, from vacant tenements. The surge in crime was correlated with an increase in heroin use and changes in the distribution and sale of heroin. Heroin use grew popular among the city's poor at the end of the 1950s. Edward Preble and John Casey estimated that at least 80 percent of the city's heroin-using population lived in slum areas by the late 1960s.[92] Both press and governmental reports attributed part of the rise in use and much of the increase in street crime to changes in the way in which heroin was sold. Due to stricter federal narcotics laws enacted in 1957, syndicated crime organizations withdrew from direct heroin sales to users but maintained their control over the supply. With the breakup of the syndicate dealers, sales to users were farmed out to street dealers via a complex web of distributors, intermediaries, and smaller operators.[93] In poorer areas throughout the city, the street dealer appeared.[94] Ned Polsky attributed the exodus of some beat users of heroin from Greenwich Village to the more plentiful dealers and lax surveillance on the Lower East Side.[95] In addition to sales on street corners and in parks, heroin dealing also took place in candy stores and grocery stores across the Lower East Side.[96] According to an informal survey of landlords, increases in crime and the exacerbated tensions between old and new residents induced many white tenants to flee the neighborhood.[97]

In a summary of the housing market in the early 1960s, a report issued by a local community organization found that the Lower East Side catered to a specific and narrow niche market of the city's poor.[98] This segment of the city's rental population barely maintained a stable demand for housing, and it could afford but very low rents. Thus, landlords could hardly fill their buildings and earned rents that did not provide sizable profits. In a pessimistic report issued in late 1965, the housing unit of the community organization Mobilization for Youth assessed local market conditions and the state of most area tenements. Its report concluded that landlords could not earn a profit from their buildings' income even if they made efforts to keep them in good repair.[99] There were few indicators that rent levels would rise. In the streets and avenues adjacent to the low-income housing projects, it appeared that low rents would remain fixed or decline further. The absence of building and infrastructure renovations or new construction reinforced fatalistic perceptions among landlords. With the exception of units constructed with government subsidies, remarkably few private market units were built in the late 1950s and 1960s.[100] Landlords continued to slowly divest their properties by withholding maintenance and allowing buildings to deteriorate in violation of the city's housing codes. The rate of property foreclosures rose appreciably, especially when the city, once again, enforced building codes in the early 1960s.[101] The number of in rem properties (parcels taken over by the city after four or more years of tax delinquency) increased. As new tenant and housing organizations formed in the early 1960s to legally combat conditions of neglect, those landlords who had not incorporated as firms did so to avoid prosecution and personal liability.[102]

Countering Decline: A Revival of Community Resistance

The behavior of landlords and other actors within the real estate industry was in response not only to the immediate conditions of their property but also to the negative discourse propagated by city officials (e.g., designating an area as "blighted") and by the media (e.g., reports of high crime zones). Some landlords, especially those associated with the local chamber of commerce and other pro-business organizations, fought against such images and rhetoric in hopes of attracting tenants who could pay higher rents. But a large portion of property owners also earned profits through disinvestment and in doing so created the material basis (dilapidation, abandonment, etc.) that perpetuated negative images of place. In short, landlords engaged in a narrative of urban decline, portraying themselves often as hapless victims of demographic shifts, rent control limitations, white flight, and a soured economy. By all accounts, the Lower East Side was indeed a harsh market for real estate capitalists to operate, but the more savvy of landlords were able to make money from degradation. Exploitation of tenants by unscrupulous landlords, for example, was rampant in apartment buildings that housed Puerto Ricans primarily or exclusively. In the early 1950s a Mayor's Committee on Puerto Rican Affairs was charged with investigating numerous episodes of rent overcharges, tenant harassment, unwarranted and illegal evictions, and intentional overcrowding in tenement apartments.[103] Like most newly arrived poor groups, Puerto Ricans were susceptible to mistreatment by discreditable landlords. In the 1950s, the peculiarities of migration and settlement and the city's urban renewal policies weakened the formation of strong community associations to resist housing and other forms of exploitation.[104] Thus, those Puerto Ricans "restricted to recognized 'poverty' areas of the City... have not been able to establish within these areas the ethnic group concentrations supportive of community projects and organizations."[105] As their economic condition worsened and their ability to pay rents or rent increases diminished, Puerto Ricans were ill equipped to offset the socially harmful effects of landlords' disinvestment strategies. In defense of their actions, landlords claimed that the area's marginal reputation caused rents to decline, thereby necessitating cutbacks in maintenance and upkeep. Landlord allegations of property destruction by youth gangs and vandalism by unruly tenants were typically exaggerated.[106]

By the late 1950s, local residents and housing organizations mounted social resistance to directly challenge not only urban blight but the discourse of urban decline that had, in effect, "written off" the neighborhood and its residents as irrelevant. Key tenant organizations were either newly founded or revived across the Lower East Side. Among the major housing organizations, the Cooper Square Committee proved to be the most durable, developing proactive strategies to insure that residents maintained a voice in local planning issues. The founding of the Cooper Square Committee in 1959 was spurred by Robert Moses' 1956 plan to demolish blocks of tenements between Delancey and East Ninth Streets that threatened to displace over seven thousand people. The proposal called for a significantly reduced amount of replacement housing at rents out of the range of affordability for most Lower East Siders. In 1963, despite the disapproval of local residents, the city expanded the size of the renewal area from twelve blocks to thirty-three. After ten years of demonstrations, sit-ins, and intense lobbying of elected officials to nix the project, the Cooper Square Committee prevailed, and the city withdrew its application for federal funds to begin redevelopment.[107] In addition to the fight against the urban renewal plan, the Cooper Square Committee was instrumental in garnering residents' input in rehabilitation schemes devised by the city and private developers.

Other organizations were formed around broader issues related to social changes within the neighborhood and across the city. The Lower East Side Committee on Civil Rights and the Negro Action Group set out to resolve immediate social problems but saw their agenda as a means of addressing long-term social injustices of economic and political marginalization. One of the more active groups, the Lower East Side Neighborhoods Association (LENA), was an umbrella organization formed in 1956 by University Settlement director Helen Hall to unite local social, civic, and religious groups against a score of health, employment, and other social problems.[108] A central goal of LENA and other organizations, such as the Educational Alliance, was to ease the tense racial climate along the Lower East Side. In 1959, for example, the Educational Alliance and six other community organizations sponsored a well-attended street fair and festival intended to bring together minority and white youths from across the neighborhood.[109] The University Settlement, LENA, and the Youth Board sought to diffuse gang tensions and offered multiple activities to occupy the spare time of local youth.[110] In the early 1960s, LENA successfully pressed the Ninth Precinct to distribute newsletters in Spanish and English that called for recruitment of Hispanic police officers and provided useful information for tenants in disputes with landlords.[111] Within minority communities, the Negro Action Group, the Council of Puerto Rican Organizations on the Lower East Side, and the Puerto Rican Mothers' Association became active in poverty issues, police brutality, and housing concerns at the block level.[112]

Perhaps the most familiar of new initiatives was the Mobilization for Youth (MFY) project, which operated from 1961 to 1967.[113] Created through funding and participation by the federal Public Health Service, Columbia University, and, later, the Ford Foundation, MFY was an experimental project in local initiatives to combat urban poverty that led to federal community assistance aid through the Economic Opportunities Act of 1964. MFY combined community action with social research, producing nearly a dozen reports on community life, housing, delinquency, and welfare. In its earliest years, the reduction of area juvenile delinquency was a high priority on the organization's agenda. Later, MFY's program was broadened and became more radicalized. MFY opened a storefront, "Casa de la Comunidad," on East Fourth Street between Avenues B and C in January 1963. The site was used for community outreach programs, including drug abuse treatment, welfare, the prevention of juvenile delinquency, voter-registration drives, and fair housing issues.[114] In 1963 and 1964, MFY opened two coffee shops — Club 169 and The Hideout — designed as recreational centers and drop-in lounges for members of local street gangs.[115]

In response to the downward spiral of living conditions in the poorest neighborhoods, community groups across the city waged a "war against slumlords" in the first half of the 1960s.[116] Over one hundred tenant associations were formed out of MFY's housing clinics.[117] Lists of housing violations on the Lower East Side were compiled and presented to city officials for housing code enforcement. Clinics were founded to represent tenants who filed claims against landlords for harassment and breach of habitability.[118] In concurrence with a local history of strike activism, residents employed the rent strike as a tool of resistance against local landlords in the early 1960s. The central theme of strike activity was livability rather than rent levels.[119] The Lower East Side chapter of the Council on Racial Equality (CORE) was especially militant, organizing strikes, protests, and acts of civil disobedience in the summer of 1963. A strike against dilapidated and unsanitary living conditions organized by CORE included the participation of one hundred tenants along Eldridge Street; the strike eventually spread to parts of Brooklyn and Harlem. In response, the city hired more building inspectors.[120] Another strike protesting hazardous living conditions was mounted in 1964 under the auspices of the University Settlement, CORE, local Puerto Rican organizations, and MFY. The strike was influential in the passage of legislation that effectively legalized the rent strike by allowing aggrieved tenants to place rents in escrow if landlords did not repair code violations within sixty days.[121] The MFY's housing activities included mounting a four-month rent strike against landlords of buildings with delinquent maintenance records in 1963, and financing the founding of the United Tenants Association on Avenue A in 1964. The intensity of the anti-slumlord crusade was widely reported in the local press and was instrumental in the city's decisions to authorize anti-rat campaigns and institute emergency heat and water repairs in privately owned buildings in the winter of 1964–65.[122] Strategic alliances and connections between local and citywide groups grew more common as the density of organizations and their causes mounted. "When mothers in one condemned building became involved in controversy," an MFY report noted, "other organizations offered assistance, and some local activists and politicians entered the fray on the side of the mothers."[123] The Metropolitan Council on Housing, a citywide pro-tenant organization, supported the Cooper Square Committee in their efforts to undo the city's renewal plan. Community groups were kept busy as private disinvestment and governmental disengagement led to further neighborhood decline.

Changes in local political organization and the wellspring of organizations culminated in the flowering of proactive democratic participation on the Lower East Side in the early 1960s.[124] This outpouring of community action was a strong corrective to the identity of despair that was partly due to tensions between older and newer residents and was stoked by the city's indifference toward and landlords' exploitation of low-income neighborhoods. The ethnic/racial, class, and cultural fragmentation that characterized the neighborhood of the 1950s was radically transformed in the 1960s when the hippie counterculture invented an "East Village" out of the Lower East Side. Unlike the muted influence of the beats and artists on community changes encountered in our survey of the 1950s, the subcultural and spatial practices of this emerging community would influence the conflict between different groups of tenants and landlords over the use versus the exchange of space and over working-class versus middle-class place identity.

CHAPTER FIVE

A Brief Psychedelic Detour:
Hip Urban Renewal and the Invention of
the East Village

At the close of the 1950s the Lower East Side resembled a patchwork quilt comprised of tightly knit groups separated by ethnic and, to a lesser degree, class differences but stitched together largely by representations *about* them and their neighborhood. The Lower East Side was an eclectic neighborhood that was visibly different in many ways from other New York neighborhoods and in most ways from the predominantly homogeneous white, middle-class, pristine new suburbs. In the district's northern and western blocks, the often barren and grim landscape was dotted with pawnshops, liquor stores, boardinghouses, lunchrooms, and ethnic groceries tucked between tenements occupied by older white ethnics, including a sizable cohort of eastern Europeans. Farther east presented a very different landscape where in summer Puerto Rican families spilled out from overcrowded and sweltering tenements onto sidewalks for a game of dominos, some gossip, and urban gardening. Jane Jacobs's well-known critique of the eviscerating effects of state intervention on the livelihood of urban neighborhoods seemed to apply to some parts of the Lower East Side and not others.[1] Viewed from the outside, however, the hybrid constellation of classes, ethnicities, and cultural practices remained lumped together in convenient labels of slum or ghetto. In short, the Lower East Side appeared as the symbolic antithesis of postwar suburban society.

When the highly public and visible critique of *suburban* America developed into the 1960s counterculture, the *anti-suburban* Lower East Side emerged as one of its cultural capitals. Between 1964 and 1968 the streets

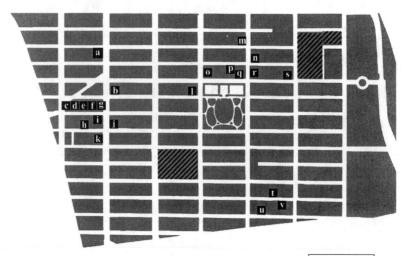

1960s Hippie Culture Sites
a. The Place
b. Sindoori Imports
c. Cricket Theater
d. Gregory's Restaurant
e. Board and Bowl; Khadejha
   Fashions
f. The Dom/Electric Circus
g. St. Mark's Playhouse
h. McSorley's Old Ale House

i. Gems Spa Newsstand
j. Orpheum Theater
k. Fillmore East
l. Office of the *East Village*
   Other
m. Stanley's Bar
n. Charles Theater
o. Psychedelicatessen
p. Engage Coffeehouse
q. Sid's Newsstand

r. Annex Bar
s. Peace Eye Book Store
t. Old Reliable Bar
u. Mobilization For Youth
v. Slug's Saloon

Moderate income housing

Map 4. Hip urban renewal and the landscape of the 1960s. Map constructed by Neil Wieloch. Source: Gruen 1966.

and avenues between Houston and Fourteenth Streets experienced a cultural explosion of art, music, theater, film, writing, and, most significantly, public performance, all of which were linked to the loosely connected hippie movement. The area was dubbed the "East Village," and for four years it became the key East Coast site of a countercultural spectacle that had an enduring influence on the cultural history of the United States and the struggle over neighborhood restructuring on the Lower East Side. This chapter reconstructs the influence of the middle-class hippie youth movement on the cultural invention and spatial development of the "East Village" as distinct from the larger Lower East Side. Unlike the beats, whose presence in the neighborhood was hardly perceptible, the hippie counterculture was highly spatialized, transforming both local identities of the Lower East Side and popular representations of it.

During the 1960s, hippies colonized the northern tier in significant numbers and sought to introduce new uses and meanings to parks, streets, shops, restaurants, and tenements already utilized by existing ethnic working-class communities. The chiefly middle-class and white hippie counterculture assumed an interventionist stance, seeking to build community by adapting, perfecting, and often including working-class and ethnic cultural practices into an overall critique of mainstream society.[2] By 1967 mention of the "East Village" in popular media supplanted those of the "Lower East Side" for the area north of Houston Street. Such representations no longer characterized the district as the old neighborhood of ethnic diversity but as the site of cultural protest and alternative lifestyles. Despite the inclusiveness of the counterculture's notion of "community" and media representations of it, the social relations between the hippie newcomers and preexisting ethnic groups were often strained. For many existing residents, the incursion of hippies onto their turf was not easily accommodated. For the real estate industry, however, the subcultural images, symbols, and rhetoric affiliated with the East Village offered to do away with the area's outdated and unprofitable working-class reputation. Landlords, developers, and real estate firms sought to channel the growing popularity of the East Village into a means of attracting a broader and more equivocal category of upscale middle-class residents. The wholesale adoption of the place-name *East Village* by tenement owners, speculators, and developers exemplified their effort to appropriate and assert a favorable identity to reshape the local housing market. Finally, it is argued, the hippie movement's highly visible and celebrated conventions were situated within the postwar changes in cultural consumption and commodification that popularized and, in turn, altered the movement itself. Together, the extremely public cultural politics of the hippie movement and the sophistication of media and culture industries in popularizing and commodifying subculture had immediate and lasting effects on the course of local struggles. The tragic close of the hippie era on the Lower East Side sowed the seeds of the symbolic representations based on danger, fear, and decline that suffused representations of the East Village and the entire Lower East Side in the 1970s.

The Desired Middle-Class Residents: Traditional and Hip

The long stretches of tenements off Second Avenue occupied by older eastern Europeans and the bustling streets of the impoverished Puerto Rican enclave to the east presented few opportunities to the real estate industry at the close of the 1950s. Yet optimism for a middle-class revitalization of the ghetto was encouraged by two different kinds of plans put forth by the private and public sectors in the late 1950s and early 1960s. First, aspirations to redevelop the entirety of lower Manhattan, beginning in the Wall Street area and continuing northward, were rekindled despite two decades of urban policies that had, in effect, cordoned off entire swaths of the Lower East Side as "poverty zones." Beginning in the late 1950s, developers and corporate executives, led by David Rockefeller, devised a blueprint to revive the declining Wall Street office district.[3] The scale of the plan and the amount of public and private funds earmarked to be spent gave hope to promises for a revitalized lower Manhattan, including, by default, residential areas on the Lower East Side. In addition to the World Trade Center (which was completed), key aspects of the plan included a crosstown freeway that would bisect the SoHo district, and the completion of a Second Avenue subway (neither of which were built). In 1963 the City Planning Commission revived the call to complete the subway line, which was first proposed prior to World War I.[4] Lower Manhattan developers quickly heralded it as a chance to increase the accessibility of the Wall Street business district.[5] The implications for property owners across the Lower East Side were clear: subway stations along the line would provide better transportation to the streets and avenues disconnected from the rest of Manhattan with the demise of the Second Avenue El (elevated) in 1942.[6] The line would reinvigorate commercial and residential rents on streets and avenues along its path. By 1974 the subway plan fell victim to the city's fiscal crisis.

Second, tenement owners were encouraged by new urban renewal proposals that included areas on the Lower East Side. While well-organized neighborhood resistance movements contested plans for the Cooper Square renewal district, the number of potential sites for middle-class development increased in the 1960s to include the areas of Fourteenth Street and Avenue B, Tompkins Square, Third Street and Avenue C, and the blocks south of Houston Street adjacent to Seward Park. Development of these urban renewal areas called for a mix of low-income rental units and moderate-income cooperatives and rentals.[7] Although municipal policies had largely favored spatial segregation of class, ethnicity, and race, other state agencies initiated programs to revitalize or stem further urban decline by "seeding" the poorest neighborhoods with middle-class developments.[8] Two middle-income developments—Village View and Village East—were constructed under a state-sponsored program known as Mitchell-Lama.[9] Mitchell-Lama's expressed purpose was to essentially anchor low-income neighborhoods with large, middle-class rental housing developments as a means to further private development. The program's subsidies allowed middle-class families to rent new apartments at less than the city's average middle-class rents. In 1964, the Village View Apartments opened a 1,236-unit complex interspersed between tenements on First Avenue. The Village East project opened in 1968 on Avenue C between Tenth and Thirteenth Streets. The project's high-rise residential tower was surrounded by modern "town houses" that gestured toward the area's dominant tenement architecture. Other middle-income "seed" developments were placed adjacent to low-income public housing projects south of Houston Street, such as Masaryk Towers (1967), which was built near Samuel Gompers Houses (1964).[10] Although a considerable number of middle-class units were built in the 1960s, the numbers paled in comparison with low-income public and private housing. In 1968, for example, 78.4 percent of the Lower East Side's housing stock consisted of low-income tenements, 15.3 percent were public low-income apartments, and only 6.3 percent were middle-income cooperatives and rental units.[11] The placement of the new middle-class complexes was not contiguous but isolated: individual apartment towers dotted the landscape. The dispersal of middle-class enclaves throughout the Lower East Side did little to contribute to the class, ethnic, or racial integration of the community. Spatially segregated, residents of these units tended not to associate with their "different" neighbors. Exceptions were religious practices and community politics: middle-class residents would associate with poor white ethnics who resided in the adjacent tenements.

New urban renewal proposals and the unfolding drama of the lower Manhattan revitalization plan revived and, later, quashed hopes to rationally develop the ill-used but valuable real estate areas on the Lower East Side. In the decade-long course of implementing parts of the urban renewal and revitalization plans and discarding others, some landlords continued to "hold out" for the elusive profits on the horizon. Others, frustrated by the uncertainty of renewal in the midst of evident and continued growth elsewhere, withdrew. If the downtown redevelopment plan and the new middle-class apartment towers failed to generate investors' interest and confidence in the area's housing, a third factor— the colonization of the neighborhood by the 1960s counterculture— once again raised the specter of an upscale transformation of the Lower East Side.

Space and the Public Spectacle of Hippie Culture: The East Village 1964–68

> Thus where the [West] Village is removed from Uptown by long subway rides, the East Village is twice removed, and this perhaps accounts for the fact that for a while it became *an underground underneath the underground.*
>
> Ronald Sukenick, *Down and In: Life in the Underground* (my emphasis)

As discussed in the previous chapter, the beats' critique of bourgeois society in the 1950s was largely intellectual—beats did not develop into a popular social movement but instead sought to influence critically particular established literary and musical genres or create new ones.[12] As such, beat culture remained a critique of middle-class, suburban society, but it never transformed itself into a public movement that would avow direct interest in expressly political or social matters.[13] The formation of a movement "broader in shape and more political in direction"[14] in the 1960s marked a departure from the beats' more passive social critique. Defining a clear demarcation between beats and hippies, however, is complicated as important features of one movement strongly influenced the other. Aspects of the early hippie movement were clearly derived from the beats. As an early critic commented, hippies were "no more than Beats plus drugs."[15] Like the small group of beats in the late 1950s, the first hippies interpreted the Lower East Side's traditions of ethnic pluralism and working-class community resistance as viable and authentic alternatives to mainstream culture. Key players in the 1950s movement (such as Allen Ginsberg and Jack Kerouac) appeared as central figures and spokespersons of the hippie lifestyle. Likewise, principal landmarks of the beat era surfaced as hangouts and meeting places for the hippie movement. The Charles Theater on Avenue B near Twelfth Street, where underground and censored films were shown in the 1950s, was a favored site for the nascent hippie community in the early 1960s.[16]

But essential differences between the two subcultures became apparent as the ideology of the hippie movement began to reflect significant social changes that were taking place across the United States in the 1960s. The beats' credo of "dropping out" and disengaging from the mainstream as a form of social critique grew less appealing to middle-class youth in the 1960s than the prospect of confronting and actively changing society. In the making of a new counterculture and identity, the description "hippie" supplanted that of beat or beatnik.[17] By the mid-1960s, the hippies had constructed a subculture based around a proactive and open critique of bourgeois society and in support of widespread social change. Consequently, the movement's rituals and characteristics and the establishment of community were infused with ideals of collectivity and public visibility. The hippie phenomenon emerged as an umbrella countercultural movement that encompassed many different social groups, cultural practices, political ideas, and beliefs, including peace, nonviolence, free use of drugs, and liberal sex, among many others. The forms in which ideals and beliefs were conveyed were equally diverse — in theater, film, and music, among others. Despite such plurality in the content and forms, the expression of hippie culture was, nonetheless, connected to and situated within local environments. An emphasis on building alternative or counter-bourgeois communities meant that the movement was *located* or spatialized first in urban areas in cities large and small across the United States and later in rural settings.

As the hippie counterculture developed in urban centers, its earliest practitioners sought to distance themselves spatially as well as ideologically from the beats. By the early 1960s, the beats' enclave of Greenwich Village had, in effect, been colonized and, consequently, commercialized by middle-class onlookers, poseurs, and other settlers. The West Coast beat equivalent — the Italian neighborhood of North Beach in San Francisco — underwent a similar phenomenon as new cafés and clubs offered more tourists than locals an arena for contrived beat experiences. Hippies settled in the Lower East Side and Haight-Ashbury in part due to the commercialization of established "bohemian" neighborhoods and their increasingly expensive rents. Yet the draw of cheap rents cannot fully explain the emergence of the hippie community on the Lower East Side.[18] In their rejection of mostly suburban, middle-class lifestyles and expectations, hippies converged on the working-class "ghetto" to construct their own countercultural space. Involved in a truly public movement that purposefully engaged in a transformation of community, the hippies brought themselves in contact with the area's existing ethnic and cultural subgroups and drew the attention of tenement landlords and real estate speculators.

Prior to 1964 there was no place popularly known as the East Village. By 1965, the place-name was used pervasively by hippie locals and owners of commercial establishments, newspaper and magazine writers and editors, and landlords. *East Village* referred exclusively to the area's hippie community and not to the communities of older white ethnics and Puerto Rican families, who were nonetheless the predominant residents. Hippies laid claim to the many cultural sites and various hangouts that were founded by the beats. As the counterculture converged onto the Lower East Side, it did not form a bounded community that sought to exist independently of the already established Ukrainian, Polish, or Puerto Rican enclaves. Unlike the beats, whose cultural critique was expressed within confined spaces of bars and clubs and apartments, the hippie scene was visible and vocal, and its audience was the general public. In mostly public and commercial forums, hippies acted out cultural practices based on notions of communalism and universality (in opposition to bourgeois individualism), creating a "virtual religion out of 'opening their heads' to other people."[19] Collective and public engagement was simultaneously a critique of mainstream society and the foundation of an alternative community. Social interaction, not personal introspection, typified the presentation of the hippie self. By 1966 a rite of passage for many neophyte hippies was a pilgrimage to either Haight-Ashbury or the East Village, where initiates experienced the subculture firsthand in parks, bars, streets, and apartments. Cultural expressions and spectacles in public settings were the preferred means to express displeasure with the mainstream and to trumpet the merits of the hippie lifestyle.

In the East Village, St. Mark's Place emerged as the central cultural spine, with the corner at Third Avenue as the symbolic gateway to the hippie community. Along the street, individuals and groups of hippies staked out sidewalk spaces in front of shops and clubs to recite poems, sing songs, chant, or proselytize ideas ranging from free love and nonviolence to the benefits of LSD for personal liberation (Sir Galahad, a well-known regular who dressed in medieval garb, was featured often in the city's press accounts). Pedestrians heading east moved through a succession of public stages where performers barefoot or in top hats and capes engaged in street theater. Hippies perfected and made popular semiorganized public affairs, called "be-ins" or "be-outs," in which performance, protest, entertainment, and audience participation were combined. In August 1967, for example, nearly five hundred hippies turned out for a "be-in" in support of nature over concrete, planting an evergreen tree in a mound of dirt dumped in the intersection of St. Mark's Place and Third Avenue.[20] To the chagrin of the neighborhood's ethnics, the most popular public arena for spectacles was Tompkins Square Park, where hippies visibly and vocally expressed themselves on a daily basis. Music (the bongo drum was extremely popular), dancing, the chanting of mantras (often led by the Society for Krishna Consciousness), and simply hanging out were prevalent activities in the park, especially during the summers of 1966 and 1967, when middle-class youth fled the dull comforts of their suburban split-levels by the thousands and overwhelmed the neighborhood. When public spectacles fell afoul of city regulations, the events were instantaneously transformed into protests against "the ultra symbol of middle class society"[21] — the police department — which led to clashes with officers from the Ninth Precinct. In what became known as the Memorial Day Riot of 1967, hundreds of youthful gatherers converged on the park for a holiday session of the usual fare of music, chanting, and dancing. The city granted permission for the event but required the gathering to be confined to the southern area of Tompkins Square adjacent to the band shell so as to not interfere with the park's other users — eastern European and Puerto Rican mothers and their children, handball players, and chess players. As the day's activities progressed, the large crowd flowed into parts of the park that police were ordered to keep clear. A cordon of police set upon the bongo-playing and chanting revelers, who refused to disperse. They arrested thirty-eight and injured several. The fury of the officers' (over)reaction evinced the long-simmering antipathy for hippies, whose verbal litany against the "establishment" was often directed toward the local police.[22] The Memorial Day Riot brought to the fore neighborhood tensions between the police and the more conservative elder white ethnics and members of the highly visible counterculture.[23] It also reaffirmed the legacy of the park as a site of turf battles over the neighborhood's identity.

Placing the Hippie Counterculture

Demonstrations, gatherings, and everyday street performances were indicative of a counterculture of public expression that soon transformed the social and physical landscape of the East Village. Countercultural *practices*, including the street-based rituals and role-playing, conspicuous devotion to the consumption of drugs, and experimentalism in artistic forms of theater, film, and music, were fully manifested in numerous *places* in the East Village. First, a local identity and, later, media representations of "downtown" were forged as the counterculture was increasingly spatialized. "Hippieland,"[24] as the media came to refer to the East Village, provided a variety of experiences, all of which were designed to "shake up the senses."[25] Since a shared premise within the hippie movement was a desire to break down static norms and codes of middle-class behavior, ambiguity and suspense were often underscored at gatherings and events. Such features played well for the sensationalist media. A venue popular across art forms was the "happening," which actively included the audience in the performance and reinforced the hippie axiom of communalism.[26] Since happenings were not scripted, they eliminated the passive spectator and emphasized participation, spontaneity, experimentalism, and the excitement of the unknown. In December 1965, the Film Makers' Cinematheque on Lafayette Street offered a series of happenings presented by the artists Claes Oldenburg and Robert Rauschenberg, among others. In Oldenburg's effort at audience-performer role reversal, the performers (including the artist's wife) became the audience to a group of bemused spectators whose reactions guided the direction of the piece. In film, passive viewings were replaced by active performances that trumpeted immediacy and uncertainty at each showing. Experimental filmmakers Barbara Rubin and Andy Warhol utilized technologies such as multiple screens, slides, and projectors, and integrated other media, such as sculpture, music, and lighting to create a total experience that varied each night.

The incursion of hippie culture transformed many of the meeting places and performance venues of the earlier immigrants. Second Avenue, the former Jewish Broadway, was modified as the showplace for rock and roll music. The Grateful Dead, Santana, and The Who were among the many musical acts who performed at the Fillmore East on Second Avenue. Andy Warhol sublet the Polish National Social Hall (atop the Dom) on St. Mark's Place and opened the Electric Circus. As Warhol wrote in 1980, the East Village provided the optimal environment for experimentation:

> Of course we had no idea if people would come all the way down to St. Mark's Place for night life. All the downtown action had always been in the West Village — the East Village was Babushkaville. But by renting the Dom ourselves, we didn't have to worry about whether "management" liked us or not, we could just do whatever we wanted to.[27]

Under Warhol's guidance, the Dom featured the Velvet Underground (with Nico) as its "house band" and was the stage for his "total environment" show *The Exploding Plastic Inevitable*.[28] The Astor Place Playhouse on Lafayette Street hosted local bands, such as the Fugs, and dance performances. Several ethnic working-class bars became favored drinking spots for the newcomers. The most popular were the Dom and Old Reliable on East Third Street. Hippies commingled with old-timers at the Annex (Tenth Street and Avenue B), and Stanley's (Twelfth Street and Avenue B) was the favored spot for artists, writers, and actors. The bars provided a "convivial social milieu"[29] for the unconventional ways of the youthful counterculture; interracial couples, for example, were welcomed without incident. St. Mark's Place from Astor Place to Tompkins Square Park emerged as the area's commercial main street or "New Bohemia's Madison Avenue,"[30] as recounted by one habitué:

> Here I am, man, getting out of the subway on the Lower East Side, man, climbing the steps, hitting the street once again, man, at Cooper Union and St. Mark's Place, back to my people, man. Feel the filth and dust, man, blowing into my eyes and the stench of piss and shit and vomit and old beer cans, man, up my nose. We're back man, where we belong. St. Mark's Place, man, with one headshop after another, man, where I will SELL A FEW FANS! Go into this weird psychedelic emporium, man, with rotating lights give me a headache and incense make my eyes water, how wonderful, man. Over to the counter, man, where the manager is sitting in a high silk hat.[31]

Between 1964 and 1968, dozens of specialty shops that catered to the hippies had opened along St. Mark's Place.[32] In 1967, a group of merchants inundated by the swarm of shoppers and onlookers proposed blocking the street from vehicular traffic at night to create an outdoor mall.[33]

Poster and bead shops, clothing stores, and drug emporia provided all the necessary lifestyle accoutrements. The Limbo was a fashion shop that catered to the androgynous look. The Diggers, a hippie subgroup that "specialized in giving things away,"[34] ran a used furniture store in the neighborhood. The Something and Psychedelicatessen were two popular eateries that catered to the hippie crowd. A proliferation of specialty, politically affiliated, and secondhand bookstores and underground movie houses provided an intellectual component to the area's rapid commercialization.

Experimental theater, once centered on the west side, matured in the East Village in the mid-1960s. Off-off Broadway theater originated in Greenwich Village in the late 1950s with the establishment of Caffe Cino, a performance space on Cornelia Street.[35] By 1964, however, most new theaters were opening on the east side. Formed in critical response to the commercialism and self-censorship of traditional Broadway theater, off-off Broadway venues were small and purposefully obscure and their theatrical styles intentionally defiant against excessive and staid professionalism.[36] The East Village shaped the identity of experimental theater and vice versa. The area's marginal reputation, snubbed by the average Broadway theatergoer, provided a suitable environment for the new and the untried. Physical, and more importantly, symbolic distance from Broadway allowed the new theater to "resist the natural escalating tendencies of theater."[37] Troupes rented spaces in church basements and coffeehouses nestled in old tenement apartment houses. Theater Genesis was founded in the church community space at St. Mark's-in-the-Bouwerie at Second Avenue and Tenth Street. Theater 62 on East Fourth Street and the Far East on East Second Street survived briefly on audience donations.[38] The most famous of avant-garde theaters, Cafe La Mama E.T.C. (Experimental Theater Club), opened at 321 East Ninth Street[39] but later relocated (due to licensing and building code problems) three times before settling in 1969 at its current address at 74A East Fourth Street. Cafe La Mama was popular among students, artists, and writers, and it attracted the occasional uptown professional.[40] Its founder, Ellen Stewart, who seldom read scripts and chose writers "more or less by hunch and intuition,"[41] provided support and a space for a new genre of experimental theater to emerge. Devoid of any censorship or pressures of commercialism, performances embraced the conventionally taboo issues, such as homosexuality, and presented the stories of marginal, underworld characters—pimps, prostitutes, and drug dealers. La Mama's influence on theater was notable, as reflected in scenes in the film *Midnight Cowboy*,[42] and the improvisational form employed in the Broadway musical *Hair*.[43]

As the neighborhood's hippie reputation developed, a variety of ideological and political countercultures gravitated to the East Village. A range of different approaches to and convictions about social issues, including drugs, sex, religion, and philosophy, among many others, were reflected in locally produced music, performance, poetry, and writing. Ed Sanders, a key figure in local politics and arts, formed the Fugs, a band that wrote songs about dirty old men, orgies, promiscuous sex, LSD, and the CIA, as well as the East Village "scene." Drug use, in particular, formed the (sometimes spiritual) basis of many cultural practices. The central spine of the East Village, St. Mark's Place, was also the place to "cop drugs" such as methamphetamine, marijuana, LSD, and mescaline (the distribution of heroin [not a popular drug among hippies] remained controlled by Puerto Rican dealers farther east). The Keristans espoused their soul-searching utopianist philosophy (favored at one time by Ginsberg) at the City Living Center on East Tenth Street, which also functioned as a hangout for the area's growing number of runaway teenagers.[44]

Issues important to hippie culture found expression not in mainstream press but in local papers that emerged in the mid-1960s. Sanders, who also made films such as *Amphetamine Head* (which authorities considered pornographic), published a local entertainment and arts newsletter in which Fugs lyrics were often reproduced. The local pamphlet *Despair* produced an issue of "poems to come down by" in July 1964. Other homemade mimeos and pamphlets with such titles as *C Magazine*, *Clothesline*, *Elephant*, and the *Marijuana Newsletter* featured lyrics and poems as well as editorials on various political issues, such as legalization of drugs.[45] The Communication Company mass produced a daily list of East Village events, including demonstrations, "be-ins," and "be-outs."[46] The newspaper the *East Village Other* began publishing in October 1965 with a mandate to cover what the editors considered to be a new social and cultural phenomenon taking shape in the East Village.[47] In short, by 1966 the hippie movement had invented a highly varied and complex countercultural community, imbuing dilapidated tenements, storefronts, streets, and parks with new meanings. Hardly taciturn, the

East Village hippie community relished highly symbolic sights and sounds that communicated the possibilities of alternative lifestyles to both believers and skeptics alike. Given the high visibility of this endeavor, the popularization of the East Village was swift and complete.

Changing Representations of the East Village

The influx of middle-class youth and the accompanying changes in the built environment drew increasing local and national media attention. Consequently, by 1966 the area once characterized as a working-class ethnic ghetto was reputed to be the center of the hippie avant-garde on the East Coast. But unlike the beats' or the earlier bohemians', that reputation did not circulate only among an elite set of devotees or a slightly larger set of curious onlookers or sympathizers. Awareness of the hippie phenomenon had reached international proportions, and national magazines, such as *Time* and *Newsweek,* were devoting pages of coverage to the movement and its capitals Haight-Ashbury and the East Village. Such attention was inevitable and unsurprising given that the primary cultural forms that articulated the hippie's critique of mainstream society were saturated with flamboyant images, flowery speech, and provocative symbolism. The immediacy of the general public's awareness of hippie culture was also attributable to technological advancements in the dissemination (and commodification) of information. The hippies were perhaps the first thoroughly modern countercultural movement. Public spectacles, such as sit-ins and demonstrations, played well for the cameras, which brought these images into the living rooms of the suburban white middle class. Technology helped circulate both countercultural practices—such as styles of music, dress, and language—and related values that questioned or outright challenged authority structures from parents to governments. Radio broadcasted the music of the counterculture, and suburban shopping malls sold the records, the clothes, and accessories to complete the hippie style. If the growing popularity of the counterculture shocked or offended a bourgeoisie that had produced suburbs, country clubs, and the Vietnam War, the hippies were keen to oblige. Importantly, such notoriety transformed the representation of (part of) the Lower East Side and, ultimately, the hippie movement itself.

For many white, middle-class adolescents and young adults, the hippie alternative to the suburban lifestyle was alluring. The pervasiveness of secondhand familiarity with hippie culture outside the East and West Coast bohemian enclaves was driven by extensive and sometimes favorable media coverage in the mid-1960s. Articles in *Newsweek, Esquire, Look,* and *Life* magazines portrayed the hippies as "mystical" and "ethereal" and presented auspicious accounts of the East Village community. Rather than being portrayed as dysfunctional dropouts or alienated and misguided youth, hippies were characterized as "generally thoughtful Americans [who were] unable to reconcile themselves to state values and implicit contradictions of contemporary Western society, and have become internal emigres."[48] Other accounts played up the hippies' communal aspects and applauded the movement as a much needed source of introspection of Western values. In 1967, the *New York Times Magazine* featured "The Intelligent Square's Guide to Hippieland," which claimed the hippie movement was "neither subversive nor violent" but "an improvement over...the destructiveness of some of the beatniks, beats and hipsters." The article posited over a half dozen hippie principles regarding, among others, property, religion, sex, and politics that were well worth considering by the "establishment."[49] In sum, hippies were presented as naively innocent, their culture appeared somewhat innocuous, and the movement was a phenomenon in which everyone (i.e., middle classes in general) was invited to partake. One particular feature, rampant drug use, never played well in the middle-class attempt to sugarcoat or co-opt dissident hippie culture. That added "mild amount of danger," however, was a strong allure to a rebellious middle-class youth.[50]

As the symbols and images associated with the hippie movement permeated middle-class suburban hamlets, young adults sought out the means of expressing their growing interest in the counterculture. The East Village (and Haight-Ashbury) loomed as places to participate in and fully experience the hippie counterculture. Suburban devotees made pilgrimages to *the site* of cultural expression, and in 1966–67, the East Village was overwhelmed by those seeking to live out some notion of a "hippie lifestyle." Thousands of newcomers—mostly white, middle-class, well-educated men and women in their late teens and twenties—descended on the neighborhood, transforming unrenovated tenement rooms into "pads" for drug parties and "love-ins." During the months of May and June 1967, it was estimated that two thousand hippies moved into the tenements adjacent to Tompkins Square Park.[51] The youthful infatuation with the East Village/hippie identity increased the demand for local commercial and residential rentals. Shops and restaurants that predated 1964 benefited from the incursion of newcomers, as hippies were touted as "the best customers they've had in years."[52] Individual property owners and real estate companies were quick to capitalize on the hippie's cultural presence as a basis for increased profits. Real estate advertisements touted the location of apartments in the city's newest district. The name East Village was used to represent the area's distinctiveness from the dowdier West Village and the stale Old World flavor of the rest of the noncolonized Lower East Side. "Behind a cloud of marijuana smoke, a new dawn is breaking on the Lower East Side."[53]

As St. Mark's Place and Third Avenue emerged as the crossroads of the hippie phenomenon, the intersection anchored the subsequent renewal that spread along the tenements and storefronts of adjacent streets and avenues. The fury of the real estate market boom was intense but brief. Anticipated demand triggered a wave of real estate speculation centered in the western blocks of the East Village that lasted between 1966 and 1967. Property foreclosure rates at that time dropped, and the number of sales transactions increased.[54] The novelty of the hippie phenomenon kept apartments and storefronts leased and rent levels increased. Rents for apartments adjacent to St. Mark's Place doubled, in part due to new leases from frequent turnover as new hippies replaced those who left.[55] In addition to students and hippies, the neighborhood's countercultural atmosphere attracted copywriters, editorial workers, fashion designers, and commercial artists, among others. At the peak of "hip affluence,"[56] the resurgence of the property market made inroads into the eastern district's primarily Latino neighborhood east of Avenue A:

> On East 7th Street, between C and D, where garbage lines the gutter and most of the residents are on welfare, there are three buildings in the middle of the block that have been recently painted and remodeled.... The windows are sparkling clean and hung with bright colored burlap curtains. Two brand new BMW motorcycles stand at the curb, along with three foreign make sports cars.[57]

Demand renewed real estate interest in the area, but it did not spark the levels of capital investment required to sustain a major rehabilitation of the area's aged housing units. Because demand for housing and commercial space was predicated solely on the East Village's prominence within the hippie movement, the revival of the local property market was susceptible to the inevitable drift in and the vicissitudes of the counterculture. Particularly, the increased mainstream commercialization of hippie culture not only weakened its defiance as a movement (and, therefore, its allure), it made pilgrimage destinations like the East Village and Haight-Ashbury unnecessary. Simultaneously, fractures in the hippies' relationships with fellow Lower East Siders and within the alternative community they had created began to be exposed.

Outsiders/Insiders: Class, Ethnic and Racial Differences and Tensions

"No matter how much the hippies beg for dimes and quarters from obvious non-hippies on avenues B, A, and First, in Tompkins Square Park, on St. Mark's Place, and on Seventh Street, that bright middle class glitter in their eyes and the underneath glow in the personalities speak of a security these natives can never know."
Quoted in Ronald Sukenick, *Down and In: Life in the Underground*

For enthusiastic landlords and developers along with the mainstream media, the hippie colonization appeared as salvation for what was considered an ill-fated, impoverished neighborhood. Hippies "breathed new life" into the ghetto and, ironically, offered some hope to the stalled notion of middle-class revival. Although the youthful movement criticized middle-class values and lifestyles, its members, nonetheless, were of largely middle-class origin living in one of the poorest working-class districts in the city. Interestingly, local and national magazine and newspaper articles reported the hippie's urban colonies as having a calming effect on otherwise dangerous neighborhoods. "In *their* own sections of cities there is little serious crime or prostitution."[58] The hippies, it seemed, were able to accomplish what private developers, urban planners, and state and local governmental agencies could not: to establish a footing in the redevelopment of the Lower East Side. Briefly and in varying degrees, the real estate industry, city agencies, and local boosters anticipated that the hippies' urban sanctuary would pave the way for subsequent and lasting urban redevelopment.[59]

Quite expectedly, the hippies viewed their presence on the Lower East Side as a positive reinforcement of the neighborhood's historic identity of diversity and radicalism. Since their cultural practices were public and inclusive, hippies had directly engaged the urban environment and, albeit naively, the older ethnic and minority communities who had called the Lower East Side home. As stated earlier, "be-ins," "be-outs," demonstrations, and hanging out on street corners and parks brought hippies in direct contact with the older, established communities. Since hippies viewed their lifestyles and their mandate(s) as parallel to those of the elderly, the poor, and the immigrant locals, such contact was viewed as unproblematic. As in previous avant-garde movements, many white, middle-class, and privileged hippies identified with the Lower East Siders, whose lives and experiences they interpreted as authentic expressions of resistance to bourgeois society. "People are here in the East Village," stated a writer in the *East Village Other* in 1967, "because they could no longer make it in Harlem or Poland or Russia or Suburbia or Puerto Rico or what have you."[60] Hippies chose to insert themselves in the multi-ethnic/racial Lower East Side, which in the 1960s offered a stark contrast to the bland, pristine suburbs. Such a positive gesture was applauded even by the occasional critic. "At a time when racial antagonisms erupt on the street," wrote a reporter in the *New York Times* in 1967, "these boys and girls appear relaxedly integrated. The problems of poverty and the ghetto — together with those of leisure — are no problems to the hippies who embrace all three."[61] Hippie culture coexisted and often participated in the artistic endeavors of the black artists and intellectuals who also formed communities on the Lower East Side — "a kind of Harlem Renaissance downtown"[62] — in the late 1950s and early 1960s. The Umbra Workshop, which included authors Askia Muhammad Toure, Ishmael Reed, and many others, proved an important vehicle for black writers. Black musicians Archie Shepp and Marion Brown were central figures in the local music scene.[63]

Despite the "Gentle People's"[64] platitudes of inclusiveness and identification with the Lower East Side locals, differences between the old-timers and newcomers were apparent. The middle-class bohemian East Village identity was positioned awkwardly vis-à-vis the identity of the working-class and ethnic Lower East Side. Tensions among resident groups within the fourteen-block area were common. By 1965, Latino residents maintained the strongest cultural presence in the area east of Avenue A, while white ethnics sustained their communities west of the park. Hippies' apartments were spread throughout the neighborhood, but their settlements were mostly clustered along St. Mark's Place, which ends at Tompkins Square Park. The park was the central public space for the neighborhood's various social groups to meet. Hippies, white ethnics, and Latinos each laid claim to sections of the park to socialize among themselves, recreate, or simply take in the view. Thus, the geography of the park's use ("turf") was a microcosm of the neighborhood that clearly signified the social and cultural distance between the three dominant groups:

> In the southeast corner, old men wearing hats were earnestly playing cards on the stone chess tables while their womenfolk sat on the benches nearby, gossiping in Slavic tongues. In the southwest corner, small children from the Riis Houses on Avenue D were playing under the eyes of their mothers. In the northeast corner, Negro and white youngsters were playing basketball. In the northwest corner, it was baseball in Spanish. . . . the hippie territory appeared to be well defined yesterday — the concrete bandstand and the two grassy areas near it.[65]

The notion of forging a new, alternative community was, in itself, somewhat patronizing to those who had sought to maintain community amidst poverty and neglect on the Lower East Side. Latinos and the elderly sometimes appeared disparagingly in the many venues of hippie entertainment and performance. John Duffy's poems in the collection *Down Worn Forgotten Streets,* for example, conveyed an uncritically positive sense of urban renewal as hippies brought the sounds of harmonicas, tambourines, and bongos to once desolate and unused streets.[66] One of the more popular hippie vocalists went by the name "Sheila the Slum Goddess." Describing the neighborhood's revitalization, one local author wrote, "It is already on the verge of ceasing to be a slum without the bulldozing away of the indigenous population."[67] In a more obvious sense, the hippies' class status and residential choice firmly distanced them from most other residents. It was these factors (rather than the hippie's unconventional beliefs or appearances) that defined how both minorities and older white ethnics viewed the newcomers. Since hippies were by and large the first wave of newcomers to willfully settle on the Lower East Side, many locals viewed their presence suspiciously. Puerto Rican residents, who struggled against deteriorating employment and housing conditions, were the least conciliatory toward those who had given up middle-class privilege, status, and economic security for voluntary poverty. The hippie reaction was one of naïveté, as one participant noted:

> The neighborhood was for a while the model of the American melting pot, polyglot with Poles, Jews, Ukrainians, Blacks, White Russians,

Italians and us, all willing to live and let live with, even, a certain amount of neighborliness. I was always surprised when the Blacks from my building, with whom I often lounged on the stoop, would nod tensely at a passing patrol car with the phrase, "here come Whitey." Or when some other ethnic neighbor would be picked up in Tompkins Square Park for drug peddling or rolling someone like me.[68]

Attacks on hippies mounted by Latinos punctuated the four years hippies colonized the Lower East Side. In the evening following the Memorial Day police clash with hippies in Tompkins Square Park, for example, a crowd of Puerto Ricans and Blacks assaulted a group of hippies in the park.[69] The attack brought to the fore simmering antagonism toward the newcomers and was, in part, retribution for the increased and unwanted police presence in the community following the Memorial Day riot.[70] At the height of the influx, more and more hippies were becoming neighbors of Latinos residing on Avenues A, B, and C. The reaction to middle-class newcomers was often hostile, and hippies complained of verbal and physical assaults. "The hippies really bug us," a black resident told the New York Times, "because we know they can come down here and play their games for awhile and then escape. And we can't, man."[71] Conversely, conscious efforts were made among residents to bridge the neighborhood's social and cultural divide. Following the attack on the hippies in Tompkins Square, "a group of neighborhood residents, representing Negro, Puerto Rican, Slav, and hippie factions, patrolled the park wearing white armbands."[72] The older white ethnics generally disliked the hippie newcomers as well. Strong proponents of civic law and order, they bristled at public displays that openly challenged authority. The prevailing attitude was that hippies were spoiled and ungrateful. By choosing to "act" poor, they had mocked and (temporarily) rejected the middle-class respectability and lifestyle that many of the residents yearned to achieve some part of.[73] In newspaper and magazine accounts of the rise of the East Village, Ukrainians, Jews, and Italians who were interviewed disapproved of the latest changes and longed for the relative quiet of their former neighborhood.[74] They tended to ignore the hippies as best they could—the streets and avenues belonged to the hippies by night and to the Ukrainian, Italian, and Jewish merchants and shoppers by day—but there were occasional incidents. The New York Times reported an episode in which a group of New York University students "with unconventional hair styles or clothes" were allegedly accosted by "blond youths with broad Slavic faces."[75] Such hostilities betrayed the degree to which the identity of the East Village was viewed as exclusively hippie (despite the hippies' best intentions). The character of the "East Village" and representations of it corresponded little with the social and cultural lives of most white ethnics, Latinos, and Blacks, for whom the area's identity remained expressly "Lower East Side." Contiguous with the much touted hippie urban renewal, the downward slide in social and economic conditions for the majority of residents continued unabated as did local resistance to such problems. Employment opportunities diminished, and labor conditions worsened for the bulk of Latino workers. The 1960s saw rising heroin use and a consequent increase in street crime.

The Death of Hippie: Real and Symbolic

> Suddenly I am aware that the East Village is being invaded by straight people who want to be hip, and who impose on it their conception of what they think the underground is like, gathered from sources such as *Time* magazine.
>
> Ronald Sukenick, *Down and In: Life in the Underground*

Neither the hippies' idyllism nor their sociospatial community on the Lower East Side lasted very long — a mere four years. Tourism and commercialization of the counterculture were the underlying reasons for the area's decline. A highly publicized sensational tragedy in the summer of 1967 assured, however, that negative stereotypes, images, and rhetoric would characterize the dissolution of the neighborhood's hippie identity.

As mentioned, thousands of young people flocked to the East Village to witness the public spectacle of hippie culture during the summers of 1966 and 1967 and on weekends throughout each year.[76] The presence of thrill seekers and curious gawkers, drawn to the "bizarre" and the unconventional, and teenage runaways from the tonier suburbs of Long Island and Connecticut began to overwhelm and redefine hippie culture — to the dismay of many seasoned hippies. In Long Island suburbs, for example, it became fashionable for well-to-do parents to place their teens in therapy and counseling in hopes of suppressing any desires to run away to the hippie mecca.[77] Worried parents of runaways cruised the streets in the East Village, searching for their teenage sons and daughters and posting "missing" flyers and photos on makeshift bulletin boards along St. Mark's Place. In 1966, police department officials estimated that eleven thousand persons were reported missing in the city and that 85 percent of these were under eighteen years old.[78] Locally, the influx took on near crisis proportions. Informal "crash pads," more organized drop-in shelters, and a teenage runaway switchboard sprung up to handle the demographic explosion. The offices of the *East Village Other* served as an information clearinghouse to assist runaways with shelter, food, transportation, or a telephone call home. Many older hippies and original "settlers" bemoaned the influx of neophytes into *their* heretofore unobtrusive (yet highly visible) community. Runaways were escaping *from* the suburbs and arrived in the East Village expecting the hippie community to welcome them (as media accounts said it would) or to provide some form of solace when uncertainty overcame initial enchantment. Without means to support themselves, many returned home or turned to begging or petty thievery especially along St. Mark's Place and Second and Third Avenues. In addition to teenage runaways, the East Village was inundated with tourists. The curious onlookers were drawn to the neighborhood not as participants in hippie culture but as consumers expecting to be entertained. In August 1967, the Diggers sponsored a "be-out" on St. Mark's Place as a demonstration against East Village tourism. Nearly two hundred hippies blocked traffic on the crowded street in protest of commercialization and weekend crowds of the fickle thrill seekers. In true hippie fashion, the protesters formed a circle and chanted Hindu mantras. When crowds of camera-toting tourists formed to watch the spectacle, the hippies returned their voyeuristic gaze through plastic binoculars.[79]

As the counterculture matured and its novelty began to fade, the relevance of the East Village as hippie cultural center was undercut. New "elements," according to contemporary reports, commodified and trivialized the environment of the East Village. Teens, tourists, and "plastic" hippies (those who lived uptown or in suburbs)[80] pandered to the overtly commercial aspects of the East Village. Boutiques along St. Mark's began to cater more to tourists than to locals, selling the requisite hippie gear at overinflated prices. Indeed, by 1967, an "authentic" hippie lifestyle was no longer limited to the East Village or its West Coast counterpart but was fully purchasable at suburban shopping malls around the country. Along with its increasingly commercial image, the neighborhood took on a more cynical and less hospitable feeling. Many "weekenders" or "part-timers" were drawn to the area's reputation for easy access to drugs, which fostered the neighborhood's more insalubrious features. As the drug of choice shifted from LSD and marijuana to methedrine or "speed," halcyon or carefree attitudes were replaced with the harsh edginess of desperation and withdrawal. Responding to complaints from older Lower East Siders, the local police staged crackdowns on open drug distribution and consumption, pushing such activities further underground and encouraging criminality. In 1967, narcotics arrests by the local police precinct increased 28 percent, and felony narcotics arrests, 51 percent. Rumors and tales of bad LSD/acid trips, aggressive panhandling, frequent street muggings, robberies, and worsening racial tensions between local minority youth and hippies painted a darker side of "Hippieland."[81] Although these social problems were not new to the East Village, they were represented as new and threatening once the idealism of the hippie movement began to wane.

Liabilities notwithstanding, the East Village hippie community continued to flourish in the summer of 1967 as thousands of revelers turned streets and avenues into a massive public venue of youthful expression. By the fall, however, critical events highlighted the community's underlying faults that would soon mark the end of the East Village's hippie identity. On October 6, 1967, dozens of mourners gathered in the panhandle of Golden Gate Park in San Francisco to mark the death of Hippie, an imaginary character killed off by overexposure and rampant commercialism. A broadside distributed at the event stated, "H/Ashbury was portioned to us by Media-Police and the tourists came to the Zoo to see the captive animals and we growled fiercely behind the bars we accepted and now we are no longer hippies and never were."[82] The mock funeral celebrated not the end of hippie ideals and beliefs but the commercialism of the culture's core site, the Haight-Ashbury. Two days later death would also mark the beginning of the demise of the East Village enclave when a hippie couple were found murdered in the basement boiler room of a tenement building at 169 Avenue B. The murders were a watershed event. The victim's profiles were representative of many East Villagers, and the highly publicized details and circumstances of their deaths described a sinister place of danger and fear. One victim, Linda Fitzpatrick, an eighteen-year-old daughter of affluent suburban Connecticut parents, had fled the suburbs for the life of an East Village "flower child."[83] The other victim, James Hutchinson, age twenty-one, was a locally renowned hippie known as Groovy who was an alleged small-time dealer of marijuana, methedrine, and LSD.[84] Groovy was reputed among the St. Mark's crowd for his generosity, often giving away drugs to friends and associates.[85] The accused killers were two black men—a hippie and an "unemployed black nationalist"—who were also accused of raping Fitzpatrick.[86] Within a few days of the Fitzpatrick-Hutchinson murders, thousands of alarmed parents registered concerns for their children's safety with local police or took to the streets of the East Village looking for their lost sons and daughters.[87]

Following the murders, the representations that had characterized the East Village as liberated from the ghetto of the Lower East Side were quickly discarded. They were replaced by a discourse of urban decline. Fueled by dozens of articles and reports in the *Village Voice, Newsweek, Time,* the *Daily News,* and the *New York Times,* news of the murders evinced a nearly instantaneous reversal of the lionized identity of the East Village: youthful innocence became reckless naïveté, and racial harmony became racial fear. As a reporter wrote, there was a "sudden realization" that the East Village was a slum.[88] Coverage of the tragedy propagated images of unsuspecting and inexperienced white suburban youth left to fend for themselves in the predatory ghetto, or as *Newsweek* termed it, "the jungle."[89] The demonization of the East Village also unleashed a barrage of attacks against the hippie lifestyle—"Trouble in Hippieland" and "Love Is Dead" to cite a few article headlines. The summer of love had "chilled into a violent harvest."[90] Often, diatribes against hippie culture and the East Village were one and the same. A fifteen-year-old girl from Queens wrote the *New York Times* confessing that prior to learning of Fitzpatrick's death, she admired and emulated the hippies as best she could under her parents' watchful gaze: "I dreamed of living in the Village with people who I liked and who wouldn't care what you did or how you dressed, or how you looked. I could do whatever I wanted and nobody would ever mind or care." The murders had compelled her to reconsider. She wrote, "How I want to accomplish something and be something in life. And I thought how the Village would ruin it all." A mother in Fort Lee, New Jersey, warned other parents of the "problem presented by certain sections of the East Village" and voiced the opinion that "such gathering places in Tompkins Square Park and a few other places in the East Village along with certain cafes and residential abodes must disappear."[91]

Both critics and supporters of hippies (and many hippies themselves) questioned the wisdom of middle-class white youths carving out an alternative space in a multiethnic, poor ghetto. That the question was posed following the murder of an affluent white suburban woman by poor black inner-city males during an era of urban riots across the United States provides strong evidence of the important connection between space, race, and class in the representation of neighborhood. Following the East Village murders, reports circulated that Blacks and Puerto Rican young males had long *encroached* on the East Village to commit crimes against hippies (the reference to minorities as outsiders is itself telling).[92] Sentiments changed to "There's no love here anymore. Everyone is scared to death."[93] The poverty, violence, and danger of the minority ghetto reemerged in dominant representations of a threatening and marginal space. Prophetically, the majority of East Village hippies chose the course taken by hundreds of thousands of earlier residents and departed the neighborhood en masse. By 1969, the spatial core of hippie culture was no longer the city but the countryside as hippie communities and communes popped up across upstate New York and Vermont and, on the West Coast, in northern California, Oregon, and Washington. "We were like busloads of tourists from Scarsdale [an affluent New York Suburb]," commented a former East Villager, "It couldn't have worked. The neighborhood was built as a slum—and that's what it still is."[94]

Both the mainstream commercialism of hippie culture and the near hysteria in the aftermath of the 1967 murders clearly illustrate the influence of symbolic representations of place on political economic changes in the disposition of urban space. As the hippie counterculture became tightly associated with the space of the East Village, property owners acted on that association in speculative ventures and limited redevelopment. The brief real estate revival of 1965–68 rested solely on the hippie place identity and representations of it. Consequently, as these were transformed, so too was the capacity of local property owners to accumulate profits from demand for housing and commercial space. The murders represented a breaking point that signaled the end of the briefly profitable juncture of counterculture and neighborhood. Rampant commercialism also proved fatal to the continuation of a renewed hippie East Village on two counts. First, the most zealous hippies, who viewed commerce and tourism as trivializing the movement's ideals, were quickly disenchanted with the East Village "experiment" and moved elsewhere. Second, the ease of obtaining countercultural commodities in smaller cities and in suburbs eliminated the East Village's competitive spatial advantage as *distinctively* hippie. As a specialized site of hippie expression in an era suffused with hippie images and commodities, the East Village identity became redundant.

In the height of the fury over hippie urban renewal, representations of minority and white ethnic communities were largely swept aside. After 1968, however, they reappeared in popular discourse in more ominous and uneasy tones, framed by the vast decline in social and economic conditions that plagued inner cities across the United States. The summer of 1967 had marked the apogee of the hippie East Village, but in 1968 the relatively peaceful era was replaced by sweeping social unrest. Police narcotic raids on East Village establishments and residences were met by violent opposition from local youths. The Yippies (Youth International Party) offered organized resistance to the police crackdown; the group's leader, Jerry Rubin, who was arrested for drug charges in June, claimed the arrests were a political effort to wear down the Yippies as they planned for social protests at the Democratic National Convention in Chicago.[95] Yippies organized a "spring be-in" at Grand Central Station in March attended by three thousand participants. The event turned violent as Yippies allegedly "went on a rampage" destroying property and confronting police. Organizers contended the violence was in reprisal for the drug raids on East Village apartments.[96]

Well-publicized incidents confirmed the fears of many shop owners, landlords, and tenement dwellers that the neighborhood's decline was again inescapable. As hippies departed the East Village, one by one the landmarks of the counterculture disappeared from the landscape and were not replaced immediately by any new uses. Andy Warhol's Electric Circus closed in 1971, as did the Fillmore East after a final concert featuring Frank Zappa, John Lennon, and Yoko Ono.[97] Storefronts along St. Mark's Place and Second and Third Avenues were vacated, and the increasingly empty streets took on a much seedier character. According to an owner of an East Village "head shop" and bookstore, "People are noticing the junkies in the area now, but they've always been here; it's just in the absence of the suburban trendie they've become more visible."[98]

Very little mention was made of owners' abandonment of housing in the immediate post-hippie discourse. Indeed, housing abandonment was seen as a consequence, not a cause, of the community's decline. For outsiders, the East Village no longer appeared immune to the ravages that were occurring in inner cities across the country. Hippies were originally drawn to the diversity of the Lower East Side but, within a few years, departed on the same basis. For Lorenzo Thomas, a participant in the East Village scene, "The fact that this atmosphere changed in the middle of the decade has, perhaps, more to do with the realities of the nation at that time than with any failure of heart among the practitioners of the avant-garde."[99] The ensuing notions of the East Village fraught with images of danger and decay were central to the policies and actions that led to neighborhood disinvestment and "blowout" between 1969 and 1979.

CHAPTER SIX

Urban Malaise, Community Abandonment, and Underground Subcultures of Decay

The representational themes of chaos, danger, and decay that resurfaced in the early 1970s were not identified exclusively with the East Village or the Lower East Side. In the aftermath of urban unrest in the late 1960s and the accompanying accelerated exodus of the white middle class to the suburbs, cities in general were increasingly vilified in media and political circles. Tributes to the thrill and wonder of New York were replaced by the public's preoccupation with the worst aspects of urban living, including crime, congestion, poverty, and alienation. The themes of urban cynicism and inner-city decline resonated in contemporary forms of popular culture. In films, for example, the city as jungle or Sodom was a common motif as were the binaries of good/evil, Whites/ Blacks, and suburb/city. In 1970, actors Jack Lemmon and Sandy Dennis played a very middle-of-the-road midwestern married couple who visit New York City in the comic film *The Out-of-Towners*. Within a short time of their arrival, George and Martha Kellerman are confronted with rude and uncaring city dwellers, pickpockets, muggers, street gangs, and a garbage strike. Their urban experiences leave them sanguine for their dull but peaceful suburban lifestyles. Other popular films of the era depict a less comical and much "darker" image of the city. In *Death-wish* (1974), Charles Bronson plays a New York businessman turned vigilante after a gang of urban thugs killed his wife and raped his daughter. Bronson's enraged character is compelled to seek justice through violence in a chaotic city that has lost the capacity to provide safety for its decreasing numbers of average middle-class citizens.

Symbolic representations of the city in the 1970s not only produced hyperbole about the state of urban affairs but also a powerful discourse of despair that influenced the types of real estate actions and state urban development policies enacted during the decade. The phrase *urban crisis,* frequently mentioned in the 1970s, came to represent middle-class hopelessness and apprehension toward a city perceived to be unsalvageable and filled with impoverished, threatening, and mostly minority residents. *Urban crisis* was not merely a discursive reflection of the white middle-class fears, it offered a cultural means to legitimize and explain the exodus of people and capital from the city and the incapacity of urban policies to deal with the consequences. "Most cities by 1980 will be black and brown, and totally bankrupt," warned the *National Urban Coalition* in 1971.[1] Increased poverty, sectoral unemployment, and other social costs related to the continued transformation of cities' economic bases from manufacturing to services fostered an air of pessimism about future urban prospects. Political intervention seemed unlikely to improve the dire situation. Solutions posed in the 1950s urban renewal programs or in the 1960s antipoverty campaigns were (re)interpreted as either outright failures or ventures whose limited successes were overwhelmed by much larger social and economic problems.

Symbolic representations of urban decline both reflected and facilitated the urban disinvestment and municipal neglect that beset many working-class neighborhoods in New York and similar older cities in the United States. Given the prevailing downward trend of the city's political economy in the 1970s, disinvestment became economically rational for landlords of low-income housing. This chapter reconstructs the decade of neighborhood abandonment and social decline, focusing especially on the streets and avenues east of Avenue A, known as Loisaida ("Spanglish" for Lower East Side), that bore the brunt of real estate disinvestment. While regional and national attention was directed toward the East Village hippie enclave in the 1960s, the area's Puerto Rican residents built the Loisaida community into a viable and vibrant ethnic enclave. Beginning in the early 1970s, many of those who owned properties in Loisaida began to walk away from their buildings, leaving uninhabitable and often burned-out shells that soon transformed the landscape into a haunting and scarred urban war zone. Scores of landlords historically had disinvested tenements during periods of anemic demand, such as the depression,[2] but in the 1970s residential abandonment was so concentrated and intense that it reached epidemic proportions within a few years. The contagion of abandonment proceeded exhaustively in Loisaida, even prompting owners of "healthy" buildings to disinvest and abandon.[3] Within a decade nearly half of Loisaida's residents were displaced.

As this chapter demonstrates, the factors that precipitated real estate disinvestment and municipal neglect were largely economic and political. In addition, it is argued, contemporary explanations and rationalizations of inner-city community abandonment during the 1970s were articulated in mostly cultural forms. Symbolic representations of urban decline, especially in terms of racial, ethnic, and class differences, provided an ideological framework for the escalation of residential abandonment from an isolated and individual occurrence to a neighborhood-wide phenomenon. The devastation of the built environment, its uniformly negative social consequences, and the prevailing discourse about the marginal ghetto also prompted new forms of local collective action and struggle to stabilize the neighborhood and institute tenant controls over the disposition of property. Local housing activists won important gains, but their efforts were largely overshadowed by the pervasiveness of disinvestment and abandonment. Physical abandonment and disparaging place images began to reinforce each other, creating a seemingly intractable stereotype of the ghetto as an oppressive and unredeemable space. Finally, the chapter examines the emergence of another middle-class youth subculture drawn to the landscape of physical and social decline and its problematic role in the ensuing redevelopment of the 1980s.

Building the Loisaida Community in the 1960s

> My memories of the seventies? Good and bad, hot and cold—like my building in summer and winter! [laughter] I miss my friends and family. We would stay up and talk late in the night about home [Puerto Rico] and the city. We knew everyone on the block but that was before. It got bad real fast—the drugs and junkies everywhere. Some left but where can we go? I paid my rent. The fires and the stories about the evictions scared me. We went without heat, hot water for so long! Then they told us to pay our rent to the city and things got no better.

The middle-aged Puerto Rican woman just quoted was responding to a question I asked in an interview referring to the widespread social changes that occurred throughout the Lower East Side in the 1960s and

Figure 15. Avenida del Loisaida — the heart of the Puerto Rican community.
Scene from a festival, 1989. Photograph used by permission of Marlis Momber.

1970s. Her statement suggests a dominant theme of vibrant community
life transformed by economic contraction, cultural adjustment, and political disavowal that marked the turbulent era of housing abandonment.
In the middle to late 1960s, while the media, politicians, and property
owners were inured with an "East Village" rather than a Lower East Side,
notable changes were well under way in the Puerto Rican community
east of Tompkins Square Park. Two decades of migration flows, urban
renewal policies, and a tightening of the city's low-income housing supply fostered the development of a sizable ethnic residential enclave. By
the late 1960s, many of the area's Puerto Rican residents had been born
on the Lower East Side. More so than the generation of migrants that
preceded them, they set out to create viable commercial and residential
spaces that reflected the fusion of island culture and the New York experience. Throughout the 1960s, beauty parlors, laundries, *bodegas,* and
Latino social clubs opened along Avenues C and D. Restaurants and lun-
cheonettes that once served Polish and Russian foods now featured island favorites, such as *cuchifritos* and *comidas criollas.* In summers, the
neighborhood streets and parks bustled with cultural activities. Salsa
music emanated from car radios and open tenement windows. Middle-
aged men peddling *piragueros* ("snow" cones made of shaved ice and

flavored syrups) were strategically positioned on street corners and along the East River Park. Young men worked late in the night in makeshift auto body shops while others played dominos with old-timers on kitchen tables brought outdoors. As prior generations of tenement dwellers had done during summer months, residents preferred to socialize on sidewalks, fire escapes, and rooftops than in their cramped, hot apartments. Other signs of an established community were manifest during the 1960s. Local churches originally founded by European immigrant congregations accommodated the area's burgeoning Latino population. Ethnic organizations flourished, emboldened by the era of civil rights and political mobilization. Puerto Rican participation in neighborhood and tenant associations, such as Pueblo Nuevo and The Real Great Society/ Charas, Inc., peaked in the late 1960s. The Real Great Society, whose agenda included economic empowerment, emerged out of two street gangs, the Lower East Side Dragons and the Assassins, who were centered in the Chelsea neighborhood.[4] Other community-based organizations, such as the Lower East Side Puerto Rican Action Committee, emerged as advocates of rapid and often radical social change.[5] The Puerto Rican version of the Black Panthers—the Young Lords Party (which split with the Chicago-based Young Lords in 1969)—was centered in the Bronx but was active on the Lower East Side and other *barrios* across the city.

The social and political organization of the Puerto Rican community was framed by larger societal struggles for ethnic and racial justice that swept across U.S. cities in the 1960s. Episodes of social unrest were infrequent on the Lower East Side, but community frustrations with unemployment, dire social conditions, and accompanying municipal disregard were vented in the explosive year of 1968. Unrest erupted over several nights in July 1968 as mostly Puerto Rican youths set fire to automobiles, smashed storefront windows, and battled police on the streets east of Avenue B. A firebombing of Jack's Bar and Grill on Avenue C and Ninth Street precipitated the confrontation between locals and members of the Tactical Patrol Force, but the dispute soon centered on the vexation of Puerto Rican residents with adverse social conditions and a history of mistreatment by the local police. The unrest was intensified by a three-day police occupation of the neighborhood leading up to the forcible dispersal of a parade organized by local associations against social and economic grievances. While local community and religious leaders appealed for calm, they also requested that the city address the underlying structural causes of the unrest. Both the Lower East Side Puerto Rican Action Committee and The Real Great Society demanded immediate creation of jobs for local residents, increased park and playground space, and low-income housing to replace deteriorated tenements.[6]

A significant corollary to ethnic-based mobilization and resistance against employment and housing discrimination on the Lower East Side and in other enclaves was the public outpouring and affirmation of Puerto Rican ethnic pride.[7] After several decades of migration, settlement, and struggle, public expressions of ethnic heritage and self-esteem proliferated in the late 1960s and were especially conspicuous at the neighborhood level. In *barrios* throughout the city, street festivals and parades highlighted Puerto Rican cultural history and folklore and the struggle for the island's political and economic independence. Visual and literary mentions of struggles with landlords, achievements against economic discrimination, and efforts to build and sustain community on the Lower East Side were prominent features of the Puerto Rican cultural renaissance. Local *hermandades* (brotherhoods), organized around island hometowns, sponsored street parties, dances, and extravagant neighborhood processions on religious feast days. In the Lower East Side *barrio*, local poets and writers recounted the life left behind on the island, the migration narrative, and the hopes and harsh realities of urban life on the mainland. Poems, music, and other cultural forms almost always made direct reference to the ancestral home, but they also acknowledged a commitment to the Lower East Side as a Puerto Rican community. In 1974, two poets and activists, Chino Garcia and Bimbo Rivas, called their adopted home east of Avenue B Loisaida to signify the area's Puerto Rican heritage and identity.[8] The name has since been retained.

Political mobilization, ethnic awareness, public recognition of Puerto Rican culture as well as demands for social justice by underrepresented groups in general led to citywide institutional changes in the late 1960s, such as bilingual education and political inclusion at the community and city level.[9] Many of these advancements were threatened or rolled back, however, in the face of urban decline in the 1970s. Puerto Rican political militancy and community action on the Lower East Side had little if any effect on deep-rooted regional and structural employment conditions that only worsened throughout the 1970s.[10] Although active just a few years earlier, many of the chief political organizations were co-opted, infiltrated, or simply disbanded.[11] Government-financed neighborhood social programs (job training, housing assistance, etc.) were the first affected by the city's looming fiscal crisis. The most significant adversity, however, came in the actions of landlords, whose choices dramatically altered the social and physical landscape of Loisaida.

The Marginalization of Loisaida in the 1970s

The cultural invention of Loisaida positively asserted and affirmed the Puerto Rican/Latino identity of the area east of Avenue B as distinct from the larger Lower East Side. That identity, however, was largely absent from mainstream representations of the hippie influence on the East Village that had circulated in the media in the mid-1960s. Within such representations, the dominant residents and places in Loisaida were collapsed or subsumed into images and discourse about the East Village. The presence of Puerto Ricans and Latino culture served as "local color" or exotica to embellish the more significant and central focus on white middle-class hippies and their positive effect on urban renewal. In the height of the hippie phenomenon, middle-class youth were applauded for rescuing the neighborhood from its moribund Old World remnant of ethnic and working-class culture.

At the close of the hippie era of urban renewal, representations of Loisaida began to appear that marginalized, rather than celebrated, local differences and reinforced the spatial division between the eastern and western sections of the East Village. Focusing on overcrowding, unemployment, delinquency, and drug sales and addiction, some non-Latino residents, landlords, and commercial interests characterized the Puerto Rican community as a threat to the East Village.[12] In the aftermath of the hippies' decline, the East Village was featured in press accounts and local lore as a community "under siege by teenage hoodlums"[13] and threatened by "rat packs" who roamed "the area in packs of six to eight beating, robbing and heaping abusive language on residents."[14] Images of a changing frontier or "DMZ" (demilitarized zone) between geographies of white and Latino and of safety and danger abounded as muggings and purse snatchings increased in the western blocks.[15] In addition to teenage gangs, social pathologies related to drug abuse were identified as contributing to an atmosphere of decline. Although the supply of heroin and methamphetamine was centered east of Tompkins Square Park, addictions impelled petty thefts, shoplifting, burglaries, and similar crimes farther west.

Government-sponsored assessments of living conditions on the Lower East Side furthered the discourse of inevitable neighborhood decline. A three-year study of land use on the Lower East Side commissioned by the city and completed in 1971 found 50 percent of the housing stock in need of replacement. The report also noted severely limited economic opportunities for the bulk of the area's population and concluded (somewhat belatedly) that the Lower East Side no longer functioned as a "spawning ground for poor people who later achieve economic success."[16] The study, conducted by the consultant firm of Abeles, Schwartz and Associates, was the basis for a planning document that called for considerable state intervention in local development.[17] Within a few years of its publication, however, there was little likelihood of such large-scale intervention because city expenditures were slashed. Census figures from the 1970s officially confirmed the poor socioeconomic conditions of Loisaida's residents. In 1970, the residents of the private apartments within Loisaida were the poorest among all East Villagers. One-third of Loisaida families earned incomes below the official poverty level (compared to 13 percent for all of Manhattan). The household median income was barely half the median household income for Manhattan. In the Wald and Riis public housing, meanwhile, one-fourth of the families existed below the poverty level, and household incomes were significantly higher than those in adjacent private housing (nearly two-thirds the median for Manhattan). Educational levels were low across the board; the eastern blocks had one of the highest high school dropout rates in the city. Reflecting the large number of new, young families, these same blocks contained the neighborhood's highest percentage of persons under eighteen years old. Loisaida also suffered the greatest unemployment and incidence of juvenile delinquency. While the larger district west of Avenue A fared better in all social indicators, rent levels there remained stagnant. White ethnics maintained scaled-down versions of the once massive immigrant communities. Slightly over 70 percent of the residents were white, although there were pockets of minority enclaves, such as the area north of Tenth Street between Avenue B and First Avenue (census tract 34 at 37 percent Latino). Compared to the adjoining east, socioeconomic conditions improved considerably. The percentage of families below the poverty level ranged from 28 percent (census tract 34) to less than 10 percent for the blocks along the western perimeter of Fourth Avenue. Household income levels were considerably higher for those residents in the western blocks of the neighborhood, as well. The long tenure of many ethnic residents appears in the census figures; the western area had the highest concentration of persons over sixty-five years old (18 percent in the area south of Tompkins Square Park).[18]

Capital, State, and Perceived Inevitability of Urban Decline

Representations that associated Loisaida with fear and danger and the discouraging socioeconomic conditions of its residents were among several conditions conducive to widespread real estate capital *disinvestment*. The resolution to disinvest and, for many landlords, to abandon their properties in Loisaida and in similar neighborhoods across the city was largely influenced by the prevailing public discourse of urban decline and several other postwar factors mentioned in earlier chapters, including

> financial disinvestment by lending institutions (redlining); tax policies which permit rapid depreciation allowances and capital gains rates, thus encouraging rapid turnover; increased property tax appraisals which penalize improvements; the level and quality of public and commercial services; public policies which produce either overzealous code enforce-ment, or years of nonenforcement; the negative side-effects of public programs in other areas of the city which trigger rapid population turnover in a deteriorating area (e.g. urban renewal relocatees moving in; or neighborhood residents moving out in large numbers to a particular new development); and overall regional and national trends promoting suburbanization and relocation of employment opportunities and economic activity away from the central city.[19]

Most of these factors had been in place since the 1950s, and housing abandonment had long been an option exercised by individual land-lords. But in the 1970s these factors not only intensified, they converged with the *perception* among landlords, tenants, and city agencies that continued disinvestment was inevitable and social and economic con-ditions within the inner city would only worsen. The profitability of other alternatives was severely limited. Selling property to earn income was not a possibility for many owners. Buyers were few, and private-based and government-secured mortgage financing was limited.[20] Without the participation of institutional and governmental lenders, low-income housing areas were also deprived of important access to capital for building improvements.[21] Since rates of abandonment were also correlated with the socioeconomic characteristics of renters, declining confidence in the housing market was, in part, influenced by judgments of the future capacity of tenants to pay existing rents or rent increases.[22]

Through campaigns and appeals to free-market principles circulated in the press and other media, the city's real estate sector directed the attention of an increasingly alarmed public toward the state's role in abetting disinvestment and abandonment. Landlords, real estate organizations, and lobbies effectively exerted pressure on the state to deregulate imposed ceilings on rents as the preferred means to arrest abandonment. Landlords and their representative agencies touted rent control as *the* cause of disinvestment and abandonment since controls prevented rents from keeping pace with rising costs of property upkeep. Landlords on the Lower East Side, where the majority of housing units were rent controlled, were especially zealous in the deregulation crusade. Under increasing political pressure to act, the city undertook reforms in rent-control policy and code enforcement. A study by the policy institution, the Rand Corporation, lent legitimacy to deregulation. The study's findings blamed the rise in the incidence of abandonment on a significant gap between the level of controlled rent and "economic rent" — the level necessary for landlords to maintain their properties.[23] In 1969–70, the city created new laws geared toward milder regulation rather than direct control of private rent levels.[24] The city's intention was to provide an economic incentive to stem the process of landlord withdrawal of building maintenance and upkeep and, ultimately, the volume of property abandonment. For example, to be eligible for the new programs, landlords were required to maintain the upkeep of their buildings (80 percent of a building's code violations were required to be removed).[25] By officially conceding that a link between abandonment and rent regulation existed, however, the city made it easier for real estate lobbyists to argue for the state to repeal rent regulations altogether. In 1971, in the midst of instituting regulation reforms, the New York State legislature passed a decontrol law eliminating rent control and stabilization for newly vacated apartments. Rent regulation was reinstated three years later.[26] These abrupt policy changes and partial victories for the real estate sector ended up having little effect on the pace of abandonment since its causes were far more complex. From the perspective of real estate capitalists, the financial incentives offered through changes in rent regulations were too limited to overcome the insuperable lack of confidence in the long-term viability of older rental housing. That is, as George Sternlieb and James W. Hughes argue in their analysis of the 1970s New York housing market, there was little certainty among landlords that savings accrued through these changes would be greater than the income collected through the more insalubrious method of gradual disinvestment.[27] If the city was at all interested in curbing abandonment, then its strategy, by all accounts, had failed. In addition, evidence of a causal link between regulation and abandonment was weakened by the fact that similar rates of disinvestment were occurring in other cities where rents were not regulated.[28]

Few new city, state, or federal urban pro-development policies were introduced in the 1970s, and those that were enacted did little to allay the fears of housing market decline for owners of low-income housing. Some initiatives knowingly exacerbated disinvestment, while others produced unintentional but nonetheless negative consequences for local communities. When the city and state did design and enact urban development policies, they tended to placate large developers and to maximize revenue (taxes) intake but offered little assistance to individual and small corporate holders of low-income housing. Most of the 1970s, however, was defined by the contraction of the state's role in social welfare and urban affairs. In New York City, the capacity and the willingness of the state to engage the increasingly severe social problems within its poorest neighborhoods declined tremendously during the fiscal crisis of the late 1970s. The effects of municipal contraction were not evenly distributed across all neighborhoods; the city chose to maintain middle-class neighborhoods and "contain" the poorest and predominantly minority communities. At the height of the fiscal crisis in April 1976, for example, New York City Housing and Development Administrator Roger Starr devised a fiscal austerity program of "planned shrinkage." Starr's austere plan advocated that an entire range of city services — from subway stations and road repair to police and fire stations, hospitals, and schools — be reduced or eliminated in marginal blighted neighborhoods. The savings would then be channeled into the provision of services for "viable" — white middle-class — communities.[29] Starr's pronouncements were publicly condemned by governmental officials and in editorials of the mainstream press. Many aspects of "planned shrinkage" were, however, implemented wholesale or piecemeal under the pretense of fiscal emergency. The city withdrew support for infrastructure improvements, cut public services, and slashed housing rehabilitation funds for areas deemed unlikely prospects for real estate capital investment.[30] This "triage" of state resignation from low-income community assistance provided further incentive for landlord disinvestment and housing abandonment.[31] Tenants in areas such as Loisaida were put at greater risk by budget cutbacks in the Emergency Repairs Program, a stopgap measure that made emergency building repairs when landlords defaulted on their maintenance responsibilities. Without the mediating role of state policies, real estate capitalists gained and tenants lost considerable influence over the disposition of urban space.

In other instances when the city attempted to arrest disinvestment and abandonment, the repercussions were typically detrimental. In periodic crackdowns (usually prompted by organized tenant complaints), city agencies levied fines against rogue landlords for such infractions as building code violations. But threats of fines and forced capital improvements unwittingly abetted or hastened landlords' decisions to abandon.[32] In 1977 the city attempted to curtail the scale of housing abandonment through the passage of Local Law 45. The law reduced the length of time landlords could forgo payment of property taxes from three years to one year before they would lose their buildings to the city. The law was intended as a disincentive for abandonment, but its effects were to the contrary. By shortening the time frame of gradual disinvestment, the law's provisions inadvertently sped up the pace and scale of abandonment, and the more deteriorated properties ended up under the city's stewardship (a condition known as in rem).

The Phases of Community Abandonment

Real estate disinvestment emerged as the most viable option for property owners given the more profitable outlets for capital investments (e.g., suburban housing), the anemic inner-city housing market, widespread landlord claims of "negative revenue flows," and ineffectual urban development policies.[33] Abandonment, despite the fact that it furthered the neighborhood's marginal conditions, was a wholly rational form of urban capital accumulation.[34] Gradual disinvestment allowed an owner of "a wasting asset" to "maximize immediate yield, minimize investment, and, perhaps, even in the very act of preparing for the worst,

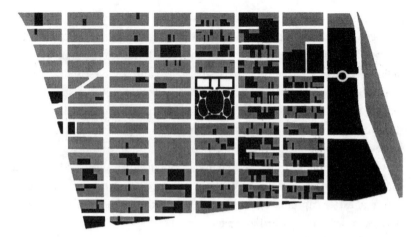

Map 5. Locations of all city-owned properties. Map constructed by Neil Wieloch.
Source: Department of City Planning, New York City, *Atlas of City Properties*,
vol. 3: Manhattan, December 5, 1990.

generate its [abandonment's] fulfillment."[35] The time frame from disinvestment to abandonment consisted of a succession of deliberate actions from a few months to a few years. Each stage of disinvestment
brought revenues in the form of savings that otherwise would have
been expended. Typically, the first expenses withdrawn were capital improvements—those repairs done to offset property depreciation due
to wear-and-tear through age and everyday use, such as new roofing,
replacement windows, or apartment renovations. Eventually, divesting
property owners withdrew a building's operating services, including heat,
hot water, and janitorial services. At the same time landlords reduced
the provision of operating services, they "earned" additional revenues
by not paying fixed costs such as mortgage payments and property taxes.

   The final act of gradual disinvestment taken by many, but certainly
not all, landlords was arson-for-profit. Widely circulated images of fires
and haunting landscapes of burned-out tenements in the South Bronx,
parts of Brooklyn, and the Lower East Side symbolized the inevitability
of decay and social decline of the city in the 1970s. In the months and,
in some cases, years preceding arson, the value of a building's insurance policy was increased to match property values falsely inflated by
arranged sales among relatives, associates, or "dummy corporations."[36]
Revenues were then generated through insurance settlements on loss
of property due to fire. In addition, many Lower East Side tenements

were insured by the Fair Access to Insurance Residuals (FAIR) program, which was instituted to underwrite properties in high-risk neighborhoods.[37] To divert accusations from themselves, insalubrious landlords hired neighborhood drug addicts and petty criminals to harass tenants and set fires.[38] A city-commissioned study of the causes of arson in residential buildings found that the highest incidence of suspicious fires (twenty-five or more per month) occurred within neighborhoods undergoing housing disinvestment and abandonment. The report concluded that arson was endemic to those neighborhoods undergoing significant housing market change.[39]

Disinvestment and abandonment overwhelmed in a cascading fashion the poorest sections of the Lower East Side. Disinvestment actions taken by an individual landlord directly affected a particular building and, indirectly, the disposition of adjacent properties. Thus, buildings in various stages of disinvestment contributed to an environment of decline and the impetus for other landlords to divest their holdings, eventually creating a spatial and temporal momentum that engulfed entire blocks of tenements. When abandoned properties on a block reached a considerable number (a "tipping point"), it was no longer economically rational for landlords of the most viable and occupied, but nonetheless devalued, apartment buildings to resist disinvestment. As buildings and then entire blocks succumbed to abandonment, adjacent property values declined, and more landlords began "milking" their buildings.

The timing and location of abandonment in Loisaida and the East Village were not haphazard but patterned. Differences in the location and timing of disinvestment, by and large, mirrored the east-to-west gradient of socioeconomic conditions: the area containing the oldest and most deteriorated housing and the poorest socioeconomic conditions suffered the most from disinvestment and abandonment. The core of disinvestment was the eastern and southern blocks of Avenues B through D and Second and Eighth Streets. From there, disinvestment and abandonment proceeded north and west. Geographer Neil Smith used local tax arrears data to provide a temporal and spatial map of the disinvestment/reinvestment "frontier" on the Lower East Side.[40] Using city records of tax data, Smith and associates classified the severity of tax arrears by the length of time of delinquency (ranging from three to twelve or more quarters of nonpayment) and correlated their findings with housing vacancies at the census tract level. This method allowed them to pinpoint the timing and location of peak years of disinvestment as well as the beginnings of a subsequent phase of reinvestment. Their analysis of the timing of disinvestment showed 1976 and 1977 as the prime years in the East Village as a whole, but variations occurred when the data were analyzed spatially. Tax arrears peaked in the late 1970s for the far eastern blocks of the neighborhood, while delinquencies in the western sections were less severe and peaked earlier.[41] Smith and associates' findings furnish an empirical picture of the block-by-block westward outflow of urban capital that correlates with the prevailing representations and perceptions of Loisaida as expendable among city policymakers, the real estate industry, and the media.

Given the relatively small area of Loisaida and its proximity to the city's midtown and Wall Street corporate business districts, the pervasiveness of abandonment in Loisaida was striking. The scale of disinvestment was demonstrative of the predominantly negative assessments of older and minority neighborhoods propagated by government, real estate, and media. Although a desperate strategy of profit making, housing abandonment should not be construed as evidence that the real estate industry had desisted in its efforts at middle-class renewal of the East Village. While some property owners were abandoning their tenements, shrewd speculators were buying up buildings at bargain prices. This trend, which we shall encounter later, proved significant to subsequent redevelopment.

The Consequences of Abandonment for Loisaida

Once the process of abandonment began to take hold in a few buildings, entire blocks were often consumed by physical and social destruction. In their retreat from Loisaida, landlords had, in effect, fulfilled the prophecy of devalorization and community decay that many claimed had driven them to disinvest initially. As the pace of abandonment began to drop off at the close of the 1970s, the social and physical effects on Loisaida were made clear.

As the census data presented in Table 1 clearly show, considerable changes in the population and housing makeup of Loisaida occurred during the 1970s as a result of real estate disinvestment and housing abandonment. Almost half of the private apartments east of Avenue B disappeared from the landscape between 1970 and 1980. Many resi-

Figure 16. Loisaida cleared of abandoned tenements. Jacob Riis Public Housing is in the background. Photograph by Christopher Mele.

dents were either directly or indirectly displaced. The population of Loisaida declined 40 percent over the decade compared to a 27 percent drop for the entire East Village and a 7.2 percent decrease for Manhattan. When public and private housing populations are considered separately, the effects of private-market disinvestment become more noticeable: 57 percent of private apartment dwellers were displaced, while public housing experienced a slight decline in tenants (−8 percent). Table 1 also shows dramatic differences in population changes between Latino and non-Latino residents of Loisaida during the 1970s. The Wald and Riis Houses along Avenue D experienced significant ethnic and racial turnover. Latinos comprised half of the residents in 1970 but over two-thirds in 1980, indicative of continued limitations in the supply of affordable low-income private housing for minorities in the city. In the adjacent tenements, ethnic turnover was as discernible. In 1970 the percentage of non-Latinos and Latinos of the area's total population was 58 percent and 42 percent, respectively. Although both populations decreased over the 1970s, their rates of decline differed. By 1980 Loisaida housed fewer Latinos but was proportionately more Latino than it was a decade earlier. Non-Latinos made up 42 percent of Loisaida's tenement population, while Latinos comprised 57 percent. The ethnic com-

Table 1.   The consequences of abandonment for housing and population in
Loisaida east of Avenue B, 1970–80

	1970	1980	1970–80 (% change)
Loisaida housing			
Total private housing units	10,944	5,725	–48%
Loisaida population			
Total population	40,145	24,093	–40%
As a percentage of all East Village	46%	38%	
Total residents living in			
Private housing[a]	26,290	11,283	–57%
Public housing	13,855	12,810	–8%
Loisaida Latinos[b]			
Total	18,031	16,492	–9%
In private housing	11,075	6,536	–41%
As a percentage of all private housing	42%	57%	
In public housing	6,956	9,956	+43%
As a percentage of all public housing	50%	78%	
Loisaida non-Latinos			
Total	22,114	7,601	–66%
In private housing	12,215	4,747	–69%
As a percentage of all private housing	58%	42%	
In public housing	6,899	2,854	–59%
As a percentage of all public housing	50%	22%	

Note: By the late 1950s, the geographic borders of Loisaida were Houston Street north to
Fourteenth Street, and Avenue A east to the East River Park. Unfortunately, census tract
boundaries do not correlate with Loisaida's borders. The data in this table are for the area
between Houston Street to Fourteenth Street and Avenue B and the East River Park.

[a]The term *private housing* intends the area's stock of apartment houses as distinct from
the large-scale Riis and Wald public housing projects. In the course of the 1970s
disinvestment, a significant number of tenements became in rem (city-owned) or tenant-
managed and thus no longer owned or controlled by private landlords.

[b]Due to changes in definitions and undercounting of illegal immigrants, longitudinal
comparisons cannot be exact. In the 1970 census, "Persons of Puerto Rican Birth or
Parentage" included persons born in Puerto Rico and persons born in the United States or
an outlying area with one or both parents born in Puerto Rico. (U.S. Census of Housing and
Population, 1970, Appendix B). In 1980, "Persons of Hispanic Origin" were those who
classified themselves as one of the specific Hispanic origin categories listed on the
questionnaire—"Mexican," "Puerto Rican," or "Cuban"—as well as those who indicated
they were of "other Spanish/Hispanic" origin. Persons of "Other Spanish/Hispanic" origin
were those whose origins were from Spain, the Spanish-speaking countries of Central or
South America, or the Dominican Republic, or they were persons of Hispanic origin
identifying themselves generally as Spanish (U.S. Census of Housing and Population, 1980,
Appendix B).

Source: U.S. Bureau of the Census, 1970 and 1980

parison is significant for understanding the dominant but nonetheless erroneous perception among media, politicians, and the real estate industry that *more* Puerto Ricans had moved into Loisaida. Latinos had increased *only in proportion* to other groups because their rate of population decline was lower than that for non-Latinos. The causes of residential attrition for Latinos and non-Latinos were also different. The reduction of the white population was caused primarily by deaths among the aging ethnic groups and the departure of hippies. For minorities, the most significant cause of population decrease was displacement caused by disinvestment. As the largest ethnic group in the area most affected, Puerto Ricans were forced to leave their homes due to arson or other forms of landlord harassment and victimization. Some fled the deteriorating conditions that inundated the neighborhood for East Harlem and Williamsburg,[42] while others doubled up illegally with friends and families in the public housing projects lining the East River.

In addition to stark demographic declines, the social consequences of disinvestment and abandonment included a considerably diminished quality of life for remaining residents. As abandonment and arson denuded numerous pockets in Loisaida, streets, empty lots, parks, and other public spaces became prone to "other criminally related commerce such as pimping, prostitution, and/or fencing and other rackets."[43] Intimately connected to neighborhood decline was the rise of a robust underground economy of heroin and cocaine sales and consumption that earned Loisaida the reputation as a premier buying site for the New York, New Jersey, and Connecticut region. Drugs moved from the interstices to the center of Loisaida street life as complex forms of distribution and sales thrived in the atmosphere of physical and social decline and severely limited economic alternatives.[44] The social geography of the Lower East Side drug economy varied depending on the type of drugs sold and the class of drug consumers. Enterprises that catered to discrete well-to-do uptown and out-of-town clients involved protected places (apartments, buildings, or occasionally an entire block) maintained by complex networks of old and young men and women acting as doormen, whistlers, appointment takers, and ushers. Drug markets that catered to the casual "off-the street" trade were more numerous but equally well organized. Lines of clients would form on a given corner or in a section of a park at a time of the day set by roaming dealers. Some drug houses required buyers to "show their tracks" to gain entry,

Figure 17. "Shooting Gallery, Abandoned Building." Photograph used by permission of Marlis Momber.

Figure 18. "Drug Buy, Empty Lot, Fourth Street at C and D." Photograph used by permission of Marlis Momber.

while others conducted transactions with baskets lowered and raised from upstairs windows. Liquor stores and *bodegas* fortressed in Plexiglas often sidelined or specialized in the lucrative commerce, selling small bags of cocaine and heroin to "shoppers." Entire blocks, such as East Second and East Seventh Streets between Avenues B and C, operated for years as successful drug emporia, thwarting infrequent crackdowns by law enforcement officials. In addition to distribution spaces, the landscape of the drug economy included well-known sites of consumption. An abundance of empty lots, deserted apartments, or entire buildings provided spaces for makeshift and temporary hangouts or more permanent "shooting galleries" that charged admission (heroin, heroin "works," or cash payments). Often desperate for cash to support drug habits, users or "junkies" pillaged the neighborhood and sold their wares at several improvised street markets off Avenue D. Addicts burgled apartments of goods that could be traded for heroin or cash. News accounts reported junkies entering abandoned buildings and breaking through walls to rob adjacent churches of religious icons and other valuables.[45] Desperate addicts were also reported to scavenge empty and sometimes even occupied buildings for copper wire and plumbing that could be sold as scrap metal for a few dollars.

By the end of the 1970s, abandonment and arson had laid waste to the housing stock in sections of Loisaida. Increased poverty, the underground drug economy, and associated criminality threatened to undo the gains of two decades of community building. In line with previous eras of the neighborhood's history, residents responded to the threat of displacement with a variety of organized and spontaneous collective actions. Unlike previous eras of struggle, however, control and ownership of large portions of Loisaida tenements were no longer in the hands of private absentee landlords. The municipal takeover of abandoned properties marked a momentous shift in how tenants' struggles for affordable and decent housing would proceed. The Office of Property Management, formed as part of the Department of Housing Preservation and Development (HPD) in 1978, managed thousands of occupied in rem apartment buildings across the city.[46] Nearly 18 percent of the total in rem stock was dilapidated, and the median income of its tenants was only 62 percent of that of all renters.[47] Citywide, over 78 percent of the occupants of in rem housing units were black or Puerto Rican.[48] As landlord, the city typically rivaled or was worse than private owners in its management practices.[49] For local housing activists, the city's takeover of buildings meant that the status of low-income housing development (i.e., rehabilitated for low-income versus middle-income residents) could be swayed by intensive and grassroots political action.

The Culture and Politics of Community Resistance

The debilitating effects of real estate disinvestment on the quality of life in Loisaida compelled many of the area's remaining poor- to moderate-income and minority residents to act collectively against capital disinvestment and political neglect. In the process of fighting to maintain their homes and retain some semblance of community, they renewed the Lower East Side's reputation for active political and cultural resistance to increasing crime, tenant evictions, and the destruction of buildings. The Puerto Rican community, which was most affected by abandonment, waged a vociferous campaign against residential displacement and social decline, coupling music, poetry, painting, and even gardening with traditional tactics, such as rent strikes and demonstrations. Puerto Rican artists painted large murals on building walls, including those exposed by the demolition of adjacent buildings, as vi-

Figure 19. "Mural: 'Don't want no cheese.'" Photograph used by permission of Robert G. McFarland.

Figure 20. Murals remain a dominant expression of Loisaida's stand against drugs and violence. Mural by Chico, 1991. Photograph by Christopher Mele.

sual public protests against community decay. The earliest murals were visual narratives of the Puerto Rican island-to-mainland migration experience, but by the mid-1970s they had begun to depict the ravages of abandonment for the Loisaida community. The ill effects of landlord greed, drug addiction, and forced evictions replaced U.S. colonialism as the dominant themes for Puerto Rican muralists. Puerto Rico was uniformly portrayed in murals as peaceful and utopian and associated with family life, music, religion, and other elements important to Puerto Rican identity. Images of life in New York City evoked mainly sorrow and unhappiness tinged with the future possibility of community betterment. Illustrations of nefarious white men (landlords) grasping money loomed in the background of murals depicting burned-out buildings, robberies, and muggings. Several murals reflected residents' growing concerns about the prevalence of neighborhood drug dealing, addiction, and overdoses. In the late 1970s, the artist Chico's paintings on walls and storefront metal shutters memorialized friends and neighbors lost to cocaine and heroin and drug-related violence. Still other murals featured Asians, Latinos, and Whites harmoniously working to rebuild a more inclusive Lower East Side.[50] In addition to the murals, Latino poetry, writing, and language reflected a pervasive sense of oppression, the lack of autonomy, and the stubborn persistence of struggle that were products of the New York migration, in general, and community disinvestment in particular. The description *Nuyorican* came to refer to an identity, a language, a genre, and a style that expressed Puerto Rican experience and frustration with the vicious marginalization and decline of the *barrios* of New York. "Nuyorican (language) is full of muscular expression. It is a language full of short pulsating rhythms that manifest the unrelenting strain that the Nuyorican experiences."[51] Nuyorican poems, such as those presented in Miguel Algarin and Miguel Pinero's *Nuyorican Poetry: An Anthology of Puerto Rican Words and Feelings* (1975), recalled the positive and negative sentiments associated with the migration and post-migration experiences.

The outpouring of a culture of dissent within the Puerto Rican community was matched in intensity by organized forms of resistance to abandonment. During the earliest stages of disinvestment, tenants and tenant associations, numerous churches, settlement houses, and local and citywide housing groups acted independently or banded together against private landlords to rescue buildings from probable destruction. In 1970 a group of neighborhood activists founded the Lower East Side Joint Planning Council as an umbrella organization to effectively represent and to coordinate the activities of local community-based organizations. The whole of these organizations represented a polyglot of diverse ideologies (secular, religious, reformist, and radical), an equal number of different visions of the neighborhood's future, and a wide range of tactics to best achieve their goals. As a result, in-fighting among the organizations was not unusual,[52] and serious strategic disagreements surfaced in the course of mobilization, especially in the 1980s (as chapter 8 documents). Despite important differences and clashes, housing organizations shared a broad objective of solidifying the property tenure rights of residents threatened with displacement and increasing such rights whenever possible. Grounded in notions of social justice, these groups concurred that widespread abandonment and its consequences clearly revealed that profit-driven, absentee landowners and the city were incapable of providing and maintaining decent housing for low-income residents. Low-income residents would be less susceptible to displacement pressures if building ownership was transferred from the private or state sectors directly to tenants themselves (the goal was, in effect, to de-commodify housing).

Traditional forms of tenant action on the Lower East Side, such as rent strikes and demonstrations, remained an essential part of the repertoire of resistance for activists in the 1970s. Threats of impending displacement often incited a building's tenants to organize and develop initiatives to forestall abandonment, such as campaigns to collect and withhold rents from the landlord and use those funds to purchase supplies for essential repairs. The city's Rent Strike Law (Article 7A) allowed tenants of dilapidated units to petition courts for the appointment of an administrator charged to funnel rent payments into escrow accounts. Rents would remain in escrow until landlords removed outstanding code violations and improved living conditions in their buildings.[53] Such actions thwarted the profitability of disinvestment strategies, and many landlords fought back with a barrage of illegal evictions, verbal and physical threats, and other forms of tenant harassment against local activists. Other, long-term tenant actions required substantial commitment and organization to sustain effectiveness. Successful urban homesteading, for example, demanded considerable organization, the solicitation of outside expertise, knowledge of building codes, and experience with property management.[54] Successful homesteading or "sweat equity" (tenant labor invested into rehabilitation) ventures had been mounted in the Bronx since the late 1960s,[55] and in the early 1970s, the community-based organization Adopt-A-Building assisted in similar initiatives in Loisaida. Groups of tenants formed planning and action committees and invested their skills, labor, time, and small amounts of capital to gut and renovate dilapidated apartment buildings. Financing for some of the "sweat equity" programs relied on funds drawn from a city loan pool that was originally intended for projects initiated by private property owners.[56] In addition to Adopt-A-Building, Rehabilitation in Action to Improve Neighborhoods (RAIN) and the Lower East Side (Catholic) Area Conference (LESAC) formed to provide assistance to emerging tenant associations interested in homesteading.

Saddled with considerable numbers of vested buildings, the city government's preference was to auction them to private individuals or real estate firms. Auctions would allow the city to relinquish its landlord status, the funds earned would repay the owed property taxes, and the buildings' new owners would contribute tax revenues to the city's coffers. When the city began to auction buildings in the late 1970s, public protest against the policy grew strident. Some of the auctioned build-

Figure 21. "Homesteaders of a RAIN/LESAC Building, Avenue C at Fifth Street."
Photograph used by permission of Marlis Momber.

ings reentered the disinvestment-abandonment cycle and ended up once again in rem, while others were bought up for purely speculative purposes, leaving deplorable low-income housing conditions unchanged. Housing coalitions from across the city joined forces against the in rem auctions and fought to transfer management and ownership of the affected buildings to tenants. The Association of Community Organizations for Reform Now (ACORN), which spearheaded the national squatting movement in the early 1970s, employed more radical tactics of immediate tenant occupation of threatened buildings. Their protest efforts and, consequently, media exposés of an embarrassing abundance of city-owned properties propelled the issue of tenant management and ownership of in rem properties to the front and center of housing politics in New York City.

Under increased pressure to act, the city responded with new homesteading programs, which briefly quieted the protests of housing organizations. Homesteading efforts were "far more palatable, politically speaking, than the vision of energetic and noisy squatters demonstrating in front of boarded-up buildings or, even more embarrassing to the authorities, simply walking in and taking over."[57] Under the increasing oversight of the city's Division of Alternative Management Programs (DAMP), homesteading soon evolved into a complex form of community-based action that required sustained tenant commitment, expertise, patience, and money.[58] The Urban Homesteading Assistance Board (UHAB), the Housing Development Institute (HDI), and LESAC were the key organizations that provided vastly different forms of technical assistance to homesteaders. They often acted as intermediaries between tenant associations and city agencies that administered an elaborate web of new housing programs.[59] Under their auspices, interested residents with limited experience in housing legalities and technicalities formed highly organized homesteading associations, which stipulated membership rules, the cost of monthly dues, and each member's amount of "sweat equity."[60] In 1978 the Tenant Interim Lease (TIL) Program, regarded as DAMP's most successful initiative, was instituted to allow tenants to first manage city-owned apartment buildings and then own them as cooperatives. Tenants acted as landlords and were responsible for collecting rents and maintaining a building's upkeep. After an interim lease period of successful self-management, tenants were approved to purchase the building as a low-income cooperative.[61] A second program, the Community Management Program (CMP), called for extensive re-habilitation by the city (using some federal funds) and eventual sale to tenants or a neighborhood housing organization.[62] Another program contracted with neighborhood associations to manage buildings in conjunction with tenants.

Not all of the community self-help initiatives were developed under the city's auspices or overseen by its agencies. Rehabilitation in Action to Improve Neighborhoods (RAIN) pursued community land trusts for low-income housing on the Lower East Side. Unlike homesteading, the basic premise of the trusts was that the community, not landlords or even tenants, owned the land. Tenants were entitled to *use* land for pur-poses such as housing, but they could never own it and, therefore, could not sell, speculate on, or divest it. RAIN acquired lots and buildings as community land trusts and retained their ownership in perpetuity. An-other popular self-help initiative, urban squatting, was illegal and did not receive full support from established housing organizations. Squat-ting actually predated the more formal homesteading programs and was influential to the founding of the homestead movement.[63] For nu-merous reasons both practical and ideological, however, squatters did not deal with the city in their building takeovers. Unlike homesteading, squatting was not legitimized by municipal recognition, and thus build-ing takeovers were unsanctioned. Once squatters occupied a building, the illegality of tenure was much less incontrovertible. During the era of rampant urban disinvestment that generated a glut of empty and de-teriorated buildings with few takers, the squatters' unwillingness to en-gage the city's bureaucratic channels and their violation of property rights were not significant political concerns for the real estate indus-try, the city administration, or more established and visible commu-nity stakeholders. Issues of legality and the legitimacy of squatting sur-faced only after real estate capital ventured back into the neighborhood in the 1980s. Private redevelopment and the ensuing tightening of the available housing stock and the competing claims by housing organi-zations (including homesteaders) for control over in rem properties pushed the squatter question to the center of local politics in the late 1980s and 1990s (see chapter 8).

Although the number of tenant-managed or tenant-owned buildings was modest compared to those abandoned, homesteading and squat-ting dominated Loisaida community politics of resistance against disinvestment. In its earliest years, the homesteading movement was in-clusive of Loisaida's minority residents; approximately 70 percent of those participating in "sweat equity" were Latino, and 30 percent were Whites, Blacks, or Asians.[64] To capitalize on their resilience in the face of urban decline, homesteaders named "rescued" buildings after leaders or im-portant political figures, such as Archbishop Oscar Romero, the priest slain in the Salvadoran civil war. Reflective of dominant issues and causes popular in the 1970s, some homesteading associations adopted unique energy-saving designs, such as solar energy panels and windmills to power their buildings. While most Loisaida residents were not home-steaders or squatters, many applauded their neighbors' efforts at com-munity betterment. Well-attended street fairs and block parties raised revenues to complete existing projects or to begin new ones. In addi-tion to providing decent self-managed housing, homesteads functioned as symbols of struggle, perseverance, and patience over despair.

Stories of pioneering and daring individuals with minimal or no in-stitutional assistance evicting drug dealers and addicts and fixing dilapi-dated buildings in frightening neighborhoods attracted national and international attention. The city's press took interest in the self-help housing movement in the Bronx and Loisaida, labeling the product as "an oasis amid desolation."[65] One case in particular dramatized both the homesteaders' devotion and the magnitude of local housing prob-lems. Under the auspices of the Adopt-A-Building organization, residents rehabilitated three tenements on East Eleventh Street between Avenues A and B. Each of the tenants paid $100 for a cooperative apartment and contributed forty hours of "sweat equity" weekly to rehabilitate a build-ing. Such slow and arduous efforts were heralded as a mixture of 1960s activism and a much older American individualist pragmatism. Inter-est in the Eleventh Street homesteaders was due in part to the severity and extent of abandonment on the block. Between 1972 and 1976, eleven buildings on the block had been abandoned by a single landlord, who owned a total of forty properties in the neighborhood.[66]

The collective work of homesteaders and squatters to stabilize an en-vironment of spiraling decline was joined by the Lower East Side's com-munity garden movement, which sought to reclaim turf from encroach-ing urban blight. The resident gardeners set out to transform vacant lots strewn with trash, bricks, old appliances, and automobiles into green spaces. The movement's first community garden began in 1973, when a

Figure 22. "Homesteaders of the Eleanor Bumpers Building, East Eighth Street between B and C, 1984." Photograph used by permission of Marlis Momber.

group of residents threw balloons containing plant seeds and bulbs into a large fenced-in parcel on Houston Street near the Bowery. The activists, who called themselves the Green Guerrillas, assisted local residents and block associations in starting gardens and, at times, gaining permission to use city-owned properties. Neighborhood women and Puerto Rican residents especially participated in the Loisaida garden movement. Over the years the movement grew to more than seventy-five community gardens (1995 figures).[67] The gardens ranged from the most lavish and elaborate "formal" plantings to the more modest and inconspicuous vegetable patches. Some of the gardens were founded and cared for by organized resident groups, while others were the domains of individual Latino families. *Casitas* (lot gardens with small wooden shacks), maintained mostly by Puerto Rican men, often featured shrines to patron saints, small murals, benches, and tables, a flower and vegetable patch, and, as was the case for a garden on Ninth Street and Avenue C during the mid-1980s, a rooster. *Casitas* functioned as a type of outdoor social club during the warmer months, providing meeting space for parties, cookouts, and respite from summer heat. Residents congregated in their gardens to vent frustrations over dire conditions of the neighborhood, to share stories, to gossip, to develop strategies for improving their block, or to simply relax. Participation in the gardens was a form of territorial resistance against threatening environs and streets often controlled by drug dealers and junkies.

Homesteading, squatting, and urban gardening were important means of grassroots resistance, whose requirements ranged from a few hours a week to long-term and exhaustive commitments. Such practices moved properties from private ownership to community control, if only temporarily. These forms of social resistance were also highly politically symbolic. By transforming the built environment, all three movements demonstrated the success of community reclamation as the means to combat physical and social decay. Although city agencies recognized some aspects of this resistance, funded some of it, or looked the other way, their policy preferences remained driven by the real estate sector's political demands to eventually return the disposition of in rem housing to private control. Homesteading, then, functioned as a stopgap measure during a period of housing market decline and as "a means to further the goal of neighborhood stabilization, recycle housing stock and increase the city's tax base."[68] Many of the city's homesteading programs looked better "on the books" than they did when put in practice in several Loisaida buildings.[69] The regulations that governed tenant eligibility, building codes, and management were oppressively bureaucratic, and funding was far less than adequate to see projects through to completion.

Despite bureaucratic hurdles, the homesteading movement had successfully legitimized self-help housing rehabilitation, as evidenced by the number of city-sponsored programs in the late 1970s. Such programs institutionalized homesteading and incorporated activists into the official working of housing policy, thus erasing the subversive character of homesteading and blurring the distinction between insider and outsider stakeholders that had consistently framed local cultural and political resistance on the Lower East Side. The legitimization of homesteading would prove costly, however, when the city's economy and housing market recovered from the fiscal crisis and the local government's urban policy radically shifted toward middle- and upper-class spatial reorganization of the city.

The decade of the 1970s played out as a continuous withdrawal from Loisaida of real estate capital and people, punctuated by the efforts of remaining residents to stabilize their streets and homes. This narrative of urban decline provides a different perspective on the relationship between representations of place and the political economy of neighborhood change. As we have seen in the preceding chapters, efforts by real estate capitalists and state actors at middle-class renewal of working-class neighborhoods were facilitated by images and rhetoric that marginalized existing uses and users of space and promoted improved, better uses. As this chapter has shown, rhetoric and images that presented the inner city as "off limits" and unsalvageable created an environment that was both permissive and conducive to gradual disinvestment and abandonment. Although structural conditions including further urban deconcentration of residential capital, people, and employment propelled inner-city disinvestment, the process itself was rationalized through rhetoric and images of urban ethnic, racial, and class differences as marginal. Cultural representations of marginal and dangerous cultures and the politics and economics of community abandonment reinforced each other. The consequences of abandonment, as we have seen, served to press forward the area's identity as criminal, dangerous, and otherwise uninhabitable, making it only more logical for landlords to walk away.

Looking ahead, we see that structural shifts in the city's postindustrial economy and changes in its post–fiscal crisis political structure served to disrupt the circular dynamic between cultural marginalization and capital disinvestment in the East Village. The call for renewal would again resurface for a new set of stakeholders drawn to the illusive profits of reconstructing the neighborhood for upscale, white-collar workers, or "yuppies." Yet, as we have seen consistently throughout this book, redevelopment opportunities fueled by structural changes in the city's economy provided little guidance to understanding the ways developers and state actors engineered their renewal efforts and policies. Once again, real estate capitalists and the state actors were faced with the task of reinventing the place identity of the East Village in ways suitable for middle-class colonization. Given the neighborhood's reputation as frightening and dangerous, representing the East Village as desirable to the middle class would have proved daunting were it not for changes that elevated the area's stature in the arts world and culture industries. Although the East Village identity as an "off-beat" or subversive cultural district would prove functional to real estate redevelopers during the city's real estate boom in the 1980s, the formation of such an identity predated the era of 1980s reinvestment and can be found in the connection between the social-spatial consequences of disinvestment and the appearance of underground urban subcultures.

The Subcultures of Urban Decay

Throughout the latter half of the 1970s, the long, slow process of disinvestment and abandonment and accompanying social problems inundated the everyday experiences of residents, compelling many Lower East Siders to flee, some to resign to despair, and others to mobilize and act for change. Sandwiched between the corporate skyscrapers of Wall Street and Midtown, the East Village landscape, particularly in sections of Loisaida, resembled the bombed-out centers of some European cities at the close of World War II. The efforts of activists and tenants to save buildings or replace lots with gardens occasionally interrupted a streetscape that was otherwise littered with discarded and rusted household appliances, hulls of cars that were stripped of tires, engines, and seats, mounds of bricks where buildings once stood, and oil barrels used as furnaces by junkies, dealers, and the homeless. The heroin and cocaine drug economy remained entrenched and vibrant, earning Loisaida the reputation as "the drug capital of America."[70] For an emerging subculture of disaffected middle-class youth, however, the social-cultural landscape of cynicism, chaos, and social decline inspired a belligerent cultural critique of mainstream and increasingly commodified society. When the subcultures of punk and related underground scenes developed in New York in the 1970s, they flourished in the landscape of the East Village amidst the abundance of signs and symbols of urban decay.

Like the former beat and hippie subcultures, the 1970s underground reflected disenchantment and alienation with dominant or mainstream society and its principal postwar creation, the suburbs. Yet the 1970s urban subcultures framed their critique of the mainstream differently than the earlier beats (who passively "dropped out") or the hippies (who sought to construct a better, alternative community). The social milieu of unemployment, hyperinflation, and the accelerated out-migration of middle classes that overwhelmed many cities across the United States and Western Europe influenced the development of various underground groups and their associated cultural practices and forms. In the United States, the urban underground consisted of several loosely connected subcultures, including "glam" or "glitter" rock and, later, various hybrids, such as "New Wave,"[71] that evolved from or in reaction to the British punk movement. Despite differences among them, these subcultures shared dominant features that were influential in the creation of an East Village countercultural identity in the 1970s and early 1980s. First and foremost, underground subcultures emerged self-consciously around particular aesthetic styles rather than from particular ideological commitments or political resistance. Whereas hippie culture was framed around a "vision of change in society and the self," underground cultures took themselves and their absence of a purpose or mission less seriously: "You get around better as an image than you can as a self. It allows you to reject an idea without taking its alternative seriously either."[72] Underground cultures in the United States in general offered disenfranchised youth rebellion without an explicit political message or means of social protest other than pure escapism (which itself may be legitimately interpreted as political). This feature set the U.S. experience apart from the defiant youth movements of the working-class districts of aging cities in the United Kingdom.[73] The lack of any form of political or artistic commitment was endemic of a second common feature: the symbolic embrace of alienation and pessimism partly reflected the material conditions of the essential setting or venue for the underground — the inner city. Underground subcultures, especially punk, were characterized by symbolic violence and aggression articulated in rituals played out in a suitable environment of decay and despair that reinforced a stylized notion of alienation. Cynicism, then, was a progressive creative force, and punk and other underground subcultures extolled and celebrated social disorder, chaos, and decay through music, fashion, and related components of style rooted in the urban experience. Outsiders perceived early punk style, for example, as not only different but, like the inner city, antagonistic, antisocial, and threatening (a perception encouraged by the punk look but seldom realized in actions).

This proclivity of "underground" subcultures toward themes of alienation and settings of urban decay was clearly shaped by national roots and local influences. Early underground, including "glitter rock" and punk, formed in the late 1960s and early 1970s when rock and roll journeyed into the mainstream and lost its subversive character.[74] The legacy of the rebellious East Village was central to the development of the early East Coast underground. At the start of the 1970s, rock bands such as the Velvet Underground, Iggy Pop and the Stooges, and the New York Dolls were writing music about angst, malaise, and other themes that would characterize "New York Punk"[75] a half decade later. The Velvet Underground (with singer Nico), which was first affiliated with Andy Warhol in the late 1960s, differed significantly from other bands of the hippie era; their music sought to "express uptightness and make the audience uptight."[76] Following the demise of Warhol's *Exploding Plastic Inevitable* in 1967, the Velvet Underground toured outside New York and recorded three albums, none of which made national charts.[77] Although the group disbanded in 1970, it remained influential to the "underground" music scene later in the decade. Iggy Pop's frantic stage performances and the exhibitionist New York Dolls continued to shape alternative music culture in the United States. The New York Dolls celebrated a deliberate amateur quality that combined eclectic "visual images and musical styles that seemed brilliantly reckless."[78] The New York Dolls' and other "glitter" bands' predilection for sexual ambiguity and performance transvestitism held considerable cachet in the underground music scene, as it precluded their recognition and easy acceptance into the mainstream music world (David Bowie's Ziggy Stardust notwithstanding).[79] All of these bands featured raw and intentionally unpolished music (marked by few notes and chords), caustic lyrics that spoke of boredom, rage, and a bleak future, and performances in an aggressive, angst-ridden style that distanced them from the mainstream music industry. These same attributes became trademarks of a diverse New York underground music subculture, whose icons included such groups as the Ramones, Television, and early incarnations of Blondie and the Talking Heads.

Punk and underground style and music extolled themes of despair and destruction that were emblematic of their mainstream critique and, at the same time, derivative of contemporary social conditions in cities. While the angst-ridden underground subcultures were partly a vituperative reaction to the rampant commercialization of rock music[80] that "no longer had anything radical to say,"[81] at the same time they found their fullest expression in an urban milieu of abandonment and increasing social despair.[82] Once again, the form of subculture and prevailing characteristics of an urban setting reinforced each other. New York City in the 1970s proved inspirational, and the East Village in particular provided a compatible environment for a subculture constructed symbolically around images of disheartenment and violence.

The connection between underground subcultures and the area "downtown," or "below Fourteenth Street," gelled as retail and performance spaces opened in the East Village. Secondhand clothing and used-record stores, boutiques that specialized in the extraordinary, hair salons, and other shops that peddled the required look of diverse subcultures opened along St. Mark's Place. But the link between underground and East Village was strengthened much further by another, grossly incompatible cultural phenomenon that occurred uptown in the late 1970s. There, large and extravagant discotheques such as Studio 54 and Xenon helped create an entertainment scene that catered explicitly to wealthy socialites, celebrities, and the city's elites and power brokers, all of whom graced the society pages of the international press. Uptown cultural life represented status and privilege played out in expensive, high-tech, and ultra-modern cavernous megaclubs complete with uniformed doormen and the ubiquitous symbol of exclusivity, the velvet rope. By the late 1970s, uptown Manhattan's stylized and studio-produced music (disco) and mimetic dance trends (the "hustle" and other group dances) grew fashionable in cities and suburbs across the country. In reaction, punk and related subcultures hunkered down in the tiny and reclusive bars and clubs below Fourteenth Street and presented themselves as the antidote

Figure 23. Destruction and despair as inspiration. Photograph by Christopher Mele.

to the sugar-coated disco phenomenon, reinforcing the cultural dissonance between uptown and downtown. Thus, the tremendous popularity of disco and its association with "uptown" conferred considerable cachet to downtown as the site of a developing underground
scene. The cultural identity of downtown (alternative, original, experimental, radical, rebellious) soon crystallized as the antithesis to that of
uptown (corporate, homogenized, orthodox, conventional). Downtown
described not only a place but an aesthetic or genre of music, dance,
fashion, hairstyle, art, and performance.[83]

From Subculture to Downtown Scene

The social and physical landscape of the East Village in the 1970s, associated with crime, fires, drug abuse, and juvenile delinquency among
other vices, allowed the underground subcultures to thrive in the midst
of chaos and decline and to remain obscure and relatively anonymous.
The rebellious middle-class youths of the 1970s flourished as a viable
subculture partly because their rituals were played out in a location
where most of their mainstream counterparts dared not to venture.

By the close of the 1970s, however, growing awareness of underground
music, art, and other cultural practices gave way to the formation of a
"downtown scene." The downtown scene was defined by the production
and consumption of the various forms of style concentrated below Fourteenth Street. Arguably, scene was specified less by any one particular
cultural style than a network of *places* where participants and spectators congregated. Central to the identity of the scene was club culture.[84]
Downtown became associated with multitudinous forms of cultural experimentation, most of which were played out in the important and
confined space of the nightclubs, where subcultural styles were imi-
tated and eventually commercialized. The club was a space where art,
music, and performance coalesced much like in the 1960s, but it was
also the central site of production, dissemination, and consumption of
subcultural practices. The clubs functioned both as meeting spaces for
subcultures, such as punks, and as showcases of exotic and erotic styles,
most of which were eventually glamorized, commodified, and then
popularized in the world outside the club. Social and sexual (hetero/
homosexual and androgynous) themes were celebrated and stylized
through particular blends of music, fashion, and art.[85] Club regulars
fabricated attitudes and creative dress around stereotypes of pimps,

hustlers, and rock stars, such as the New York Dolls. In director Slava Tsukerman's 1982 sci-fi/fantasy film about downtown "new wave" subculture, *Liquid Sky*, the nightclub is featured as the central space, where men and women adorn makeup and costume to pose and be seen, to network, to find drugs, to meet sexual partners, and to dance. The Bowery's CBGB, the Mudd Club, and Danceteria (the latter two located downtown but not in the East Village) and Club 57 on St. Mark's Place were the nightclubs most influential in defining the underground scene.

The most famous of these underground landmarks was the performance space CBGB-OMFUG, located on the edge of the East Village along the Bowery. Originally founded as a country, bluegrass, and blues bar (hence the acronym CBGB; OMFUG is an acronym for Other Music for Uplifting Gormandizers[86]), CBGB showcased live music and emerged as the most significant venue for punk, underground, and alternative bands in the United States.[87] In the mid-1970s, when most record companies eschewed the experimental, CBGB was one of the few spaces where punk and related music and styles were heard and seen. The close networks of bands that played and frequented CBGB in the 1970s and early 1980s spawned several music and style scenes. The Ramones, repeat performers who acted the part of street thugs addicted to drugs, were a popular draw for both the curious and their dedicated fans. The group Blondie first performed at CBGB in August 1974 and continued to do so after gaining international fame. CBGB's location on Manhattan's "skid row," the Bowery, and its connection to the East Village together provided the appropriate ambience of rebellious dysfunction for music experimentation. As one of CBGB's frequent callers noted, "Not too many people were coming down to the East Village in those days. . . . It was a dangerous place for white kids from the suburbs to be hanging out, but it also had the cheapest apartments in the city—which made it a haven for starving rock musicians, many of whom began congregating at CBGB."[88]

The Mudd Club opened in 1978 and gained a reputation as space hostile to the uptown scene and scornful of "bridge and tunnel" (non-Manhattanite) revelers (which only served, of course, to attract those same individuals). Danceteria's response to uptown was the egalitarian club; it offered multiple floors, each with a different scene (people, music, dance, art), and was an important showcase for alternative music. Club 57, which opened originally as a screening room and later as a club in 1979, was downtown's first "art-driven club."[89] It catered to downtown artists seeking a platform to present their work. The early 1980s saw the opening of several other dance, performance, and after-hours clubs, many short-lived and each defined by their patrons' style, favorite drug, or sexual preferences. The landmark of the hippie era, the defunct Fillmore East on Second Avenue, reopened in 1980 as the Saint, an immense, high-tech, gay disco that became a focal point for dancing, sex, and drugs.

Club spaces with their flair for the exotic and shocking were representative of a larger cultural transformation that transpired in tandem with the physical and social decline of the East Village, and Loisaida in particular. Underground developed as an urban aesthetic that characterized a wide variety of cultural forms in addition to music, including fiction, poetry, fashion, and visual arts. In the 1980s the underground aesthetics that reflected the underbelly of the city emerged as a nationally and internationally recognized cultural genre. And as the aesthetic of urban decay was adopted by the established and mainstream culture industries, the hard edges of the East Village identity were softened. The developing reputation of the East Village as a site of cultural innovation would provide an important means for the real estate industry to reintroduce the middle-class renewal of the local housing market.

CHAPTER SEVEN

Developing the East Village: Eighties Counterculture in the Service of Urban Capital

Traversing eastward from Fifth Avenue to the East Village and on to Loisaida in the early 1980s provided a journey from the vibrant center of Manhattan to its margins, from a landscape of townhouses and boutiques to one of tenements, *bodegas,* and *carnicerías.* Just before the imposing phalanx of public housing projects on Avenue D, the remnants of the 1970s were manifest in blocks of buildings with bricked-up windows and doorways and overgrown lots strewn with debris. But sandwiched between spaces of destruction were pockets of freshly painted and renovated shops, art galleries, and restaurants that foreshadowed the possibility of a different future. As the previous chapters have suggested, the effect of the presence of middle-class subcultures on the political economic dimensions of restructuring was secondary to the broader discourses that marginalized the Lower East Side and the struggles that unfolded among working-class residents, state actors, and the real estate industry over its future. That changed significantly in the 1980s as the images, symbols, and rhetoric of emerging subcultural communities began to resonate in conventional representations and discourse about the East Village. The characterization of the East Village as desirable occurred initially within art, fashion, music, and design circles, and later, through circulation in the media, among particular segments of the middle class. Symbolic representations of downtown slowly transformed from marginal and inferior to central and intriguing.

This chapter first examines housing market conditions in the East Village, focusing on the shift from abandonment to the beginning stages of redevelopment. The limitations of these early efforts at redevelopment are attributed to the neighborhood's dominant reputation as threatening and menacing. The second part of the chapter recounts the development of the artistic and subcultural communities in the East Village in the late 1970s and early 1980s, focusing especially on their social relations with existing residents and their colonization of the depreciated landscape of half-emptied tenements and lots. It simultaneously analyzes the shift in conventional representations of East Village cultural differences from marginal to central and the effect of that shift on the struggle over middle-class urban renewal. As the previous chapter has noted, subcultures that comprised the East Village underground scene in the late 1970s symbolically embraced all that had been formerly represented as the detritus of community abandonment. Thus, the symbols and images of abandoned buildings, empty lots, graffiti, and a thriving drug economy served as the foundation of an urban aesthetic inclusive of music, art, fashion, and literature. By the mid-1980s critics and cultural observers could refer to an East Village "style" that translated into a particular and, most importantly, a recognizable appearance, sound, attitude, or affect. Advances in communication technologies and changes in middle-class consumption patterns facilitated the migration of the downtown style from obscure to conventional. In addition, this transformation from subculture to mainstream was authored by the artists, musicians, designers, and writers through active promotion of themselves, their work, and, of significance to this chapter, their setting. The underground scene rehabilitated the maligned reputation of the East Village and in the process of doing so provided to developers the images, symbols, and rhetoric to reinvent the neighborhood for middle-class consumers.

The third part of the chapter analyzes how the shift of subcultural difference from the margins to the center influenced local real estate development. Emboldened by the extensive media coverage of the "improved" East Village, new sets of real estate actors — larger firms, holding companies, and lending institutions — set aside their former aversion to financing the development of the tenement district and invested in local real estate. An analysis of the geography, scale, and pace of the capital investment flow into the neighborhood during the 1980s and 1990s is presented.

Speculation and the Prospect of Renewal

The connections of the East Village underground scene to mainstream culture industries and real estate investment happened, not coincidentally, during the halcyon days of the 1980s when fascination with the lifestyles of young urbanites flush with cash and immersed in Wall Street capitalism reached full stride. After the city's near bankruptcy in the late 1970s, and with considerable help from a corporate-friendly political administration, New York emerged as a global city in finance, banking, insurance, and real estate. Popular culture embraced the corporate lifestyle, elevating brokers and accountants to heroes and Donald Trump to the status of civic savior. While light manufacturing industries continued to vanish from the city's landscape, the development of producer services industries trebled, causing significant changes in the composition of employment. Growth in the specialized services sector created more skilled occupations and midlevel positions in finance, insurance, international commerce, law, and communications. In the midst of recovery euphoria, however, the divisions between the city's richest and poorest classes widened. The increase in the number of new corporate service positions was outmatched by the disappearance of semiskilled jobs, creating a condition that drove parts of the city's poor and minority labor force into an expanding formal and informal low-wage service economy.[1] Such social polarization was mirrored in the spatial reorganization of the city. The incumbent real estate boom threatened to further segregate the city's social geography, making Manhattan a gilded core of office and luxury residential towers and the "lesser" boroughs its servicing periphery. The early 1980s witnessed a surge in the construction of office towers and luxury housing and conversions of existing units into owner-occupied condominiums and cooperatives. Overall, the city's housing market tightened as increases in luxury conversions removed middle-class rental units from the housing stock.[2] As the supply of desirable rental units dwindled, existing housing in low-income neighborhoods within or near the core became targeted for upgrading, pushing those who could no longer afford Manhattan rents to "less desirable" areas within the city.

The East Village and Loisaida in particular first appeared as unlikely venues for middle-class redevelopment. Many blocks remained plagued with drug dens, and a high incidence of crime unnerved even the most thick-skinned of New Yorkers. Despite the area's obvious liabilities and associated financial risks, real estate activity shifted gradually from capital disinvestment to reinvestment. Beginning in 1978, the rate of disinvestment slowed considerably, as evidenced by a reduction in tax arrears.[3] While many of the existing property owners continued to divest, savvy investors had begun to purchase dilapidated tenements. Real estate transactions occurred "below the surface" with few visible clues of impending social and spatial changes. In some instances, resourceful investors checked court records of properties listed in tax default and scheduled to be vested, approached their owners, and offered to pay owed taxes plus a nominal fee in return for ownership title to the properties.[4] Speculative investment was fueled not by *known* need or demand for affordable, low-income housing units but by *anticipated* consumption of apartments and condominiums by "upscale urbanites."[5] Increased confidence in investments in East Village real estate was the result of three factors: (1) the middle-class redevelopment of adjacent neighborhoods, prompting expectations of a "spillover" effect, (2) the rapid pace of the speculative market itself, and (3) the symbolic representation of the East Village as an alluring arts district.

In the late 1970s, risks associated with speculative investment in the East Village were diminished by the extensive redevelopment of the adjacent areas of lower Manhattan.[6] A complex fusion of real estate capital, government development incentives, and an expanding art market spurred the transformation of the SoHo district to the south and west from a light manufacturing district into an upscale residential and retail district.[7] Changes in immigration laws and the expansive Pacific Rim political economy were responsible for tremendous population growth in Chinatown and its continued enlargement into the southern tier of the Lower East Side.[8] Across the city, the contraction of the middle-class housing supply jolted an otherwise stagnant low-income housing market. There was a significant drop in dilapidated vacant housing units within the city between 1981 and 1984. During the same time period, rents for substandard housing rose a staggering 20 percent.[9] Citywide, nearly a third of apartments vacated by Puerto Ricans and Blacks were rented to non-Puerto Ricans and non-Blacks while the proportion of white single-person households increased.[10] Within this context of market changes, the Lower East Side emerged as the last low-income residential enclave south of Ninety-sixth Street. Because changes in Manhattan's economy were favorable to high-end corporate producer services and, subsequently, to an upgrade in housing market conditions, the devalorized real estate in the East Village was recast as a potentially profitable investment opportunity.

Incipient speculative investment generated further speculation. That is, speculation was partly self-fulfilling as inquisitive entrepreneurs perceived a steady increase in investment behavior as evidence of revived confidence (and a lessening of risk) in the local land market. A profile of speculative investors and their activities emerged from interviews conducted with former East Village speculators and property developers.[11] Speculators purchased properties at substantially low prices in the late 1970s and early 1980s. Most five-story walk-up Old Law and New Law tenements east of Avenue A were priced from $17,000 to $21,000, and the average sale price of empty lots was from $9,000 to $12,000, far below comparable building and land prices in adjacent neighborhoods in 1978.[12] Although a few prominent investors engaged in a land grab in the East Village (e.g., Peter Kalikow, former owner of the New York Post, participated indirectly through his brother Richard), most were small-time operators. Speculators considered themselves risk-taking maverick entrepreneurs out to make a quick profit and an even quicker exit once the stakes were no longer in their favor. They typically acted individually, although small corporations were formed to manage the buying and selling of often more than a half-dozen properties at one time. Many of the speculators in the East Village tenement market used secure rental properties (usually) in the outer boroughs of the city as collateral for borrowing capital to invest.

A speculation frenzy occurred in the East Village in the late 1970s and early 1980s as more investors entered the fray, and the rate of "flipping" (continued reselling of a single property within a short time at successively higher prices) escalated. Flipping frequently involved "dummy" or holding corporations, "creative" financing schemes, and often the same individuals entered and exited the buying-selling game over short periods of time. In more than a few cases, speculators sold their properties at two to three times the initial buying price. The transactions involving the Christodora House are a case in point. The property was auctioned by the city in 1973 for $60,000. Real estate speculator-cum-developer Harry Skydell led a group of investors in 1984 in purchasing the Christodora for $1.2 million. Shortly thereafter, the group flipped it to another player, Robert Weiss, who immediately turned the deed over to Samuel Glasser for $3 million. Glasser had made his money buying nearby East Village walk-up tenements and renting out units, mostly to white artists. Interestingly enough, to procure financing for the Christodora's rehabilitation, Glasser turned to Skydell as a partner.[13] The experience of the Christodora, although one of the largest projects in the area with eighty-five condominiums, was not exceptional. Recurrent flipping and large sale price increases occurred even in the "riskiest areas" east of Avenue A.

The logic of speculative investment was to procure profit by resale — not redevelopment — of properties. Speculators anticipated higher sale prices to be generated solely by renewed interest in the local housing market; capital improvements on purchased properties were rare. The appearance of the neighborhood's built environment therefore remained fundamentally unchanged. When the flipping of properties was most heated, speculators showed little interest in converting or upgrading their buildings — procedures that given the predominance of rent regulations, would have required tenant evictions. Only after the speculative market was glutted did speculators resort to wide-scale displacement of their poorest (and least rent-paying) residents to attract prospective buyers. The cleverest speculators, however, had already exited the market by that time. For the tenants of the majority of flipped buildings, few differences were noticeable; the downward spiral in their living conditions continued, resulting in less heat and fewer repairs. As more investors appeared and the pace of flipping accelerated in the first half of the 1980s, market prices for properties increased exponentially to the level where the principle of speculative accumulation — investing in undervalued commodities for resale — was violated. Eventually, speculative investment burned itself out as profit margins from resale alone diminished. The result of the speculation market was an overvalued housing stock that could no longer yield a return on investment *without* substantial redevelopment intended for new, middle-class consumers.

The subsurface movement of capital would begin to manifest itself in the actual reconstruction of the built and social environments. We return to the issue of neighborhood upgrading later in this chapter.

The city's economic growth, the development of lower Manhattan neighborhoods surrounding the East Village, and the inflow of speculative investment in undervalued tenements once again revived the possibility of middle-class renewal. As our analysis of previous efforts at renewal has shown, political and economic actions alone are unlikely to trigger the propitious social and cultural changes required to displace existing uses of space and to attract a desired class of housing consumers. For investment in housing to be profitable in the 1980s, developers were compelled to reinvent place in ways conducive to new, more profitable forms of consumption. Developers' interest in East Village real estate was impeded by the perception among potential middle-class renters of the neighborhood's poor housing, rampant drug abuse, and related social problems. As the following section demonstrates, the solution to this marginal reputation would be realized in the emerging East Village arts district. Both developers and the state viewed the "cultural renaissance" of the Lower East Side as a mechanism to attract the elusive middle-class renters.

The Transformation from Subculture to Mainstream: Art in the Service of Capital

By 1983, the national media spoke of the various cultural forms emanating from the East Village as belonging to a genre, what would later be referred to as a "culture of insurgency."[14] Underground music was transformed from obscurity to greater mainstream recognition in the form of the less angry and more commercial (pop) post-punk "New Wave." Some of the former underground musicians, such as Debbie Harry of Blondie, made the crossover to mainstream, while others emerged directly from the post-punk scene. The persona of Madonna provided the best example of utilizing symbols and images of the downtown aesthetic for self-promotion.[15] In fiction, authors Tama Janowitz, Joshua Whalen, and Jerome Charyn comprised a "downtown genre" of writing.[16] Janowitz, author of *Slaves of New York*, packaged herself as both writer and celebrity of the downtown scene.

As was the case in the late 1960s, both the corporate culture industries (the record industry, the established art and fashion worlds) and the media (especially advertising) remained important catalysts of the commodification of cultural forms. What was different and unprecedented in this transformation of subculture to mainstream, however, was the active role of the "cultural radicals" — the artists, designers, club sponsors, filmmakers, photographers, and musicians — in the celebration of the downtown scene *for the purpose of promoting themselves and their craft in the mainstream marketplace.* When their self or work was publicized through association with the scene, individuals were hyper-inflated into personalities and celebrities, subcultural practices and forms into commodities, and, most importantly for this work, a marginalized neighborhood into a desirable living space. When musicians and artists became experts at hype in the commodification of subcultural forms, downtown became a venue or conduit for their success uptown. The linkage between promotion of self, commodification, and the construction of place identity was most obvious in the case of the East Village art scene.

Place Identity in Art and Real Estate

> When Jean-Michel [Basquiat] writes in almost subliterate scrawl "Safe plush he think" it is not on a Park Avenue facade that would be totally outside the beggar's venue but on a rusted-out door in a godforsaken neighborhood. Plush to whom safe from what?
>
> Rene Ricard, "The Radiant Child"

The burgeoning East Village art scene of the 1980s invented new forms of cultural and economic linkages between the avant-garde and urban space. Artist and contributing editor of *Art in America* Walter Robinson claimed that the East Village art scene was "about making an 'art movement' seem more real by anchoring it to a concrete physical area."[17] The commercial art scene that developed in the East Village was short-lived, lasting roughly from 1980 to 1984. In the late 1970s, the East Village's profusion of underground subcultures offered an environment where artists could exhibit work that was experimental, untried, and, consequently, ill suited for the established corporate art market centered uptown and in SoHo. The first galleries were makeshift exhibition spaces started by artists or their friends in apartments and eventually in storefronts. By 1984, however, the East Village art scene was fully entrenched within the workings of the New York art world with over seventy commercial galleries located in the space of fourteen blocks. All but a few of these galleries closed by the late 1980s. This rapid growth and decline may be accounted for by the international wave of art speculation and investment that was fueled largely by the profits from the finance and producer services growth sector. Despite the brevity of the East Village art scene, an account of its rise and fall is an important means to understanding the relationship between subculture and urban development and the role of the artist and media in the promotion of place.

Like other cultural forms, such as music and fashion, underground art in the 1970s was influenced by aesthetic resistance to the staid and predictable culture industry. Both the form and content of (early) East Village art was rebellious and agitated, like the larger scenes in which they originated and flourished.[18] The association between punk style and art, for example, was realized in the most popular local art form, graffiti. Graffiti were the expression of disenfranchised, mostly minority youth[19] "who are not well represented in the dominant culture, who have no real access to its media."[20] Graffiti's authenticity and lawlessness appealed to the underground subcultures.[21] Graffiti-as-art first made its appearance in the New York art world in the 1970s in alternative storefront galleries such as Fashion Moda in the South Bronx and P.S. 1's "New York/New Wave" exhibition in 1981.[22] Art critics referred to graffiti, scrap/junk sculpture, and related mainstays of the East Village as neo-Expressionist, neo-Conceptualist, and "funk assemblage."[23]

The East Village proved an agreeable place for the exhibition of the rebellious art genre. Ann Mesner made use of the streetscape, mounting small sculptures (made from urban scrap materials) to street lampposts in the East Village.[24] Other artists made use of the underground scene, incorporating music and performance in exhibitions held in alternative galleries, clubs, and makeshift storefronts across the neighborhood. In 1979, the painter Kenny Scharf organized a single-night art exhibition at the nightclub Club 57 on St. Mark's Place; in 1980, Keith Haring followed suit.[25] According to Haring, "The result was that we disrupted the legitimate definition of what being an effective or successful artist is. Our success was in terms of reaching people and having direct contact with our audience."[26] Similar one-night shows were held at the Pyramid Club on Avenue A. The "Beyond Words" show at Mudd Club displayed photographs of graffiti-ridden subway trains and spray-painted pieces of scrap metal. In addition to exhibitions at clubs, paintings and sculpture were displayed in small, unpolished galleries that artists began to operate in the ground-floor storefronts of tenements. The Fun Gallery opened in the fall of 1981 in an unheated commercial space on East Tenth Street.[27] Fun was an important exhibition site for East Village–based artists such as Futura 2000 and Keith Haring. Its "minifestivals of the slum arts, featuring rap music and break-dancing, along with the graffiti paintings exhibited on its walls" were well attended by locals, critics, and dealers.[28] Artist-owned Gallery 51X on St. Mark's Place showed work that "captured the stylish look of the punk rock scene."[29] East Tenth Street's Nature Morte, which specialized in neo-Expressionist art,[30] and Civilian Warfare on East Eleventh Street were both opened by artists in 1982. More galleries opened in the spring of 1983, including New Math on East Twelfth Street and Gracie Mansion's gallery, relocated from St. Mark's to East Tenth Street and Avenue B. Along with the galleries appeared new art bars (most notably the Red Bar and the Pyramid) that conspicuously promoted the mix of fashion, music, performance, video, and painting.

Important to the projected image of the East Village art scene was the collapsing of spaces of production and consumption of art. Art made there was to be shown there. And despite the fact that it was being exhibited in commercial galleries, purchased by collectors, and panned by art critics in well-read journals, downtown art continued to be packaged as uncorrupted ghetto street culture. The lore that developed and circulated in the leading art magazines claimed that there were no demarcations between the sprawlings on brick walls and the art product; the boundary between the street and the gallery was eliminated. East Village art was vaunted as having evolved from (rather than being simply influenced by) graffiti on subway cars, billboards, or sides of buildings and the twisted metal, rubble, and spare parts found about the city's empty lots. Critics, dealers, and buyers began to speak of a particular style, an East Village "look" in which art featured "cartoony figuration, painted quickly, probably meant to register quickly, often helped to that end by simple shocking imagery."[31] This was the art supposedly not welcome in the galleries ("palaces"[32]) of SoHo and uptown but shown in the apartments of the struggling artists and their friends. East Village galleries, according to the more obsequious local art narratives, were opened in response to a crisis of space and not as showrooms to sell art. The story of why Gracie Mansion opened her gallery—because her former art space (the bathroom walls in her flat) was too limiting—was repeated often in stories and retrospectives in numerous art journals. Galleries were hyped as "urban museums" and authentic, proper places to view art in the ambient environment in which it was made. Graffiti, after all, were "the visible manifestations of a system gone wrong,"[33] and the East Village was the ideal setting for their display. In a gesture to its reputation for tolerance, one of the more supportive critics in *Arts Magazine* wrote that the East Village "is a neighborhood that encourages one to be the person he is with greater ease than other parts of the city." He continued, "The integrity of the art *produced or shown* there is therefore not surprising."[34] Claims of uncorrupted authenticity belied the growing reality that the galleries provided a highly visible opportunity for new artists to present and, perhaps, sell their work to the increasingly curious uptown and SoHo-based dealers.

The organization of the nascent East Village art market differed from the conventional industry in the uptown and SoHo art districts in ways that, ironically, made the promotion of both art and artists easier. The fast-paced commodification of the East Village art scene was propelled not only by the type of art presented but by how that art was featured and by the relationship between artists and gallery owners. Like their uptown Fifty-seventh Street counterparts, SoHo galleries had grown overly cautious and predictable in the kinds of art they featured and sold, in part because the premium cost of space in these areas proscribed taking risks. Since commercial storefront rents were inexpensive in the East Village, galleries there could afford to take chances in the type of work exhibited. Indeed, many galleries were started expressly to show the experimental work not seen elsewhere in the city. The focus on the new and experimental, however, attracted established art world dealers and buyers to the East Village galleries.[35] Gallery hopping became a regular activity for tourists, buyers, critics, and the curious in summer and on Sundays (when galleries elsewhere were closed). Also noteworthy was the absence of dealers who ordinarily represented artists to gallery owners. East Village artists dealt directly with gallery owners and were instrumental in decisions about what art was presented and how it was shown.[36] Greater control over the showcase of their art allowed artists to hype their personalities as well as their work and to introduce music, fashion, and other elements of the downtown "scene" into exhibition. Although the works of certain artists became associated with specific

galleries, East Village gallery owners were not contractually tied to ex-
hibiting particular artists and maintained no "artist stable." Consequently, the "free-agent" character of the East Village art scene allowed
artists who attracted attention to easily migrate to SoHo or uptown galleries, as those who eventually gained international fame did. "It's okay
with us if the artists we show run off to SoHo or 57th Street," commented
the owners of the Nature Morte Gallery. These features relegated the
East Village galleries to stepping stones on an artist's path toward success (as measured by international exposure and huge sales); the art scene
was a "kind of finishing school for young artists who later graduated to
the major leagues."[37]

The founding of art galleries amid an environment of social decay and
the footloose and unstructured quality of gallery-artist relations were
two essential components of the early 1980s East Village scene. A third important feature was the artists' celebrity status. For critics, the East Village had emerged as "a state of mind . . . an open, unwalled ghetto of talent and understanding."[38] Its clubs and galleries functioned as a means
for artists to promote their work and themselves. They "entrepreneured
the crossover" into mainstream acceptance.[39] Artists like Jean-Michel
Basquiat spent their days of obscurity enmeshed in the downtown subculture, hanging out in the clubs and social spaces of the East Village.
Basquiat socialized in the downtown scene before his recognition by
uptown and SoHo dealers. His fame was first local and tied to his status
as a Mudd Club and Club 57 regular who networked with other club
patrons, building his image among the downtown culture elite.[40] His
graffiti, tagged by the slogan SAMO, brought him recognition in the underground art world, but his fame came as one of a second generation
of graffiti artists who "capitalized on the innovations of the first."[41] From
his start, Basquiat expressed interest in "crossing over" into the successful and corporate art industry. A few years later, in 1984, he was exhibit-
ing in one of SoHo's top galleries, Mary Boone.[42] Basquiat, although
perhaps the most renowned, was not the only self-promoting artist.
AVANT, a group that performed/painted to accompanying music at Club
57, plastered SoHo and the East Village with flyers that blended "self-
advertisement and graffiti."[43] Keith Haring's "hieroglyphic cartoons"[44] propelled him into the limelight in the early 1980s. Haring opened a retail
outlet, The Pop Shop on Lafayette Street, to sell his images emblazoned
on, among other things, T-shirts, buttons, and postcards. Later, Haring's

images were used in announcements for AIDS fund-raising and, more recently, in corporate advertisements.

When artists migrated from the East Village to the corporate art world of Fifty-seventh Street or SoHo, they (with considerable assistance of art critics) elevated the awareness of the East Village and its "rogue" cultural scene among elites. The obscurity of the East Village art scene disappeared quickly as speculation in the fine arts industry (tied to the burgeoning profits on Wall Street) escalated. Within two years of the appearance of the first commercial galleries, a "second wave" of new, more professional galleries were opened by "dealers who live[d] outside the neighborhood."[45] Area X on East Tenth Street, for example, was founded by a former assistant to an uptown art dealer. In addition to new spaces for showing painting and sculpture, video and photographic galleries appeared. As the speculative art market continued to expand in the early 1980s, the professionalization of the East Village gallery scene began to mimic that of SoHo.[46]

The promotion of self and personality, artistic product, and neighborhood became the overwhelming characteristics of the downtown scene in the mid-1980s. The press devoted pages to the art, artists, galleries, art bars, and clubs in Manhattan's "third art district" after Greenwich Village and SoHo.[47] Several articles featured the details of where artists lived and played and included more commentary on the intimate aspects of their social lives and personas than on the art produced. The importance of someone's work was measured often by the scope of his or her presence in the public spheres of parties and clubs. Media (over)-exposure of the local art scene was, then, a promotion of the East Village as simultaneously interesting and desirable. In the fall of 1983, the show "The Best of the East Village" opened in Amsterdam. In 1984, two East Village retrospectives opened in the United States at the University Art Museum in Santa Barbara and the Institute of Contemporary Art at the University of Pennsylvania. Testimony to the importance of art, artist, and place to promotion, the Pennsylvania exhibition was titled the "East Village Scene" and featured only those artists who lived and worked in the neighborhood. Back downtown, the commercial marketing of art, celebrity, and space altered the subcultural landscape. The Fun Gallery and Civilian Warfare, once hole-in-the-wall art spaces, were by 1983 selling art to bankers and European millionaires. After the closing of Club 57, the Mudd Club and earlier underground clubs disappeared. The Pyramid and new spaces, such as Bohemia After Dark, catered to those looking to consume the renowned downtown scene. In 1985, the Palladium dance club, which resembled the uptown clubs in size and expense, opened on East Fourteenth Street. The club's owners, Ian Shrager and Steve Rubell, were, in fact, the creators of the vaunted, upscale disco Studio 54 in the 1970s—the rejection of which was a key catalyst for the opening of downtown clubs. The Palladium was modeled after the earlier clubs, and efforts were made to appropriate stylized attributes of the increasingly defunct downtown scene. Its owners commissioned artists Clemente, Scharf, Basquiat, and Haring to affix their designs to architecture, decorating the walls, backdrops, and bar spaces of the club's interior. The opening of the Palladium marked the symbolic end of a long subcultural journey from youthful angst and mainstream rejection to full-blown commodification and assimilation into the mainstream.

The Cultural Radical and Middle-Class Development: Culpable or Unwitting?

The increasing national and international media spotlight on East Village subculture presented the public with new ways of perceiving the landscape of dilapidated tenements and trash-littered sidewalks and streets. While the images and symbols of urban decay remained the same, their representations and attached meanings shifted from fear and repulsion to curiosity and desire. Real estate developers were quick to capitalize on the interest in the cultural scene, issuing in an arts-driven phase of redevelopment. Yet before we introduce the uses of new representations in local redevelopment, it is advantageous at this point to discuss the artist as agent in the processes of arts-driven neighborhood renewal. As discussed earlier, a central feature of the downtown scene was the interconnectedness of the artist/agent, the art itself, and the site of its production, the East Village. Artists' self-advertisement to the middle-class audience, therefore, equally promoted the East Village to these same consumers. Long-term residents and housing organizers, as well as some journalists and academic observers, have examined this connection between the role of the artist and a *particular kind* of neighborhood promotion. Neighborhood organizers viewed the artists (as well as other cultural radicals) and their self-promotion as politically threatening to the interests of the low-income and minority communities in the East Village. Media attention to the art scene elevated the status of the subcultural community among the broader public and real estate developers, thereby threatening to swallow up or displace the majority of the neighborhood's population. As one activist answered when questioned about the influx of artists, "People with choices should choose not to move to the Lower East Side."[48] Some artists, however, viewed their status as that of cultural radicals and questioned the culpability of their role in arts-driven redevelopment. Indeed, local development, it was argued, would make the many lesser-known artists themselves victims of displacement. "We made our own art world, with an entire range of different styles, as if to prove that anyone could free themselves from institutional authority. . . . For a while it looked like we actually might get away with it, pretending the real art world was irrelevant."[49] Art critics, as well, viewed the link between art and urban renewal as an unfortunate consequence of the success of the art scene. The artists' motives were, nonetheless, innocent: they had moved into the East Village for its low rents and vibrant culture, not to initiate a hugely successful art movement — "the surprise attention of collectors and curators [from Chase Manhattan and the Whitney and Metropolitan museums]" was serendipitous but completely unexpected.[50]

The concerted effort at promotion of self, subculture, and space contradicted this notion of an accidental or ad hoc burgeoning of the downtown art scene. A more accurate and less sympathetic explanation was presented in an influential article by authors Rosalyn Deutsche and Cara Gendel Ryan, who claimed that the artists' attitudes toward the neighborhood's poorest residents were mercenary, if not exploitative, creating an inviting atmosphere for real estate investments. The art scene promulgated a middle-class environment that made it possible for a "resettling of a white population in neighborhoods where they would never have dared to venture."[51] The authors questioned the interests of those artists who created the scene, since many openly and flagrantly courted (and were embraced by) the established art world, journalists, collectors, and public and private institutions.[52] While many artists had proclaimed to socially and politically acknowledge and often incorporate the plight of the everyday Lower East Sider in their work, such efforts were hollow gestures, or worse still, an appropriation of social misery as the basis of a marketable aesthetic. David Wojnarowicz's (who was also a writer) work of "spray-painted stencils of such objects as burning houses, fighter bombers and running infantrymen"[53] is illustrative of this criticism. His painting *Junk Diptych* (1982), which portrays the social problems of drugs, money, and overdose that plagued the neighborhood, is arguably an uncritical representation that verges on the sensational. An alternative perspective questioned the culpability of the artists' role in urban development. According to this view, the agency of artists must be seen as interconnected with other actors in the East Village scene, including art dealers, the larger culture industry, and real estate interests. Compared with these larger, more powerful interests, the responsibility for urban development falls less on the artists and more on the stakeholders with a vested interest in renewal — the city government and the real estate industry.[54]

The debate over artists as willing agents or unwitting pawns in arts-driven urban development overlooked the evolution of underground subcultures that included not only artists but other creative actors and their relationship to place. Deutsche and Ryan's central argument that artists were culpable was correct for the scene *after 1980*. The complicity of the key East Village artists with the commercial agenda and class interests of the established art world most certainly necessitated that the neighborhood's pressing social and economic conditions would not be addressed. "We can pick and choose from the past," stated an article in a 1984 art exhibition catalog, "which is telescoped into a single dimension to match the unity of the present."[55] It is this critical absence of inclusion of the poorest residents that allowed the real estate industry to so successfully attach itself to and capitalize on the subcultural place identity to serve developers' interests. What Deutsche and Ryan's argument did not include was the evolution of the downtown scene (as presented here) in the 1970s and its transition to a venue for self-aggrandizement and commodification in the 1980s. Artists' promotion of self and their art and the written word of art critics presented a particular place identity of the East Village that included notions of an urban renaissance and excluded the social and economic conditions of the majority of people who lived there. Such a place identity was ready-made for the interests of the real estate industry who sought to displace low-income residents and to entice middle- and upper-class consumers. The identity of a packaged East Village scene was easily fused to the agenda of real estate and the entrepreneurial city government of the 1980s.

Forging the Link between Culture and Real Estate: Urban Policy and Real Estate Development

In the midst of artists' and musicians' self-promotion and hype, the social and built environment of the East Village was further objectified in representations as a backdrop of a flourishing downtown cultural renaissance. In Steven Spielberg's 1987 film *Batteries Not Included,* which was filmed in Loisaida, tiny robotic beings from outer space help a group of distraught residents fight against the demolition of their tenement by developers. The film's happy ending suggests a humane form of urban restructuring in which minorities and Whites, rich and poor, and old-timers and newcomers coexist harmoniously in a pluralist urban landscape. Other media coverage presented experimental cultural forms as an awakening and salvation from the years of neighborhood decline and decay. The blocks between Avenues A and D that had constituted Loisaida became known as "Alphabet City" in the more playful mainstream media representations. The real estate sector brought into the image of decay an image of danger, seediness, and the mystique of "living on the edge," at the same time its investment ventures sought to displace it.[56] In retail, restaurants, and other commercial space, the area's rawness was cleverly packaged as suspense, intrigue, and adventure for those who imagined their visit to the area as an outing to the underworld. Bernard's, a restaurant located on the corner of Avenue C and East Ninth Street, specialized in French organic cuisine and catered to the uptown advertising executive crowd, whose chauffeur-driven limousines were parked out front. The corner of Avenue C and East Ninth Street was also an outdoor drug bazaar where crack cocaine was primarily sold. What went on inside Bernard's and what happened outside were related as patrons consumed a "glamour of poverty" along with their food.

Throughout the mid-1980s, the downtown scene was transformed by media, spectators, and participants from the marginal and rebellious to an urban genre well suited for urban revitalization. Both real estate developers and the city government employed representations of the downtown scene to legitimize neighborhood restructuring practices and policies, to exculpate the social costs of community displacement, and to challenge the validity of resistance efforts mounted by threatened residents. First, the rhetoric of cultural renewal facilitated various development policies that encouraged real estate investment and threatened to wrest control of public space away from low-income residents. Second, symbolic representations positively redefined the image of the East Village to attract once-skeptical middle-sized real estate developers, brokers, and large lending institutions. Finally, East Village developers employed the allure of downtown to attract mostly white, middle- and upper-income, well-educated people as tenants.

At the height of the city's fiscal crisis, politicians and policy analysts reconceptualized post–World War II urban policies in general and subsidized low-income housing in particular as too economically inefficient and overly generous to the poor. Under the ideological leadership of the Reagan administration, the (few remaining) Great Society urban programs and policies were subject to extensive criticism, disavowal, and ultimately blame for the lack of private growth in the central city. The new urban initiatives and policies developed in the 1980s were shaped and defined by a post–fiscal crisis discourse that emphasized increasing tax revenues through development incentives and the rollback of governmental provision of low-income housing. Political leaders and policymakers drew lessons from the fiscal crisis, which was reconfigured as a crisis of disincentives for urban investment rather than the city's inability to address or contain mounting social problems. City agencies with any degree of authority over private or public land use and development were brought in line with an aggressive entrepreneurial and pro-growth ideology. During the budgetary crisis, for example, the city's planning department was restructured to be less acquiescent to costly neighborhood and community initiatives (roughly, the 1960s democratic planning model) and more amenable to private redevelopment needs (e.g., granting developers exceptions to zoning ordinances).[57] With respect to low-income neighborhoods in particular, the city's position was to encourage and subsidize efforts by the middle-sized and large developers and lending institutions to enter and transform working-class housing markets for middle- and upper-class consumers.[58]

In the 1980s, the city administration sought to undo most of the programs that had transferred some control over neighborhood space to low- and moderate-income residents. The Koch administration utilized its authority over a large percentage of housing stock to leverage entrepreneurial middle- to upper-class redevelopment of housing in the

East Village. The agency ostensibly created to protect low-income neighborhoods from the ravages of disinvestment, the Department of Housing Preservation and Development (HPD), became the institutional
strong arm for private revitalization. Many of the city's tenant self-
management and ownership programs were severely curtailed, underfi-
nanced, or totally eliminated to promote private redevelopment rather
than community empowerment.[59] Throughout the 1980s, HPD demolished city-owned buildings (some occupied by squatters), leaving empty
parcels that were more attractive to developers seeking to construct new
housing. In addition to undermining the gains of community activists
over land use, the city administration devised ways to transfer its control of in rem units to private developers. In 1982, HPD announced its
plan to auction part of its stock of TIL (Tenant-Interim Lease) buildings to the highest bidders. Protest by community groups and housing
organizations thwarted the auction plan, forcing the city to reinstate a
moratorium on sales. In a similar vein, the city's position on the urban
garden movement shifted drastically. In the 1970s the city was supportive of gardens, often leasing unkempt lots to residents to grow vegetables
and flowers. With the rebound of the housing market, however, the city
placed a moratorium on leasing lots to gardeners.[60]

While city officials devised ways to retract the gains of low- and moderate-income residents and their representative housing organizations,
they explored new ways to take full advantage of the media attention
on the East Village's middle-class cultural settlement. In 1981–82, the Koch
administration proposed the Artists Homeownership Program (AHOP)
to convert in rem properties into artists' housing. The program called
for conversion of abandoned buildings into cooperative housing for
artists of moderate incomes ($40,000-$50,000 per year) and was billed
as a means to prevent displacement of East Village artists.[61] The city's
Department of Housing Preservation and Development chose a site on
East Eighth Street between Avenues B and C for the program's first phase.
Ten contiguous tenements were to be gutted and rebuilt into small lofts
for living and working. The city's Board of Estimate defeated AHOP in
1983, however, after community groups protested the availability of subsidies for middle-income rather than low-income housing development.
The Lower East Side Joint Planning Council mobilized against the plan
on the basis that its obvious intention was to heighten the neighborhood's allure to investors and private developers.[62] The councilwoman

representing Loisaida and the surrounding district referred to the plan as "a front for gentrification."[63] AHOP was a blatant attempt to re-create SoHo-styled development—that is, to harness the downtown culture scene to trigger a domino effect of upscale redevelopment.

Municipal agencies sought to promote their own interests and those of developers through manipulation of certain symbols representative of the East Village art scene and not others. That is, the city's gesture to promote the local arts was not an unequivocal acceptance of downtown subculture but rather of its milder representations conducive to the development agenda. Indeed, the Koch administration's pro-development agenda contained draconian policies to rid the neighborhood of its "unsavory elements," to sanitize its public spaces, and to rein in the area's free-wheeling, chaotic social environment. City policies, in short, threatened to fundamentally undermine the subcultural basis of the downtown scene that was completely enmeshed in the local drug culture and reputedly derived its creative energy from an environment of despair. In the early 1980s, the police mounted an antidrug effort called Operation Pressure Point, sending over 230 officers and 40 detectives along with numerous vehicles and helicopters to begin what locals described as a military invasion of Loisaida. To drive out the entrenched two-decade-old drug economy, the police occupied streets, corners, empty lots, and parks: within a month 14,285 (!) people were arrested on drug-related charges. Operation Pressure Point was a public relations victory for the Koch administration as sensational scenes of drug busts and police occupation were widely circulated by the media and played well with the image of a neighborhood renaissance. Operation Pressure Point had a less significant effect on the elimination of the local drug economy, pushing transactions farther underground and into apartments and tenement hallways. Under the guise of enforcement, the police also periodically cracked down on ad hoc outdoor flea markets along St. Mark's Place, Second Avenue, and Avenue A, which were a source of income for some residents and many homeless persons. Anti-loitering campaigns along neighborhood streets and corners, ostensibly to curb the drug and prostitution trade, restricted a long Lower East Side tradition of "hanging out," especially among youth. In the mid-1980s, the area's many lots were fenced in, preventing their use as gardens or makeshift junkyards, as well as for nefarious drug transactions. While poor and minority residents felt the brunt of the city's policing and surveillance, the subcultural communities were not left untouched. The downtown scene was, after all, thoroughly steeped in the drug consumption culture. City policies sought to sanitize the area's seamy reputation and to rein in the very same free-wheeling, chaotic social environment that initially gave impetus to the downtown creative scene. Police raided and closed down several of the neighborhood's illegal after-hours clubs, dampening the area's hedonistic atmosphere. The surveillance and regulation of activities within Tompkins Square Park that escalated throughout the 1980s fueled intense neighborhood resistance beginning in 1988, as discussed in chapter 8.

Most of the *public* social and cultural practices of Loisaida emerged within the landscape of wide-scale abandonment and disenfranchisement in the 1970s. As discussed in the preceding chapter, such practices were an assertion of community identity and a collective challenge to the drugs and crimes that plagued the area. All of the city's social control practices in the 1980s were aimed ostensibly at eliminating illicit activities, but no effort was made by the city to stipulate for Latino social and cultural functions that had occurred in these same public spaces. By proclaiming to have improved the "quality of life" for *all* residents through social control of public space, the city also complicated the politics of resistance against neighborhood redevelopment. Operation Pressure Point cleared notorious drug blocks, such as East Second Street, and benefited residents, such as the elderly or couples with children, who felt trapped by the drug trade. Yet the neighborhood's increasing safety also made its housing more attractive to developers and increased the threat of displacement for these same populations. Support for "quality of life" concerns among the area's threatened low-income residents frequently led to their alliances with wealthier newcomers on such issues. City policies shrouded the obvious political economic cleavage and, consequently, diluted political opposition to the intended outcome, redevelopment. "Quality of life" improvements, such as those made to parks, streets, and public buildings, were often used to justify and exculpate the social cost of residential displacement that was the consequence of private redevelopment efforts.

By controlling the use of public space, the city helped construct an identity more inclined toward the middle-class residents that developers ultimately were seeking to attract. Less subtle were city programs that directly encouraged displacement of low-income communities and promoted private upscale residential and commercial initiatives. In the early 1980s, the city capitalized on the burst in economic activity and launched several initiatives to subsidize new business, commercial, and residential construction as well as rehabilitation. Corporations and large developers received extensive tax abatements for the building of office towers, such as AT&T's multimillion-dollar tax break for its new headquarters on Madison Avenue (later sold to the Sony corporation)[64] or the more recent redevelopment of Times Square. The city also subsidized large multiuse development projects, including South Street Seaport and Battery Park City, both in lower Manhattan.[65] Although neither as obvious nor as spectacular, other government intervention policies were geared toward small-scale, piecemeal redevelopment of the city's older neighborhoods. These incentives sought to draw real estate money into low-income and capital-deficient neighborhoods to radically transform their landscapes into middle- and upper-class enclaves. Development programs known as MCI, J-51, and 421-a were the foundation of an ambitious coalition between city agencies and private developers to renew the older housing stock unit by unit, building by building.

The city's pro-development agencies instituted incentives and subsidies for owners to substantially renovate units in their buildings.[66] Because of the design of the incentive programs, they were profitable to landlords only if they could charge substantially higher rents for the renovated units. A program offered by the Division of Housing and Community Renewal (DHCR) called the Major Capital Improvement (MCI) subsidized buildingwide improvements such as new windows, furnaces, and boilers.[67] The program allowed owners to pass on all direct and indirect costs of improvement to tenants by increasing regulated rents gradually and permanently (once the costs were paid, rent hikes remained as profit).[68] Two tax reduction programs, J-51 for old buildings and 421-a for new construction, also promoted neighborhood upgrading. J-51 offered two forms of benefits to owners in return for certain improvements: (1) tax abatements that lowered the amount of property tax for a period ranging from twelve to twenty years, and (2) exemptions from any tax increases that resulted from reassessments based on capital improvements made. The Section 421-a program was part of the State of New York's Real Property Tax Law. For properties constructed under

421-a subsidy, property taxes were phased in incrementally over a ten-year period, including a total exemption during construction and the first two years of operation. Eligible owners agreed to offer rent-stabilized units during the period in which the tax abatement was applied. The construction of Red Square, a massive apartment complex located on Houston Street between Avenue A and First Avenue, was subsidized by the Section 421-a program.

Since these programs fostered significant building renovations or new construction, they directly encouraged the displacement of minority and/ or low-income residents.[69] Significant "loopholes" in rent regulation laws also provided owners a means to quick (re)development. The "substantial alterations" exemption clause to regulated rents was a popular tool in the East Village. Rent regulation procedures determine the new rent when a unit is vacated, typically a 12 percent increase of the former rent. Landlords circumvented this regulation, however, by substantially altering vacated apartments.[70] In addition to "gut" rehabilitation, developers frequently redesigned interior spaces (e.g., combining two units or converting tenement dumbbell airshafts into elevators[71]). If apartments were altered so that they no longer approximated the size or dimension present when the base (original) rents were first determined, then landlords were eligible to charge much higher "first" rents based on the current free-market value.[72] Significant modifications allowed landlords to escalate rents unit by unit, creating wide discrepancies in rents charged within the same building. When regulated one-bedroom apartments that rented from $90 to $125 per month became vacant, the incentive to renovate was strong.

Real Estate Development in the 1980s

> "This [the East Village] can't be a slum forever. I'm a Manhattanite and I know what young professionals are thinking. This could be another SoHo."
>
> Lynne Griffiths, assistant vice president of Citibank,
> quoted in *Real Estate Newsletter* 1985: 1

In the course of the 1980s, real estate development and management firms and lending institutions expended large amounts of capital on purchasing East Village properties and upgrading them.[73] Their expectations of profit earnings from their investments increased as well. For developers, the image of a bohemian arts district served to popularize the East Village, but it offered little advantage as the basis of a future place identity. Continued redevelopment of the East Village held promise that the alternative art and culture scene itself would be replaced by a more permanent, high-income-earning class of residents. An analyst for L. B. Kaye Associates, one of the largest commercial and residential real estate and brokerage firms in Manhattan, offered a favorable prognosis in which the neighborhood "once transient in character, is being transformed into a neighborhood of young professionals."[74] Those working in the city's thriving culture industry who "wouldn't be caught dead buying apartments in stuffy uptown buildings"[75] were targeted by developers. Developer Samuel Glasser, who purchased the vacant and run-down Christodora House on Avenue B and then renovated it for luxury rentals, banked on the neighborhood's exotic allure. "I really do believe that an all-poor neighborhood is a bore," he claimed. "The same goes for an all-rich neighborhood. In between is where the fun is. When you've got all these types rubbing shoulders — yuppie, Ukrainian, Polish, black and Spanish — that's the spark, that's what causes creativity and art."[76]

Given the long history of development schemes, one of the more ironic features of the drive toward redevelopment of the East Village in the 1980s was a growing consensus among developers, lending institutions, and other real estate actors that the tenement was viable as a built form for the upscale, even luxury housing market. Following the collapse of the immigrant slum housing market in the 1920s, the real estate industry had steadfastly maintained its position that both tenements and 25-by-100-foot lots were not only impractical but were impediments to profitable large-scale redevelopment of the Lower East Side (see chapters 3 through 6). In the 1980s, the real estate industry no longer viewed piecemeal redevelopment as inefficient.[77] The pro-growth ideology of the state and city had accomplished an incredible feat — redevelopment policies and incentives had effectively recast century-old "cold-water" flats occupied by low-income residents paying regulated rents into lucrative commodities. In the 1980s, the means for displacing low-income tenants, converting apartments into co-ops or condominiums, renovating Old Law and New Law tenement units, circumventing rent regulations, and obtaining mortgages from banks and savings institutions developed as a specialty industry within real estate. Periodicals geared toward developers of low-income neighborhoods, such as the *Apartment Law Insider*, featured articles such as "What to Do When Rent-Controlled Tenant Vacates" (March 1985), "17 Improvements That Get You a Rent Hike" (June 1986), and "How to Evict Drug Dealers from Your Building" (September 1988).

Speculation gave way to development in the 1980s, and the rules of the "real estate game" and the type of players changed dramatically. Because of risks inherent in investing in an area still reeling from the physical and social consequences of abandonment, the pace of speculative investment was hectic and often impulsive. Speculators were maverick risk takers who typically earned profits or suffered losses within months, not years. Development, or upgrading of a property's "use," was a more time-consuming and protracted process that involved displacing existing residents, renovating units, and attracting higher-rent-paying tenants. Since development required large amounts of capital, the type of investors who entered the local land market changed, and new players — institutional lenders — appeared. Prior to the 1980s, landlords operating in the East Village were primarily petty capitalists, rarely holding more than a few buildings and viewing their property as a supplemental source of income. As the costs (purchase price and tax costs) of entry into the neighborhood land market skyrocketed in the early 1980s, the form of ownership shifted heavily to mid-sized firms and corporations capable of paying exorbitant property costs.[78] Small-scale or single "mom and pop" owners began to drop out, and brokerage firms, property management corporations, and individuals with extensive property holdings within the neighborhood and in similar neighborhoods, such as Harlem or Hell's Kitchen on Manhattan's west side, began to purchase and develop properties.[79] Large firms were more professionally organized and maintained support personnel, such as in-house lawyers, maintenance personnel, and construction personnel. New holding companies and real estate corporations specialized in the upscale marketing of the low-end property market. Urban development policies facilitated this shift in ownership patterns. Larger firms, rather than individual owners, were more likely to gain local and state redevelopment tax incentives, mount legal eviction proceedings, or convert units into condominiums or cooperatives. Local and state redevelopment incentives were geared toward developers with access to capital, rather than to individuals, small landlords, or local housing cooperatives. Tax abatement programs required expensive renovations and improvements to be made. In the absence of low-interest loans, small-time property holders were incapable of embarking on ambitious renovation projects and, therefore, were ineligible for many of these programs' benefits. Rehabilitation loans, which could have been utilized by individual owners or tenant-managed buildings, were phased out by the early 1980s.

Increases in real estate activity and the prevalence of firms and individuals with extensive property portfolios as investors also triggered the appearance of banks, savings and loans, and other lending institutions. Changes in institutional lending patterns in blighted neighborhoods provide an important indicator of the status of redevelopment.[80] Since loans offered access to capital necessary for redevelopment, the participation of these institutions had implications for both the pace and scale of neighborhood upgrading in the East Village. The propensity of banks to lend was not determined just by individual borrowers' credit histories or collateral but also by an assessment of risk based on the neighborhood's current socioeconomic characteristics and indicators of future improvement. Prior to the early 1980s, prospective buyers in the East Village were systematically denied mortgages (redlined) by lending organizations.[81] Banks declined to lend in the East Village based on such indicators as depressed rental market, weak sales, and declining property values. In turn, institutions' aversion to lending in the neighborhood compounded these very same conditions. Speculators and early developers operating in the late 1970s and early 1980s had relied on noninstitutional sources of capital for purchasing property. (Indeed, the lack of access to institutional lending was a bargaining chip for speculators when negotiating sale prices.[82]) Purchase money mortgages (PMMs)[83] — also called "contracts for deed" or "holding the mortgage" — were commonly used to finance speculation and early development in the area deemed riskiest by institutional lenders, Alphabet City/Loisaida in the early 1980s.[84] As speculation waned and was fully replaced by development in the mid-1980s, the importance of PMMs as a source of financing declined, from a mean of 36 percent in 1982 to 28 percent in 1985.[85] By 1984 a record of accelerated real estate sales activity, steadily increasing property values, and the entry of large real estate firms provided institutional lenders evidence of a turnaround in the local land market. Large institutional lenders, such as Citibank (the area's leading lender), Chemical Bank, Barclays, and Bank Leumi, were active in development financing as confidence levels in the neighborhood increased.[86] Their presence allowed developers access to significant sums of capital for extensive rehabilitation and new construction of luxury rental units and condominiums. Penthouse condominiums in Heath House on Avenue A and Fifth Street were sold for nearly $500,000, while smaller units on lower floors were selling for $250,000. At "3 on B" on Avenue B and Third Street, financing allowed for a total rehabilitation of the former tenement. At $1,100 per month for one-bedroom apartments, the rents at "3 on B" rivaled those of uptown units.[87] The participation of large lending institutions in local redevelopment signified the inclusion of the formerly marginal East Village into the fold of the Manhattan housing market.

The Struggle over Redevelopment:
Unit by Unit, Building by Building, Block by Block

The city's and state's piecemeal development incentives, the fragmented redevelopment of small real estate parcels, rent regulations, the abundance of city-owned properties throughout the neighborhood, and the mobilization of residents against displacement of their community were all central factors that together explain the unevenness of restructuring in the East Village in the 1980s. Since restructuring occurred as a protracted battle between residents and developers played out unit by unit, building by building, its effects on the use of space are best revealed in an analysis of street-level changes over time.

To further illustrate the process of restructuring, sales trends and capital flows on a single East Village street were analyzed and are presented in figures 24 to 26. The data are derived from real estate transactions along East Seventh Street from First Avenue to Avenue D. The length of the block bisects the east-west pathway of reinvestment; it straddles the historically better-off western area near First Avenue, the southern half of Tompkins Square Park, and the eastern section most ravaged by abandonment near Avenue D, ending at the Riis Houses (public housing). Properties along the street consisted of Old and New law tenements with storefronts and bars, as well as empty lots, squatted buildings, a synagogue, and churches. Approximately 20 percent of the properties

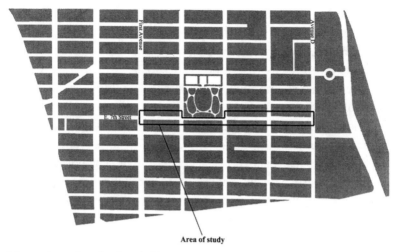

Area of study

Map 6. Area of study of capital investment and sales transactions. Map constructed by Neil Wieloch.

were city-owned, as opposed to 26 percent for the entire neighborhood east of First Avenue. Over 85 percent of the city-owned properties were vacant lots. Most of these lots were clustered in the blocks east of Avenue B, mirroring the trend of widespread abandonment and arson that occurred in Alphabet City in the late 1970s. Despite residential turnover and displacement pressures over two decades, cohorts of once larger ethnic enclaves continued to populate the blocks. Eastern European residents maintained a strong presence between First Avenue and Avenue A, supported by a handful of commercial establishments, including a well-frequented ethnic restaurant and St. Stanislaus Church (between First Avenue and Avenue A). Many of the parishioners of St. Brigid's Church (corner of Avenue B) and of the students who attended its adjacent school were Puerto Rican residents. Puerto Ricans predominated in the apartment buildings between Avenues B and D. The number of newcomers — white young adults — steadily increased throughout the blocks in the mid-1980s.[88]

The analysis of restructuring along Seventh Street included statistical calculations and mapping of real estate sales transactions data between 1982 and 1995, and fieldwork, including participant-observation and interviews with developers and city officials. Data from transactions and investments in all privately owned five-to-six-story Old Law and New Law walk-up apartments on East Seventh Street were collected and analyzed using the Sanborn Manhattan Land Use Book and the Real Estate Data Inc. (REDI) surveys. The results show the temporal and spatial patterns (or the pace and direction) of subsurface real estate capital flows over the thirteen-year period.[89]

Figure 24 depicts the number of properties sold along the entire length of Seventh Street from First Avenue to Avenue D by year between 1983 and 1995. The graph shows that most sales occurred in the mid-1980s, then declined in the early 1990s, only to rebound between 1992 and 1995. Such changes correlate with overall neighborhood sales activities: property development was pronounced in the mid-1980s but was hampered by the community anti-displacement efforts and the 1989–92 citywide real estate bust. Figure 25 charts the dollar amount of real estate capital invested in building purchases on Seventh Street during the same thirteen-year period. The diagram shows that the peak investments occurred in the years 1986 through 1988 during the height of East Village reinvestment. Again, the city's property market decline brought down building sale prices; more recent sales show a considerable increase in market value. Both diagrams in figures 24 and 25 are consistent with analyses of the restructuring process presented here and elsewhere.[90] They clearly show temporal patterns in the level of sales and capital investments. Presenting real estate transactions and investment levels in the entire stretch of Seventh Street alone, however, masks important spatial differences in redevelopment between the eastern and western blocks. Using the same data from Figure 25, Figure 26 shows the dollar

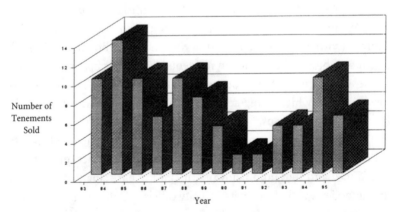

Figure 24. Sales of tenement buildings on East Seventh Street between First Avenue and Avenue D, 1983–95.

amount of real estate capital investment *for each block* along Seventh Street between 1983 and 1995. The diagram clearly visualizes the east-west spatial gradient of sales values as well as temporal changes in the level of capital inflow.

The spatial and temporal unevenness of capital flow along Seventh Street reveals the importance of existing social conditions such as residential makeup, quality of life factors, and residential resistance in the pace and scale of restructuring. For most of the 1980s, socioeconomic conditions were not uniform even *within* buildings along East Seventh

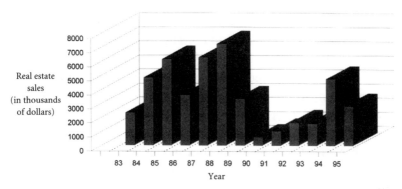

Figure 25. Real estate capital investments in tenement buildings on East Seventh Street between First Avenue and Avenue D, 1983–95.

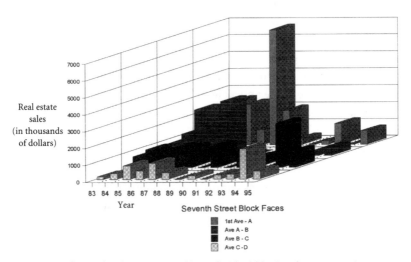

Figure 26. Flows of real estate capital by individual blocks of East Seventh Street between First Avenue and Avenue D, 1983–95.

Street from First Avenue to Avenue D. Tenants included many generations of Puerto Rican families paying modest rents, squatters, college
students living with roommates paying exorbitant rents, drug addicts,
blue-collar workers, and single mothers, alongside fashion designers, musicians, and management trainees. In a nineteen-unit walk-up between
Avenues B and C that was purchased for redevelopment, rents for a one-
bedroom apartment ranged from a low of $256 to a high of $835 per
month.[91] Drug sweeps in the early and middle 1980s attempted to "sanitize" the block but were mostly unsuccessful. Raids drove established
drug distribution off the streets but into foyers, hallways, and apartments
of walk-up buildings.

A focus on the Seventh Street case distorts some features of the redevelopment process and clarifies others. The mix of old tenants and new
on Seventh Street tends to understate the otherwise significant levels of
displacement that occurred in the entire neighborhood between 1980
and 1990. Comparison of demographic data reveals significant changes
in who lived in Alphabet City/Loisaida.[92] Although the increase in total
population of East Village residents was negligible, there were considerable changes in the ethnic and socioeconomic composition of the residents. The groups most vulnerable to displacement were primarily low-
income Latinos, the elderly, and families with children. During the 1980s,
many Puerto Rican residents relocated to the outer boroughs.[93] From
1980 to 1990 the percentage of Latino residents of the total population
dropped 14.5 percent, as compared to an increase of 13.2 percent for all
of Manhattan. In the southern and eastern blocks of the neighborhood, displacement was significant; the percentage of Latino residents
of the total population dropped between 25 and 50 percent. The majority
of newcomers were white and well-educated with higher income levels.
Census data revealed a significant change in the level of educational attainment of neighborhood residents. The percentage of East Villagers
over twenty-five years of age with college degrees increased 14.5 percent, as compared to 8.4 percent for all of Manhattan. The East Village
median household income as compared to Manhattan increased as well
by 19 percent. The notable exception was public housing, where Latinos
remained the majority, and both education levels and median household income increased only slightly between 1980 and 1990. A larger
study of demographic changes across the Lower East Side published in
1987 presented similar findings.[94]

A comparative snapshot of 1980 and 1990 demographic data for the East Village provides strong indication of displacement and redevelopment, but it masks the important spatial and temporal processes of neighborhood restructuring that occurred *during* the decade. As the Seventh Street case exemplifies, low-income residential displacement and upscale redevelopment proceeded incrementally and never totally overwhelmed the East Village. After a frenzy of speculative reinvestment in the early 1980s and the developers' efforts to transform the neighborhood's social and physical landscape, change was neither thorough nor pervasive; revitalization was instead remarkably lopsided, uneven, and irregular. The encroaching signs of gentrification occasionally popped up in the least likely locations and at other times evaded what seemed to be the most plausible sites for neighborhood renewal. Renovated Old and New Law tenements stood adjacent to vacant lots and burned-out buildings. Banners hung in front of a scattering of newly brickfaced buildings advertised "luxury units" with amenities such as terraces, gardens, and laundry facilities.[95] The sixteen-story landmark Christodora House located on the eastern edge of Tompkins Square Park—the heart of the "untamed" East Village—reopened in July 1986. Converted at the cost of $10 million,[96] the Christodora was the flagship of the real estate industry's efforts to reclaim the Lower East Side.[97]

Both historical and current factors accounted for such unevenness. Part of the explanation for the extreme unevenness of redevelopment has already been suggested earlier and in previous chapters of this book: the East Village real estate game included many players dealing large sums of money for small parcels with limited investment returns. No large-scale strategic development plan existed that would allow developers and the state to undertake evictions and condemnation or finance renovation and new construction on a massive scale. Despite the inroads of larger developers and lenders, property ownership remained essentially fragmented in small parcels. On virtually every street and avenue east of Avenue A, city-owned buildings and lots were sandwiched between privately owned apartment buildings.

Structural factors endemic to the New York City housing market prevented the wholesale dislodging of incumbent residents and immediate wide-scale redevelopment. Most low-income renters lived in apartments with state-regulated rental leases that gave legal tenure to tenants and (theoretically) protection against unwarranted evictions to their holders.

Figure 27. Corner of Fourth Street and Avenue C, before development, 1977. "Community Center and Headquarters of Adopt-A-Building." Photograph used by permission of Marlis Momber.

The large number of rent-regulated housing units slowed the pace of neighborhood redevelopment, but it did not arrest it. Landlords invented strategies to deal with individual units, if not entire buildings. To circumvent state rental restrictions, developers resorted to both legal and illegal means to empty their buildings of low-income and often minority tenants. Illegal persuasion and intimidation dominated the early years of development. Tactics included curtailment of heat and hot water in winter, tenant harassment by superintendents or hired drug dealers or addicts, and intentional fires to create unlivable conditions. Illegal means were customary for emptying out entire buildings where a significant proportion of the units were rent controlled, and were frequently employed by some of the more notorious landlords in the East Village.[98] Many of those threatened, especially older Latinos, were less likely to register complaints of tenant abuse because of fear, language barriers, and a lack of information about assistance. As units within buildings were rehabilitated, most were rented out at increased rents to new tenants,[99] making illegal eviction tactics for remaining low-rent units difficult. Landlords resorted to buying out tenants — offering sums in the thousands of dollars that were attractive to many low-income resi-

Figure 28. Corner of Fourth Street and Avenue C, after development, 1984.
"Luxury Apartments." Photograph used by permission of Marlis Momber.

dents. Once vacated, these apartments were either "warehoused" (withheld from the market in anticipation of upscale condominium or cooperative conversion) or renovated for newcomers. Some 16 percent of the 446 Lower East Side households surveyed in the 1987 Community Service Society displacement study indicated that their landlords were keeping apartments vacant for the purpose of conversion.[100] Warehousing was rampant in the heated real estate market in the mid-1980s[101] but petered out by 1989. Landlords renovated and rented individual units one at a time as they were vacated by poor and minority tenants. Whereas new tenants lived in apartments that were uniformly modernized and freshly painted, the majority of their Puerto Rican neighbors remained in the untouched and substandard apartments they had lived in for years.

The unevenness of redevelopment and the accompanying idiosyncratic social relations between newcomers and existing residents were most apparent in those blocks between Avenues B and C where the informal drug economy was pervasive. In contrast to blocks like East Eighth Street, which succumbed to abandonment and displacement in the 1970s, the demography of blocks with historically entrenched drug trades had remained remarkably intact. Few buildings were intentionally set afire or left unoccupied, and most of the Puerto Ricans who had arrived in the early 1960s remained tenured. Dense social networks existed in drug-dealing operations that involved mostly Latino residents linked by kin and friendship networks and employed as whistlers and lookouts, chaperons, and dealers. During business hours (usually the evening), large numbers of residents were engaged in the trade: lookouts were stationed on rooftops and at the entrances to the block, while teenagers and the elderly kept an eye out for suspicious persons and the police. Often, the boundary between licit (grocery worker) and illicit (dealer) activities was permeable. The trade functioned as a "cash and carry operation"; consumption of drugs on these blocks was most often strictly prohibited, and all sales were based on repeat customers and word of mouth rather than solicitation. In the deindustrialized labor market of New York, the thriving drug trade had provided a certain economic and social stability on these blocks. Residents involved in the trade were not easily displaced as a consequence of real estate disinvestment or reinvestment. Interactions between existing residents and new occupants of those apartments that had been renovated were more accommodating than hostile. Since most of the public activities on such blocks were monitored by residents involved in the drug trade, a remarkable social order was maintained; petty crimes, apartment break-ins, and assaults were virtually unheard of. This "order" prevented an unwanted police intrusion that would have interrupted business. Operating as classic free riders, some new residents spoke glowingly of this added safety factor.[102]

Redevelopment during the 1980s was a protracted process undertaken by hundreds of individuals and real estate firms and carried out literally unit by unit, building by building, and block by block. But the fragmented and disjointed form of real estate investment and the legal protections of New York rental housing cannot fully explain these uneven effects. The area's prevailing severe socioeconomic conditions and, more importantly, local political and cultural resistance to development prevented the wholesale homogenization of the East Village.

CHAPTER EIGHT

Targeting the Middle Class:
Cultures of Resistance and Class Warfare

Efforts toward arts-based development of the East Village were predicated on an expectation that changes in the neighborhood's reputation would attract the illusive middle-class residents who long considered the area too destitute and displeasing. Positive media coverage of the arts scene contributed to the growing popularity of the East Village, yet the commensurate arrival of newcomers (and the displacement of existing residents) did not follow suit in a continuous or smooth fashion. Several factors account for the uneven landscape of pockets of development mixed with sections of entrenched poverty. As we have seen, the fragmented geography of ownership and rent regulations hindered redevelopment in some areas but not others. This chapter examines the cultural and political dimensions to uneven redevelopment, focusing first on changes in the art scene and the alliances and cleavages among various community actors engaged in resistance. Second, the chapter recounts three incidents of resistance in 1988–89: the battles over the curfew in Tompkins Square Park, the homeless encampments, and the eviction of squatters. These three incidents provide details of the class and ethnic fissures in grassroots politics and the relationship of art and performance to urban resistance.

The Limits to Middle-Class Redevelopment: Community Politics and Fissures in Urban Resistance

By the close of the 1980s, the celebrated East Village art scene that ushered in the neighborhood's "renaissance" went bust. The frenzy of art magazine articles, celebrity artist interviews, and shows in elite SoHo and uptown art galleries was replaced by the near disappearance of "East Village art" in New York. Graffiti art, in particular, was never institutionalized into the mainstream art world. Several explanations for the precipitous fall have been posited. These include arguments pointing to the culture and class dissonance between graffiti artists and their work and the elitist art establishment, the disorganization of graffiti artists and dealers that led to only a brief courtship with the mainstream art world, and the fateful consequence of the paradox of a rather public and democratic art form and the exclusive and privileged private art market.[1] The East Village commercial art galleries that had transformed the landscape in the beginning of the 1980s largely disappeared. A few capitalized on the early success of local art and migrated to SoHo, but most simply closed as the neo-Expressionist hype dissipated. At the same time, the credibility of the East Village "underground" scene was under attack. Michael Musto, entertainment columnist for the weekly *Village Voice*, pronounced the underground cultural life in downtown Manhattan dead. What had once been an elusive "below Fourteenth Street" scene of alternative music, new talent, and creative expression had become vernacular, its rough edges softened.[2] The rapid decline of the art scene undermined the strategy of both developers and the state to employ a "SoHo model" of arts-based and middle-class urban redevelopment. With the fallout of the most obvious and glaring forms of hype, those artists and (mostly not-for-profit) galleries that remained and had resisted commercialization meshed cultural venues with political resistance against development and displacement. A handful of groups and organizations, such as the collective Political Art Documentation and Distribution (PADD), which sponsored the "Not For Sale" anti-displacement project in the early 1980s, consistently contested the agenda of developers and the city.[3] The gallery ABC No Rio featured local minority artists and highlighted issues critical of the social changes occurring in the neighborhood.[4] Other cultural organizations distanced themselves from rampant commercialism. The Kenkeleba Gallery collective of black artists and writers operated out of a city-owned tenement on Second and B,[5] the El Bohio community center on East Ninth Street run by Charas, and the WOW Cafe, a theater space for women that emerged after the 1980 Women's One World Festival in the East Village, eschewed com-

mercialism and allied themselves with the area's low-income populations and often with the most radical and visible of protesters.

The developers' intent to dislodge the character of the East Village
and replace it with one appealing to the middle and upper classes was
met with various and effective forms of political and cultural resistance.
Popular resistance to the threat of bland, middle-class aesthetics mixed
art forms and antidevelopment politics together as a culture of protest.
The message "Die Yuppie Scum" was scrawled ubiquitously on buildings
and sidewalks throughout the neighborhood. "Mug a Yuppie" and ad-
monitions to newcomers were coupled with calls for boycotts of upscale
boutiques and groceries. While protest culture presented a nuisance, developers and the state viewed the brewing dispute with local organized
housing organizations over the fate of city-owned lots and buildings as
an obstacle to redevelopment. After a decade of fighting the effects of
disinvestment, political aloofness, and marginalization, long-time activists were faced abruptly with the surreal notion that spaces once abandoned as worthless were now coveted by developers and hawked by the
city to white, middle-class renters. For dozens of community-based organizations and loose affiliations of activists in the East Village and across

Figure 29. "Loisaida War Party; Performance at Charas." Photograph used by
permission of Marlis Momber.

the Lower East Side, the shift from housing abandonment in the 1970s to housing redevelopment in the 1980s meant a minor retooling of their strategies to preserve housing and community for low-income residents. The switch in the land-use intentions of the state and capitalists did nothing to alleviate the threat to the low-income and ethnically diverse character of the Lower East Side. As proprietor of nearly six thousand properties scattered across the Lower East Side, the City of New York was in the position to tilt the balance in favor of development. Nearly one hundred of the city's properties were empty lots, one-third were vacant buildings, and another one-third of the buildings were administered under some form of tenant management program, such as Tenant-Interim Lease (TIL).[6] There was no master plan for the disposition of in rem properties, especially after the funding for tenant self-management was substantially reduced. For developers, city-owned properties blocked contiguous redevelopment, either by serving as contentious spaces or by acting as pockets of low-income housing that could not be displaced easily. Since the investment frenzy in the early 1980s, developers had expressed concerns about the potential saturation of public housing in the area, or, put more directly, community pressures to build more housing units for low-income and mostly minority tenants threatened to frustrate plans for a white, middle-class housing market. Despite their substantial displacement from privately owned buildings in the 1980s, Latinos maintained a significant percentage (79 percent) of the population of the Riis and Wald Houses along Avenue D. Most of the tenants in these subsidized units lived on fixed incomes and relied on the Housing Authority's below-market rents to maintain homes in the neighborhood. As in other New York neighborhoods (e.g., Chelsea, the Upper West Side) the detrimental effect of a contiguous row of public housing buildings on real estate development was strictly limited to adjacent properties.

The city intended to auction off in rem properties to the highest bidders. But that plan—a blatant gesture toward real estate interests—was thwarted consistently by a sundry of community organizations, including Cooper Square, Good Ole Lower East Side (GOLES), and, especially, the umbrella organization to which they belonged, the Lower East Side Planning Council. For activists, the central issue that defined the fight over community was the future disposition of in rem properties. They sought and gained a moratorium against the auctioning of city-owned housing and lots to developers in 1983 through mass demonstrations. In addition to such time-honored tactics, the local community board and the Joint Planning Council (JPC) supported plans for Mutual Housing Associations (MHAs) to rehabilitate and manage some of the city-owned properties. MHAs had operated in other cities, such as Baltimore, as nonprofit cooperatives providing affordable housing to low-income populations.[7] Prospective tenants paid a fee to join, and if they later moved, they received the original amount paid (with interest) but no equity share in the building. Rents were set at levels to insure a building's long-term upkeep and maintenance and were generally affordable. A plan was forwarded to convert five city-owned properties on Second Street and Avenue B into MHAs. However, the city first moved slowly on site approval and later folded the site into the discussion over a much larger in rem agenda, the cross subsidy plan.[8]

In the early 1980s, key activists and organizations proposed a new legislative means to combat the root of urban restructuring—removing in rem property from the profit-oriented private housing market.[9] Most local housing activists had witnessed the power of real estate capital to abet both the neighborhood's deterioration in the 1970s and its miraculous "renaissance" in the 1980s. They also expressed concerns over how each process had, at best, left the working poor community behind or, at worst, displaced a significant number of low-income residents. The auction of all city-owned properties to private owners offered no guarantee against repeat occurrences of disinvestment-reinvestment and its consequences for residents. Yet financing for a major community initiative to purchase in rems was unlikely given the pro-development focus of city and federal housing policies in the 1980s. In June 1984, a task force representing the key organized low-income housing organizations in the neighborhood broached the notion of using monies from the sale of some of the newly valorized in rem properties to subsidize low-income housing development. City-owned properties, according to the proposal, would be sold to developers who would provide a one-to-one match of market-rate housing and low- to moderate-income housing. In turn, the proceeds from the sale of market-rate housing would be used to develop vacant lots and other in rem buildings. The city's HPD responded with its own plan in which one low-income housing unit would be provided for every four market-rate units. The developer would then rehabilitate another in rem building to be managed by a nonprofit organization.[10] After a series of negotiations and compromises between the Joint Planning Council and the city, the result was the 1987 50/50 Cross Subsidy plan. The plan called for both real estate and local housing coalitions to share in the disposition of city-owned lots and buildings. The cross subsidy plan proposed to allocate one thousand dwelling units in existing city-owned tenements for low- to middle-income occupants to be rehabilitated using revenue gained from the sale of a comparable number of empty lots to real estate developers constructing market-value units.[11]

Despite contention between local housing organizations over details of the brokering of the plan with the city, the 50/50 cross subsidy successfully tied the provision of the low-income housing to redevelopment. Since 1992, several blocks in Loisaida, especially along Avenue C, have been reconstructed under the auspices of the 50/50 cross subsidy. By temporarily (and, in some cases, permanently) securing the disposition of these properties as low-income housing units, the potential for private development to engulf the area was thwarted.[12] The precedent was also important. Community ownership and control over the disposition of housing units have improved the uncertain housing situations of some low-income residents.

The successful efforts of organized housing organizations to hammer out the cross subsidy deal with the city over the fate of the neighborhood's in rem properties were a partial defeat for the exclusively middle-class development proffered by developers. Clearly developers would have preferred open sales of all of the city's property stock rather than the compromise arrangement that limited market-rate private development. The 1987 cross subsidy deal meant that low- and moderate-income units would be interspersed among middle-class housing (if only temporarily), making uniform redevelopment difficult if not impossible east of Avenue A. Nonetheless, further private redevelopment of the East Village was built into the deal. And for impatient developers, the cross subsidy plan promised to put an end to the highly visible conflict between state and community over the future of the city's properties. While the plan was in the process of negotiation, real estate capitalists expressed concerns about the controversy. In 1985, a special segment on the East Village property market in *Real Estate Newsletter* documented the hesitancy of large developers to continue to invest, citing those who "are tiring of battles over the future of properties."[13] Although the 50/50 cross subsidy was not the preferred outcome for developers, the dispute over the city-owned properties was resolved, and the harangue against redevelopment by community groups who signed on to the plan was, in effect, silenced.

The cross subsidy plan formalized a compromise between the *organized* detractors of East Village redevelopment and the city, but popular community dissent was not silenced. In fact, after 1987 the level of social resistance against neighborhood redevelopment reached such levels that the East Village was nationally and internationally identified with riots, protest, and housing demonstrations. Cleavages between formal housing organizations and loosely organized self-styled urban radicals over antidevelopment ideology and tactics grew pronounced after the 50/50 cross subsidy deal. The cross subsidy plan had bypassed the housing interests of a vocal group of squatters who had taken control and made homes in over a dozen in rem buildings when the moratorium on auctions of city-owned properties was in effect. While the fate of such properties was left hanging during the negotiations between the city and local housing groups, squatters and other individuals opposed to private development were busy fixing up their new homes and, at times, defending them from eviction efforts by HPD and the police. Although squatters were not part of the negotiations, their homes were counted among the properties encompassed by the cross subsidy plan. The relationship between squatters and organized housing groups transformed from neighborly in the 1970s, to chilly during the plan's inception in the 1980s, to outright hostile. Squatters charged that the plan was a sellout to developers, that the JPC benefited from the right to renovate and manage squatter properties. In exchange for this benefit, the Community Board had conceded the rest of the properties to developers.[14] The proponents of the cross subsidy countered that, under present circumstances, the plan was the best option for low-income housing. Finally, squatters and other radical housing activists claimed that the plan's provision for low-income housing units was short-term. The key providers of new units, low-income housing development corporations, were not obligated to maintain permanent, affordable housing; units would revert to private-market rents after a set period.

Characterizing the deal as a "sellout" and "betrayal," the more radical activists and squatters mounted their own resistance tactics to "stop the real estate attack on the Lower East Side." They called for an immediate moratorium on evictions from squatted buildings and the opening of abandoned buildings for homesteading by the neighborhood's growing homeless population.[15] Several confrontations between city agencies and the police and neighborhood radicals escalated rebellion and antiauthoritarianism as the defining features of the East Village's identity in 1988–90. The overview of the violent episodes of 1988–89 offered next demonstrates the complexity of neighborhood politics and focuses on the class and ethnic/racial cleavages over issues and actions. The analysis also illustrates the influence of place symbols and images on Lower East Side protest politics.

The Turf Battles of 1988–89:
Radical Politics and the East Village Identity

As redevelopment of the East Village intensified in the mid-1980s, the effects on the landscape became more obvious and glaring. The sometimes stark physical contrasts between new developments and the area's nearly century-old worn features were matched in social and cultural tensions between groups of old-timers and newcomers. Such tensions erupted several times as heated turf battles occurred over the control of Tompkins Square Park and the tenure rights of squatters who occupied several buildings east of Avenue B. The immediate causes of each of the confrontations between police and locals were different, but they shared key aspects. Each incident involved similar sets of actors and tactics with only minor variations. By virtue of their visible and vocal presence at demonstrations, marches, and local meetings, the squatters[16] emerged as the unofficial leaders of an otherwise disconnected assortment of punks/skinheads, anarchists, ex-hippies, artists, and other cultural radicals, who expressed a wide range of commitments to opposition to redevelopment and authority. The resistance tactics typically employed were insurgent, disruptive, highly flamboyant, and intentionally obnoxious — a mix of 1960s social protest with 1970s/1980s underground/punk stylized alienation. The strategic marriage of art and subversion in the form of spectacles (concerts, parties, etc.), music, sculpture, graffiti, video making, "fanzines," and mimeographed leaflets was highly effective in attracting public turnout and media attention. Despite rare moments of neighborhood unity on a particular issue, such tactics further separated the radicals from critical long-term activists, the more moderate residents who referred to them as "thugs," "toughs," "disrupters," and "bullies" who "held the neighborhood hostage."[17] Through repetition, resistance became highly symbolic and ritualized. Resistance slogans, associated music, and art styles became autonomous forms in themselves, contributing to an East Village identity of antiauthoritarianism.

Tompkins Square Park: The Curfew

Over the course of nearly a decade, pro-development city policies intended to slowly regulate and redefine the use of streets, empty lots, and tenements. In the wake of these efforts, violence erupted in the site where the antagonisms over the importance of neighborhood space for local use versus profitable exchange and the desires of the community versus those of capital seemed visibly conspicuous — Tompkins Square Park. As previous chapters suggested, the use of the park and its territorialization by various local groups often led to conflicts that were highly representative of social changes that enveloped the Lower East Side. The circumstances were no different in the summer of 1988 when simmering tensions over the use of the park were resonant with friction between residents new and old over middle-class redevelopment. On the evening of August 7 and in the early hours of August 8, 1988, a few hundred diverse protesters, sympathizers, and bystanders faced off an army of riot-geared police fortified by helicopters, advanced communications, and a high-tech mobile command center. The event had begun as a relatively small gathering of "punks, politicos, and curious neighbors"[18] who gathered to protest a newly enforced midnight curfew of the well-attended twenty-four-hour neighborhood meeting place. The demonstration soon escalated into a riot when police officers, emboldened by the tacit consent of their commanders, swept the park and adjacent overcrowded neighborhood streets, indiscriminately clubbing anyone caught in the onslaught. As witnesses would later testify and homemade videotapes clearly showed, police officers on horseback set upon pedestrians without apparent provocation. Unsuspecting bystanders were forced to scatter to avoid flailing nightsticks. Businesses along Avenue A, which were typically packed with weekend revelers, were quickly deserted as the police chased protesters through restaurant dining rooms and bars. Following the initial sweep of the park, the riot was transformed into a series of mini-confrontations and "standoffs" between the police and a swelling number of protesters, aggrieved bystanders, and residents determined to "hold and defend" the intersection of Avenue A and St.

Mark's Place. For several hours, alarmed and outraged punks, post-hip-pies, housing activists, and innocent bystanders joined together in chants of "No police state" and "It's our fucking park, you don't live here!" With organizers carrying banners of "1988 = 1933, Revolt" and "Gentrification Is Class War," the crowd intermittently challenged the cordon of mounted police, hurling insults along with bottles and exploding firecrackers. The police responded swiftly and ruthlessly, charging the crowd and forc-ing them to retreat. Mayhem ensued only to be replaced by another standoff. After nearly three hours of attack, retreat, regroup, and then attack again, a local parish priest sympathetic to low-income housing concerns brokered a truce and defused the tense standoff over control of the intersection. Members of the makeshift community delegation voiced some of the issues that angered the demonstrators: "There's been no dialogue. Rents are going up."[19] It soon became obvious that the park's curfew enforcement was the flash point of deeper tensions over control of the redevelopment of the neighborhood. Before dawn, a handful of protesters, feeling victorious from the police back-down, descended on the touchstone of real estate colonization, the Christodora House. Chanting "Die Yuppie Scum!" and using parts from a wooden sawhorse police barricade, they rammed the glass doors of the entrance way, ripping down a light fixture and overturning a potted fern. Outside, to the cheers of a small band of onlookers, they mounted a banner car-ried earlier in the evening; it read, "Gentrification + Class War = Geno-cide."[20] All told, forty-four people, many of whom were bystanders caught in the fray, were injured in what has become known as the Tompkins Square Police Riot.[21] Clearly, locals were not going to allow developers and the state to upgrade the East Village and rid its subversive charac-ter without a fight.

Like most urban riots, the events of August 1988 in Tompkins Square were a watershed that reflected the frustrations of past and present social conditions and unleashed new social forces to atone or address com-munity grievances. The significance of the riot of Tompkins Square for community collective action is twofold. First, the melee revealed political, economic, and cultural tensions among class- and ethnic-based resi-dent factions over ways to deal with or combat real estate intentions and actions and the city's local development policies. Second, the riot legitimized, if only briefly, a radical and highly symbolic form of com-munity resistance to redevelopment that eventually only furthered existing cleavages among local resident groups and organizations. In the aftermath of the "riot," real estate supporters, pro-development community associations, the police, and city leaders presented the uprising as a result of differences in opinion over quality-of-life concerns, respect for law and order, and appropriate uses of public space. And while meetings and official proclamations prior to the riot emphasized concerns over homeless encampments and noise in and around the park, the events in Tompkins Square Park were clearly a manifestation of deeper conflict over the restructuring of the East Village.

A brief review of the events that led to the riot reveals the heightened intrigue coupled with mistrust and suspicion across ethnic and class lines that saturated local politics of neighborhood development and resistance in the 1980s. The immediate issue that prompted the melee — enforcement of a park curfew — had been repeatedly broached by older working-class residents (both white and non-white) *and* wealthier, mostly white middle-class newcomers who lived adjacent to the park. Despite obvious class differences, the two groups joined forces to complain to the Community Board 3 about late night and excessive noise emanating from the park and surrounding bars. Cognizant of local residents' attachments to and the diverse uses of the park, the local community board declined to call for the park's midnight closing but did author a letter of support for increased police presence in the park late at night. For older residents, the board's hesitancy to enforce the curfew evinced its failure to maintain order and deal with the neighborhood's "rogue element." Newer residents charged that the board's apparent complicity with the old guard was out of touch with the new revived East Village. The city, meanwhile, interpreted the board's request for added police as an opportunity to "clean up" the park. Within a few days of the local board's resolution, city park workers had painted on the asphalt entrances to the park a warning that Tompkins Square would close at 1 A.M.[22] "The mystery of the Tompkins Square Park riot," wrote a journalist seeking to reconstruct the events leading up to the riot, "lies somewhere between the order, which calls for increased police protection, and the call for a park curfew."[23] In the weeks following the meeting, the local police incrementally began to usher in curfew enforcement. Around midnight on July 11 and periodically on nights thereafter, all persons were ordered to vacate the park except the homeless, who were confined to the park's southeast corner. Local activists, squatters, punks, anarchists, and other supporters of a variety of radical political interests interpreted the closings as municipal approval of property owners' development plans. The curfew enforcement, according to the popular sentiment on the street, was a clear and aggressive effort to eliminate particular behaviors and associated persons who did not conform to the idealized representation of a developed East Village. Older residents who were in favor of the park curfew, including eastern Europeans and some Latinos on fixed incomes, were dismissed as an ill-informed or ultra-conservative political element.

In the weeks preceding the riot, local radical activists, including squatters, skinheads, and punks, mobilized against the planned curfew, posting leaflets throughout the neighborhood reporting the curfew crackdown as a police effort to take the park away from the public. In an obvious mix of political and cultural radicalism, a protest rally in the park featured a concert of several local bands and a crowd of three hundred people. When police officers arrived to enforce the curfew, they scuffled with protesters but were well outnumbered and withdrew to the delight of the jubilant demonstrators.[24] In response to the growing crisis, a meeting among the officials of the local police precinct, the mayor's office, and "right-wing elements" of the local community board was hastily called.[25] Police officials left that meeting with the understanding that they were authorized to enforce the curfew. Unbeknownst to most actors until the evening of the riot, the local police precinct, from the leadership to the rank and file, began to regard the successful implementation of the curfew as a "make-or-break" issue of authority. The degree of advanced preparation and the size of force sent to engage the small group of protesters on August 7 suggests both the local precinct's exasperation with local resistance and its resolve to assert control.

The story of the Tompkins Square riot and the uncertain events that led to it captures the obvious and less obvious elements of neighborhood politics of resistance in the 1980s. Clearly, the riot was an outcome of simmering and underlying conflicts over development. Yet the riot also brought to the fore the strains over strategies, goals, and representations of the neighborhood that ranged from the subversive notions put forth by "radicals" to the more unassuming and conservative ideals of the older residents. A second, albeit short-term effect of the Tompkins Square Park riot was the radicalization of local resistance politics. The brutal misbehavior of the police sparked extensive condemnation, and that reaction worked in favor of a new, more radical episode of antidevelopment collective action. Although the city never rescinded the curfew, Tompkins Square Park remained open following the riot. The collective meaning of the riot's aftermath disregarded cleavages in grassroots opposition: those opposed to the park's curfew as a statement against the neighborhood's development had "won" this round against the city; those in favor of the curfew, regardless of class, ethnic, or tenure status, were agents of redevelopment. With the media in full gaze of local events following the riot, local activists, community sympathizers, and many residents chided the police department's actions and explained the rationale for such actions as city policy to clean up the neighborhood in support of development. Indeed, the riot seemed to convince even the most skeptical of the very real possibility of widespread development and displacement. Immediately following the riot, the scope of resistance widened to include residents from across class and ethnic lines, including the most vocal of the more radical activists and, ironically, some newcomers. In the late hours of the Tompkins Square Park riot, the protesters seemed a representative sample of the late-1980s East Village: white, young, well-dressed adults, aging bearded ex-hippies, and Puerto Rican and black men and teenagers together singing and screaming, "This land is our land." "The streets were full of people who I see coming out of their houses every morning with briefcases," said Phil van Aver, a member of Community Board 3. "I mean people who work on Wall Street, and they're standing in the street screaming, 'Kill the pigs.' "[26] One week after the police riot, a similarly diverse crowd of five hundred gathered in Tompkins Square Park and sat under a banner stating, "Gentrification Is Class War" to listen to defiant speeches along with plenty of rock music performed by local bands.[27] In the offices of suited real estate developers and banking officials, the riot and the social inclusiveness of the ensuing outrage did little to palliate their concerns about the rough image of the East Village.

In the aftermath of the riot, threats to defend the park pervaded activists' discourse and tactics. "Arrest us! Try us! We'll have another riot!" was a familiar refrain of demonstrators at community board meetings, homelessness demonstrations, and police actions that dealt with the park or other issues tinged with the slightest relevance to development and displacement. At small ad hoc protests and large planned ones, spectators and the media anticipated a repeat of August 1988, and protesters employed familiar images, slogans, and signs in their repertoires. Activists exploited the sweeping post-riot realization that the city's quality-of-life policies thinly concealed an aggressive endorsement of private re-development. The riot, in essence, had proved the naysaying activists cor-rect. In local political terms, that realization translated into a broadly supported tolerance of the use of the park. But the tolerance of an un-regulated public space was soon tested by events in the following year.

Tompkins Square Park: The Homeless

Following the riot, both local reactions and larger media spotlights high-lighted the rhetoric and actions of the East Village's more radical polit-ical contingent consisting of squatters, punks, anarchists, and politicos. The voices of the more formal low-income housing organizations had been silenced, and their leadership of the antidevelopment movement questioned. With their focus on housing needs, many organized groups had ignored the simmering tensions over the park's closure, while oth-ers were suspected of having supported the curfew. By the fall of 1988, the public's fascination as well as that of the committee formed to inves-tigate the riot soon turned to an increasing homeless population that had "settled" in Tompkins Square Park.[28] Word of the nonenforced cur-few spread among the homeless, who were increasingly fenced out of most public spaces across the city. By the summer of 1989, over two hundred homeless individuals lived in makeshift shacks and lean-tos in Tompkins Square Park. In July 1989, 250 police officers sealed off the park, informed the "residents" they were being evicted, and gave them fifteen minutes to gather their belongings.[29] The rationale for the evic-tion, according to park and police officials, was rampant prostitution and drug use in the park.[30] The effect of the July clearance was tempo-rary, however. By fall a considerable number of homeless had resettled the park. The debate over a Tompkins Square Park curfew was revis-ited, this time complicated by the presence of a sizable homeless en-campment. The political fallout of the 1988 riot remained tangible. In meetings, on street corners, and in bars, the "park problem" was con-structed as an overly simplified political dichotomy: those who sup-ported the removal of the homeless were in support of the curfew and, therefore, redevelopment and displacement. Those many residents who wanted a "usable park" but also supported the housing demands of the homeless and were opposed to an enforced curfew faced a "lose-lose" dilemma.

In the fall and winter of 1989, activists and protesters capitalized on the link between quality-of-life issues (a usable park not occupied by homeless) and support for real estate development. In public meetings, anyone expressing concern over the park's condition or the need to displace the homeless was accused (and very often silenced) of being a coconspirator with real estate developers and banks. Activists successfully commandeered local meetings, shouting down any discussions of options to relocate or remove the homeless. In a raucous October community board meeting, police in riot gear were called on to intimidate a large crowd of protesters but left after a half hour of taunting and name calling.[31] Interestingly, several homeless persons who lived in Tompkins Square Park resented the symbolic use of their plight in a larger battle over land use.[32]

A local city councilwoman who advocated low-income housing initiatives pressed for a compromise between the polar opposites of sweeping the park and leaving it untouched. By fall, individuals and groups supporting a solution to the homeless encampment problem grew in-

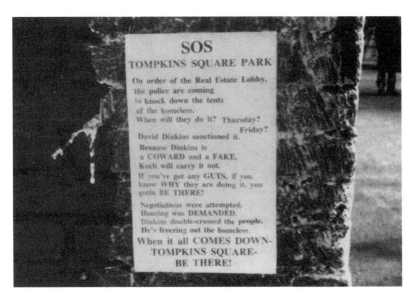

Figure 30.   Activists' flyer warning of coming eviction. Photograph by Christopher Mele.

creasingly interested in a third option: the closing down of the park for much needed extensive renovations.[33] The compromise solution was implemented to both satisfy the demands to "restore the park" and placate the concerns about a callous and potentially violent eviction of the homeless left to fend for themselves. By opening a social service outreach "help center" in the park, the plan's sponsors hoped most of the homeless would leave voluntarily and prevent forced evictions. While some of the park dwellers utilized the service, few left on the basis of assistance provisions. A few isolated evictions of homeless camps occurred in the fall of 1989, but the size of the park's population continued to swell, and the makeshift structures grew more elaborate. The cold of winter seemed to amplify the homeless presence in the park. Smoke from fires that burned in trash barrels day and night inundated the park and adjacent blocks, shopping carts and belongings were chained to park benches, and numerous blue plastic tarps used for weatherproofing sharply contrasted with the leafless trees and gray skies. As the size of the contemporary Hooverville expanded, the number of complaints from residents (ranging from reports of prostitution, drug abuse, and crime to an inability to use the park) increased, and even the most ardent supporters of the homeless reconsidered their position against a curfew or closure.

In early December a resident group, the Tompkins Square Neighborhood Coalition, posted a "Statement of Principles" throughout the neighborhood calling for the eviction of the homeless. The Coalition railed against the intimidation by radical protesters who disrupted public meetings "by throwing cat feces, and other objects, smoking marijuana, shouting abuse... and appearing with tires emblazoned with the names of local officials whom they said should be 'necklaced,' like those accused of Government collaboration in South Africa."[34] Clergy from local churches, meanwhile, argued that the first priority of any solution to the shantytown was the provision of affordable housing, not the park's beautification or the unenforced curfew. They campaigned for renovation of abandoned city-owned buildings adjacent to the park for homeless occupancy.[35]

While the various grassroots opposition factions fought among themselves, the city acted. On an unbearably cold December 14, workers from the city's park department, protected by uniformed and plainclothes police and "peace officers," subdivided the park into six sectors, roused

Figure 31. Removal of homeless possessions in homeless eviction, Tompkins Square Park, 14 December 1989. Photograph by Christopher Mele.

the homeless from their shelters and ordered them to vacate the park. Garbage trucks and five flatbed trucks were ready to haul away the debris and material that formed the structures. Organized resistance was noticeably absent during the eviction, but nearly two dozen of the homeless set fire to their shanties before walking away, adding a surreal appearance to the mix of park workers clad in green jackets, rubber gloves, and surgical masks and dozens of homeless scampering to collect what belongings they could carry. Later in the day, a group of protesters occupied an empty building on East Tenth Street across from the park and made several speeches from its third-floor windows to a crowd of spectators below before being arrested. Interviewed in the local press, park officials voiced the concerns of "tax-paying" residents as justification for the eviction. Echoing the officials' stance, a resident who lived near the park for a year and a half voiced his support of the action: "We're taxpayers. We want a place to walk our dogs."[36] In 1991, the park was closed for over a year for extensive renovations.

Battle over the Squats

Tompkins Square Park was not the only site of violent contests among factions of residents and the state at the end of the 1980s. In 1989 and

Figure 32. Protesters demonstrate against eviction of homeless from Tompkins Square Park. Photograph by Christopher Mele.

periodically in the 1990s, city agencies and the police department sought to rid Loisaida of the most vocal, subversive, and flamboyantly radical critics of urban redevelopment, those squatting abandoned city-owned properties. As discussed in earlier chapters, the position of squatters vis-à-vis the neighborhood politics of restructuring had been transformed since the 1970s. Squatting was embraced initially by embattled Lower East Siders as a welcome alternative to wide-scale abandonment, drug dens, and depopulation. In the late 1970s, the city hesitantly imparted official status to "urban homesteading" through a handful of financing and management programs. The curtailment and elimination of home-steading programs further radicalized squatting. The city interpreted its part of the 50/50 cross subsidy deal with neighborhood organizations as community support to remove the squatters. As a result, enforce-ment exacerbated existing antagonisms among antidevelopment fac-tions. Conflict over rightful use of the numerous city-owned lots and buildings proliferated after the 1987 cross subsidy agreement.

In the late 1970s, a local Latino resident organization, Charas, had transformed an abandoned, trash-strewn lot into a park, playground, and outdoor concert/theater space called La Plaza Cultural. The issue of own-ership and use of La Plaza did not come into question until the late

1980s when the Lower East Side Coalition for Housing Development, Inc., (LESCHDI), whose director at the time, area councilman Antonio Pagan, petitioned the city to turn over the land to develop housing for the elderly. The plan won the approval of key city agencies and the local community board but was met with protest by a loose affiliation of community-active white residents (most of whom had lived in the area since the 1970s), sympathetic Latinos, and squatters and anarchists. The debate centered not on the need for elderly housing (indeed, all parties agreed more should be built) but on the selection of the site. La Plaza's supporters were angered that given so much adjacent unused and abandoned property, valuable community green space would be sacrificed instead.[37] Community Board 3, supporting LESCHDI, retorted that empty lots, abandoned buildings, and other city-owned properties had already been slated in the 50/50 cross subsidy formula.

In the late 1980s and early 1990s, similar rifts between squatters and community organizations were touched off by the city's escalated in rem eviction-demolition policy in the heavily squatter-occupied area east of Avenue B. In the late 1980s, HPD began a policy of demolition of several city-owned buildings deemed unsafe and officially listed as "vacant," although it was well known that many had been occupied by squatters since the late 1970s. Although some of the targeted buildings were occupied, even renovated, and equipped with running water and electricity, the New York City Buildings Department ruled them in "immediate danger" of collapse so as to warrant demolition by HPD workers. The sudden interest in clearing the neighborhood of buildings left vacant for over a decade can only be explained by the terms of the 50/50 cross subsidy plan that were favorable to the city. The arrangement with the organized housing coalitions enabled the city to sell *vacant* lots to real estate developers to build private market housing. A policy of clearing old, dilapidated, and abandoned tenements would increase the stock of vacant lots to the advantage of both the city and developers.[38] When HPD began to lay claim to the properties it had long ignored, it confronted squatters and community activists prepared to do battle over the control and disposition of homes, gardens, and community spaces.

Turf battles between the city and local activists over buildings on East Eighth Street brought the city's policies and neighborhood resistance to middle-class development to the media limelight. HPD's effort to evict a fifty-two-year-old mother of two from a six-story squat at 316 East

Eighth Street was featured in the *Village Voice* and the *New York Times*.[39] News of the impending demolition spread via a highly organized neighborhood eviction watch, to other squatters and squatter sympathizers who amassed at the site and occupied the building's foyer until being forcibly removed by the police.[40] As the police began the evictions, M-80 explosives were thrown from the roof of a nearby squatted tenement, which was quickly commandeered by the police. Last minute legal efforts mounted by supportive paralegals to stave off the eviction and demolition failed. Hours later a crane was ripping the roof off the nineteenth-century tenement. And once again, a phalanx of protesters moved their demonstration to the Christodora House high-rise condominium on Ninth Street and Avenue B, after one squatter shouted to the crowd of angry onlookers, "To the Christodora!"[41] In a chorus of cheers, demonstrators hurled cement bricks at the building, threw rocks at windows, and dumped a bag of garbage in the lobby.[42]

Two weeks later, the New York City Building Department declared another East Eighth Street building unsafe due to a 1987 fire that had weakened its rear wall. This building too was occupied by "a rare mix, exemplifying the diversity that is being ground out of the Lower East Side,"[43] including a Puerto Rican poet active in the Nuyorican Poets Cafe, an artist, a "professional slam-dancer," a local activist, and the family of a former coal miner from West Virginia.[44] Crews sent to demolish the structure were met with resistance by squatters who hurled bottles of urine (used to ward off drug dealers) and pulled down the temporary scaffolding.[45] At the peak of the protest, two hundred demonstrators alerted by the eviction watch and carrying the now familiar banner, "No Housing No Peace," had gathered. Confrontation began after the demonstrators marched around Tompkins Square Park and were confronted on Avenue B by about twenty police officers, who began to corral them toward Seventh Street. Three hundred police officers were called to the scene to put down the melee. Despite interventions of lawyers, two architects, and a licensed contractor who concurred that the building was indeed salvageable[46] and a brief restraining order from a local judge, the HPD demolition crews returned on May 5, protected by two hundred police officers, and razed the remainder of the building. For several days following the demolition, police from the local precinct implemented virtual martial law. Access to East Eighth and Ninth Streets between Avenues B and C was denied to all except residents, who were often compelled to show proof of residency to gain admittance. Both on the streets and in Tompkins Square Park, plainclothes police monitored pedestrian comings and goings and discouraged loitering.[47]

In the fall, police and city workers again clashed with squatters and protesters over the city's attempt to evict squatters from PS 105, an abandoned four-story school, once commandeered by drug dealers, at 269 East Fourth Street (at Avenue B). The squatters, many of whom lived in encampments in Tompkins Square Park prior to moving into the school in September 1989, had established the ABC Community Center catering to homeless people in Tompkins Square Park, who numbered over two hundred at the time.[48] The community center acted like the earlier settlement houses, providing such services as emergency and permanent housing, tenants' rights assistance, a free medical clinic, job training and placement, meeting halls for neighborhood organizations, drug and alcohol rehabilitation, high school equivalency classes, dances, concerts, art shows, and poetry readings.[49] The city had other plans for the building. HPD had ceded control of the building to the New York Foundation for Senior Citizens, a nonprofit organization that planned to convert the school into eighty-two units for homeless senior citizens.[50] When police officers and city workers attempted to break into the build-

Figure 33. "P.S. 105 East Fourth Street between B and C; Eviction of Demonstrators." Photograph used by permission of Marlis Momber.

Figure 34. "P.S. 105 East Fourth Street between B and C; Police Action during Eviction." Photograph used by permission of Marlis Momber.

ing's entrance, they were met by a masked squatter who flung garbage bags of dry cement, eggs, and bottles of urine from the fourth floor.[51] Protests occurred over a period of eleven hours (parts of which were broadcast live on local television networks). Demonstrators and supporters from behind police barricades set bonfires in nearby intersections, launched powerful firecrackers, and occasionally scuffled with police. The police retreated and attempted to negotiate a settlement with a lawyer representing the squatters.[52] Again, sympathetic lawyers argued the squatters' rights to formal hearings since they had already occupied the PS 105 for thirty days.[53] An injunction was granted but was overturned by the efforts of city lawyers less than three hours later.[54] By late evening most of the squatters had left the school in return for immunity from trespassing charges. Nonetheless, skirmishes between police and protesters continued into the next day. Over thirty-eight people were arrested during twelve hours of occasional clashes as city workers sealed the emptied building.[55]

Cleavages in Resistance

The overview of the turf battles over Tompkins Square Park and the squats underscores the complexity of resistance politics in a diverse urban community. The many social cleavages among groups and individuals who opposed unchecked neighborhood redevelopment were often realized as political cleavages over the best ways to deal with the state and developers. The uncertainty of events leading up to the riot followed by accusations and denials of responsibility in its aftermath fueled the production of a political rift and a local lore of neighborhood "sellout" and betrayal by some community leaders in collusion with real estate interests. In addition, organized housing coalitions had laid claim under the 50/50 plan with the city to the properties occupied by protesting squatters. The squatters' claim to represent the interests of the community's disenfranchised was first legitimized in the aftermath of the 1988 riot but later was effectively challenged not only by the city (as it had been all along) but by those individuals and low-income housing organizations who signed on to the cross subsidy plan. In addition to the differences over key issues, other cleavages were apparent. Differences in the politics of antidevelopment among squatters and their supporters, long-term activists, and other locals only rarely fell on ethnic and racial lines, and then not so neatly. Eastern Europeans and Ukrainians represented one group of older East Villagers, and Latinos the other. Rarely did they form alliances, but they did rally together in particular instances, such as the call to evict the homeless and institute changes in the park. The race and ethnicity of squatters and other protesters did not differ greatly from those of the local residents who opposed them and their tactics (but not necessarily their antidevelopment position). The homeless camped in the park and their advocates, for example, were comprised of individuals from Latin America as well as Europe. Class positions among factions factored little in political alliances as well. The often intense hostility between squatters and some housing organizers, and the "quality-of-life" alliances between poorer white ethnics and minorities and middle-class newcomers clearly demonstrate that political interests and actions cannot be imputed to roughly similar class or ethnic categories.

The cleavages in the resistance politics of the late 1980s mirrored a long-standing debate among resident groups over definition of the best interests of the community and which population was best entitled to speak on its behalf. A central factor determining leadership and legitimacy was a resident group's length of tenure. In turbulent meetings about park issues or squatted tenements, speakers would boast to the audience about the number of months, years, or decades they had resided in the neighborhood as a means of conferring legitimacy to themselves and the points they made. Punks, squatters, and anarchists, according to older residents, were outsiders who were "too young" to have witnessed the desperate years of the 1970s. Following the 1988 riot, various groups briefly allied in their opposition to the park curfew mainly in response to the brutality of the police. Yet the community's sense of outrage did not translate into sustained political alliance primarily because its most vocal leaders—radicals—were not sanctioned by the more organized and reformist neighborhood groups. Another cleavage occurred in how different groups read contested issues and acted on them. In their public statements, squatters and other protesters decoded "quality-of-life" issues as thinly veiled pro-development policies. Old-timers were well aware of the linkages between city policies and redevelopment but supported them anyway with the belief that displacement would not affect them individually. As they had the drug sweeps of the early 1980s, many of the low-income minority residents welcomed the quality-of-life improvements, in this case a clean park, less homeless presence, and the promise of quieter and safer streets in addition to their rent-protected leases. Neighborhood improvement issues concerned not only middle-class gentrifiers but the long-term low-income and minority residents as well. This shared interest in neighborhood enhancement partly explained an otherwise peculiar alliance between those whose presence threatened displacement and those threatened to be displaced. Finally, the conflicts revealed the employment of symbols, images, and rhetoric to facilitate implementation of contested urban policies and to promote or magnify factionalism among local resistance groups. Urban policies that clearly aided private redevelopment were coded as quality-of-life improvements for *all* residents regardless of class, race, and ethnic background. The police, the mayor's office, and, at the time, the local community board presented contested policies in feel-good terms of clean and safe streets, playgrounds for children, and lush park spaces. Several proclamations issued by the parks department and the police played up local antipathy toward radical activists and squatters. Urban policies that promised to rid the East Village of political agitation and deviance by misfits, weirdoes, and experimenters played well to the more conservative elements in the neighborhood. Hence, tactical differences in resistance styles furthered the cultural and lifestyle cleavages among those opposed to redevelopment. Squatters and other radicals acted on their very politically astute rejection of the city's "quality-of-life" improvements with "in-your-face" tactics that alienated many locals. For some residents, especially old-timers, support for quality-of-life programs and neighborhood improvement was opposition to bothersome squatters and the homeless. For the city and developers, the quality-of-life issues were instrumental to cleaning up and sanitizing the disruptive image of the Lower East Side.

The unrest in the East Village in 1988–89 revealed the saliency of production and manipulation of symbols in resistance to urban restructuring efforts. The radical protests of the late 1980s were successful in reaffirming images of resistance to the East Village identity and thereby thwarting developers' efforts to sell the working-class enclave as a desirable middle-class district. A key strategy of the protesters was to keep the publicity of the 1988 riot fresh in the minds of local players, developers, the state, and the media. This "culture of conflict" partially impeded middle-class development plans. The 1980s rush of real estate firms and brokers into the East Village housing market never achieved the wholesale gentrification of the type experienced on Manhattan's west side and in neighboring SoHo. By the end of the decade, it was appar-

Figure 35. "Gargoyles to Scare Away Developers, by Dina Bursztin." Photograph used by permission of Robert G. McFarland.

ent that prototypical white, upper-class professionals would never flock to the neighborhood in great numbers. Likewise, the built environment never surrendered to the "brownstoning" of tenements or to condominium conversions that inundated adjacent neighborhoods. A 1990 *Crain's New York Business* report attributed the decrease in property sales on the Lower East Side to the city's real estate slump and to the area's reputation for demonstrations and virulent protests.

While the city's real estate slump in the early 1990s slowed the rate of local property sales (see figures 24–26), it did not affect the local rental market. In fact, low-income housing availability continued to shrink, and the market for middle-income apartments continued to expand. High-end luxury rentals and condominiums in other Manhattan neighborhoods, on the other hand, were plentiful, and their rents were falling. Units in the East Village remained in demand and earned premium rents. The latest viability of East Village development, however, was no longer predicated on the invention of a neighborhood attractive to white, middle-class professionals, as developers were able to turn the symbols of antidevelopment politics to their favor and against the interests of the very activists who employed them.

CHAPTER NINE

The Production of Desire:
Urban Development and Community
Resistance at the End of the Twentieth Century

As the struggle over the redevelopment of the East Village resembled a contested deadlock among developers, state actors, and residents in the initial years of the 1990s, two central paradoxes of nearly one hundred years of urban strife rose to the fore. First, given the combination of the Lower East Side's choice Manhattan location and comparably under-valued land prices, successive generations of property owners and developers ventured to develop the tenement district to attract middle-class renters. Each generation of zealous entrepreneurs and jaded landlords faced the paradox of the seeming permanence of a working-class neighborhood in the center of an international city. While potential profits lured the real estate sector, the Lower East Side's reputation proved clearly inimical to easy and profitable upgrading. The social construction of marginality, rooted in nineteenth-century representations of the working-class immigrant district, remained salient, preventing middle-class redevelopment from proceeding wholesale. Over the course of a cen- tury, symbolic representations of the working-class immigrant "Other" eventually gave way to those of the stereotypical ethnic and racial mi-nority. Across successive episodes of restructuring, the real estate indus-try and the state manipulated prevailing cultural representations to fa-cilitate social and spatial changes on the Lower East Side. Preexisting (and unprofitable) reputations of "ghetto" or "slum" were employed to call for and legitimize necessary changes (i.e., private development funded with public subsidies). Conversely, in order for middle-class development to proceed favorably, the marginal reputation of the Lower East Side

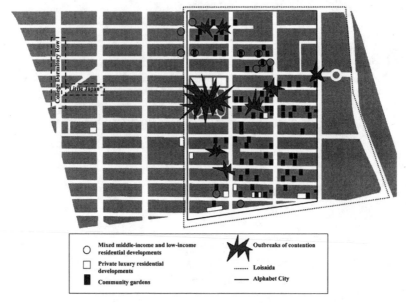

Map 7. Community destruction and creation: the landscape of the 1980s and 1990s. Map constructed by Neil Wieloch.

needed to be dissolved, or, as efforts commenced in the 1980s and 1990s disclose, reworked in ways advantageous to urban capitalists.

Alongside the century-long narrative of persistent real estate restructuring was another paradox of community resistance and urban allure. In the discourse about the urban ghetto, representations of the Lower East Side primarily emphasized the social problems, ethnic and racial divisions, and the cultural deviance that differentiated the "ghetto," the "slum," or the "DMZ" from the rest of Manhattan. The everyday realities for most residents, including commonplace interactions, the banal routines of work and home life, and the extraordinary but uncelebrated efforts to preserve home and community, were effectively ignored in the broader discourses that marginally defined the politics, economics, and culture of the inner city. The deployment of these series of discourses, as we have seen, facilitated and legitimized the efforts at neighborhood restructuring and understated the consequences of residential displacement. Lower East Siders consistently rejected both the symbolic and material threats of community displacement through collective action. Local activism, including rent strikes, marches, and demonstrations, frequently posed effective challenges to the real estate sector's endeavors to redevelop or abandon the Lower East Side. Contrary to prevailing representations, locals were active and innovative in cultural and political resistance within the very unspectacular social spaces often glossed over or written off by social workers, newspaper feature writers, politicians, and urban planners. Thus, the continuity of the Lower East Side's reputation for social resistance depended on the efforts of generations of disenfranchised residents and a larger sociocultural framework that constructed their communities as both dysfunctional and inferior. Out of such marginalization developed a political and cultural legacy of subversion and community resistance.

It was this legacy of insurrection and defiance that attracted successive waves of middle-class subcultural or avant-garde movements to the Lower East Side. The nearly continuous presence of subcultures on the Lower East Side added to the neighborhood's identity and representations as subversive, thus complicating the middle-class redevelopment efforts of real estate and state actors. The unfolding of radical protest *and* the presence of idiosyncratic subcultures reinforced the neighborhood's long-standing identification with difference among the middle classes (much to the chagrin of powerful stakeholders). Although the subcultures were uniformly sympathetic politically to the plight of their low-income neighbors faced with possible displacement, their presence often complicated local struggles against development. Indeed, the effect of the hippie presence on urban renewal in the 1960s seemed to portend the incongruous and even hostile relationship between middle-class subcultures and the East Village working-class community over development that transpired in the 1980s. As our survey of the 1980s has shown, the presence of subcultures and their contribution to the neighborhood's prevailing characterizations presented significantly less hindrance to the redevelopment efforts of the state and the real estate industry.

This chapter further explores the break with past patterns in which the dominant reputation or characterization of the Lower East Side frustrated political and economic efforts at middle-class development. It accounts for the break through an analysis of the increasingly sophisticated shift in the representation of local cultural differences from marginal to central, first introduced in chapter 1. The initial section of the chapter outlines changes in corporate cultural production and middle-class consumption that accommodated East Village subcultural artistic practices and forms. When the 1980s economy and culture of Wall Street mergers and corporate buyouts gave way to the 1990s information and entertainment brokers, hypermedia, and the "content" industry, the idiosyncrasies of the East Village identity were clearly no longer hindrances but assets to private middle-class redevelopment. In the following section, the chapter examines the strategies of real estate developers and state actors to manipulate and control *symbolic* representations of cultural differences. The appropriation of difference by developers created new opportunities for urban entrepreneurs to restructure and market low-income communities. Under the guise of "quality-of-life" initiatives, municipal leaders, meanwhile, have employed strategies that restrict *public expressions* of social and cultural diversity, according "authenticity" to the contrived representations of difference employed in the culture industry and by the real estate sector. The final section addresses the challenge of new forms of urban development to the legacy of East Village resistance.

Place and the Differentiation of Production and Consumption in Late Capitalism

Our journey into past episodes of urban conflict provided us ample evidence of the ways a "culture of difference" has shaped the contested processes of neighborhood change and development. The real estate sector and state actors consistently put forth notions of a desired, revitalized East Village or Lower East Side that contradicted existing sociocultural conditions. Couching descriptions in glowing terms of "renaissance" or "revival," proponents of development envisioned a community populated by a relatively circumscribed, idealized middle-class who were otherwise drawn to the suburbs. The status of intended or targeted consumers was defined in terms of prevailing middle-class occupational and income categories, typically stipulated as white-collar professionals or office workers (1920s) or, more recently, as yuppies (1980s) or new media "content" industry workers (1990s). Even more emphatically, however, the desired class of new residents was defined in *negation* to the characteristics of existing residents and their lifestyles — poor, working-class minorities and the numerous dysfunctions assigned to them in official and public discourses. Thus, state actors and urban capitalists articulated development in references to the class, race, and ethnic status of *extant* and *intended* (or preferred) residents. This left little doubt that a fundamental feature of neighborhood restructuring was residential displacement.

Oversimplified cultural representations of the opposition between normal and deviant, white and ethnic, middle-class and working-class, and uptown and downtown were salient to forms of urban development premised on the physical and cultural displacement of old tenants and the attraction of new ones. As previous chapters have shown, bourgeois representations of difference did more than mark off the Lower East Side territory as peculiar and marginal. They sustained the political and economic legitimation and often the moral obligation for developers and state actors to "fix the ghetto" primarily through its elimination and reinvention as proper and middle-class. While such binary oppositions continue to prevail (especially in structural terms), representations based on the cultural distances between classes in particular have given way to more inclusive ones that *symbolically* bridge the (former) divisions between normal and deviant, white and ethnic, middle-class and working-class, and uptown and downtown. A core feature of the East Village identity consisted of its reputation as an urban sanctuary for subcultures that defined themselves and their avant-garde practices in defiance and opposition to the mainstream. Consequently, the symbolic appropriation and commodification of cultural differences have influenced both the neighborhood's identity and the struggle among developers, the state, and residents over its social and spatial arrangements.

As chapter 7 noted, cultural intermediaries — artists, musicians, designers, among others — partly initiated the accommodation of the cultural margins into the center (i.e., commercialism). The "eminently marketable pose" of dissent and subversion was incorporated into the status quo.[1] Within hyper-consumerist society, notions of avant-garde, bohemian, or underground become the basis of lifestyle options that correlate directly to a multitude of consumption niches. Rooted in changes in the culture industry that date back to the immediate post–World War II era, contemporary consumption of cultural forms, such as high or low cultures, can no longer be roughly equated with particular class statuses but is instead tied to a widening range of lifestyle options.[2] The ascendancy of global flows of information and sophisticated forms of media and communications has contributed to new middle-class consumption patterns that are collapsed or mixed into numerous hybrid variations. Consumption has been elevated as a primary signifier of so-

cial identity. The replacement of the rigid middle-class cultural dichotomies of acceptable/unacceptable or marginal/central with pluralistic and relativized perceptions of differences has allowed individuals
to concoct their own lifestyles primarily through the act of consuming
the associated products. For a person with adequate means, what one
wears and where one lives not only can articulate an individual's lifestyle
but may differentiate that person from *others within their own class*. Thus,
the wide field of consumption options translates into an equally diverse range of middle-class lifestyles. There has been, as Mike Featherstone writes, "a movement away from agreed universal criteria of judg-
ment of cultural taste towards a more relativistic and pluralistic situation
in which the excluded, the strange, the other, the vulgar, which were
previously excluded can now be allowed in."[3]

Changes in middle-class consumption of cultural forms are predicated on similar processes of differentiation in the realm of production.
Shifts in middle-class consumption patterns from rigid and fixed to flex-
ible and situational allow for a broader range of products and commodities, *including housing*. Producers supply a vast range of stylized
commodities that consumers use to define their social position vis-à-
vis other consumers. Producers' strategies of segmentation, or "niche
marketing," result in the development of specialized commodities geared
toward lifestyles formerly considered marginal (and unprofitable). Consequently, the corporate-driven transgression of low and high culture
has appropriated and transformed symbols and images from once "hidden" or submerged urban cultures into global commodities. The push
for increasing diversification of cultural products translates into an unrelenting search for marketable difference, to "commodify meaning, that
is try to make images and symbols into things which can be bought and
sold."[4] The symbolic culture of politically and economically disenfranchised social groups who live in the marginalized zones of the inner city
is encouraged, cultivated, and, ultimately, appropriated for the marketplace of culture.[5] Likewise, the individual identities, reputations, and
characteristics of places have become implicated in submarket formation because localities constitute potential sites of different cultural practices and, therefore, stylized products. As a consequence, the symbols
and images tied to certain urban ghettos in Western global cities are no
longer stigmatized in middle- and upper-class circles as marginal and
inferior but as different and unique, dissolving the symbolic binary op-

positions between uptown and downtown. The formerly stigmatized ghetto instead functions simultaneously as a site *for* consumption and *of* consumption.

East Village as Place for and of Consumption

With the increasing corporate differentiation of middle-class consumer culture, neighborhood identity or distinguishing cultural features become vehicles for advertising goods, products, and lifestyles: the East Village exists as *brand name.* What constitutes the East Village "brand" is a stylized and depoliticized subversion borrowed from past and present images, symbols, and rhetorics of protest, resistance, and experimentation. The media's engrossment with local radical politics and culture and the popularization of sexual subcultures linked to local sites provide but two examples of branding and "niche" marketing. The several encounters between squatters and their supporters and the police in the early 1990s led to heightened national and international currency of the area's radical reputation. While state political and legal repression of squatters intensified, the media increasingly focused attention on the squatters' cultural expressions — the familiar symbols, images, and icons of protest — downplaying (largely by ignoring) their political missives. To the dismay of the squatters (who eventually mounted a protest outside the theater), the Broadway show *Rent* set the otherwise highly politicized struggle between capitalists and community to melody and theatrical dance. Politically defrocked, the representation of squatting emerged as a romanticized and nonthreatening bohemian lifestyle. Indeed, representation and actuality were further blurred during a squatter eviction in 1996 when the city's mayor, Rudolf Giuliani, bemoaned the "whole romantic thing about squatters," charging that most of the residents had freely elected squatting solely to avoid paying rent.[6]

The media elevation of once marginalized and "hidden" gay and drag subcultures has also implicated the East Village as a culturally radical site. Within the New York gay scene of the 1980s and early 1990s, nonconformity associated with the East Village served as cultural antipode to the West Village's reputation as post-Stonewall, white, middle-class, and accommodating to the mainstream "straight" world. Reactions to the onslaught of HIV/AIDS and the mobilization of gay, lesbian, bisexual, and transgender activists against government inaction to the health crisis contributed to the rise of a younger, more radical, inclusive, and vocal queer culture, much of it centered in East Village bars, clubs, coffee shops, and other meeting spaces. Wigstock, a yearly festival held at the close of summer in Tompkins Square Park, promoted the fabrication of an East Village gay identity.[7] Within a few years, the event, which featured a hybrid mix of drag transvestitism and performance art, drew audiences in the thousands. The Wigstock Labor Day tradition grew so popular that it relocated to larger venues outside the neighborhood and has since been the subject of a feature film. During the 1980s, the East Village "brand" of drag performance was further popularized in two local nightclubs, the Pyramid Club on Avenue A and Seventh Street, and the Boy Bar on St. Mark's Place near Third Avenue. Driven by a friendly rivalry between the two clubs, performances purposefully rejected celebrity mimicry and realism and instead featured political lampoons, satire, and commentary on race and social issues often concocted by the performers themselves.[8]

New forms of telecommunications also allow for the rapid and pervasive dissemination of "place brands" associated with a set of commodities. These multiple venues include the Broadway show, the boutiques, television shows, and Internet Web sites. In the mid-1990s, the Marinex Multimedia Corporation's cybersoap *The East Village* allowed Internet Web browsers to interact with a cast of characters said to represent the youthful and artistic character of the neighborhood; less glamorous working-class families were absent. Through the Internet, browsers were offered different avenues of "experience," including correspondence with the struggling actress, the heroin-addicted rock musician, other "residents," and each other and influencing the story's plot lines. For an audience of thousands, the soap featured "unknown" local rock bands and virtual tours of "obscure" underground nightspots, fusing real places with particular representations of them. The success of the cybersoap triggered the production of an accompanying compact disc sound track that featured the music of local bands and a description of their past performances in neighborhood bars and clubs (lest they seem "inauthentic").[9]

Symbols and signs that address an East Village identity, public memory, and history are linked together in a narrative that enables or embellishes the consumption of particular lifestyle products. But these images contrived from locality not only sell products, they mediate particular impressions of the East Village for nonresident consumers and potential new residents. Representations of the East Village land-

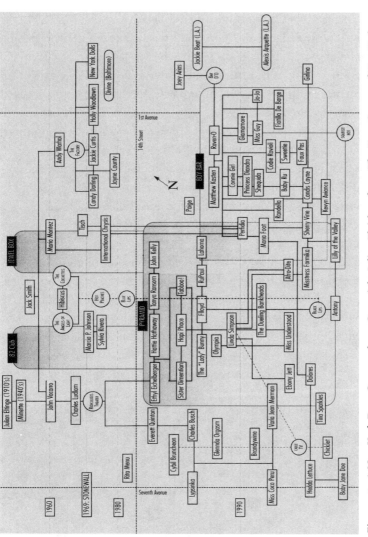

Figure 36. A New York Drag Queeneology. Copyright Julian Fleisher, from *The Drag Queens of New York: An Illustrated Field Guide* (New York: Riverhead Books, 1996). Used by permission.

scape correlate with those of the urban subversive aesthetic or (life)style: exciting, cutting-edge, exotic, hip, and unusual but not life-threatening or depressing. Cultural symbols relative to local landscape and architecture, politics, drug culture, community lore, and customs are assembled to construct multiple and contrived place identities. In such packaged constructions, the East Village exists to allow individuals to experience (consume) the related lifestyle more fully and *authentically*. Consumers, visitors, and potential new residents come to "know" and "experience" the East Village through representations of ethnic, racial, sexual, and cultural differences mediated by film, music, television, writing, and cybercultures or various other merchandise. Idealized and concocted "East Villages" are themselves consumed from afar; the landscape has become a cultural commodity.[10]

The reality and fantasy of an offbeat and unconventional neighborhood are fused together in pictures and dialogue in magazines, films, and television programs. In Japan, for example, an idealized subversive East Village is presented extensively in youth-oriented magazines, such as *Clique: New York Style* and *Street,* and in other media, such as Web sites.[11] Through such means, Japanese youth are "familiarized" with a prepackaged underground urban culture and an inflated importance of

Figure 37. "Teriyaki Boy" in Little Japan. Photograph used by permission of Robert G. McFarland.

the East Village in alternative design, art, fashion, fiction, music, and film. A pilgrimage and extended stay in the East Village have become a desired endeavor for curious middle- and upper-middle-class young Japanese with creative aspirations. Since the 1990s, an influx of some six thousand as residents and many more as visitors has given rise to a small "Japantown" on East Ninth Street. Karaoke bars, video stores specializing in Japanimation, grocery stores, saloons, and other businesses that cater to the newcomers have opened in the immediate area. The international success of a handful of Japanese bands in New York, such as Cibo Matto, has enhanced the allure of the counterculture havens among Japanese youth.

Although the East Village has long functioned as an incubator of diverse forms of music, fashion, art, writing, and film, that function has been heightened by the corporate production, marketing, and distribution of cultural products that constitute a symbolic economy.[12] The making and selling of content are the industry of the symbolic economy. Growth in the symbolic economy depends on continuous diversification of content. Consequently, the industry has flourished in New York because of the ample pool of easily mobilized creative talent. In addition, the corporatized creative or symbolic sector has flourished under the auspices and encouragement of large international media distribution companies located in Manhattan. Small "shops" engaged in the production of content for emerging multimedia technologies are concentrated in lower Manhattan (the area near lower Broadway has been dubbed "Silicon Alley"). Documents issued in 1996 by the Regional Plan Association and the consulting firm Coopers and Lybrand suggested private-public initiatives to realize the vast potential for job creation and revenues from the information and knowledge sector.[13] As the report was issued, New York State and New York City governments were creating public-private development initiatives and tax-based incentives for entrepreneurial investment in content provision industries. Lower Manhattan, with its glut of older, unused office buildings, has been targeted for "smart infrastructure" — an amalgam that links talent, technology, capital, and know-how through urban political and corporate alliances.[14] Companies ranging in size from small workshops that employ a handful of workers to multinational giants, such as Time Warner, utilize advanced technologies (and development incentives) to draw on New York's unrivaled advantage in human capital in the arts, literature, music, and related cultural fields as resources for the development and dissemination of products.[15]

Within the symbolic economy, urban subcultures exist as a pool of cultural intermediaries who possess "a close knowledge of the inner dynamics of the cultural field" and whose purpose is "to interpret, package, transmit and manipulate symbols and knowledge in a way that produces new value."[16] The information-entertainment industry's emphasis on creativity and diversity in production and marketing requires, in a sense, a space like the East Village as a prime site for living, socializing, and networking among graphic artists, designers, filmmakers, and musicians. Content production sites tend to agglomerate in urban areas where face-to-face interactions facilitate social networks, including workshops, office spaces, and boardrooms, and, especially for the freelance sector, restaurants, coffeehouses, and bars. With its reputation as novel and subversive, the East Village attracts cultural intermediaries who consider themselves and their work as "cutting edge."

The shift in the representation of the East Village from marginal to central is predicated on its function as an incubator for consumption and production of highly stylized, and increasingly commodified, subversive or alternative culture. The area's dominant population of working-class and impoverished families, minorities, informal workers, drug dealers, prostitutes, petty criminals, and homeless persons are not left out of these symbolic representations or necessarily shown in a disparaging way. Rather, they function as a cast of background players in an abstracted environment themed around carefully managed representations of dysfunction and difference. Within the context of such theming,[17] their lifestyles and everyday activities exist to contribute the necessary ambiance stripped of politics and resistance but filled with excitement and the thrill of the unanticipated. The stylization of local cultural differences is symbolically representative of its place of origin — but just barely. Such images of the East Village as exotic and interesting, when circulated globally or expressed in a Broadway theater, are distanced from the collective process of invention or the political and economic realities of where they were spawned. Poverty, crime, and despair, as such, do not sell clothes, makeup, music, or housing, but sanitized and playful symbolic references to them can and do. Consequently, the production of the built environment for middle-class consumption begins to resemble less the harsh realities and more the sugarcoated representa-

Figure 38. Resistance as art. Photograph by Christopher Mele.

tions of a subversive and alternative East Village. As the culture industry reaches deep into the urban milieus of street corners, alleyways, basement bars, and clubs to appropriate content to merchandise to consumers across the globe, it presents new opportunities for the urban redevelopment of neighborhoods where such forms originate. New cultural production and consumption practices based on lifestyle engage "the enterprise of culture to manufacture differentiated urban or local identities."[18] The real estate industry and state institutions act on these corporate-produced "imagined" identities, producing new landscapes that reflect the East Village allure in profitable ways.

Venerating/Controlling Difference:
Real Estate Development and Urban Development Policies
in the 1990s

> The most effectively appropriated spaces are those that make symbolic use of what is around them and turn it to their advantage, whether by subverting the codes of the dominant space or by representing an alternative form of social space alongside them.
>
> John Allen and Michael Pryke, "The Production of Service Space"

The consumption-oriented stylization of the East Village identity and its increasing symbolic importance as a site of cultural invention for the city's symbolic economy have significantly influenced contemporary forms of middle-class urban development. By the early 1990s, developers and landlords no longer interpreted the East Village's stubborn "subterranean" countercultural features as harbingers of future middle-class development. The 1980s call to invent another SoHo arts district or a West Village historic district in the East Village has since been drowned out by the emerging niche rental market.[19] The promotion of a specialized residential market — the selling of "bohemian mix" — has mirrored the corporate promotion of specialized consumer goods. Developers have abandoned the goal to produce an environment that conveys typically middle-class corporate status (e.g., that of the "yuppies" of the Wall Street era) or a focus on occupation and "family" quality-of-life issues, such as convenience to office, concern for local schools, available playgrounds, and so on. The newly targeted middle class reflects the changes in consumption patterns and the city's information-based economy — the more contrived urban "radical" *lifestyles* of singles in their twenties and thirties. In this spatialization of difference, developers and the state appropriate images, symbols, and themes to valorize their commercial and residential properties. Signage and visual cues produce an environment symbolically familiar to the media-circulated representations of place. "The neighborhood's funkiness seems to include graffiti-covered buildings, garbage strewn by the homeless collecting redeemables and heavy drug traffic," according to the *New York Times,* adding, "the allure of bohemian decadence keeps housing prices up."[20]

Real estate developers have been successful in spatializing the subversive cultural image of the East Village for both commercial and residential markets. In commercial development, the themed environment has proven conducive to lifestyle retailing and entertainment-enhanced consumption, prompting the occasional *Vogue* magazine exposé of the "hottest scene."[21] Along St. Mark's Place, Second and Third Avenues, and Avenue A the appearance of underground culture is staged in the interior spaces of bars, restaurants, and clothing shops. The controlled atmosphere of interior consumption spaces, such as the Anarchy Cafe and alt.coffee, and the semipatrolled but more chaotic public sidewalks and streets tend to bundle sightseeing, experience, entertainment, and retail together. Many of the independently owned "mom and pop" stores cultivate the area's counterculture reputation. Independent, or "indie," designers have opened shops along East Ninth Street, adding to the block's retail theme a place "where fashion, furniture, music, art, architecture and hip nostalgia come together."[22] The number of retail giants and chain stores has increased, mimicking a trend familiar throughout the city. Multiplex theaters (Third Avenue and Twelfth Street) and other entertainment "anchors" attract large numbers of consumers who spill over to adjacent shops and restaurants. Increasingly, the same merchandise is available in similar, if not identical, "chain" or franchised stores (e.g., The Gap clothing stores and Starbucks coffee shops) in different neighborhoods throughout the city and in the suburbs. Yet when the chain stores are situated in and associated with location-based themes, they are perceived as "different" and attract market segments tied to associated lifestyles. The rock/pop band U2, for example, held a CD-release party at the K-Mart department store on Astor Place. A McDonald's fast-food restaurant with Kandinsky prints secured to the walls above its prefabricated dining booths does business on Third Avenue near St. Mark's Place, the gateway to the East Village. The alternative, experimental, and subversive themes, then, provide "an experience unlike those available in shopping malls or other urban entertainment sites—an experience that is authentic to setting."[23]

The residential housing market has benefited from the association with themed commercial spaces. The real estate market rebounded in the mid-1990s, emboldened by the continued short supply of middle-class housing and the city government's commitment to Manhattan's cosmetic upgrading. Burned by the local failure of the cooperative and condominium conversion trend in the 1980s, developers have expressed little interest in doing away with rental units. New construction of rental buildings has been substantial in the former "DMZ"—the blocks east of Avenue A. Cheek by jowl with Old Law tenements occupied by low-income Puerto Rican families, such developments have increased residential displacement and the cultural dislocation of Loisaida. Sixty-four luxury rental units have replaced the Gas Station, a squatted performance space at the corner of Second Street and Avenue B. Vacant lots on East Seventh Street between Avenues B and C—the site of an open-air cocaine drug market in the 1980s—are slated for the development of twenty-five luxury apartments. A massive, multistory luxury apartment complex rises over the tenements and empty lots on East Second Street between C and D in proximity to the monolithic column of Lillian Wald low-income public housing towers.

Figure 39. "CD280: Building Facade" and "CD280: Rental Office Sign," luxury apartments between Avenues C and D, one block from Wald Public Housing. Photographs used by permission of Robert G. McFarland.

Without exception the new private market buildings, complete with plush amenities and expensive leases, use architectural symbols to convey a downtown exoticism to attract renters. The Red Square apartment building on East Houston Street has attracted individuals employed in the city's art, fashion, design, publishing, or music industries. They were drawn to Red Square because, as one resident said, "it is playful, which is what the East Village is all about."[24] Red Square does exemplify playful. The numerals on the clock face positioned atop the thirteen-story building were arranged randomly. Balconies afford views of either the Wall Street or midtown skyline or the adjacent landscape with its remnants of scarred tenements and empty lots. The facade of Red Square and other buildings like it may symbolize "downtown," but inside "uptown" amenities, such as a uniformed doorman and dry cleaning laundry services, are offered at premium rents. Luxury rental buildings combine the appeal of two extremes — the indulgence within and the worn urban landscape outside. On a smaller scale, apartments that have been redesigned for households of unrelated individuals (e.g., university students) sacrifice traditional dining and living areas for additional bedrooms or include built-in sleeping lofts or room subdivisions. Designers of one building included built-in drafting tables in their units. In another, a landlord used her J-51 tax abatement to install expansive loftlike windows for anticipated rentals to artists. Like Red Square, these buildings, despite extravagant rents, were not attracting the prototypical urban gentry of the white-collar professional, financial ana-

Figure 40.   Red Square luxury apartments. Photograph by Christopher Mele.

lyst, or banker ilk. Regardless of the structural accommodations, it is the representation of cultural differences that differentiates a two-room tenement flat in the East Village from one in Brooklyn or Queens and, consequently, attracts a very different segment of the urban middle class.

Representations of Difference and Recent Changes in the East Village Housing Consumers

It is important to note that the efforts of developers to incorporate historically disenfranchised populations into a favorable identity of the East Village have been *wholly symbolic*. Commercial and residential developments based on representations of an ethnically, sexually, and culturally diverse community have sold housing to a submarket of the middle class who are capable of paying significantly higher rents to consume such an identity. Based on the caricatured image as a countercultural haven, the East Village has become "an appealing address for young professionals seeking a less costly alternative to neighborhoods like Greenwich Village and SoHo."[25] This submarket consists of mostly white, college-educated individuals in the twenty-to-forty-year age range who live alone or in shared households. Students attending nearby colleges and universities have also remained a readily available market of East Village tenants. In the late 1980s, three large dormitories were constructed on or adjacent to Third Avenue for students of New York University, the New School for Social Research, and the Cooper Union. The presence of dormitories brought hundreds of first-year college students to socialize, shop, and recreate nearby.[26]

According to real estate brokers and downtown rental agents, a sizable cohort of East Village newcomers consists of freelance artists, writers, graphic designers, musicians, and other creative entrepreneurs employed in the information and entertainment economy. As a residential cohort, content workers pay high rents to tolerate the area's above-normal levels of crime, noise, and drug-related social problems that are viewed as integral to the ambience of downtown urban living. Thus, they derive social capital from occupying an area that the stereotypical middle class are reputed to avoid. Simultaneously, they contribute to the area's aura of youth and unconventionality. Overall, newcomers have demonstrated little intention of remaining in the area, or in a single apartment within the area, for any considerable length of time. "We didn't expect to get so many transients and so few families," bemoaned a pro-development member of Community Board 3. Given the area's media-influenced reputation, the East Village tends to attract renters who "see the neighborhood as a place to party, and when they grow up, they'll move elsewhere."[27] Roommate turnover, job promotions and relocations, and "East Village overexposure" account for the high rate of apartment turnover among these groups.[28]

Controlling Difference: State Urban Development Initiatives

In tandem with urban policies of the 1980s, the state in the 1990s intensified its role in the provision of direct and indirect development incentives for the private real estate sector. In addition to facilitating investment and development through subsidies such as tax abatements and zoning exemptions, the Giuliani mayoral administration has increasingly employed city agencies to regulate and modify the uses of public space, from sidewalks to parks. The political regulation of public space and social behavior has advanced the commercialism of the East Village legacy of subversion and counterculture. Under the guise of "improved quality of life," city policies have driven the once *public* expression of cultural radicalism and subversion into the *private* realm — most notably, into commercial and residential real estate spaces where desirable references to difference are employed as themes. With the power of effective new policies, both significant and banal (such as public passageway laws, park regulations, and even jaywalking ordinances), the city has systematically regulated and controlled public spaces, fundamentally excluding many of Loisaida's low-income and minority residents from the "revived" Lower East Side.

Despite the inroads of speculators and developers in the 1980s, the streetscape of Loisaida had remained the domain of squatters and other cultural radicals, low-income Puerto Rican families, and, increasingly, Dominican immigrants. The eviction of the homeless encampment, or "shantytown," from Tompkins Square Park in 1989 and, months later, from the empty lots east of Avenue B marked the first of a series of initiatives undertaken by the state to rid the area of its "eyesores." Since the 1980s, unwelcome, intrusive, or unappealing social behaviors — panhandling, soliciting, occupying public space — have been increasingly criminalized. In actions sanctioned by real estate developers, the more conservative community groups, and certain members of the local community board, the city has utilized its police force and other agencies to hem in the public social and cultural activities of undesirables, namely the homeless and some minority and poor residents. Labeling them "thieves' markets," the police forbade the peddling of wares on public sidewalks and in empty lots, thus depriving the poorest individuals a source of much-needed revenue. The popular practice among the homeless of displaying and selling salvageable garbage-picked items (including clocks, old magazines, books, and discarded furniture) on the sidewalk of well-traveled Second Avenue was prohibited.

In addition to efforts to "clean up" East Village parks, empty lots, and sidewalks, the city has deployed a "zero tolerance" strategy for dealing with neighborhood squatters. Demonstrations and violence over the status of occupied abandoned buildings resurfaced in the 1990s as private developers and service providers (whom squatters disparagingly referred to as "poverty pimps") pushed to utilize city-owned property. The implementation of cross-subsidy development projects also heightened demands on "officially unoccupied" land. In 1994, the city evicted squatters from the Glass House (an abandoned former glass factory) on Avenue D and Tenth Street. Plans to renovate the building for housing for persons with AIDS, however, were never realized. The city and police had honed their skills acquired from previous conflicts and laid full military siege to evict two squatted buildings on East Thirteenth Street

Figure 41. "Fire on East Seventh Street between B and C; Squatter Building, 1990." Photograph used by permission of Marlis Momber.

chosen for low-income housing development by the Lower East Side Coalition Housing Development (LESCHD). On Memorial Day weekend several dozen police, SWAT teams, sharpshooters, and a tank (actually, a fifty-thousand-pound armored personnel carrier) stormed the fortified and defended squats, arresting thirty-one residents and demonstrators. Months later several hundred police cleared some fifty squatters and seventy-five demonstrators who had barricaded themselves inside three other city-owned buildings on Thirteenth Street. The police maintained a highly visible presence for weeks following the evictions, requiring residents to show identification to get to their homes. Although the occupants of the Thirteenth Street buildings included Central American refugees, unskilled laborers, and Vietnam veterans, the city characterized the squatters as middle-class bohemian artists who lacked respect for law and order. Typically under the pretense of protecting public safety, the city's Department of Housing Preservation and Development (HPD) systematically condemned and issued evictions to squats throughout the Lower East Side. While legal struggles between HPD lawyers and the squatters' counsel tended to buy the squatters time, the city regularly prevailed, often by disregarding unfavor-

able legal rulings. Evictions and demolitions regularly led to street violence. After a minor fire in a squatted building on East Fifth Street between Avenues A and B, for example, HPD declared the tenement
structurally unsafe and a public safety hazard. Despite a temporary restraining order against demolition, the city razed the building and displaced twenty-six squatters. The silence of local housing organizations
and the lack of community outrage at events added to the city's bravado
in handling the squatters. The political isolation of the squatters, according to a sympathetic commentator, is evidence of the co-optation
of the "old guard" of Lower East Side organized resistance:

> [T]he squatters are setting precisely the type of example that no one in
> power — neither the politicians nor the bureaucrats, neither the land-
> lords nor the real estate "developers," neither the community groups nor
> the local educators — want anyone else to follow. The squats are demon-
> strating — neither in words nor in speeches, but in acts — exactly how
> much is possible for small autonomous groups of people to accomplish
> outside of the dominant institutions, the most basic of which is
> landlordism.[29]

As evidenced by the lack of organized community resistance, the appeal of "quality-of-life" initiatives among various classes and cultures
of residents outweighs the political and economic ramifications of such
measures (namely, the continuation of low-income residential displacement). Most older residents, for example, sanction the occasional un-
dercover prostitution "stings" on notoriously troublesome areas such
as Eleventh and Twelfth Streets between Second and Third Avenues.
Some of the city's measures have reaped the dismay and outrage of East
Village residents, however. The development of projects geared ostensibly
to the housing needs of disadvantaged populations has not occurred
without controversy. The construction of the Del Este Village project
on East Eleventh Street required the demolition and clearance of several community gardens. Del Este Village consists of eight newly constructed state-subsidized buildings that house a mix of middle-income,
first-time condominium buyers and low-income renters. Adding to the
controversy, the site is privately managed by LESCHD. According to local activists, LESCHD is controlled by a former pro-development city
councilman.[30] Displacement tied to other projects, including new and
renovated moderate-income apartment buildings affiliated with the 50/50

cross subsidy plan, housing for the elderly (Casa Victoria on the site of formerly squatted lots on East Eighth Street between Avenues B and C), and a day center for homeless adults, has stirred controversies.

In July 1998, the city auctioned properties it owned in Manhattan and other boroughs. Claiming the lots were "officially" empty and a misuse of valuable space, city leaders argued that the auctions would stimulate further development and restore those neighborhoods most devastated by earlier abandonment and arson. As chapter 6 disclosed, residents and block associations had transformed many of the empty lots in the East Village into community gardens. Most parcels auctioned, in fact, were utilized as community gardens.[31] Activists and residents alike turned out to protest the auction, shouting down and disrupting the bidding and releasing thousands of live crickets into the police department's central headquarters.[32] Only a few East Village gardening groups were able to collectively purchase and preserve their plots. Included among those sold was the neighborhood's nineteen-year-old central theater place, Charas/El Bohio Cultural Center at Avenue B and East Ninth Street.[33]

The Giuliani administration's drive to purge the public landscape of uses, practices, and behaviors labeled deviant, unpleasant, or simply unorganized fits squarely into the themed development purported by the real estate sector. Driven from the streets, parks, lots, and sidewalks, the expression of East Village cultural and political radicalism is plainly enduring in its most contrived forms in bars, nightclubs, restaurants, and themed apartment buildings. Ironically, these concocted commercial and residential spaces have become the last bastion of avant-garde culture and radicalism.

The Symbolic Accommodation of Dissent and the Challenge to Local Resistance

Despite their symbolic incorporation in the imaging of the East Village, the area's low-income and minority populations remain threatened by development. Although the city's and developers' representations of the East Village symbolically celebrate its demographic diversity, the displacement of poor and minority communities continues unabated. Evictions forced from arson are less likely, but legal threats, rent overcharges, sporadic provision of services, and other forms of tenant harassment continue. Working-class residents, the elderly on fixed incomes, and oth-

Figure 42. "Stop the Auction! Lamppost with Political Fliers." Photograph used by permission of Robert G. McFarland.

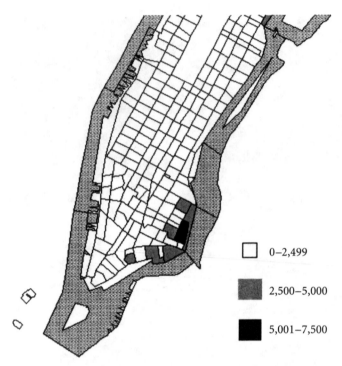

Figure 43. The demography of poverty in 1997: the Hispanic population. Source: U.S. Department of Census, Demographic Estimates, 1997.

ers in need of decent and inexpensive housing continue to be priced out of expensive, renovated apartments. Consequently, doubling-up and overcrowding persist in occupied tenements and in the adjacent public housing projects along Avenue D. Minorities and the poor are also indirectly "pushed out" or made to feel like strangers in their own neighborhood by the city's restrictive policies and new commercial spaces geared toward middle- and upper-class consumers. The cultural dislocation of Loisaida abounds as new shops, restaurants, and groceries open to serve more-affluent newcomers rather than the remaining underprivileged families. Ironically, the vibrancy of ethnic community life is threatened to be replaced by the fabricated commercial artifices of ethnic restaurants and clothing shops. In short, the negative social consequences of middle-class development (even in its new and subtle form) have not diminished for many longtime residents of the East Village. The livelihood of the working class, the indigent, and the minorities in the neighborhood — indeed in all of Manhattan — has been made more

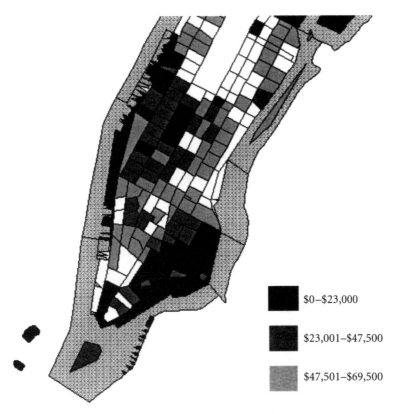

$0–$23,000

$23,001–$47,500

$47,501–$69,500

Figure 44. The demography of poverty in 1997: median household income.
Source: U.S. Department of Census, Demographic Estimates, 1997.

precarious by the cumulative effect of related social problems and inadequate policy solutions. In her ethnographic portrayal of Latinos on
the Lower East Side, Jagna Sharff documents how changes in city, state,
and federal welfare laws, the crack epidemic, and the police crackdown
on small-time dealers coupled with draconian mandatory sentencing
laws and the AIDS crisis have harmed community life. She writes:

> The active presence of the Grim Reaper on the Lower East Side was not
> confined to deaths from AIDS, "overdosing" on illicit drugs (usually the
> result of poisonous admixtures rather than overdoses per se), alcohol
> abuse, or accidents. It was a combination of these factors and additional
> stresses that put the population at an increased risk. Real estate pressures
> on the housing of the poor that left them homeless and more vulnerable
> to infections in crowded or congregate housing, lawlessness by the police
> that ended in maiming and deaths, and the increasing push for "moving

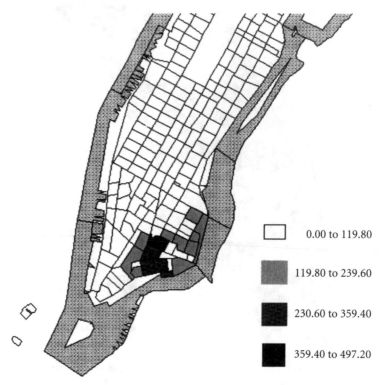

☐	0.00 to 119.80
■	119.80 to 239.60
■	230.60 to 359.40
■	359.40 to 497.20

Figure 45. The demography of poverty in 1997: households with six or more persons. Source: U.S. Department of Census, Demographic Estimates, 1997.

on," causing constant internal migrations, created conditions that were inimical to maintaining ordinary life.[34]

The miserable living conditions of the impoverished on the Lower East Side are, of course, not new, and neither is resistance among organized and unorganized groups of residents. Local resistance has not been weakened by the representation of local cultural differences as central rather than marginal to upscale development. Although global marketing and representations of previously marginal places purposefully conceal and mask conflicts of class, race, and ethnicity over space, such inequalities persist and remain the basis for social action.

Local Resistance as Performative and Political

As the previous chapters have documented, the social construction of the Lower East Side as a culturally marginal space shaped the ways in which local resistance to political and economic restructuring was ar-

Figure 46. "Homeless Shelter: Empty Lot at Fourth and Fifth Streets between B and C." Photograph used by permission of Marlis Momber.

ticulated. Often, local resistance was expressed in art forms that contradicted or challenged external representations or public discourses that denigrated the Lower East Side and its residents. Within the confines of ideological marginalization, even cultural practices that expressed residents' attachments to community (but not framed as intentional resistance to its displacement) were radicalized and viewed as threats to a middle-class upgrade of the neighborhood. The symbolic accommodation of cultural differences as a theme for the development of the East Village problematizes the use of traditional repertoires of local resistance — especially cultural expressions of discontent, subversion, and radicalism that are quickly assimilated into the redevelopment agenda.

As we have seen, the social production of residential and commercial spaces geared toward middle-class consumption symbolically indulges and absorbs difference — including the symbols, image, and rhetoric critical of or directed against urban displacement and renewal. When images and slogans related to local histories and pivotal events such as riots are confiscated and reassembled as place themes, consumption-oriented meanings of such acts are superimposed atop intended or implied political meanings. Middle-class newcomers, tourists, theatergoers, film audiences, and Web surfers "experience" or consume mediated "bohemian" or "subversive" identities of the East Village that are devoid of political content and invoke few, if any, profound references to the struggle over housing. Cultural representations, such as *Rent*, present neighborhood radicalism and protest as entertainment, myth, a human-interest story, or a peculiar spectacle to be gazed at by a curious middle class. Thus, the predicament for East Village cultural resistance is that traditional forms of resistance feed into the area's mediated image as a counterculture breeding ground. The more visual and flamboyant the resistance, the more it *appears* to enhance themed development. Whereas control over the uses of space remains the central point of contention between landlords and tenants, the discourse of struggle has been altered by the co-optation of local symbols (including those of resistance) and developers' efforts to channel the area's (contrived) subversive identity toward profits.

The symbolic accommodation of difference in the private realm of real estate development and the political exclusion of difference in the public realm have confined what James Scott has referred to as "the sites of antihegemonic discourse."[35] Under the gaze of cultural intermediaries eager for the next innovation, the increasing and rapid dissemination of images and rhetoric of locale undermines the distinctions between neighborhood "insider" and "outsider" that were historically essential to group solidarity and resistance. "When small groups emerge in order to visibly confront the political authorities on specific issues," Alberto Melucci writes, "they *indicate* to the rest of society the existence of a systemic problem and the possibility of meaningful alternatives."[36] The inside/outside dichotomy breaks down, however, when those images migrate beyond the literal and figurative boundaries of neighborhood and take on different interpretations. With the niche production and consumption of "hidden" or subcultural forms, the ability of social groups to control the dissemination of their messages or to define even the broadest parameters of their interpretation has been reduced. A logo for a record label, for example, depicts a graffiti image employed by local radicals once spray painted on buildings and door frames across the East Village (the year "1993" adjacent to an image of an upside-down martini glass). Local systems of meaning attached to symbols come to exist simultaneously with commodified meanings.

Most local activists continue to argue that political and cultural resistance can and does motivate and generate positive changes in urban circumstances despite the symbolic blurring of marginal and central categories of difference. Yet the niche marketing has made it increasingly more difficult for local activists to build consensus around issues of social inequities and injustice. It is difficult to demand accountability for such problems when responsibility for displacement and other urban ills is cloaked in the illusion of cultural inclusiveness.

If new symbols, images, and rhetoric of urban resistance are to be found, they are in the *unmediated* spaces left untouched by the culture industry, the real estate image makers, or city officials bent on ridding public expression of difference in the name of "quality-of-life" improvements. Evidence exists of networks and circuits of subversive discourse centered around culture production and, often simultaneously, issues of decent and affordable housing and control over public space. A collective of squatters and cultural radicals broadcast a "pirate" (nonlicensed), low-wattage radio station, aptly titled *Steal This Radio* (at 88.7 FM). With used and borrowed broadcast equipment and an antenna made from salvaged plumbing supplies, the radiocasters move to a different location each week, broadcasting dates and locations of squatter benefits as well as live music, poetry, fiction, and drama.[37] Thus, the challenge to local resistance is to remain at least a step ahead of the symbolic economy or content industry by manipulating the realm of ordinary activity and coding it with political meaning. Of course, these constantly shifting spaces of subversion exist in relation to the efforts of niche marketers, who are highly motivated to quickly co-opt images before they become cliché. Local cultural and political resistance is framed in opposition to the symbolically inclusive but nonetheless still mainstream bourgeois culture—a condition resonant with the neighborhood's past.

As the subordinate and marginal have moved front and center in the realms of cultural production and consumption, we see how the historical connection between subculture and urban space—that is, the allure and the attraction of difference and desire—has become the source of representations in the production of middle-class spaces. In our survey of a century of social conflict over land use, it is easy to view such development as progressive. Past representations tied to urban restructuring were hostile to local cultural practices and forms and were used as a means to legitimate and facilitate political and economic displacement of existing working-class populations. Recent practices no longer code local ethnic, racial, sexual, political, and cultural differences to eliminate them but rather to acknowledge them as symbols and themes for the development of residential and commercial real estate property. We need to scratch just barely beneath the surface of this veneer of accommodation and plurality, however, to see that the struggle that has defined the local history for the past century endures in the present.

Within the historical context of local struggles over the Lower East Side, the sustainability of the latest phase of middle-class urban development seems questionable. The symbolic appropriation of difference and the widespread commercialism of subversive cultural forms threaten the legacy of the East Village as a place outside the mainstream. Yet the mainstream corporate acceptance of such a legacy undermines the very basis of allure that, as we have seen, attracts a certain segment of the middle class to the East Village. Under the glaring spotlight of media exposure and increased commercialism, East Village subversion is demystified, and its cultural cachet is forfeited. The very forces that threaten to swallow up the radical legacy of the East Village — especially middle-class development — may themselves be consumed by overkill.

Notes

1. The Struggle over Space

1. Lury 1996: 93–108.
2. Bourdieu 1984.
3. Lury 1996: chapter 2.
4. Featherstone 1991.
5. Weiss 1988.
6. See Gottdiener 1985: 219; and Feagin and Parker 1990.
7. Fainstein and Fainstein 1988; Shefter 1992; Cerillo 1991.
8. Costikyan 1993: 422.
9. Shefter 1988.
10. See Shefter 1992: 34.
11. Tabb 1982: 12–15.
12. Both traditional and critical urban sociologists have treated displacement as an outcome of a process of neighborhood transformation. Proponents of a consumer market explanation of neighborhood revitalization viewed displacement as an unfortunate, yet "natural" consequence of the dynamics of the housing market (Lee and Hodge 1984: 141–42). Since data had consistently shown high levels of residential mobility for poor renters in inner-city neighborhoods, analyses proved inconclusive in determining whether what appeared as gentrification-caused displacement was, in actuality, voluntary mobility (Sumka 1979; Palen and London 1984: 260–63). Analyses by critical urban sociologists contradicted the view of displacement as epiphenomenal or accidental to the process of revitalization (Hartman 1979a, 1979b). Instead, they considered involuntary outmigration of the poor as a negative structural outcome (Marcuse 1985; Smith 1988: 147; Feagin and Parker 1990) or a "vicious side-effect" (Goldfield 1980) of profit-driven urban restructuring.
13. Park, Burgess, and McKenzie 1925: 95.
14. Hammon 1992: 262.
15. In his 1945 study of land use in Boston, the ecologist Walter Firey resurrected the inclusion of cultural factors to account for "locational processes that seem to

defy a strictly economic analysis" (Firey 1945: 141). More recently, the sociologist Gerald Suttles reasserted the significance of cultural factors to spatial processes. Suttles criticized the conceptualization of cultural factors as residual or nonrational and viewed attachments, sentiments, and place identities as integral to understanding how urban places change (1984).

16. Gottdiener and Feagin 1988. Urbanists influenced by poststructuralism argue that discourses, images, symbols, and representations that cohere as conventions simultaneously reflect and shape social practices within specific spaces and time frames (Hastings 1999). The focus on discourses is relevant insofar as it informs analyses of social, cultural, political, or economic processes; that discourse "produces something else (an utterance, a concept, an effect), rather than something which exists in and of itself and which can be analyzed in isolation" (Mills 1997: 17). There are, nonetheless, various approaches. Studies that examine the city as site of complex processes of identity construction and fragmentation underscore the centrality of discourses about the city (Ghani 1993; Chambers 1993; Robins 1995). Here, the meaning of urban is the diverse and often conflicting representational forms (city as text) that both produce and are products of the formation of a wide range of subjectivities, including ethnic, racial, gender, and sexual identities (Imrie et al. 1996: 1257). The focus on discourse as the subject of such research may tend to ignore spatial (or material) processes and structural relations of power, including class and other bases of inequality (Imrie et al. 1996: 1258). For Badcock (1996), the end result of privileging identity and performance in urban studies is a scholarly indifference to the social consequences of spatial practices, such as uneven development and displacement. In the pages that follow, I develop the argument that the circulation of prevailing discourses about the city is intrinsic to political economic processes of sociospatial change, such as community abandonment and redevelopment.

17. Alexander 1979; A. Cohen 1985: 16–18.

18. Strauss 1961: 17.

19. Strauss 1961: 8.

20. Gottdiener (1997), Zukin (1995), and Shields (1996) also provide a comprehensive overview of the treatment of representations in contemporary urban theories.

21. Hall 1997: 259.

22. Lefebvre 1991: 51–52.

23. Hall 1997: 6.

24. Hall 1997: 232; see Foucault 1972.

25. Gold and Ward 1994; Philo and Kearns 1993.

26. Beauregard 1993: 21.

27. Davis 1991: chapter 1.

28. Katznelson 1981: 210.

29. Pile 1997: 2–3; Melucci 1989; J. Cohen 1985.

30. Scott 1990: 140.

31. For a critique of sociologists' neglect of the social significance of art, see Zolberg 1990: 29–52.

32. This discussion is not intended to provide a theoretical overview of the formation of avant-garde movements or subcultures or their relation to dominant, mainstream society. Rather, the purpose here is to investigate the connections between the presence of avant-garde movements and subcultures and the processes and outcome of struggles over the Lower East Side over time. Burger (1984) provides an excel-

lent theoretical source on avant-gardism. Overviews of the American avant-garde are found in Parry (1960), Miller (1977), and Hobbs (1997). Hobbs's work contains a useful bibliographical essay of works on the avant-garde.

33. Rosenberg 1973: 79.
34. Gross 1995: 3.
35. Crow 1983: 235.
36. Clarke et al. 1976: 13.
37. Crow 1983: 252.
38. Crane 1987: 84; Zolberg 1990: 62–65.
39. Owens 1984: 162.
40. Hobbs 1997: 150.

2. Different and Inferior

1. Dos Passos 1925.
2. Arthur 1873.
3. Phillips 1977.
4. Riis 1971: 6.
5. Katznelson 1992: chapter 6; Katznelson 1985.
6. Taylor 1992: 71–72.
7. Taylor 1992: 76–78.
8. Campbell 1892: xi; italics and capitalization in the original.
9. Zajkowski 1982.
10. Documents of the Assembly of the State of New York, Eightieth Session, no. 205, 1857, quoted in Ford 1936: 95.
11. Contemporary Sanborn insurance maps still show the property lines of the predevelopment-era land uses.
12. Malon 1981: 394.
13. Veiller 1970c: 382.
14. Veiller 1970c: 370.
15. Gould 1970; Veiller 1970b.
16. Real Estate Record Association 1967: 221.
17. Real Estate Record Association 1967: 221; Veiller 1970c: 372.
18. Ford 1936: 867. The initial year a building was expressly constructed to house more than two families is cited as 1833.
19. Veiller 1970c: 370–72.
20. Claghorn 1970: 75.
21. Webster 1970.
22. Gould 1970: 357–58.
23. Rischin 1962: 84–85.
24. Claghorn 1970: 88.
25. *Charities and the Commons*, January 18, 1908.
26. Claghorn 1970: 71.
27. Claghorn 1970: 72.
28. "Tenement Evils as Seen by the Tenants" 1970: 398.
29. Roth 1934: 406.
30. Bernheimer 1905: 286.

31. "Tenement Evils as Seen by the Tenants" 1970: 401.

32. Gilfoyle 1992: 217.

33. Sante 1992: 122–24.

34. Crane 1966.

35. Kusay 1916.

36. Kaufmann 1910.

37. Kildare 1905.

38. See Park 1921.

39. Brace 1880.

40. The purpose and scope of this chapter does not permit a full review of the diverse historical and sociological literature on immigrant/ethnic community building. Rather the purpose here is to offer a framework of the sociospatial conditions and the political and cultural boundaries that both contained and sustained the types of communities that existed on the Lower East Side during this time period. For fuller treatments of community building, see, especially, Ewen 1985 and Kessner 1977.

41. Bogen 1987; Ernst 1949.

42. Maffi 1995: 99.

43. Nadel 1990: chapter 3.

44. Lieberman 1976: 40.

45. Peiss 1986: 22.

46. Schoener 1967: 58.

47. Nadel 1990: 110.

48. Lieberman 1976: 65.

49. Lieberman 1976: 62; emphasis in the original.

50. Iorizzo 1970: 55–57.

51. Nelli 1970.

52. Nelli 1964.

53. Nelli 1970.

54. Maffi 1995: 117.

55. Lieberman 1976: 40–44.

56. Regional Plan Association 1931: 2.

57. Rischin 1962: 97

58. Nadel 1990: 101.

59. Rischin 1962: 91. The reactions of established ethnic groups to displacement pressures caused by waves of new and different migrants were not always peaceful. Jews were targeted for violence by Italian and Irish youth gangs. In 1902, mourners at the funeral of a Lower East Side rabbi were attacked by a contingent of Irish residents reacting to displacement pressures from growing numbers of Jewish residents.

60. Rischin 1962: chapter 5.

61. Peiss 1986: 26.

62. Maffi 1995: 118.

63. Rischin 1962: 141.

64. Maffi 1995:125.

65. Rischin 1962: 134.

66. Sanders 1977: 243–44.

67. Rischin 1962: 134.

68. Maffi 1995: 239.

69. Leinenweber 1981: 50.
70. Gutman 1965: 53.
71. Gutman 1965: 53.
72. Rischin 1962: 179–80.
73. Leinenweber 1977: 153.
74. Joselit 1986: 41.
75. See Frieburger 1984.
76. Joselit 1986: 42.
77. Maffi 1995: 166–67.
78. Spencer 1986.
79. Joselit 1986: 40.
80. Joselit 1986: 40.
81. Joselit 1986: 41.
82. Joselit 1986: 43.
83. *Charities and the Commons*, January 18, 1908: 1403.
84. Joselit 1986: 45.
85. *Charities and the Commons*, January 11, 1908: 1379.
86. Joselit 1986: 47.
87. Joselit 1986: 47.
88. Scott 1990: 140.
89. Higham 1975: chapter 1.
90. Rischin 1962: 97.
91. Higham 1975: 41–42.
92. Iorizzo 1970: 44.
93. Myers 1971.
94. Bridges 1988: 63.
95. Mandelbaum 1965: 76–86.
96. The 1919–20 proceedings of the New York State Legislature's Joint Legislative Committee to Investigate Seditious Activities [the Lusk Committee] include maps outlining concentrations of ethnic groups, correspondence and administrative files, investigation subject files, legal papers relating to searches and prosecutions of suspected radical individuals and organizations, newspaper clippings files, and mass meetings investigation files.
97. Hofstadter 1963: 2.
98. Wasserman 1990: 64.
99. Schoener 1967: 58.
100. Steel 1995: 220; Caroli 1995: 1059–61.
101. Quoted in Veiller 1970a: 89.
102. Veiller 1970a: 90.
103. Plunz and Abu-Lughod 1994: 66–67.
104. Veiller 1970a: 96.
105. Veiller 1970a: 102.
106. "Tenement Evils as Seen by the Tenants" 1970: 401–2.
107. Veiller 1970a: 103.
108. Friedman 1978: 40.
109. Lubove 1962: 122–25.
110. Plunz and Abu-Lughod 1994: 71.
111. Lubove 1962: 135.

112. Rischin 1962: 85.
113. Plunz and Abu-Lughod 1994: 72.
114. See Grebler 1952: 100.
115. Lubove 1962: 156–57.
116. Peiss 1986: 74–87.
117. Kaufmann 1910.
118. *Appleton's Dictionary of Greater New York and Its Neighborhoods* 1905: 65–66.
I thank Val Marie Johnson for bringing this source to my attention.
119. The phenomenon of slumming makes up a large part of the story in Caleb
Carr's novel *The Alienist* (1995).
120. Parry 1960; Grana 1964; Fishbein 1982.
121. Grana 1964: chapter 7.
122. Hapgood 1910: 114.
123. Fishbein 1982: 171.
124. Parry 1960: 314–15.
125. Parry 1960: 325.
126. Jackson 1984.

3. Utopian Metropolis versus the Legacy of the Slum

1. Johnson 1996: 37–38.
2. Lampard 1986: 70.
3. Gluck and Meister 1979: 131.
4. Rosenwaike 1972: 90.
5. Grebler 1952: 221.
6. Grebler 1952: 49.
7. Wasserman 1994: 100.
8. Grebler 1955: 184.
9. Grebler 1952: 44.
10. Grebler 1952: 44.
11. Grebler 1952.
12. Caroline Zachary Institute of Human Development 1950.
13. Living standards for significant numbers of Lower East Side residents were
improved slightly due to unionization drives in the garment industry. By 1920, most
shops were unionized, and increased wages facilitated the exodus from downtown.
See Grebler 1952: 118.
14. Lasker 1931: 587.
15. Grebler 1952: 143.
16. Grebler 1952: 144.
17. Wasserman 1994.
18. Grebler estimated the black population of the Lower East Side at 185 persons in 1910 and 1,372 in 1940. In Manhattan, during this same period, the black
population increased from 60,000 to 300,000 (1952: 149).
19. What Grebler ignored was the discrimination black newcomers inevitably
faced when they engaged (as did waves of newcomers before them) in a process of
settlement that dislodged preexisting and entrenched social and cultural institutions
from the last major wave of immigration. See Grebler 1952: 149.

20. Lower East Side Planning Association 1932: 15.
21. Gries and Ford 1931: 31.
22. Gries and Ford 1931: 32.
23. Gries and Ford 1931: 33.
24. Gries and Ford 1931: 31.
25. Perry et al. 1929: 128.
26. Gries and Ford 1931: 9.
27. Gries and Ford 1931: 10; emphasis added.
28. Lasker 1931: 627.
29. Jackson 1984: 328.
30. McAneny 1931: 133.
31. Haig 1927.
32. Schwartz 1993: 36.
33. Lasker 1931.
34. Haig 1927: 100.
35. Lasker 1931: 587.
36. Haig 1927: 103.
37. Wasserman 1994: 103.
38. Lasker 1931: 588.
39. The Chrystie-Forsyth site was purchased by the city in 1930 and cleared of tenements. Although housing and the parkway plan were proposed, the site was developed as the Sarah Roosevelt Park.
40. Adams et al. 1931: 394–406.
41. Buttenwieser 1986: 394.
42. Buttenwieser 1986: 395.
43. Buttenwieser 1987: 171–75.
44. Buttenwieser 1986: 397.
45. Wasserman 1990: 117–18.
46. Holden 1932.
47. Perry 1936.
48. Wasserman 1994: 104.
49. Wasserman 1994.
50. Gries and Ford 1931: 93.
51. Wasserman 1994: 107.
52. Wasserman 1994: 107.
53. Gries and Ford 1931: 136.
54. Wasserman 1994: 104–5.
55. Wasserman 1994: 106.
56. Lower East Side Planning Association 1932: 47.
57. Regional Plan Association 1931: 10.
58. Teaford 1990: 7.
59. Hoyt and Badgley 1939: 23.
60. As cited in Wasserman 1990: 105.
61. Wasserman 1990: 131.
62. Schwartz (1986), Naison (1986), Wasserman (1990), and other students of this era and its tenant-based social movements include the famous rent strike mounted by the Knickerbocker Village Tenants Association in 1935–36 over the shoddy and incomplete construction of units in the towers. Although the strike was important—

the tenant association joined forces with the City-Wide Tenants Council (CWTC) to push for collective bargaining with landlords — it would be inappropriate to cite it as a form of resistance against middle-class redevelopment of the Lower East Side since the majority of the Knickerbocker strikers were lower-middle and middle-class tenants drawn from outside the neighborhood.

63. Naison 1986: 96.
64. Naison 1986: 112–13.
65. Wasserman 1990: 128–29.
66. Wasserman 1990: 148.
67. Wasserman 1990: 130.
68. Buttenwieser 1987: 170.
69. Wasserman 1990.
70. Schwartz 1986: 415.
71. Wasserman 1990: 83.
72. Regional Plan Association 1931: 6.
73. *New York Times*, June 2, 1929.
74. Wasserman 1990: 143.
75. Grebler 1952: 43.
76. Grebler 1952: 97.
77. Grebler's (1952) otherwise thorough study neglected to include developer Fred French's purchase of several hundred lots on blocks between the Manhattan and Brooklyn Bridges for the development of Knickerbocker Village. According to Wasserman (1994: 107), French had "secretly purchased 14.5 acres of land in some 250–300 separate parcels, buying up the properties through four dummy corporations."
78. Holden 1932.
79. Schwartz 1993: 62–63.
80. Schwartz 1993: 26.
81. Radford 1996: 197–98.
82. Only through reconstructing the emergence and application of state policy in response to known social ills and within the specific historical circumstances of local community can we see the intended and unintended consequences of state intervention in the changing place identity of the Lower East Side.
83. Schwartz 1993: 37.
84. Wasserman 1990: 141.
85. Plunz 1990: 227.
86. New York City Housing Authority 1935.
87. Plunz 1990: 208.
88. Lumsden 1936: 103–5.
89. But for two, all of the original tenements were owned by the well-to-do Vincent Astor, who agreed to exchange title ownership for bonds issued by the housing authority. The two holdout properties were owned by an intractable landlord whose demand for an exorbitant cash payment held up the project's initiation. See Post 1938: 183–84.
90. Cited in Post 1938: 185. The State Court of Appeals 1936 ruling on eminent domain was far-reaching. In 1935, in *United States v. Certain Lands in City of Louisville*, a federal court ruled that the federal government could not employ the power of eminent domain to purchase slum properties for public housing development. This

ruling did not apply to slum clearance and public housing constructed by state or local government agencies. These rulings were reflected in the 1937 Housing Act, which stipulated federal subsidies for programs enacted only by local public housing authorities.

91. Kessner 1989: 325.

92. Schwartz 1993: 40–41.

93. In the 1930s, urbanists, such as Lewis Mumford, argued against older urban sites for public housing and favored less dense construction in outlying, undeveloped land. Beyond aesthetic or socially progressive reasons, advocates argued that public housing sites in undeveloped land promised cheaper acquisition costs than central city land. Savings in purchase costs and clearance would allow for creative and expansive housing designs, such as low-density garden apartments. See Genevro 1986: 340.

94. Genevro 1986: 337.

95. The 1937 Housing Act's requirement that tied slum clearance to the new construction of low-income housing was subjected to intense lobbying efforts between 1937 and 1959. The National Association of Real Estate Boards, the United States Savings and Loan League, and the Mortgage Bankers Association campaigned simultaneously to decouple subsidies for slum clearance and public housing and to allow for higher reuses of cleared land other than low-income housing. Business and real estate supporters sought to connect slum clearance with *middle-class* developments, such as housing, office buildings, parking areas, and transportation improvements. The chief backer of the 1949 Housing Act, Senator Robert Taft, disagreed. Taft rejected federal aid as a program to subsidize older cities' alteration of land use and canvassed for a continuation of the slum clearance–low-rent housing linkage enacted in 1937. The outcome was Title I of the Housing Act of 1949, which stipulated the use of federal funds for reducing the costs of acquiring land in depreciated areas that were "predominantly residential in their original use or would be in their re-use" (Lowe 1967: 32). Despite Taft's efforts, federal housing policies became increasingly watered-down in amendments to the act made in the 1950s. While maintaining the initiative to remove blighted areas, revisions in 1954 and 1959 de-emphasized the role of the federal government as a low-income housing provider and allowed easier access to funds for private middle-class redevelopment of urban renewal areas (defined as blighted areas and, importantly, those *threatened* by blight). The 1954 act allowed nonresidential development to take place in urban renewal areas, breaking ground for the ubiquitous parking garages and convention centers found in today's older cities. In 1959, the act permitted up to 20 percent of grant authorizations for nonresidential development. The 1959 act also eliminated the requirement that eligible targeted urban renewal areas have a significant amount of substandard housing, opening up non-blighted areas for physical restructuring. Thus, while preserving its goal of eliminating slums, the evolution of postwar housing policy had shifted its main (and brief) objective from the betterment of low-income housing to funding new uses for urban space.

96. Foard and Fefferman 1966: 96–98.

97. Bratt 1986: 337.

98. Wasserman 1990: 151.

99. Plunz 1990: 245. The Riis and Wald Houses were built with federal, state, and city funds. The specifications are as follows: Jacob Riis Houses, located between

FDR Drive and Avenue D and Sixth to Thirteenth Streets, were constructed with federal and city funds. The development comprised nineteen buildings that covered 18 percent of the 17.6-acre site. The buildings housed 6,865 people in 1,768 apartments. The Lillian Wald Houses housed 7,168 people in 1,861 apartments within sixteen towers. Built with state funds, the development covered 18.6 percent of 16.5 acres. The Wald Houses were built adjacent to the Riis complex, between FDR Drive and Avenue D and Houston to Sixth Streets.

100. Dates in brackets refer to the year of final completion of the projects.

101. Contributing to the functional isolation of the Lower East Side as a poverty zone was the construction of Stuyvesant Town, a "whites-only" middle-income project, on the north side of Fourteenth Street. With financial backing from Metropolitan Life Insurance Company, master builder Robert Moses developed the complex using eminent domain to clear away tenements housing eleven thousand working-class residents. Stuyvesant Town hemmed in the Lower East Side, further isolating it materially and symbolically as lower Manhattan's poorest district. Many of those displaced by the complex relocated south of Fourteenth Street, and the construction of the Riis and Wald Houses was quickened to help settle displaced tenants (Schwartz and Abeles 1973: chapter 4). Later, when the influx of ethnic and racial minorities into the Lower East Side trebled, Fourteenth Street became an obvious spatialized class (middle-class/lower-class) and racial (white/minorities) boundary.

102. Friedman 1978: 21.

103. Bratt 1986: 337.

104. *New York Times*, April 19, 1949.

105. Stegman 1985: 30–31.

106. Stegman 1985: 54–55. The level of government responsible for the determination of rent regulations has shifted since 1942, when the federal government first enacted rent control laws. In 1950, that authority was assumed by New York State, which created a rent commission that periodically assessed the need for continuation of rent control. In 1962, New York City was granted the power to administer regulation, and on April 1, 1984, once again, New York State took charge of rent regulations.

107. Lett 1976: 13–18.

108. *New York Times*, March 22, 1949.

109. *New York Times*, April 29, 1950.

110. Rosenblatt 1964: 16.

111. Van den Haag 1961: 278.

112. Miller and Werthman 1961: 285.

4. Reengineering the Ghetto

1. Bell 1961.

2. Jackson 1985.

3. Moses' extraordinary sway over the direction of New York's development is best documented in Robert Caro's biography of Robert Moses, *The Power Broker* (New York: Knopf, 1974).

4. *New York Times*, August 30, 1953; Friedenberg 1961: 275.

5. Grebler 1952: 147–48.

6. Postwar fluctuations in Puerto Rican migration to the mainland have been extreme. The largest influx was in the 1950s. During that decade, an average of forty-six thousand persons migrated to the mainland per year; migration peaked in 1953 with a net influx of seventy-three thousand persons. In the 1960s, migration rates oscillated yearly with no clear trend. Throughout the 1970s, reverse migration was dominant. Forty-four thousand persons returned to Puerto Rico in 1970. See Rogler and Cooney 1984: 50.

7. Rogler and Cooney 1984: 38; Chenault 1938.

8. Sanchez-Korral 1983: 12–13.

9. Rosenwaike 1972: 121.

10. Rosenwaike 1972: 138.

11. Sanchez-Korral 1983.

12. History Task Force 1979.

13. New York City Department of Welfare 1949.

14. New York City Department of Welfare 1949: 48.

15. Rodriguez 1974: 121; Herberg 1953.

16. U.S. Department of Labor 1975: 62–63.

17. Graduate School of Public Administration and Social Service 1957: 22.

18. Helfgott et al. 1959.

19. Rosenberg 1974: 43.

20. See inter alia Torres 1991.

21. Laurentz 1980: 239.

22. *New York Times*, June 28, 1962.

23. The predominantly white ethnic leadership of the ILGWU feared the restructuring occurring in the garment industry as a result of the growing postwar standardization and suburbanization of production. Their own positions would be lost if the garment industry folded or set up shop elsewhere. With this in mind, union leadership, without consulting the rank and file (the majority of whom were African American and Puerto Rican), negotiated contracts that maintained low wages to forestall an exodus of the garment industry. In his study of those contracts, Herbert Hill wrote, "In reality, there are two categories of workers in the ILGWU: a relatively small number of highly skilled white workers with seniority and stability of employment who earn high wages and for whom the union performs a variety of protective functions, and the great mass of unskilled, low-paid workers, mostly Negro and Puerto Rican, who exist in a permanent condition of semipoverty and are the base of the industry's workforce as well as the union's membership in New York City." See Hill 1974: 406.

24. Laurentz 1980: 240.

25. Helfgott et al. 1959.

26. Zukin 1989.

27. Rapkin 1963: 38–40.

28. Hill 1974: 406.

29. Kessner 1977.

30. Mele 1994a.

31. Eagle 1960: 149–53.

32. Kantrowitz 1973: 49.

33. *New York Times*, February 23, 1953; *New York Times*, September 28, 1959.

34. *New York Times*, August 30, 1953.

35. *New York Times,* January 20, 1958.

36. *New York Times,* September 25, 1959.

37. *New York Times,* March 26, 1958.

38. *New York Times,* September 28, 1959.

39. In a speech given at the seventieth anniversary of the founding of the University Settlement House on the Lower East Side, Moses made clear his unwavering commitment for the demolition of entire neighborhoods by government decree: "The first job is to eradicate the slum, primarily by uncompromising large-scale rebuilding and only incidentally by dispersion and filling up vacant spots.... Piecemeal rebuilding leaves untouched bad blocks in between new housing. These rookeries cannot be assembled except by condemnation, and cannot be torn down or improved automatically by individual owners" (Moses 1956: 3).

40. Lowe 1967: 32; and Friedman 1978: 148–61. The costs of the Title I program were shared, with the federal government paying two-thirds and the city paying one-third of the subsidy.

41. Subsequent revisions to the Housing Act in 1954 and 1959 de-emphasized the role of the federal government as low-income housing providers and allowed easier access to funds for private middle-class redevelopment of urban renewal areas (defined as blighted areas and, importantly, those *threatened* by blight). See chapter 3, note 95.

42. Toll 1969: 289.

43. Proceedings of "Puerto Ricans Confront Problems of the Complex Urban Society," 1967: 359.

44. Bratt 1986: 339.

45. Sanchez 1986: 210.

46. *New York Times,* June 2, 1963.

47. Sanchez 1986: 203

48. Mobilization for Youth 1962b.

49. Rosenblatt 1964: 18.

50. Population figures are problematic as Ukrainians do not show up in immigration "country of origin" statistics (Ukraine constituted a republic of the USSR).

51. Caroline Zachary Institute for Human Development 1950: 73.

52. Wakefield 1959: 465.

53. Quoted in Wakefield 1959: 468.

54. Quoted in Miller and Werthman 1961: 282.

55. Rosenblatt 1964: 23.

56. Lopez 1974: 328.

57. Included among the tenants shaken by the arson was Nicholas Wyeth, the son of painter Andrew Wyeth.

58. *New York Times,* July 2 and 9, 1964.

59. *New York Times,* April 10, 1960.

60. *New York Times,* September 5, 1959.

61. Rosenblatt 1964.

62. *New York Times,* September 11, 1960.

63. Jenkins 1963.

64. Powell 1962: 78.

65. Powell 1962: 78–79.

66. Powell 1962: 79.

67. Proceedings of "Puerto Ricans Confront Problems of the Complex Urban Society," 1967: 169.

68. These organizations were active but not very successful. In my search of publications on Puerto Rican organizations operating in neighborhoods in the 1950s, I have found few references to successful movements organized around social issues in general and housing issues in particular. Instead, I have found citations of contemporaries addressing concerns that few if any such organizations exist. See Lopez 1974.

69. Lopez 1974: 329–37.

70. Although in *The Urban Villagers*, Herbert Gans (1962) portrayed the population of Boston's West End in the 1950s as diverse in ethnic and class composition, the working-class Italians had clearly defined the identity of the community. No such group accomplished this on the Lower East Side.

71. Since the late 1940s, when writer Herbert Huncke (author of *Guilty of Everything* and *The Evening Sun Turned Crimson* and influential associate of beat writers William S. Burroughs, Allen Ginsberg, and Jack Kerouac) is said to have coined the term, the original meaning of *beat* has remained somewhat contested. When the term first appeared in the *New York Times* in 1952, it conveyed meanings of poverty, depression, and dissatisfaction. Beat author Jack Kerouac interpreted the meaning of beat in a far more positive sense and noted its association with contemporary music, especially bebop jazz. See DeYoung Museum 1996.

72. Although the beat scene was pluralistic, we should not impute equality of status among and between the various subgroups that comprised the movement. Polsky (1961) wrote: "Nowhere is there greater disparity between beat theory and practice than in the role that Negro beats, wittingly or unwittingly, are forced to play for white beats" (356–57).

73. Polsky 1961: 340.

74. Polsky 1961; *New York Times*, September 29, 1959.

75. Polsky 1961: 351–52.

76. In addition to the movement to the Lower East Side, there was considerable migration of writers, artists, musicians, and intellectuals to the Upper West Side (Solomon 1961). In contrast to the Lower East Side, the cultural attachment of this community proved to be more durable in the tumultuous decade of the 1970s.

77. Polsky 1961: 341.

78. Wakefield 1959: 466.

79. Wakefield 1959: 466.

80. Sandler 1978; Ashton 1973.

81. Sandler 1978: 2.

82. Sandler 1984: 62.

83. Rosenberg 1973: 101.

84. Sukenick 1987: 58.

85. Quoted in Sukenick 1987: 58.

86. Rosenberg 1973: 106.

87. Rosenberg 1973: 104.

88. Sandler 1978: 21.

89. A similar labor influx of southern African Americans to New York set off housing speculation in neighborhoods in northern Manhattan and in Brooklyn. In the Lower East Side, the newcomers were predominantly Puerto Rican. The average percentage of housing units occupied by nonwhite persons between Houston and

Fourteenth Streets for 1950 was 3.2, for public housing (tracts 20 and 24), the average was 10.2, and for all of Manhattan, 16.24. Source: U.S. Census of Population and Housing 1950.

90. Proceedings of "Puerto Ricans Confront Problems of the Complex Urban Society," 1967: 115.

91. Mobilization for Youth 1966: 79.

92. Preble and Casey 1969: 1.

93. Preble and Casey 1969: 7.

94. Polsky 1961: 350.

95. Polsky 1961: 350.

96. Sales of heroin and other narcotics and drugs became firmly entrenched on Lower East Side streets and remain so today. Since the onset of drug markets in the late 1950s, landlords and tenants have petitioned the state to rid the area of a major source of crime and other social problems, albeit for very different reasons.

97. Mobilization for Youth 1966.

98. Mobilization for Youth 1967.

99. Weissman 1969: 69.

100. Abeles, Schwartz and Associates 1969.

101. Mobilization for Youth 1967: 30–32.

102. In response to incorporated landlords' claiming of immunity from prosecution by the city and lawsuits from tenants, the New York State legislature passed a law in 1966 holding individuals of a corporation personally liable. The law applied to damage suits related to property as a public nuisance brought about by tenants or the city (Mobilization for Youth 1967: 17).

103. *New York Times*, July 24, 1953.

104. Fitzpatrick 1971: 57–58; Rosenberg and Lake 1976: 1149.

105. Mobilization for Youth 1966.

106. Mobilization for Youth 1966.

107. *New York Times*, July 26, 1966.

108. Wakefield 1959: 470.

109. *New York Times*, September 28, 1959.

110. *New York Times*, December 22, 1959.

111. *New York Times*, January 5, 1962.

112. Mobilization for Youth 1962a: 75, 80.

113. The scale of programs offered by Mobilization for Youth was significantly reduced once its original mandate expired in 1965. In 1969, the Ford Foundation granted a $200,000 loan guarantee for the organization's operating expenses. See Weissman 1969: 69.

114. Weissman 1969: 29.

115. Mobilization for Youth 1962a: 141–44.

116. Lipsky 1967: 132.

117. Mobilization for Youth 1962a: 74.

118. Weissman 1969: 64.

119. Lipsky (1967, 1970) and Naison (1986) note that the actual participation rate of tenants in rent strikes was quite low. In most instances, however, sponsoring organizations used highly visible demonstrations, marches, and pamphleteering to increase media attention and, hence, public awareness of the strike and its causes.

120. Lipsky 1967: 114.

121. Lipsky 1967: 128–29.

122. Lipsky 1967: 132.

123. Mobilization for Youth 1962a: 77.

124. One of the key organizational changes was the creation of community boards—advisory bodies comprised of various neighborhood leaders—in 1963. Community boards were founded in response to citizen demand for inclusion in neighborhood decisions. In 1975, the boards' role was expanded to include resident advisement in the development of neighborhood plans.

5. A Brief Psychedelic Detour

1. Jacobs 1961.

2. Lee and Shlain 1985: 195.

3. Robison 1976.

4. Grava 1980: 35.

5. Robison 1976: 97.

6. Grava 1980: 34.

7. Turner 1984.

8. DeSalvo 1974.

9. New York State's Limited-Profit Housing Companies program (more commonly referred to as the Mitchell-Lama program) was passed by the state legislature in 1955. The program provided tax abatements and low-interest, long-term loans to developers to build rental or cooperative housing within distressed neighborhoods. State or city loans were made available to developers for up to fifty years at 4 to 4.5 percent interest, covering up to 90 percent of development costs. New York City also granted property tax abatements for up to 50 percent. The program often was offered in combination with land cost write-downs in federally aided renewal areas. See Frieden 1964: 136–37.

10. Other middle-income projects were built in the 1960s. These include Seward Park Cooperative (1961), Governeuer Gardens (1964), David Podell Houses (1967), Haven Plaza (1967), and Village East Towers (1968).

11. Abeles, Schwartz and Associates 1969: 4.

12. Cook 1971: 10–11.

13. Cook 1971: 96.

14. Cook 1971: 100.

15. Quoted in Cook 1971: 196.

16. Sukenick 1987: 144.

17. According to Cook (1971: 200), the term *hippie* slowly replaced *beatnik*. It first appeared in print in the *San Francisco Examiner* on September 5, 1965. *Hip* was used much earlier, in the 1940s, and its root meaning has been slightly contested. Cook (94) maintained that *hip* emerged from *hep*, a term used to describe a quality of "instant understanding" (i.e., to be hip to a situation). He also quoted Norman Mailer's piece "The White Negro" published in *Dissent* in 1957 in which "hipsters" were defined as urban types who sought out dangerous scenarios for thrills and adventure (93). Herbert Huncke, the Times Square hustler and author, was the ultimate "hipster." For Polsky (1961), also writing in *Dissent, hip* and *hep* were derived from drug culture, and most specifically the phrase "to be on the hip," referring to the

position of lying on one's side while smoking opium. Regardless of distinctions between being in the know, being a hustler, or being a thrill seeker, all such meanings of *hip* are tied to drug consumption.

18. Communities in Haight-Ashbury in San Francisco and in the East Village in New York in the 1960s were expressions of the hippie movement, and they shared many cultural practices, such as drug consumption and public displays ("happenings," "be-ins," "be-outs," etc.). There were also obvious links between the two enclaves, such as the music performance venues of the Fillmore (San Francisco) and the Fillmore East (New York). Comparisons can be made, but the analysis of the hippie enclaves in the Haight and in the East Village (Lower East Side) should be situated within the historical narratives of social and cultural change in each neighborhood. My purpose here is to understand the sociospatial changes within the Lower East Side that were linked to the hippie phenomenon. As such, I do not imply that similar forces gave rise to the Haight-Ashbury district in San Francisco.

19. *New York Times*, June 4, 1967.

20. *New York Times*, August 13, 1967.

21. *New York Times*, June 5a, 1967.

22. *New York Times*, June 5b, 1967; *New York Times*, June 4, 1967.

23. The issue of antagonism between the police force (comprised of mostly middle-class and suburban personnel) and countercultural groups resurfaced in the analysis in the aftermath of another, similar "riot" in Tompkins Square Park in August 1988.

24. *Newsweek*, October 30, 1967: 84.

25. Gruen 1966: 110.

26. Gruen 1966: 11. Performance "happenings" did not originate in the East Village, nor were they unique to any particular hippie community. Stuart Hobbs wrote: "The first happening is generally considered to be an event staged by [John] Cage and others at Black Mountain College in 1952. In a college dining room in which paintings by Rauschenberg and Franz Kline were displayed, Cage stood reading on one ladder, poet Charles Olson read another text from another ladder, Rauschenberg played scratched phonographic records, David Tudor played the piano and the radio, and Merce Cunningham danced among them all" (Hobbs 1997: 109). Most of the cultural practices identified in this chapter were neither original nor exclusive to the East Village or to Haight-Ashbury. What was distinctive about these places was the coming together in a single area of key figures in the counterculture and thousands of other hippies who engaged in these and other practices and rituals.

27. Quoted in Henry 1989: 26.

28. Cagle 1995: 88.

29. Gruen 1966: 29.

30. Gruen 1966: 43.

31. Kotzwinkle 1974: 133.

32. *Village Voice* 1972.

33. *New York Times*, August 25, 1967.

34. *New York Times*, August 13, 1967.

35. Little 1972: 186; Greenberger 1971: 198.

36. Little 1972: 185.

37. Little 1972: 186.

38. Gruen 1966: 76.

39. Greenberger 1971: 200.
40. Little 1972: 189.
41. Little 1972: 187
42. Little 1972: 188.
43. Greenberger 1971: 201.
44. Gruen 1966: 55–58.
45. Gruen 1966: 12; Sanders 1966.
46. *New York Times*, August 7, 1967.
47. *East Village Other* 1965: 1.
48. Cited in Cook 1971: 201.
49. *New York Times Magazine*, September 24, 1967.
50. *New York Times Magazine*, September 24, 1967.
51. *New York Times*, June 3a, 1967.
52. *New York Times*, August 25, 1967.
53. Nusser 1967: 1.
54. Mobilization for Youth 1967: 30.
55. Rent regulations allowed a 13 percent rental increase for new leases.
56. Nusser 1967 1: 1.
57. Nusser 1967 1: 1.
58. *New York Times Magazine*, September 24, 1967, emphasis added.
59. See Carey 1972.
60. Mitchell 1968: 226.
61. *New York Times Magazine*, September 24, 1967.
62. Wright 1993: 592.
63. Thomas 1993: 576.
64. *New York Times*, June 4, 1967.
65. *New York Times*, June 5a, 1967.
66. Duffy 1975.
67. Mitchell 1968: 230.
68. Sukenick 1987: 148.
69. *New York Times*, June 3b, 1967.
70. There was a great deal of ill ease toward the police among the Lower East Side Latino and black communities. In the early 1960s, local residents leveled charges of brutality against the police force. See the *New York Times*, June 5b, 1967.
71. Cited in Goldstein 1968: 257.
72. *New York Times*, June 3b, 1967.
73. *New York Times*, June 3b, 1967.
74. *New York Times*, August 25, 1967.
75. *New York Times*, June 3a, 1967.
76. *New York Times*, June 5b, 1967.
77. *New York Times*, October 19, 1967.
78. *New York Times*, October 18, 1967.
79. *New York Times*, August 7, 1967.
80. *New York Times Magazine*, October 29, 1967.
81. *New York Times Magazine*, October 29, 1967.
82. Kornbluth 1968: 267.
83. *Newsweek*, October 30, 1967.
84. *New York Times*, October 29, 1967.

85. *Daily News,* October 11, 1967; *Time,* October 20, 1967.
86. *Newsweek,* October 23, 1967.
87. *Newsweek,* October 30, 1967; *New York Times,* October 29, 1967.
88. Goldstein 1968: 257.
89. *Newsweek,* October 30, 1967.
90. Goldstein 1968: 257.
91. *New York Times,* October 29, 1967.
92. *Newsweek,* October 30, 1967.
93. *Newsweek,* October 30, 1967.
94. Cited in *New York Post,* July 25, 1969.
95. *New York Times,* June 15, 1968.
96. *New York Times,* March 26, 1968.
97. Haden-Guest 1997: 86.
98. *New York Post,* December 7, 1971.
99. Thomas 1993: 573.

6. Urban Malaise, Community Abandonment, and Underground Subcultures of Decay

1. Quoted in Regional Plan Association 1973: 13.
2. Housing abandonment was a consistent feature historically of the land market on the Lower East Side. Individual buildings were abandoned due to bad management, too much real estate speculation, or high mortgage rates, but abandonment was viewed as an isolated, rather than widespread, phenomenon.
3. Interview by author, September 21, 1989.
4. The Real Great Society became Charas, Inc., whose members were politically active in community resistance to displacement in the 1970s and 1980s (Maffi 1994: 142).
5. Lopez 1974: 330.
6. *New York Times:* July 23, 1968; July 24, 1968; July 26, 1968; July 27, 1968.
7. Rogler and Cooney 1984: 51.
8. Maffi 1994.
9. Lopez 1974: 332.
10. See Lopez 1974: footnote 34.
11. Lopez 1974: 333.
12. *Daily News,* December 11a, 1971.
13. *Daily News,* January 2, 1972.
14. *Daily News,* December 11b, 1971.
15. *Daily News,* December 11b, 1971.
16. *New York Times,* May 20, 1971.
17. Schwartz and Abeles 1973.
18. U.S. Census 1970.
19. Davidson 1979: 229–30.
20. Schwartz and Abeles 1973: 56.
21. Bradford and Rubinowitz 1975: 77–86; Myerson 1986.
22. Sternlieb and Burchell (1973) found strong correlations between tenant characteristics and the conditions of buildings in their study of factors related to hous-

ing abandonment. The rate of tenant welfarism, for example, was negatively correlated with the condition of buildings (65).

23. Lawson and Johnson 1986: 211.

24. In 1969, the city passed the Rent Stabilization Law, and in 1970 it instituted a complex formula for allowing rent increases, called the maximum base rent program (MBR). The MBR was intended to close the gap between existent rents and "economic rents." The MBR set and defined the rent level of controlled units in 1970 as a "base rent." The dollar amount of a unit's base rent reflected an income "sufficient to cover the cost of operating, maintaining, and financing rental housing while allowing a fair rate of return to the owner" (Sternlieb and Hughes 1976: 241). The MBR would be adjusted every two years (maximum increase 7.5 percent) to take into account any increases or decreases in costs due to changes, for example, in the rate of inflation.

25. Sternlieb and Hughes 1976: 241–43.

26. Rent stabilization was reinstated with the passage of the 1974 Emergency Tenant Protection Act. The act did not stipulate rent stabilization as permanent but instead required periodic renewals. The renewals have not been pro forma or uncontroversial; continued successful passage has been the result of mobilization by pro-tenant forces. See Lett 1976: 10–26; Lawson and Johnson 1986; Niebanck 1985.

27. Sternlieb and Hughes 1976: 7.

28. Davidson 1979: 236; see also Marcuse 1986.

29. *Amsterdam News*, April 24, 1976.

30. Sanchez 1986: 217.

31. Marcuse 1980.

32. Davidson 1979: 245–46.

33. Analyses of abandonment decision making typically stress the importance of landlord perceptions of future trends in addition to an assessment of existing conditions. See Rapkin 1959; Sternlieb 1972; Sternlieb et al. 1972; and Sternlieb and Hughes 1976.

34. Smith 1986; Marcuse 1986; Myerson 1986.

35. Sternlieb and Hughes 1976: 64.

36. Hartman et al. 1982: 43.

37. *East Village Eye* 1979: 1.

38. Interfaith Adopt-A-Building 1978: 14; Wallace 1981: 433–64.

39. Department of Housing Preservation and Development 1983: 7.

40. Since nonpayment of property taxes signaled divestiture in an official way, bureaucratic records of neighborhood levels of tax arrears present a clear measure of the timing and location of disinvestment. See, for example, the study of Pittsburgh in Lake 1979.

41. Smith et al. 1994.

42. 1989 interviews with residents whose relatives relocated in the 1970s.

43. Interfaith Adopt-A-Building 1978: 14.

44. Sharff 1987: 19–50.

45. *New York Times*, October 31, 1976.

46. In-Rem Working Group 1986.

47. Lawson and Johnson 1986: 240.

48. Sanchez 1986: 217.

49. White and Saegert 1997: 163.

50. Strong 1982; interviews by author and field notes, 1987.

51. Algarin and Pinero 1975: 16.

52. Turetsky 1993: chapters 3 and 4.

53. Although the law formally recognized this decades-old strategy, its byzantine regulations and eligibility requirements kept many rent withholdings technically illegal.

54. Hughes and Bleakly 1975.

55. Ward 1974: 97.

56. Lawson and Johnson 1986: 222.

57. Von Hassell 1996: 21.

58. DeRienzo and Allen 1985.

59. Von Hassell 1996: 73.

60. Von Hassell 1996: 75–76.

61. White and Saegert 1997: 164.

62. Lawson and Johnson 1986: 240.

63. Van Kleunen 1994.

64. Von Hassell 1996: 2.

65. *New York Times,* October 6, 1977.

66. *Daily News,* February 20, 1976.

67. Schmelzkopf 1995: 366.

68. Von Hassell 1996: 23.

69. Von Hassell 1996: chapter 5.

70. *New York Times,* September 5, 1982.

71. Cognizant of its imprecise meaning, I use "punk" to describe initially noncommercial music, culture, dress, and other elements of style appearing after 1975. As Henry (1989: 7) writes: "Though 'punk' did not become a generic term used in reference to a certain type of rock-and-roll music and the youth subculture associated with it until the emergence of the punk scene in Britain in 1975, it has also been used, mainly in retrospect, to describe noncommercial rock music of the early 1970s as well as highly commercial rock music of the early 1980s. In addition, 'punk' has sometimes been used synonymously with other terms such as 'underground rock,' 'new wave,' 'new music,' 'street rock,' 'power pop,' 'avant punk,' and 'hardcore.'"

72. Sukenick 1987: 270.

73. Swearingen 1996a.

74. See Cagle 1995 and Marcus 1989.

75. Swearingen 1996b.

76. Frith and Horne 1987: 112, as quoted in Cagle 1995: 84.

77. Henry 1989: 135.

78. Cagle 1995: 158.

79. Henry 1989: 34.

80. Harron 1988: 195.

81. Harron 1988: 193.

82. In a 1973 interview, David Johansen, the lead singer of the New York Dolls, told how the band's music was reflective of urban decay and the ways people related to an environment of social and economic decline (Savage 1993: 58).

83. Musto 1986; Haden-Guest 1997.

84. Bolton 1989: 16.

85. Kitsis (date unknown).
86. Henry 1989: 51.
87. Kozak 1985.
88. Henry 1989: 53.
89. Musto 1986: 106.

7. Developing the East Village

1. Sassen 1989.
2. Stegman 1984: 37.
3. Smith 1996: 200–205.
4. Interview by author, September 1987.
5. Weiss 1988.
6. *New York Times*, September 28, 1977.
7. Zukin 1989.
8. Lin 1998.
9. Stegman 1984: 105.
10. Stegman 1984: 53, 33.
11. Interviews by author, 1987–88.
12. Analysis of Sanborn real estate data.
13. *Real Estate Newsletter* 1985: 1.
14. Siegle 1989.
15. Harron 1988: 214–16.
16. Siegle 1989.
17. Siegel 1988: 177.
18. For a discussion of art genres that influenced the East Village art scene, see Hsieh 1994.
19. Lachmann 1988: 235–36.
20. Foster 1982: 15.
21. Hsieh 1994: 107.
22. Gablik 1982: 34.
23. *New York Times*, February 8, 1987.
24. Plous and Looker 1984: 41.
25. Hershkovits 1983: 90.
26. Hershkovits 1983: 90
27. Robinson and McCormick 1984: 138.
28. Robinson and McCormick 1984: 138.
29. Robinson and McCormick 1984: 138.
30. Cameron 1984: 13.
31. *Village Voice*, April 3, 1984.
32. Moufarrege 1982: 69.
33. Parks 1982: 73.
34. Moufarrege 1982: 69; emphasis is mine.
35. Hershkovits 1983: 89.
36. *New York Times*, June 26, 1983.
37. Siegel 1988: 178–79.
38. Moufarrege 1983: 37.

39. Ricard 1982: 43.

40. Hoban 1988: 39.

41. Ricard 1981: 40.

42. *Art News*, September 1984: 167.

43. Moufarrege 1982: 72.

44. Moufarrege 1982: 69.

45. Robinson and McCormick 1984: 144.

46. *Village Voice*, October 18, 1983.

47. *New York Times*, June 26, 1983.

48. Deutsche and Ryan 1984: 104.

49. Siegel 1988: 179.

50. Robinson and McCormick 1984: 141.

51. Deutsche and Ryan 1984: 94.

52. Deutsche and Ryan 1984: 92.

53. Hershkovits 1983: 90.

54. Bowler and McBurney 1991.

55. Robinson 1984: 14.

56. *Village Voice*, December 14, 1982.

57. Huxtable 1987.

58. Huxtable 1987.

59. Sites 1994: 201.

60. Schmelzkopf 1995: 377.

61. *New York Times*, August 11, 1981.

62. *The Villager*, May 13, 1982: 5.

63. *New York Times*, May 4, 1982.

64. Sleeper 1987: 437.

65. Fainstein 1994: 49.

66. The incentives were typically tax abatements, but certain programs also allowed landlords to pass the costs of renovation on to tenants.

67. Division of Housing and Community Renewal 1987.

68. *Apartment Law Insider,* January 1990: 1.

69. Interviews by author with real estate developers, 1990.

70. The setting of the base rent for rent stabilization was determined not solely by the year the initial lease began but also by the original spatial dimensions of the apartment. The alteration clause in the regulation read that a new first rent surpassed the original base rent when a unit was substantially altered to the extent that it was not in existence in its present form on the base date. Landlords could charge a new "first" rent only if the outer walls of a regulated apartment had been changed. After renovation, the apartment's outer dimensions were required to be either larger or smaller than before.

71. *New York Times*, January 3, 1988.

72. *Apartment Law Insider,* December 1989: 1.

73. *Real Estate Newsletter* 1985: 1; *Real Estate Newsletter* 1986: 1; *Real Estate Newsletter* 1987: 1.

74. *Real Estate Weekly* 1989.

75. *New York Newsday,* March 3, 1988, part 2: 8.

76. *New York Newsday,* March 3, 1988, part 2: 8.

77. *New York Times*, January 3, 1988.

78. Using the *Sanborn Real Estate Directory*, a list was compiled of properties that were sold since 1983 in the East Village, and their owners were categorized as individual owners, holding corporations, or real estate corporations. While the latter two categories expanded throughout the decade, individual owners declined. Since the 1950s, many individual landlords have incorporated themselves and formed real estate companies for a variety of reasons (limited liability, etc.). By including only those properties that changed ownership, I have tried to exclude these cases since they would give the false impression of a substantial decrease in individual owners and an increase in corporate owners.

79. The *Sanborn Real Estate Directory* was used to compile a sample of the names of new property owners who had entered the neighborhood since 1983. This was cross-checked against the *Real Estate Directory of Manhattan*, which listed individual owners and their holdings in the borough of Manhattan. Developers with multiple holdings were found not to be limited geographically to the Lower East Side but had invested as well in similar neighborhoods of the city.

80. Ahlbrandt and Brophy 1975: 26–35.

81. Schwartz and Abeles 1973: 53–57.

82. Interviews by author with real estate agents, 1990.

83. PMMs were contractual agreements between buyer and seller, in which some portion of the cost of purchase (after down payment) is paid by the buyer directly to the seller over a specified period.

84. Sagalyn 1983: 101.

85. Survey Data Security Corporation, New York State Banking Mortgage Activity Reports, Numbers 19 and 20, 1986. Banking Mortgage Activity Reports provided geographical statistics on types of mortgages used in sales between 1982 and 1986. Mortgages were classified as five types: Institutional (from banks, thrifts, holding corporations, and savings and loans); The City of New York (financing through various agencies, namely the Department of Housing Preservation and Development); Realty Firms (financing by real estate firms that are developers and landlords of properties); Purchase Money Mortgages (financing by the seller); and Private (financing by outside investors or miscellaneous lenders).

86. *Real Estate Newsletter* 1985: 1; *Real Estate Newsletter* 1987: 1.

87. *New York Newsday*, September 12, 1988: 7.

88. Author's field notes, 1987–88.

89. A random sample from the entire neighborhood was not feasible since pace and direction of investment do not occur randomly.

90. Mele 1994b; Smith et al. 1994.

91. New York State Department of Law 1989.

92. Data related to demographic changes in Loisaida are from 1980 and 1990 census figures for census tracts 22.02, 26.01, 26.02, 28, 30.02, 32, and 34.

93. Aponte-Pares 1988.

94. DeGiovanni 1987.

95. *New York Times*, April 1, 1988.

96. *New York Newsday*, March 3, 1988.

97. *Real Estate Newsletter*, 1985: 1.

98. *Village Voice*, January 17, 1989: 11.

99. DeGiovanni 1987.
100. DeGiovanni 1987: vii.
101. New York State Department of Law 1985: 8–9.
102. Mele 1995.

8. Targeting the Middle Class

1. *Village Voice*, December 22, 1987; Lachmann 1988; Drew 1995.
2. Musto 1987.
3. *Village Voice*, April 3, 1984.
4. Moore and Miller 1985.
5. Hershkovits 1983: 92.
6. Department of Housing Preservation and Development 1987. The city's presentation of in rem data does not allow for disaggregation into subareas such as East Village or Loisaida.
7. Bratt 1988: 8.
8. *New York Times*, December 28, 1986.
9. The Cooper Square organization had fought a similar strategy in the 1950s and 1960s for low-income residents displaced by middle-class cooperatives built under urban renewal programs (see Abu-Lughod 1994b: 320–21).
10. Herb 1989.
11. Abu-Lughod 1994b.
12. Community land trusts and public-private housing coalitions operate differently and have distinct forms of ownership. Local not-for-profit housing associations retain indefinite ownership of land in community land trusts. Associations sell the housing units to individual low-income residents and lend money to occupants for renovations. Occupants are permitted to sell their property only at original cost in addition to improvements made. Private-public coalitions create an equity trust from corporate investments. Using trust money, coalitions purchase and rehabilitate properties. These units are rented as low-income housing for a period of ten to fifteen years. They may be sold to private developers at market rate only after the period expires. Both of these community redevelopment initiatives attempt to direct growth to include the needs of at-risk populations, thus curtailing displacement. See Abu-Lughod 1994b.
13. *Real Estate Newsletter*, November 4, 1985: 2.
14. Van Kleunen 1994.
15. Alphabet City Community Center 1989.
16. For a detailed overview of the sociodemographic makeup of East Village squatters and various squatter ideologies, see Van Kleunen 1994.
17. Author's field notes, Community Board 3 meetings 1988–89.
18. *Village Voice*, August 16, 1988.
19. Videotape of riot by Clayton Patterson, August 7–8, 1993 (field notes of video by Janet Abu-Lughod). A fuller treatment of the Tompkins Square Riot and its aftermath can be found in Abu-Lughod 1994a.
20. Abu-Lughod 1994a.
21. *East Villager* 1988: 1. In one well-publicized incident of police violence, "an officer [was] seen jamming his nightstick into the spokes of a passing bicycle. The

rider fell to the ground and was set upon and clubbed by several officers"; *New York Times*, August 14a, 1988.

22. *New York Times*, August 14a, 1988.
23. *New Common Good*, September 1988.
24. *New Common Good*, September 1988.
25. *New Common Good*, September 1988.
26. *New York Times*, August 14b, 1988.
27. *New York Times*, August 14a, 1988.
28. Greshof and Dale 1994.
29. *New York Times*, July 7, 1989.
30. *New York Times*, July 7, 1989.
31. Author's field notes; *New York Times*, October 25, 1989.
32. Author's field notes, 1989.
33. Abu-Lughod 1994a: 253–58.
34. *New York Times*, December 7, 1989.
35. *New York Times*, December 7, 1989.
36. *New York Times*, December 15, 1989.
37. *New York Times*, December 18, 1989.
38. Abu-Lughod 1994a: 252.
39. *New York Times*, April 2, 1989; *Village Voice*, April 11, 1989.
40. *Village Voice*, April 11, 1989.
41. *Village Voice*, April 11, 1989.
42. *New York Times*, April 2, 1989.
43. *Village Voice*, May 6, 1989.
44. *Village Voice*, May 16, 1989.
45. *New York Times*, May 6, 1989.
46. *Village Voice*, May 16, 1989.
47. *New York Times*, May 6, 1989.
48. *New York Times*, October 27, 1989.
49. ABC information handout.
50. *New York Times*, October 27, 1989.
51. Author's field notes; *New York Post*, October 27, 1989.
52. *New York Times*, October 27, 1989.
53. *Daily News*, October 27, 1989.
54. *New York Times*, October 27, 1989.
55. Author's field notes; *New York Times*, October 28, 1989.

9. The Production of Desire

1. Hebdige 1979: 93.
2. Featherstone 1991.
3. Featherstone 1991: 106.
4. Abercrombie 1994: 51.
5. Lyotard 1984: 76; Featherstone 1991.
6. *New York Times*, August 14, 1996.
7. "History of Wigstock."
8. Interviews by author and field notes, 1987 and 1996.

9. *Billboard* 1996: 72.

10. Zukin 1991.

11. Wise 1997: 41; Condon 1991; *New York Times*, May 31, 1991.

12. Zukin 1995: chapter 1.

13. Yaro and Hiss 1996; Coopers and Lybrand 1996.

14. Smart infrastructure is a political economic initiative created to advance a locality's strategic advantage in knowledge- and information-based economies. Initiatives typically include planning and development of advanced information infrastructure projects (such as wired buildings), linking public institutions of government with corporate interests to encourage the knowledge and entertainment sector, providing incentives for the private sector to take a leadership role in the establishment and operation of trial projects, developing contacts between government, corporations, and research, and locating and furthering diverse cultural entertainment as content provision sites.

15. *New York Times*, February 13, 1995.

16. O'Connor and Wynne 1996: 62.

17. Gottdiener 1997.

18. Morley and Robins 1995: 37.

19. Interviews by author with real estate brokers specializing in area rentals, March 1996, May 1997, and April 1998; *New York Times*, August 29, 1997: B5.

20. *New York Times*, June 14, 1992: 7.

21. *Vogue*, September 1998.

22. *New York Times*, August 11, 1998: 1.

23. Davis 1998: 2.

24. *New York Times*, June 14, 1992: 7.

25. *New York Times*, August 29, 1997.

26. Interviews with students from Eugene Lang College of the New School for Social Research and the Cooper Union.

27. *New York Times*, August 9, 1998.

28. Frequent turnovers permitted landlords to increase rents with the signing of every new lease. New rentals to multiple but usually unrelated householders with separate incomes yielded increasingly higher rent fees.

29. *Not Bored Magazine* 1996.

30. *The Shadow* 1998.

31. *New York Times*, July 26a, 1998.

32. *New York Times*, August 9, 1998.

33. *New York Times*, July 26b, 1998.

34. Sharff 1998: 220–21.

35. Scott 1990: 112.

36. Melucci 1989: 60.

37. *The Shadow* 1995.

Bibliography

Abeles, Schwartz and Associates. 1969. *The Lower East Side's Housing Inventory: 1960–1968*. New York: Mobilization for Youth.

———. 1970. "Forging a Future for the Lower East Side: A Plan for Action." Prepared for the City of New York Planning Commission. Reproduced in part in Schwartz and Abeles 1973.

Abercrombie, Nicholas. 1994. "Authority and Consumer Society." In *The Authority of the Consumer*, ed. Russell Keat et al. London: Routledge: 43–57.

Abu-Lughod, Janet L. 1994a. "The Battle for Tompkins Square Park." In *From Urban Village to East Village: The Battle for New York's Lower East Side*, Janet L. Abu-Lughod et al. Cambridge, Mass.: Blackwell: 233–66.

———. 1994b. "Defending the Cross-Subsidy Plan: The Tortoise Wins Again." In *From Urban Village to East Village: The Battle for New York's Lower East Side*, Janet L. Abu-Lughod et al. Cambridge, Mass.: Blackwell: 313–34.

Abu-Lughod, Janet L., et al. 1994. *From Urban Village to East Village: The Battle for New York's Lower East Side*. Cambridge, Mass.: Blackwell.

Adams, Thomas, et al. c1931. *The Building of the City, Regional Plan*, vol. 2. New York: Regional Plan of New York and Its Environs.

Ahlbrandt, Roger S., Jr., and Paul C. Brophy. 1975. *Neighborhood Revitalization: Theory and Practice*. Lexington, Mass.: Lexington Books.

Alexander, Christopher. 1979. *The Timeless Way of Building*. New York: Oxford University Press.

Algarin, Miguel, and Miguel Pinero. 1975. *Nuyorican Poetry: An Anthology of Puerto Rican Words and Feelings*. New York: William Morrow and Co.

Allen, John, and Michael Pryke. 1994. "The Production of Service Space." *Environment and Planning D: Society and Space* 12, no. 4 (August): 453–76.

Alphabet City Community Center. 1989. "Seven Point Statement on Tompkins Square Park and Surrounding Issues." New York: By the authors. Mimeographed.

Amsterdam News. 1976. "Starr Advocates Controlled Ethnic Communities." April 24: 1.

Apartment Law Insider. 1989. "Get Free Market Rent for Substantially Altered Apartment." December: 1.

————. 1990. "How to Beat 13 Common Challenges to MCI Rent Hikes." January: 1.

Appleton's Dictionary of Greater New York and Its Neighborhoods. 1905. New York: D. Appleton and Co.

Aponte-Pares, Luis. 1988. "Housing and Puerto Ricans: No Place for Community." Working paper presented at the Conference for Puerto Ricans and New York City Government, May 14. New York: Institute for Puerto Rican Policy.

Art News. 1984. "New York Reviews," vol. 83 (September): 167.

Arthur, Timothy S. 1873. *Cast Adrift*. Philadelphia: J. M. Stoddart.

Ashton, Dore. 1973. *The New York School: A Cultural Reckoning*. New York: Viking Press.

Badcock, Blair. 1996. " 'Looking-Glass' Views of the City." *Progress in Human Geography* 20, no. 1: 91–99.

Beauregard, Robert. 1993. *Voices of Decline: The Postwar Fate of U.S. Cities*. Cambridge, Mass.: Blackwell.

Bell, Daniel. 1961. "The Three Faces of New York." *Dissent* 8, no. 3 (summer): 222–32.

Bernheimer, Charles S. 1905. *The Russian Jew in the United States*. Philadelphia: J. C. Winston Co.

Billboard. 1996. "East Village Setting of Cybersoap," vol. 108, no. 15 (April 13): 72.

Bogen, Elizabeth. 1987. *Immigration in New York*. New York: Praeger Publishers.

Bolton, Richard. 1989. "Enlightened Self-Interest: The Avant-Garde in the '80s." *Afterimage* 16, no. 7 (February): 16.

Bourdieu, Pierre. 1984. *Distinction: A Social Critique of the Judgement of Taste*. London: Routledge and Kegan Paul.

Bowler, Anne, and Blaine McBurney. 1991. "Gentrification and the Avant-Garde in New York's East Village: The Good, the Bad and the Ugly." *Theory, Culture, and Society* 8, no. 4 (November): 49–77.

Brace, Charles Loring. 1880. *The Dangerous Classes of New York and Twenty Years' Work among Them*, 3d ed. New York: Wynkoop and Hallenbeck.

Bradford, Calvin P., and Leonard S. Rubinowitz. 1975. "The Urban-Suburban Investment-Disinvestment Process: Consequences for Older Neighborhoods." *Annals of the American Academy of Political and Social Science* 422 (November): 77–86.

Bratt, Rachel G. 1986. "Public Housing: The Controversy and the Contribution." In *Critical Perspectives on Housing*, ed. Rachel Bratt et al. Philadelphia: Temple University Press: 335–61.

————. 1988. *Mutual Housing Associations*. Washington, D.C.: Neighborhood Reinvestment Corporation.

Bridges, Amy. 1988. "Rethinking the Origins of Machine Politics." In *Power, Culture, and Place: Essays on New York City*, ed. John Hull Mollenkopf. New York: Russell Sage Foundation: 53–73.

Browett, J. 1984. "On the Necessity and Inevitability of Uneven Spatial Development under Capitalism." *International Journal of Urban and Regional Research* 8: 155–76.

Bürger, Peter. 1984. *Theory of the Avant-Garde*, trans. Michael Shaw. Minneapolis: University of Minnesota Press.

Buttenwieser, Ann L. 1986. "Shelter for What and for Whom? On the Route toward Vladeck Houses, 1930 to 1940." *Journal of Urban History* 12, no. 4 (August): 391–413.

————. 1987. *Manhattan Water Bound: Planning and Developing Manhattan's Waterfront from the Seventeenth Century to the Present.* New York: New York University Press.

Cagle, Van M. 1995. *Reconstructing Pop/Subculture: Art, Rock, and Andy Warhol.* Thousand Oaks, Calif.: Sage Publications.

Cameron, Dan. 1984. "East Village, USA." In *Neo York: Report on a Phenomenon,* ed. Phyllis Plous and Mary Looker. Santa Barbara, Calif.: University Art Museum: 10–13.

Campbell, Helen. 1892. *Darkness and Daylight, or Lights and Shadows of New York Life.* New York: A. D. Worthington.

Carey, George W. 1972. "Hippie Neighborhoods and Urban Spatial Systems." In *The City in the Seventies,* ed. Robert K. Yin. Itasca, Ill.: F. E. Peacock Publishers: 62–64.

Caro, Robert A. 1974. *The Power Broker: Robert Moses and the Fall of New York.* New York: Alfred A. Knopf.

Caroli, Betty Boyd. 1995. "Settlement Houses." In *The Encyclopedia of New York City,* ed. Kenneth T. Jackson. New Haven, Conn.: Yale University Press: 1059–61.

Caroline Zachary Institute of Human Development. 1950. *Around the World in New York: A Guide to the City's Nationality Groups.* New York: Common Council for American Unity.

Carr, Caleb. 1995. *The Alienist.* New York: Bantam.

Cerillo, Augustus, Jr. 1991. *Reform in New York City: A Study of Urban Progressivism.* New York: Garland Publishing Co.

Chambers, Iain. 1993. "Cities without Maps." In *Mapping the Future: Local Cultures, Global Change,* ed. Jon Bird et al. London: Routledge: 188–98.

Charities and the Commons: A Weekly Journal of Philanthropy and Social Advance. 1908. "The Rent Strike Grows," vol. 19, January 11: 1379; "High Rents on New York's East Side," vol. 19, January 18: 1403.

Chenault, Lawrence. 1938. *The Puerto Rican Migrant in New York City.* New York: Columbia University Press.

Claghorn, Kate Holladay. 1970. "Foreign Immigration and the Tenement House in New York City." In *The Tenement House Problem,* ed. Robert W. DeForest and Lawrence Veiller. New York: Arno Press: vol. 2: 67–89. Reissued from 1903, New York: Macmillan Company.

Clarke et al. 1976. "Subcultures, Cultures and Class." In *Resistance through Rituals: Youth Subcultures in Post-War Britain,* ed. Stuart Hall and Tony Jefferson. London: Hutchinson: 9–74.

Cohen, Anthony P. 1985. *The Symbolic Construction of Community.* London: Tavistock Publications.

Cohen, Jeanne. 1985. "Strategy or Identity? New Theoretical Paradigms and Contemporary Social Movements." *Social Research* 52: 663–716.

Condon, Bernard. 1991. "Young Japanese Take a Walk on the Wild Side." *The Manhattan Spirit.* June 18: 8.

Cook, Bruce. 1971. *The Beat Generation.* New York: Scribner.

Coopers and Lybrand. 1996. *New York New Media Industry Survey: Opportunities and Challenges of New York's Emerging Cyber-Industry.* New York: Coopers and Lybrand, April 15.

Costikyan, Edward N. 1993. "Politics in New York City: A Memoir of the Post-War Years." *New York History* 74, no. 4 (October): 414–52.

Crane, Diana. 1987. *The Transformation of the Avant-Garde: The New York Art World 1940–1985*. Chicago: University of Chicago Press.

Crane, Stephen. 1966. *Maggie: A Girl of the Streets, A Story of New York, New York*. London: Cassel and Company. Reissued from 1892.

Crow, Thomas. 1983. "Modernism and Mass Culture in Visual Arts." In *Modernism and Modernity*, ed. Benjamin H. D. Buchloh et al. Halifax: The Press of Nova Scotia College of Art and Design: 215–64.

Daily News. 1967. "A Night in the East Village." October 11: 64.

———. 1971. "From Hippie Haven to Desolation Row." December 11a: 4; "East Village Asks Cops to Stamp Out 'Rat Packs.'" December 11b: 5.

———. 1972. "East Village: Fear Replaces Atmosphere." January 2: 4.

———. 1976. "Tenants Working to Save Buildings on Lower East Side." February 20: 7.

———. 1989. "Lower East Side Melee." October 27: 3.

Davidson, Flora Sellers. 1979. "City Policy and Housing Abandonment: A Case Study of New York City, 1965–1973." Ph.D. diss., Columbia University.

Davis, Jim. 1998. "Pursuing Urban Entertainment." *Kansas City Business Journal*. March 9: 1–3.

Davis, John Emmeus. 1991. *Contested Ground: Collective Action and the Urban Neighborhood*. Ithaca, N.Y.: Cornell University Press.

DeForest, Robert W., and Lawrence Veiller. 1970. "The Tenement House Problem." In *The Tenement House Problem*, ed. Robert W. DeForest and Lawrence Veiller. New York: Arno Press: vol. 1: 1–68. Reissued from 1903, New York: Macmillan Company.

DeGiovanni, Frank. 1987. *Displacement Pressures in the Lower East Side*. New York: Community Service Society.

Department of Housing Preservation and Development. 1983. "Analysis of Arson in Residential Buildings." Report, November 1: 7.

———. 1987. Lower East Side Housing Data.

DeRienzo, Harry, and Joan B. Allen. 1985. *The New York In Rem Housing Program: A Report*. New York: New York Urban Coalition.

DeSalvo, Joseph S. 1974. "Neighborhood Upgrading Effects of Middle-Income Housing Projects in New York City." *Journal of Urban Economics* 1, no. 3 (July): 269–77.

Deutsche, Rosalyn, and Cara Gendel Ryan. 1984. "The Fine Art of Gentrification." *October* 31 (winter): 91–111.

DeYoung Museum. 1996. "Rebels with a Cause: Beat Culture and the New America: 1950–1965, Fine Arts. 1996 Exhibition of Beat Culture." Museum Catalog, October-December. San Francisco: DeYoung Museum.

Division of Housing and Community Renewal. 1987. "Major Capital Improvements (MCI)." New York: Division of Housing and Community Renewal.

Dos Passos, John. 1925. *Manhattan Transfer*. New York: Harper and Brothers.

Drew, Robert S. 1995. "Graffiti and Public and Private Art." In *On the Margins of Art Worlds*, ed. Larry Gross. Boulder, Colo.: Westview Press: 231–48.

Duffy, John. 1975. *Down Worn Forgotten Streets*. New York: Cymric Press.

Eagle, Morris. 1960. "The Puerto Ricans in New York City." In *Studies in Housing and Minority Groups*, ed. N. Glazer and D. McEntire. Berkeley: University of California Press: 144–77.

East Villager. 1988. "On the Road to Chaos," vol. 12, no. 9 (September): 1.

East Village Eye. 1979. "Aftermath on the Avenues." May: 1.

The East Village Other. 1965. New York: Joint College of Patarealism.

Ernst, Robert. 1949. *Immigrant Life in New York City, 1825–1863.* Port Washington, N.J.: I. J. Friedman.

Ewen, Elizabeth. 1985. *Immigrant Women in the Land of Dollars: Life and Culture on the Lower East Side 1890–1925.* New York: Monthly Review Press.

Fainstein, Norman I., and Susan S. Fainstein. 1988. "Governing Regimes and the Political Economy of Development in New York City, 1946–1984." In *Power, Culture and Place: Essays on New York City,* ed. John Hull Mollenkopf. New York: Russell Sage Foundation: 161–99.

Fainstein, Susan S. 1994. *The City Builders: Property, Politics, and Planning in London and New York.* Cambridge, Mass.: Blackwell.

Feagin, Joe, and Robert Parker. 1990. *Building American Cities: The Urban Real Estate Game.* Englewood Cliffs, N.J.: Prentice Hall.

Featherstone, Mike. 1991. *Consumer Culture and Postmodernism.* London: Sage Publications.

Firey, Walter. 1945. "Sentiment and Symbolism as Ecological Variables." *American Sociological Review* 10: 140–48.

Fishbein, Leslie. 1982. *Rebels in Bohemia: The Radicals of the Masses, 1911–1917.* Chapel Hill: University of North Carolina Press.

Fitzpatrick, Joseph P. 1971. *Puerto Rican Americans: The Meaning of Migration to the Mainland.* Englewood Cliffs, N.J.: Prentice-Hall.

Foard, Ashley A., and Hilbert Fefferman. 1966. "Federal Urban Renewal Legislation." In *Urban Renewal: The Record and the Controversy,* ed. James Q. Wilson. Cambridge: MIT Press: 96–98.

Ford, James. 1936. *Slums and Housing, with Special Reference to New York City.* 2 vols. Cambridge: Harvard University Press.

Foster, Hal. 1982. "Between Modernism and Media." *Art in America* 70 (summer): 13–17.

Foucault, Michel. 1972. *The Archaeology of Knowledge.* London: Tavistock.

Frieburger, William. 1984. "War Prosperity and Hunger: The New York Food Riots of 1917." *Labor History* 25, no. 2 (spring): 217–39.

Frieden, Bernard J. 1964. *The Future of Old Neighborhoods.* Cambridge: MIT Press.

Friedenberg, Daniel M. 1961. "Real Estate Confidential." *Dissent* 8, no. 3 (summer): 260–76.

Friedman, Lawrence M. 1978. *Government and Slum Housing.* New York: Arno Press. Reissued from 1968, Chicago: Rand McNally and Co.

Frith, Simon, and Howard Horne. 1987. *Art into Pop.* London: Methuen.

Gablik, Suzi. 1982. "Report from New York: The Graffiti Question." *Art In America* 70: 33–39.

Gans, Herbert J. 1962. *The Urban Villagers: Group and Class in the Life of Italian Americans.* Glencoe, Ill.: The Free Press.

Genevro, Rosalie. 1986. "Site Selection and the New York City Housing Authority, 1934–1939." *Journal of Urban History* 12, no. 4 (August): 334–52.

Ghani, Ashraf. 1993. "Space as an Arena of Represented Practices." In *Mapping the Futures: Local Cultures, Global Change,* ed. Jon Bird et al. London: Routledge: 47–58.

Gilfoyle, Timothy. 1992. *City of Eros: New York City, Prostitution and the Commercialization of Sex, 1790–1920.* New York: W. W. Norton and Co.

Gluck, Peter, and Richard J. Meister. 1979. *Cities in Transition: Social Change and Institutional Responses in Urban Development.* New York: New Viewpoints.

Gold, John R., and Stephen V. Ward, eds. 1994. *Place Promotion: The Use of Publicity and Marketing to Sell Towns and Regions.* New York: John Wiley and Sons.

Goldfield, David R. 1980. "Private Neighborhood Redevelopment and Displacement: The Case of Washington, D.C." *Urban Affairs Quarterly* 15, no. 4 (June): 453–68.

Goldstein, Richard. 1968. "Love: A Groovy Idea While He Lasted." In *Notes from the New Underground*, ed. Jesse Kornbluth. New York: Viking Press: 255–58.

Gottdiener, Mark. 1985. *The Social Production of Urban Space.* Austin: University of Texas Press.

———. 1997. *The Theming of America: Dreams, Visions and Commercial Spaces.* Boulder, Colo.: Westview Press.

Gottdiener, Mark, and Joe R. Feagin. 1988. "The Paradigm Shift in Urban Sociology." *UrbanAffairs Quarterly* 24: 163–87.

Gould, Elgin R. L. 1970. "Financial Aspects of Recent Tenement House Operations in New York." In *The Tenement House Problem*, ed. Robert W. DeForest and Lawrence Veiller. New York: Arno Press: vol. 1: 355–66. Reissued from 1903, New York: Macmillan Company.

Graduate School of Public Administration and Social Service. 1957. *The Impact of Puerto Rican Migration on Governmental Services in New York City.* New York: New York University Press.

Grana, Cesar. 1964. *Modernity and Its Discontents.* New York: Harper.

Grava, Sigurd. 1980. "Is the Second Avenue Subway Dead in Its Tracks?" *New York Affairs* 6, no. 3: 32- 41.

Grebler, Leo. 1952. *Housing Market Behavior in a Declining Area: Long-Term Changes in Inventory and Utilization of Housing on New York's Lower East Side.* New York: Columbia University Press.

———. 1955. *Experience in Urban Real Estate Investment.* New York: Columbia University Press.

Greenberger, Howard. 1971. *The Off-Broadway Experience.* Englewood Cliffs, N.J.: Prentice-Hall.

Greshof, Dorine, and John Dale. 1994. "The Residents in Tompkins Square Park." In *From Urban Village to East Village: The Battle for New York's Lower East Side*, Janet L. Abu-Lughod et al. Cambridge, Mass.: Blackwell: 267–84.

Gries, John M., and James Ford, eds. 1931. *Slums, Large-Scale Housing and Decentralization.* Washington, D.C.: The President's Conference on Home Building and Home Ownership.

Gross, Larry. 1995. "Art and Artists on the Margins." In *On the Margins of Art Worlds*, Larry Gross, ed. Boulder, Colo.: Westview Press: 1–16.

Gruen, John. 1966. *The New Bohemia.* New York: Shorecrest.

Gutman, Herbert G. 1965. "The Tompkins Square 'Riot' in New York City on January 13, 1874: A Re-Examination of Its Causes and Its Aftermath." *Labor History* 6, no. 1 (winter): 44–70.

Haden-Guest, Anthony. 1997. *The Last Party: Studio 54, Disco and the Culture of the Night.* New York: William Morrow and Company.

Haig, Robert Murray. 1927. *Major Economic Factors in Metropolitan Growth and Arrangement.* New York: Regional Plan of New York and Its Environs.

Hall, Stuart. 1997. *Representations: Cultural Representations and Signifying Practices.* London: Sage Publications.

Hammon, David M. 1992. "Community Attachment: Local Sentiment and Sense of Place." In *Place Attachment,* ed. Irwin Altman and Setha M. Low. New York: Plenum Press: 253–78.

Hapgood, Hutchins. 1902. *The Spirit of the Ghetto.* New York: Funk and Wagnalls.

———. 1910. *Types from City Streets.* New York: Garrett Press.

Harron, Mary. 1988. "McRock: Pop as a Commodity." In *Facing the Music,* ed. Simon Frith. New York: Pantheon: 173–220.

Hartman, Chester. 1979a. "Comment on H. J. Sumka's 'Neighborhood Revitalization and Displacement: A Review of the Evidence.'" *Journal of the American Planning Association* 45: 488–90.

———. 1979b. "Displacement: A Not So New Problem," *Social Policy* 9, no. 5: 22–27.

Hartman, Chester, et al. 1982. *Displacement, How to Fight It.* Berkeley, Calif.: National Housing Law Project.

Hastings, Annette. 1999. "Discourse and Urban Change: Introduction to the Special Issue." *Urban Studies* 36: no. 1: 7–12.

Hebdige, Dick. 1979. *Subculture: The Meaning of Style.* London: Methuen.

Helfgott, Roy B., et al. 1959. "Women's and Children's Apparel." In *Made in New York: Case Studies in Metropolitan Manufacturing,* ed. Max Hall. Cambridge: Harvard University Press: 19–134.

Henry, Tricia. 1989. *Break All Rules! Punk Rock and the Making of a Style.* Ann Arbor: University of Michigan Press.

Herb, Marie. 1989. "Gentrification and Public Policy: New York City's Lower East Side." Master's thesis, Graduate School of Management and Urban Professions, New School for Social Research.

Herberg, Will H. 1953. "The Old-Timers and the New-Comers: Ethnic Group Relations in a Needles Trade Union." *Journal of Social Issues* 9, no. 1: 12–19.

Hershkovits, David. 1983. "Art in Alphabetland." *ARTnews.* September: 88–92.

Higham, John. 1975. *Send These to Me: Jews and Other Immigrants in Urban America.* New York: Atheneum.

Hill, Herbert. 1974. "Guardians of the Sweatshops: The Trade Unions, Racism, and the Garment Industry." In *Puerto Rico and Puerto Ricans: Studies in History and Society,* ed. Adalberto Lopez and James Petras. New York: John Wiley and Sons: 384–416.

History Task Force. 1979. *Labor Migration under Capitalism: The Puerto Rican Experience.* New York: Monthly Review Press.

"History of Wigstock." Online at http://www.at-beam.com/wigstock.

Hoban, Phoebe. 1988. "Samo Is Dead." *New York* 21, no. 38 (September 26): 36–44.

Hobbs, Stuart D. 1997. *The End of the American Avant-Garde.* New York: New York University Press.

Hofstadter, Richard, ed. 1963. *The Progressive Movement, 1900–1915.* Englewood Cliffs, N.J.: Prentice-Hall.

Holden, Arthur C. 1932. "Facing Realities in Slum Clearance." *Architectural Record* 7, no. 1 (February): 75–82.

Hoyt, Homer, and Durward Badgley. 1939. *The Housing Demand of Workers in Manhattan: An Income Analysis of the Workers in Manhattan to Determine Rent Levels for New Apartments in the Lower East Side and Other New York Areas*. Washington, D.C.: United States Federal Housing Administration.

Hsieh, Tungshan. 1994. "The Critical Foundations of American Neo-Expressionism: 1980–1984." Ph.D. diss., Texas Tech University.

Hughes, James W., and Kenneth D. Bleakly Jr. 1975. *Urban Homesteading*. New Brunswick, N.J.: Center for Urban Policy Research, Rutgers University.

Huxtable, Ada Louise. 1987. "Stumbling toward Tomorrow: The Decline and Fall of the New York Vision." *Dissent* 34 (fall): 453–62.

Imrie, Rob, Steven Pinch, and Mark Boyle. 1996. "Identities, Citizenship and Power in the Cities." *Urban Studies* 8: 1255–61.

In-Rem Working Group. 1986. *Building from Experience: Next Step for In-Rem Housing*. New York: New York Urban Coalition.

Interfaith Adopt-A-Building. 1978. "Report on Arson and Abandonment." Mimeographed.

Iorizzo, Luciano. 1970. "The Padrone and Immigrant Distribution." In *The Italian Experience in the United States*, ed. Silvano Tomasi and Madeline H. Engel. Staten Island, N.Y.: Center for Migration Studies: 43–76.

Jackson, Kenneth. 1984. "The Capital of Capitalism: The New York Metropolitan Region, 1890–1940." In *Metropolis 1890–1940*, ed. Anthony Sutcliffe. London: Mansell Publishing: 319–53.

———. 1985. *Crabgrass Frontier: The Suburbanization of the United States*. New York: Oxford University Press.

Jacobs, Jane. 1961. *The Death and Life of Great American Cities*. New York: Random House.

Jenkins, Shirley. 1963. *Comparative Recreation Needs and Services in New York Neighborhoods*. New York: Research Department of the Community Council of Greater New York.

Johnson, David A. 1996. *Planning the Great Metropolis: The 1929 Regional Plan of New York and Its Environs*. London: E. and F. N. Spon.

Joselit, Jenna Weissman. 1986. "The Landlord as Czar." In *The Tenant Movement in New York City, 1904–1984*, ed. Ronald E. Lawson. New Brunswick, N.J.: Rutgers University Press: 39–50.

Kantrowitz, Nathan. 1973. *Ethnic and Racial Segregation in the New York Metropolis: Residential Patterns among White Ethnic Groups, Blacks and Puerto Ricans*. New York: Praeger.

Katznelson, Ira. 1981. *City Trenches: Urban Politics and the Patterning of Class in the United States*. Chicago: University of Chicago Press.

———. 1985. "Working-Class Formation and the State." In *Bringing the State Back In*, ed. Peter B. Evans et al. New York: Cambridge University Press: 257–84.

———. 1992. *Marxism and the City*. New York: Oxford University Press.

Kaufmann, Reginald Wright. 1910. *House of Bondage*. New York: Moffat, Yard and Co.

Kessner, Thomas. 1977. *The Golden Door: Italian and Jewish Immigrant Mobility in New York City, 1880–1915*. New York: Oxford University Press.

———. 1989. *Fiorello H. LaGuardia and the Making of Modern New York*. New York: McGraw-Hill Publishing Company.

Kildare, Owen. c1905. *The Wisdom of the Simple: A Tale of Lower New York*. New York: F. H. Revel Company.

Kitsis, Krystina. n.d. "Nightlife: Subcultural Sexuality." *ZG Magazine*. New York: Ultra Thin Management.

Kornbluth, Jesse, ed. 1968. *Notes from the New Underground*. New York: Viking Press.

Kotzwinkle, William. 1974. *The Fan Man*. New York: Avon Books.

Kozak, Roman. 1985. *This Ain't No Disco: The Story of CBGB*. New York: Proteus Publishing Company.

Kusay, Nathan. 1916. *The Abyss*. New York: Macmillan Company.

Lachmann, R. 1988. "Graffiti as Career and Ideology." *American Journal of Sociology* 94, no. 2 (September): 229–50.

Lake, Robert W. 1979. *Real Estate Tax Delinquency: Private Disinvestment and Public Response*. New Brunswick, N.J.: Center for Urban Policy Research, Rutgers University.

Lampard, Eric E. 1986. "The New Metropolis in Transformation: History and Prospect. A Study of Historical Particularity." In *The Future of the Metropolis: Berlin, London, Paris, New York: Economic Aspects*, ed. Hans-Jurgen Ewers et al. Berlin; New York: W. de Gruter: 27–110.

Lasker, Loula D. 1931. "Putting a White Collar on the East Side." *Survey Graphic* 65, no. 11 (March 1): 584–627.

Laurentz, Robert. 1980. "Racial and Ethnic Conflict in the New York City Garment Industry, 1933–1980." Ph.D. diss., State University of New York, Binghamton.

Lawson, Ronald E., and Reuben B. Johnson III. 1986. "Tenant Responses to the Urban Housing Crisis, 1970–1984." In *The Tenant Movement in New York City, 1904–1984*, ed. Ronald E. Lawson. New Brunswick, N.J.: Rutgers University Press: 209–76.

Lee, Barrett A., and David C. Hodge. 1984. "Social Differentials in Metropolitan Residential Displacement." In *Gentrification, Displacement and Neighborhood Revitalization*, ed. J. John Palen and Bruce London. Albany, N.Y.: State University of New York Press: 140–69.

Lee, Martin, and Bruce Shlain. 1985. *Acid Dreams: The Complete History of LSD, the CIA, the Sixties and Beyond*. New York: Grove Press.

Lefebvre, Henri. 1991. *The Production of Space*. Cambridge, Mass.: Blackwell.

Leinenweber, Charles. 1977. "Socialists in the Streets: The New York City Socialist Party in Working Class Neighborhoods, 1900–1918." *Science and Society* 2 (summer): 152–71.

———. 1981. "The Class and Ethnic Bases of New York City Socialism, 1904–1915." *Labor History* 22, no. 1 (winter): 31–56.

Lett, Monica R. 1976. *Rent Control: Concepts, Realities, and Mechanisms*. New Brunswick, N.J.: Center for Urban Policy Research, Rutgers University.

Lieberman, Richard Kenneth. 1976. "Social Change and Political Behavior: The East Village of New York City, 1880–1905." Ph.D. diss., New York University.

Lin, Jan. 1998. *Reconstructing Chinatown: Ethnic Enclave, Global Change*. Minneapolis: University of Minnesota Press.

Lipsky, Michael. 1967. "Rent Strikes in New York City: Protest Politics and the Power of the Poor." Ph.D. diss., Princeton University.

———. 1970. *Protest in City Politics: Rent Strikes, Housing and the Power of the Poor*. Chicago: Rand McNally and Co.

Little, Stuart W. 1972. *Off Broadway: The Prophetic Theater*. New York: Coward, McCann and Geoghegan.

Lopez, Adalberto. 1974. "The Puerto Rican Diaspora." In *Puerto Rico and Puerto Ricans: Studies in History and Society,* ed. Adalberto Lopez and James Petras. New York: John Wiley and Sons: 316–46.

Lowe, Jeanne R. 1967. *Cities in a Race with Time: Progress and Poverty in America's Renewing Cities.* New York: Random House.

Lower East Side Planning Association. 1932. *Plans for Major Traffic Thoroughfares and Transit. Lower East Side, New York City.* St. Louis, Mo.: Bartholomew and Associates.

Lubove, Roy. 1962. *The Progressive and the Slums: Tenement House Reform in New York City 1890–1917.* Pittsburgh, Pa.: University of Pittsburgh Press.

Lumsden, May. 1936. "First Families." *Survey Graphic* 25 (February): 103–5.

Lury, Celia. 1996. *Consumer Culture.* London: Polity.

Lyotard, Jean-François. 1984. *The Postmodern Condition: A Report on Knowledge.* Minneapolis: University of Minnesota Press.

Maffi, Mario. 1994. "Appendix: The Other Side of the Coin: Culture in Loisaida." In *From Urban Village to East Village: The Battle for New York's Lower East Side,* Janet L. Abu-Lughod et al. Cambridge, Mass.: Blackwell: 141–47.

———. 1995. *Gateway to the Promised Land: Ethnic Cultures on New York's Lower East Side.* New York: New York University Press.

Malon, Patricia F. 1981. "The Growth of Manufacturing in Manhattan: 1860–1900: An Analysis of Factoral Changes and Urban Structure." Ph.D. diss., Columbia University.

Mandelbaum, Seymour J. 1965. *Boss Tweed's New York.* New York: John Wiley and Sons.

Marcus, Greil. 1989. *Lipstick Traces: A Secret History of the Twentieth Century.* Cambridge: Harvard University Press.

Marcuse, Peter. 1980. "Triage: Programming the Death of Communities." New York: Working Group for Community Development Reform. Report.

———. 1985. "Gentrification, Abandonment, and Displacement: Connections, Causes, and Policy Responses in New York City." *Journal of Urban and Contemporary Law* 28: 195–240.

———. 1986. "Abandonment, Gentrification and Displacement: Linkages in New York City." In *Gentrification in the City,* ed. Neil Smith and Peter Williams. Boston: Allen and Unwin: 153–77.

McAneny, George. 1931. "The Beauty of Regional Planning." *Creative Art* 9, no. 2 (August 9): 133–37.

Mele, Christopher. 1994a. "Neighborhood 'Burn-out': Puerto Ricans at the End of the Queue." In *From Urban Village to East Village: The Battle for New York's Lower East Side,* Janet L. Abu-Lughod et al. Cambridge, Mass.: Blackwell: 125–40.

———. 1994b. "The Process of Gentrification in Alphabet City." In *From Urban Village to East Village: The Battle for New York's Lower East Side,* Janet L. Abu-Lughod et al. Cambridge, Mass.: Blackwell: 169–88.

———. 1995. "Private Redevelopment and the Changing Forms of Displacement in the East Village of New York." *Comparative Urban and Community Research* 5: 69–94.

Melucci, Alberto. 1989. *Nomads of the Present: Social Movements and Individual Needs in Contemporary Society,* ed. John Keane and Paul Meier. Philadelphia: Temple University Press.

Miller, Mike, and Carl Werthman. 1961. "Public Housing: Tenants and Troubles." *Dissent* 8, no. 3 (summer): 282–88.

Miller, Richard. 1977. *Bohemia: The Protoculture Then and Now.* Chicago: Nelson-Hall.

Mills, Sara. 1997. *Discourse: The New Critical Idiom.* London: Routledge.

Mitchell, Lionel. 1968. "Look at Down Here." In *Notes from the New Underground,* ed. Jesse Kornbluth. New York: Viking Press: 224–31.

Mobilization for Youth. 1962a. "Action on the Lower East Side." New York: Mobilization for Youth.

———. 1962b. "The Lower East Side Today: Emphasizing the Mobilization Area." New York: Mobilization for Youth.

———. 1966. "The Real Estate Market of Nine Blocks on the Lower East Side. A Close Look at Realtor Techniques Peculiar to the Tenement Market." New York: Mobilization for Youth.

———. 1967. "Economic Description of the Real Estate Market on the Lower East Side of New York." New York: Mobilization for Youth.

Moore, A., and M. Miller, eds. 1985. *ABC No Rio Dinero: The Story of a Lower East Side Art Gallery.* New York: ABC No Rio and Collaborative Arts Projects.

Morley, David, and Kevin Robins. 1995. *Spaces of Identity: Global Media, Electronic Landscapes and Cultural Boundaries.* London: Routledge.

Morris, Lloyd. 1955. "Cosmopolis under the El." In *The Empire City,* ed. Alexander Klein. New York: Rinehart and Co: 239–43.

Moses, Robert. 1956. "Talk by Robert Moses on the Occasion of the Celebration of the 70th Anniversary of the University Settlement in America at the Commodore Hotel, November 6." Mimeograph at the City of New York Municipal Archives.

Moufarrege, Nicolas A. 1982. "Another Wave, Still More Savagely Than the First: Lower East Side, 1982." *Arts Magazine.* September: 69–73.

———. 1983. "East Village." *Flash Art* 111, no. 37 (March): 36–41.

Musto, Michael. 1986. *Downtown.* New York: Vintage.

———. 1987. "The Death of Downtown." *Village Voice.* April 28: 15–20.

Myers, Gustavus. 1971. *The History of Tammany Hall.* New York: Dover Publications. Reissued from 1917, New York: Boni and Liveright.

Myerson, Ann. 1986. "Housing Abandonment: The Role of Institutional Mortgage Lenders." In *Critical Perspectives on Housing,* ed. Rachel G. Bratt et al. Philadelphia: Temple University Press: 184–201.

Nadel, Stanley. 1990. *Little Germany: Ethnicity, Religion and Class in New York City, 1845–80.* Urbana: University of Illinois Press.

Naison, Mark. 1986. "From Eviction Resistance to Rent Control: Tenant Activism in the Great Depression." In *The Tenant Movement in New York City, 1904–1984,* ed. Ronald Lawson. New Brunswick, N.J.: Rutgers University Press: 94–133.

Nelli, Humbert S. 1964. "The Italian Padrone System in the United States." *Labor History* 5 (spring): 164–67.

———. 1970. "Italians in Urban America." In *The Italian Experience in the United States,* ed. Silvano M. Tomasi and Madeline H. Engel. Staten Island, N.Y.: Center for Migration Studies: 77–102.

The New Common Good. 1988. "Tompkins Square Police Riot: Before the Deluge." September: 1.

Newsweek. 1967. "Linda's Last Trip." October 23: 33; "Trouble in Hippieland." October 30: 84–90.

New York City Department of Welfare. 1949. "The Puerto Rican Problem of the New York City Department of Welfare." Report submitted to Mayor William O'Dwyer, September 6. Mimeographed.

New York City Housing Authority. 1935. *First Houses.* New York: New York City Housing Authority.

New York Newsday. 1988. "Neighborhood Beacon." March 3: part 2: 8; "Lower East Side's Changing Face." September 12: 7.

New York Post. 1969. "The East Village Today: A Tougher Turf." July 25: 24.

———. 1971. "Hip Era Over in East Village." December 7: 2.

———. 1989. "Cops Hit with Cement and Eggs Battling with PS 105 Squatters." October 27: 5.

New York State Department of Law. 1985. "Report on Warehousing."

———. 1989. Report. Real Estate Financing Bureau, January.

New York Times. 1929. "Creating New Apartment Area on Lower Second Avenue." June 2: Real Estate Section: 1.

———. 1949. "Housing Project Gets 1st Tenants." April 19: 27; "Tenants Fight Evictions." March 22: 4.

———. 1950. "Families End Sit Down." April 29: 17.

———. 1953. "Spanish Linguists in City Posts Urged." July 24: 1; "Fight on City's Slums So Far Losing Battle." August 30: 10; "Flow of Puerto Ricans Here Fills Jobs, Poses Problems." February 23: 1.

———. 1958. "Puerto Rican Migration Off; Recession in U.S. Is Cited." January 20: 1; "The 'Shook-Up' Generation: Problem Youngsters Spring from Public Housing." March 26: 32.

———. 1959. "Governor, Mayor Agree on Policy to Combat Gangs." September 5: 1; "Leibowitz Urges Cut in Migration to Combat Crime." September 25: 1; "The Puerto Rican Problem." September 28: 30; "Growing Threat of Violence." September 29: 41; "East Side Urges Report on Gangs." December 22: 37.

———. 1960. "City Is Thwarted on 60s Gang Bills." April 10: 1; "Youth Gangs Quiet on Lower East Side." September 11: 75.

———. 1962. "Police on Lower East Side." January 5: 31; "Study Here Finds Job and Pay Lag." June 28: 1.

———. 1963. "Study Confirms Racial Job Bias." June 2: 71.

———. 1964. "A Feud on East 3rd; Terrified Tenants Flee after a Fire." July 2: 1; "4 Arrested as Fights Break Out at Protest on 3rd Street Landlord." July 9: 36.

———. 1966. "Cooper Square Plan Revised By City." July 26: 37.

———. 1967. "Hippies Heighten East Side Tensions." June 3a: 16; "City Hall Talks on Hippies Held." June 3b: 16; "Policeman's Lot: Is Not a Happy One." June 4: 3; "The Two Worlds of the East Village." June 5a: 63; "Hippies' Hangout Draws Tourists." June 5b: 63; "200 Hippies Stage an 8th Street 'Be-Out.'" August 7: 26; "500 Hippies Dance and Plant a Tree." August 13: 71; "Block Party Held to Create Mall." August 25: 23; "Police Hopeful of Easing Hippie Problem Here." October 18: 1; "The Case of a Runaway Flower Child." October 19: 1; "Story of Girl Hippie Slain in 'Village' Arouses Wide Concern." October 29: 57.

———. 1968. "Officials Fear That Provocateurs 'Turn-On' Hippie Violence." March 26: 21; "Policeman Accused of Kicking Suspect after His Arrest." June 15: 29; "8

Seized in East Village Confrontation with Police." July 23: 26; "Police Reinforcements Sent into East Side Area." July 24: 26; "Demands Heard in East Village." July 26: 39; "Lower East Side Has a Calm Night." July 27: 14.

———. 1971. "A New Lower East Side Envisioned in City Report." May 20: 1.

———. 1976. "Lower East Side Churches Mobilize against Vandalism and Fires." October 31: 58.

———. 1977. "Reclamation Is Starting in the East Village." September 28: 15; "A Loan and Some 'Sweat Equity' Create an Oasis Amid Desolation." October 6: 1.

———. 1981. "The Mayor's Lower East Side Story: Tenements into Co-ops for Artists." August 11: 9.

———. 1982. "16 Tenements to Become Artist Units in City Plan." May 4: 6; "The Fortunes of the Lower East Side Are Rising." September 5: 1.

———. 1983. "A Gallery Scene That Pioneers in New Territories." June 26: 27.

———. 1986. "Mutual Housing Awaits a Decision." December 28: section 8: 5.

———. 1987. "Art: Quieter Times for East Village's Galleries." February 8: C28.

———. 1988. "Tenements of 1880s Adapt to 1980s." January 3: Real Estate Section: 1; "Lower East Side Buildings Rehabilitated." April 1: 1; "Park Curfew Protest Erupts into a Battle and 38 are Injured." August 8: 1; "Heavily Tested by the Crowd in Tompkins Square, Police Discipline Broke." August 14a: 1; "One Week after Clash, Protesters Hold a Quiet Tompkins Square Rally." August 14b: 1.

———. 1989. "9 Held in Protest Near Tompkins Square Park." April 2: 31; "Melee Site Quiet, But Police Stand Guard." May 6: 29; "City Moves to Clean Up Tompkins Square after Raid." July 7: B1; "4 Held in Tompkins Square Skirmish at Symbolic Tents." July 9: 24. "Tension Eases in Tompkins Park Protest." July 10: B3; "Police Called to Meeting on Tompkins Park." October 25: 35; "24 Are Arrested during Clashes over Squatters." October 27: B1; "Police Seal Building after a Protest by Squatters." October 28: 29; "Neighbors' Attitudes Shift as Park Declines." December 7: B1; "Tent City in Tompkins Square Park Is Dismantled by Police." December 15: B1; "A Neighborhood Battle: Apartments or a Park?" December 18: B1.

———. 1991. "The East Village Becomes Japan West." May 31: C1.

———. 1992. "If You're Thinking of Living in the East Village." June 14, Real Estate Section: 7.

———. 1995. "New York Striving to Become Technology's Creative Center." February 13: 1.

———. 1996. "Police Evict Squatters from Three City-Owned Tenements in the East Village." August 14: B3.

———. 1997. "In East Village, a Spirited Pace for Rental Project Development." August 29: B5.

———. 1998. "Watching Patches of Green Turn to Greenbacks." July 26a: 5; "Separate Fates for Two Hispanic Cultural Centers." July 26b: 5; "A New Spell for Alphabet City." August 9, section 14: 1; "The Indie Scene Revs Up." August 11: 1.

New York Times Magazine. 1967. "The Intelligent Square's Guide to Hippieland." September 24: 6; "Love Is Dead." October 29: 27.

Niebanck, Paul L., ed. 1985. The Rent Control Debate, Chapel Hill: University of North Carolina Press.

Not Bored Magazine. 1996. "Squatters Evicted from East 13th Street." Vol. 26: 1. http://www.thorn.net/~rose.

Nusser, Richard. 1967. "New Dawn Breaks for 'Hippieville.'" *S.S. Advance*. March 9: 1. Mimeograph at Municipal Library of the City of New York.

O'Connor, Justin, and Derek Wynne. 1996. "Left Loafing: City Cultures and Post-modern Lifestyles." In *From the Margins to the Centre: Cultural Production and Consumption in the Post-Industrial City*, ed. Justin O'Connor and Derek Wynne. Manchester, England: Arena: 49–89.

Owens, Craig. 1984. "Commentary: The Problem with Puerilism." *Art In America* 72, no. 6 (summer): 162–63.

Palen, J. John, and Bruce London, eds. 1984. *Gentrification, Displacement and Neighborhood Revitalization*. Albany: State University of New York Press.

Park, Robert E. 1921. *Old World Traits Transplanted*. New York: Harper and Brothers.

Park, Robert E., Ernest Burgess, and Roderick D. McKenzie. 1925. *The City*. Chicago: University of Chicago Press.

Parks, Addison. 1982. "One Graffito, Two Graffito . . ." *Arts Magazine*. September: 73.

Parry, Albert. 1960. *Garrets and Pretenders: A History of Bohemianism in America*. New York: Dover Publications. Reissued from 1933, New York: Covici-Friede.

Peiss, Kathy. 1986. *Cheap Amusements: Working Women and Leisure in Turn-of-the-Century New York*. Philadelphia: Temple University Press.

Perry, Clarence A., et al. 1929. *Neighborhood and Community Planning Comprising Three Monographs*. New York: Regional Plan of New York and Its Environs.

Perry, Clarence A. 1936. *Housing for the Machine Age*. New York: Russell Sage Foundation.

Phillips, David Graham. 1977. *Susan Lenox: Her Fall and Rise*. Carbondale: Southern Illinois University Press. Reissued from 1917, New York: Appleton.

Philo, Chris, and Gerry Kearns, eds. 1993. *Selling Places: The City as Cultural Capital*. London: Pergamon.

Pile, Steve. 1997. Introduction to *Geographies of Resistance*, ed. Steve Pile and Michael Keith. London: Routledge: 1–32.

Plous, Phyllis, and Mary Looker, eds. 1984. *Neo York: Report on a Phenomenon*. Santa Barbara, Calif.: University Art Museum.

Plunz, Richard. 1990. *A History of Housing in New York City: Dwelling Type and Social Change in the American Metropolis*. New York: Columbia University Press.

Plunz, Richard, and Janet Abu-Lughod. 1994. "The Tenement as a Built Form." In *From Urban Village to East Village: The Battle for New York's Lower East Side*, Janet L. Abu-Lughod et al. Cambridge, Mass.: Blackwell: 63–80.

Polsky, Ned. 1961. "The Village Beat Scene: Summer 1960." *Dissent* 8, no. 3 (summer): 339–59.

Post, Langdon W. 1938. *The Challenge of Housing*. New York: Farrar and Rinehart.

Powell, Dawn. 1962. *The Golden Spur*. New York: Viking Press.

Preble, Edward, and John J. Casey Jr. 1969. "Taking Care of Business — The Heroin User's Life on the Street." *International Journal of the Addictions* 4, no. 1 (March): 1–24.

Proceedings of "Puerto Ricans Confront Problems of the Complex Urban Society: A Design for Change." 1967. Conference Sponsored by Mayor Lindsay, April 15–16.

Radford, Gail. 1996. *Modern Housing for America: Policy Struggles in the New Deal Era*. Chicago: University of Chicago Press.

Rapkin, Chester. 1959. *The Real Estate Market in an Urban Renewal Area*. New York: New York City Planning Commission.

————. 1963. *South of Houston Industrial Area: Economic Significance of Structure in a Loft Section of Manhattan.* New York: New York City Planning Commission.

Real Estate Newsletter. 1985. "Lower East Side Real Estate Profile: Speculators Less Active, Renovators Push to Get Market Rate Projects Going, City Mulls Sale of In-Rem Buildings, Yuppies Like It Even If Drug Dealers Share the Streetscape." 16, no. 51 (November 4): 1.

————. 1986. "Developers and Rehab Specialists Vie for Lower East Side Properties Not Controlled by City." 18, no. 2 (November 24): 1.

————. 1987. "Real Estate Resurgence Continues in East Village as Property Values Soar." 19, no. 2 (November 23): 1.

Real Estate Record Association. 1967. *A History of Real Estate, Building and Architecture in New York City during the Last Quarter of a Century.* New York: Arno Press. Reissued from 1898, New York: Real Estate Record Association.

Real Estate Weekly. 1989. "Investors Reported to Find 'Good Deals' in Pocket Areas." 35, no. 33 (March 22): 1.

Regional Plan Association. 1931. "The Lower East Side: Its Past and Present. What Should Be Its Future? Certain Projects and Proposals." *Regional Plan Information Bulletin.* No. 2 (April 20): 1–10.

————. 1973. *How to Save Urban America.* New York: New American Library.

Ricard, Rene. 1981. "The Radiant Child." *Art Forum* 20 (December): 35–43.

————. 1982. "The Pledge of Allegiance." *Art Forum* 21 (November): 42–49.

Riis, Jacob. 1971. *How the Other Half Lives.* New York: Dover Publishers. Reissued from 1890, New York: Scribner's.

Rischin, Moses. 1962. *The Promised City: New York's Jews 1870–1914.* Cambridge: Harvard University Press.

Robins, Kevin. 1995. "Collective Emotion and Urban Culture." In *Managing Cities: The New Urban Context,* ed. Patsy Healey et al. London: John Wiley: 45–62.

Robinson, Walter. 1984. "The East Village Goes to School: History, Geography, Civics, Economics." In *Neo York: Report on a Phenomenon,* ed. Phyllis Plous and Mary Looker. Santa Barbara, Calif.: University Art Museum: 14–15.

Robinson, Walter, and Carlo McCormick. 1984. "Slouching toward Avenue D." *Art in America* 72 (summer): 135–61.

Robison, Maynard T. 1976. "Rebuilding Lower Manhattan: 1955–1974." Ph.D. diss., City University of New York.

Rodriguez, Clara. 1974. *The Ethnic Queue in the United States: The Case of the Puerto Ricans.* San Francisco: R. and E. Associates.

Rogler, Lloyd H., and Rosemary Santana Cooney. 1984. *Puerto Rican Families in New York City: Intergenerational Processes.* Maplewood, N.J.: Waterfront Press.

Rosenberg, Harold. 1973. *Discovering the Present: Three Decades in Art, Culture and Politics.* Chicago: University of Chicago Press.

Rosenberg, Terry J. 1974. "Residence, Employment, and Mobility of Puerto Ricans in New York City." Chicago: University of Chicago, Department of Geography, Research Paper No. 151.

Rosenberg, Terry J., and Robert W. Lake. 1976. "Toward a Revised Model of Residential Segregation and Succession: Puerto Ricans in New York, 1960–1970." *American Journal of Sociology* 81, no. 5, March: 1142–50.

Rosenblatt, Aaron. 1964. *Older People on the Lower East Side: Their Interest in Employment and Volunteer Activities and Their General Characteristics, Report for the*

Committee on Aging, Department of Public Affairs. New York: Community Service Society.

Rosenwaike, Ira. 1972. *Population History of New York City.* Syracuse, N.Y.: Syracuse University Press.

Roth, Henry. 1934. *Call It Sleep.* New York: Cooper Square Publishers.

Sagalyn, Lynne Beyer. 1983. "Mortgage Lending in Older Neighborhoods: Lessons from Past Experiences." *Annals of the American Academy of Political and Social Science* 465: 98–108.

Sanchez, Jose. 1986. "Residual Work and Residual Shelter: Housing Puerto Rican Labor in New York City from World War II to 1983." In *Critical Perspectives on Housing,* ed. Rachel Bratt et al. Philadelphia: Temple University Press: 202–20.

Sanchez-Korral, Virginia. 1983. *From Colonia to Community: The History of Puerto Ricans in New York City, 1917–1948.* Westport, Conn.: Greenwood Press.

Sanders, Ed. 1966. *Ed Sanders Newsletter.* New York: by the author.

Sanders, Ronald. 1977. *The Downtown Jews: Portraits of an Immigrant Generation.* New York: New American Library. Reissued from 1969, New York: Harper and Row.

Sandler, Irving. 1978. *The New York School: The Painters and the Sculptors of the Fifties.* New York: Harper and Row.

———. 1984. "Tenth Street Then and Now." In *The East Village Scene,* ed. Janet Kardon. Institute of Contemporary Art, University of Pennsylvania.

Sante, Luc. 1992. *Low Life: Lures and Snares of Old New York.* New York: Vintage. Reissued from 1991, New York: Farrar, Strauss and Giroux.

Sassen, Saskia. 1989. "New York City's Informal Economy." In *The Informal Economy: Studies in Advanced and Less Developed Countries,* ed. Alejandro Portes et al. Baltimore: Johns Hopkins University Press.

Savage, Jon. 1993. *England's Dreaming: Anarchy, Sex Pistols, Punk Rock and Beyond.* New York: St. Martin's Press.

Schmelzkopf, Karen. 1995. "Urban Community Gardens as Contested Space." *Geographical Review* 85, no. 3 (July): 364–81.

Schoener, Allon. 1967. *Portal to America: 1870–1925.* New York: Holt, Rinehart and Winston.

Schwartz, Harry, and Peter Abeles. 1973. *Planning for the Lower East Side.* New York: Praeger Publishers.

Schwartz, Joel. 1986. "Tenant Unions in New York City's Low-Rent Housing, 1933–1949." *Journal of Urban History* 12, no. 4 (August): 414–43.

———. 1993. *The New York Approach: Robert Moses, Urban Liberals, and Redevelopment of the Inner City.* Columbus: Ohio State University Press.

Scott, James C. 1990. *Domination and the Arts of Resistance.* New Haven, Conn.: Yale University Press.

The Shadow. 1995. "Steal This Radio!" Vol. 38: 1.

———. 1998. "Community Gardens Destroyed for Yuppie Condo." Vol. 43: 1.

Sharff, Jagna. 1987. "The Underground Economy of a Poor Neighborhood." In *Cities of the United States: Studies in Urban Anthropology,* ed. Leith Mullings. New York: Columbia University Press: 19–50.

———. 1998. *King Kong on 4th Street: Families and the Violence of Poverty on the Lower East Side.* Boulder, Colo.: Westview Press.

Shefter, Martin. 1988. "Political Incorporation and Containment: Regime Transformation in New York City." In *Power, Culture and Place: Essays on New York City*, ed. John Hull Mollenkopf. New York: Russell Sage Foundation. 135–58.

———. 1992. *Political Crisis/Fiscal Crisis: The Collapse and Revival of New York City*. New York: Columbia University Press.

Shields, Rob. 1996. "A Guide to Urban Representation and What to Do about It: Alternative Traditions of Urban Theory." In *Re-presenting the City: Ethnicity, Capital, and Culture in the 21st-Century Metropolis*, ed. Anthony D. King. New York: New York University Press: 227–52.

Siegel, Jeanne. 1988. "Walter Robinson: Eye on the East Village." In *Artwords 2: Discourse on the Early 80s*, ed. Jeanne Siegel. Ann Arbor: University of Michigan Research Press.

Siegle, Robert. 1989. *Suburban Ambush: Downtown Writing and the Fiction of Insurgency*. Baltimore: Johns Hopkins University Press.

Sites, William. 1994. "Public Action: New York City Policy and the Gentrification of the Lower East Side." In *From Urban Village to East Village: The Battle for New York's Lower East Side*, Janet L. Abu-Lughod et al. Cambridge, Mass.: Blackwell: 189–212.

Sleeper, Jim. 1987. "Boom and Bust with Ed Koch." *Dissent* 34 (fall): 413–52.

Smith, Michael Peter. 1988. *City, State and Market*. New York: Blackwell.

Smith, Neil. 1986. "Gentrification, the Frontier and the Restructuring of Urban Space." In *Gentrification of the City*, ed. Neil Smith and Peter Williams. Boston: Allen and Unwin: 15–34.

———. 1996. *The New Urban Frontier: Gentrification and the Revanchist City*. New York: Routledge.

Smith, Neil, et al. 1994. "From Disinvestment to Reinvestment: Mapping the Urban 'Frontier' in the Lower East Side." In *From Urban Village to East Village: The Battle for New York's Lower East Side*, Janet L. Abu-Lughod et al. Cambridge, Mass.: Blackwell: 149–67.

Solomon, Barbara Probst. 1961. "The Person Alone." *Dissent* 8, no. 3 (summer): 404–7.

Spencer, Joseph A. 1986. "New York City Tenant Organizations and the Post–World War I Housing Crisis." In *The Tenant Movement in New York City, 1904–1984*, ed. Ronald Lawson and Mark Naison. New Brunswick, N.J.: Rutgers University Press: 51–93.

Steel, Robert Sangel. 1995. "Christodora House." In *The Encyclopedia of New York City*, ed. Kenneth T. Jackson. New Haven, Conn.: Yale University Press: 220.

Stegman, Michael A. 1984. "Housing in New York: Study of a City." Report prepared for the City of New York, Department of Housing Preservation and Development.

———. 1985. "The Model: Rent Control in New York City." In *The Rent Control Debate*, ed. Paul L. Niebanck. Chapel Hill: University of North Carolina Press: 29–56.

Sternlieb, George. 1972. *The Urban Housing Dilemma: The Dynamics of New York City's Rent Controlled Housing*. New York: Housing and Development Administration.

Sternlieb, George, et al. 1972. "Residential Abandonment: The Environment of Decay." Council of Planning Librarians, Exchange Bibliography no. 342.

Sternlieb, George, and Robert W. Burchell. 1973. *Residential Abandonment: The Tenement Landlord Revisited.* New Brunswick, N.J.: Center for Urban Policy Research, Rutgers University.

Sternlieb, George, and James W. Hughes. 1976. *Housing and Economic Reality: New York City, 1976.* New Brunswick, N.J.: Center for Urban Policy Research, Rutgers University.

Strauss, Anselm. 1961. *Images of the American City.* New York: Free Press of Glencoe.

Strong, Mary Clare. 1982. "An Ethnography of New Yorican Mural Communication." Ph.D. diss., Temple University.

Sukenick, Ronald. 1987. *Down and In: Life in the Underground.* New York: Beech Tree Books.

Sumka, H. J. 1979. "Neighborhood Revitalization and Displacement: A Review of the Evidence." *Journal of the American Planning Association* 45: 480–87.

Survey Data Security Corporation. 1986. New York State Banking Mortgage Activity Reports, Nos. 19 and 20.

Suttles, Gerald D. 1984. "The Cumulative Texture of Local Urban Culture." *American Journal of Sociology* 90, no. 2: 283–304.

Swearingen, Jessamin. 1996a. "I Belong to the Blank Generation: The Beat's Influence on the Punks," The Emergence of Punk http://www.inch.com/~jessamin/.

———. 1996b. "We Created It: Let's Take It Over," The Emergence of Punk http:///www.inch.com/~jessamin/.

Tabb, William K. 1982. *The Long Default: New York City and the Urban Fiscal Crisis.* New York: Monthly Review Press.

Taylor, William R. 1992. *In Pursuit of Gotham: Culture and Commerce in New York.* New York: Oxford University Press.

Teaford, Jon C. 1990. *The Rough Road to Renaissance: Urban Revitalization in America, 1940–1985.* Baltimore: Johns Hopkins University Press.

"Tenement Evils as Seen by the Tenants." 1970. In *The Tenement House Problem,* ed. Robert W. DeForest and Lawrence Veiller. New York: Arno Press: vol. 1: 385–417. Reissued from 1903, New York: Macmillan Company.

Thomas, Lorenzo. 1993. "Alea's Children: The Avant-Garde on the Lower East Side, 1960–1970." *African American Review* 27, no. 4 (winter): 573–78.

Time. 1967. "Speed Kills." October 20: 23.

Toll, Seymour. 1969. *Zoned American.* New York: Grossman Publishers.

Torres, Andres. 1991. "Labor Market Segmentation: African American and Puerto Rican Labor in New York City." *Review of Black Political Economy* 20 (summer).

Turetsky, Doug. 1993. *We Are the Landlords Now: A Report on Community-Based Housing Management.* New York: Community Service Society.

Turner, Joan. 1984. "Building Boundaries: The Politics of Urban Renewal in Manhattan's Lower East Side." Ph.D. diss., City University of New York.

U.S. Census of Population and Housing. 1950, 1960, 1970, 1980, 1990.

U.S. Department of Labor. 1975. *A Socioeconomic Profile of Puerto Rican New Yorkers.* Washington, D.C.: U.S. Department of Labor.

Van den Haag, Ernst. 1961. "Notes on New York Housing." *Dissent* 8, no. 3 (summer): 277–81.

Van Kleunen, Andrew. 1994. "The Squatters: A Chorus of Voices . . . But Is Anyone Listening?" In *From Urban Village to East Village: The Battle for New York's Lower East Side,* Janet L. Abu-Lughod et al. Cambridge, Mass.: Blackwell: 285–312.

Veiller, Lawrence. 1970a. "Tenement House Reform in New York City, 1834–1900." In *The Tenement House Problem*, ed. Robert W. DeForest and Lawrence Veiller. New York: Arno Press: vol. 1: 69–118. Reissued from 1903, New York: Macmillan Company.

———. 1970b. "A Statistical Study of New York's Houses." In *The Tenement House Problem*, ed. Robert W. DeForest and Lawrence Veiller. New York: Arno Press: vol. 1: 191–240. Reissued from 1903, New York: Macmillan Company.

———. 1970c. "The Speculative Building of Tenement Houses." In *The Tenement House Problem*, ed. Robert W. DeForest and Lawrence Veiller. New York: Arno Press: vol. 1: 367–82. Reissued from 1903, New York: Macmillan Company.

The Villager. 1982. "Artists' Housing Program Meets Resistance from Local Residents Who Fear Displacement." May 13: 5.

Village Voice. 1972. "One Way Street." N.d., from City of New York Municipal Archives Clipping File.

———. 1982. "Space Invaders: Land Grab on the Lower East Side." December 14: 10.

———. 1983. "The East Village." October 18: 78.

———. 1984. "The Hot Bottom: Art and Artifice in the East Village." April 3: 38.

———. 1987. "Graffiti R.I.P.: How the Art World Loved 'Em and Left 'Em." December 22: 37–41.

———. 1988. "Night Clubbing." August 16: 10.

———. 1989. "Loisaida's Predators: This Year's Model." January 17: 11; "An Eye for an Eye: Squatters Attack Christodora after Loisaida Demolition." April 11: 10; "Squatters' Victory?: Protesters Piss Off Demolition Crew—For Now." May 6: 29; "How to Unify a Neighborhood." May 16: 10.

Vogue. 1998. "Eastward Ho!" September: 432.

Von Hassell, Malve. 1996. *Homesteading in New York City, 1978–1993: The Divided Heart of Loisaida*. Westport, Conn.: Bergin and Garvey.

Wakefield, Dan. 1959. *Island in the City*. New York: Corinth Books.

Wallace, Rodrick. 1981. "Fire Service Productivity and the New York City Fire Crisis: 1968–1979. *Human Ecology* 9, no. 4: 433–64.

The Wall Street Journal. "The Art Scene Moves to the East Village." May 2: 28.

Ward, Colin. 1974. *Tenants Take Over*. London: The Architectural Press.

Wasserman, Suzanne. 1990. "The Good Old Days of Poverty: The Battle over the Fate of New York City's Lower East Side during the Depression. Vols. I and II." Ph.D. diss., New York University.

———. 1994. "Déjà Vu: Replanning the Lower East Side in the 1930s." In *From Urban Village to East Village: The Battle for New York's Lower East Side*, Janet L. Abu-Lughod et al. Cambridge, Mass.: Blackwell: 99–120.

Webster, Albert L. 1970. "Tenement House Sanitation." In *The Tenement House Problem*, ed. Robert W. DeForest and Lawrence Veiller. New York: Arno Press: vol. 1: 301–28. Reissued from 1903, New York: Macmillan Company.

Weiss, Michael J. 1988. *The Clustering of America*. New York: Harper and Row Publishers.

Weissman, Harold H. 1969. *Community Development in the Mobilization for Youth Experience*. New York: Association Press.

White, Andrew, and Susan Saegert. 1997. "Return from Abandonment: The Tenant Interim Lease Program and the Development of Low-Income Cooperatives in New York City's Most Neglected Neighborhoods." In *Affordable Housing and Ur-*

ban *Redevelopment in the United States, Urban Affairs Annual Reviews,* vol. 46, ed. William van Vilest. Thousand Oaks, Calif.: Sage Publications: 158–80.

Wise, Jeff. 1997. "Tokyo 10003." *New York* 29, no. 51 (January 6): 38–43.

Wright, Sarah E. 1993. "The Lower East Side: A Rebirth of World Vision." *African American Review* 27, no. 4 (winter): 592–97.

Yaro, Robert D., and Tony Hiss. 1996. *A Region at Risk: The Third Regional Plan for the New York-New Jersey-Connecticut Metropolitan Area.* Washington, D.C.: Island Press.

Zajkowski, Robert Stephen. 1982. "Five Ways of Looking at a City: A Study of Images in the New York Novel from the 1840s to the 1930s." Ph.D. diss., Indiana University.

Zolberg, Vera. 1990. *Constructing A Sociology of the Arts.* New York: Cambridge University Press.

Zukin, Sharon. 1989. *Loft Living: Culture and Capital in Urban Change.* New Brunswick, N.J.: Rutgers University Press.

———. 1991. *Landscapes of Power: From Detroit to Disney World.* Berkeley: University of California Press.

———. 1995. *The Cultures of Cities.* Cambridge, Mass.: Blackwell.

Index